Data Structures & Algorithms in Dart

by Jonathan Sande

Data Structures & Algorithms in Dart

By Jonathan Sande

ISBN: 978-1-950325-89-4

Table of Contents

Book License 13

Before You Begin 15

What You Need 17

Book Source Code & Forums 19

About the Authors 22

About the Editors 22

Acknowledgments 23

Content Development 23

Introduction 25

How to Read This Book 25

Section I: Introduction 29

Chapter 1: Why Learn Data Structures & Algorithms? 31

The Goal of This Book 33

Chapter 2: Complexity 35

Time Complexity 36

Space Complexity 44

Other Notations 45

Key Points 46

Chapter 3: Core Data Structures in Dart 47

List 47

Map 51

Set 52

Key Points 53

Where to Go From Here? 53

Section II: Elementary Data Structures 55

Chapter 4: Stacks 57
Stack Operations 58
Implementation 58
Challenges 62
Key Points 62

Chapter 5: Linked Lists 63
Node 64
LinkedList 66
Adding Values to a List 67
Removing Values From a List 71
Making a List Iterable 76
Challenges 81
Key Points 82
Where to Go From Here? 82

Chapter 6: Queues 83
Common Operations 84
Example of a Queue 85
List-Based Implementation 86
Linked List Implementation 90
Ring Buffer Implementation 94
Double-Stack Implementation 99
Challenges 106
Key Points 108

Section III: Trees 109

Chapter 7: Recursion 111
Recursion in Computing 112
When Recursion Is Useful 115
How Recursion Works 119
When Not to Use Recursion 125
Challenges 130

Key Points 131

Chapter 8: Trees 133
Terminology 134
Implementation 136
Traversal Algorithms 137
Challenges 144
Key Points 145

Chapter 9: Binary Trees 147
Implementation 148
Traversal Algorithms 150
Challenges 155
Key Points 156

Chapter 10: Binary Search Trees 157
List vs. BST 158
Implementation 162
Challenges 174
Key Points 174

Chapter 11: AVL Trees 175
Understanding Balance 176
Implementation 177
Challenges 190
Key Points 191
Where to Go From Here? 191

Chapter 12: Tries 193
List vs. Trie 194
Implementation 196
Challenges 204
Key Points 204

Chapter 13: Binary Search 205

Linear Search vs. Binary Search 206
Implementation 207
Challenges 210
Key Points 211

Chapter 14: Heaps 213
What's a Heap? 213
The Heap Property 214
The Shape Property 215
Heap Applications 215
Fitting a Binary Tree Into a List 216
Implementation 218
Challenges 236
Key Points 237

Chapter 15: Priority Queues 239
Applications 239
Common Operations 240
Implementation 240
Challenges 244
Key Points 244

Section IV: Sorting Algorithms 245

Chapter 16: $O(n^2)$ Sorting Algorithms 247
Bubble Sort 248
Selection Sort 252
Insertion Sort 254
Stability 257
Challenges 259
Key Points 260

Chapter 17: Merge Sort 261
Example 262

Implementation 264
Performance 267
Challenges 268
Key Points 268

Chapter 18: Radix Sort 269
Sorting by Least Significant Digit 270
Sorting by Most Significant Digit 276
Challenges 284
Key Points 285

Chapter 19: Heapsort 287
Example 288
Implementation 292
Performance 296
Challenges 297
Key Points 297

Chapter 20: Quicksort 299
Example 300
Naïve Implementation 302
Partitioning Strategies 303
Challenges 318
Key Points 319
Where to Go From Here? 319

Section V: Graphs 321

Chapter 21: Graphs 323
Types of Graphs 324
Common Operations 326
Adjacency List 330
Adjacency Matrix 338
Graph Analysis 346

Challenges.... 348
Key Points 348

Chapter 22: Breadth-First Search.... 349
How Breadth-First Search Works.... 350
Implementation 354
Performance.... 357
Challenges.... 358
Key Points 359

Chapter 23: Depth-First Search.... 361
How Depth-First Search Works.... 362
Implementation 368
Performance.... 371
Cycles.... 371
Challenges.... 375
Key Points 375

Chapter 24: Dijkstra's Algorithm.... 377
How Dijkstra's Algorithm Works.... 378
Implementation 386
Performance.... 394
Challenges.... 395
Key Points 395

Conclusion.... 397
Approaching a Difficult Problem 397
Learning Tips 398
Where to Go From Here?.... 398

Section VI: Challenge Solutions.... 399

Chapter 4 Solutions 401
Solution to Challenge 1.... 401

Chapter 5 Solutions 403

Solution to Challenge 1 403
Solution to Challenge 2 404
Solution to Challenge 3 407

Chapter 6 Solutions 411
Solution to Challenge 1 411
Solution to Challenge 2 412
Solution to Challenge 3 416
Solution to Challenge 4 417

Chapter 7 Solutions 421
Solution to Exercise 1 421
Solution to Exercise 2 421
Solution to Challenge 1 422
Solution to Challenge 2 422
Solution to Challenge 3 423

Chapter 8 Solutions 425
Solution to Challenge 1 425
Solution to Challenge 2 427

Chapter 9 Solutions 429
Solution to Challenge 1 430
Solution to Challenge 2 430

Chapter 10 Solutions 435
Solution to Challenge 1 435
Solution to Challenge 2 437
Solution to Challenge 3 438

Chapter 11 Solutions 439
Solution to Challenge 1 439
Solution to Challenge 2 440
Solution to Challenge 3 441

Chapter 12 Solutions 443

Solution to Challenge 1 443
Solution to Challenge 2 444

Chapter 13 Solutions 447
Solution to Challenge 1 447
Solution to Challenge 2 448
Solution to Challenge 3 448

Chapter 14 Solutions 451
Solution to Challenge 1 451
Solution to Challenge 2 452
Solution to Challenge 3 452
Solution to Challenge 4 453

Chapter 15 Solutions 455
Solution to Challenge 1 455
Solution to Challenge 2 457

Chapter 16 Solutions 463
Solution to Challenge 1 463
Solution to Challenge 2 464
Solution to Challenge 3 465
Solution to Challenge 4 465

Chapter 17 Solutions 469
Solution to Challenge 1 469
Solution to Challenge 2 470

Chapter 18 Solutions 473
Solution to Challenge 1 473
Solution to Challenge 2 474
Solution to Challenge 3 475

Chapter 19 Solutions 477
Solution to Challenge 1 477
Solution to Challenge 2 478

Chapter 20 Solutions 481
Solution to Challenge 1 481
Solution to Challenge 2 482
Chapter 21 Solutions 483
Solution to Challenge 1 483
Chapter 22 Solutions 485
Solution to Challenge 1 485
Solution to Challenge 2 485
Solution to Challenge 3 487
Chapter 23 Solutions 489
Solution to Challenge 1 489
Solution to Challenge 2 489
Chapter 24 Solutions 493
Solution to Challenge 1 493
Solution to Challenge 2 494

Book License

Before You Begin

This section tells you a few things you need to know before you get started, such as what you'll need for hardware and software, where to find the project files for this book, and more.

What You Need

To follow along with this book, you'll need the following:

- **Recommended: A computer with the Dart SDK and supporting IDE installed.** The code in this book was all tested using Visual Studio Code, but IntelliJ IDEA is another good IDE. Read more at dart.dev.
- **Alternative: Any web browser that supports JavaScript.** It's also possible to run the code in this book online. Open a web browser and navigate to dartpad.dev. If you're using a phone, you'll have an easier time if you choose the desktop view in your browser page settings.

If you haven't installed the latest version of Dart, be sure to do that before continuing with the book. The code covered in this book depends on Dart 3.0 — you may get lost if you try to work with an older version.

Book Source Code & Forums

Where to Download the Materials for This Book

The materials for this book can be cloned or downloaded from the GitHub book materials repository:

- https://github.com/kodecocodes/dsad-materials/tree/editions/2.0

Forums

We've also set up an official forum for the book at https://forums.kodeco.com/c/books/data-structures-and-algorithms-in-dart. This is a great place to ask questions about the book or to submit any errors you may find.

“Thank you to Dalai, OJ, Anand and Temuujin for helping me think through many of the data structures and algorithms in this book. You came up with novel solutions and asked questions that I didn’t always know the answer to. This book is better because of your input.”

— Jonathan Sande

About the Authors

Jonathan Sande is an author of this book, converting *Data Structures & Algorithms in Swift* by Kelvin Lau and Vincent Ngo to the current Dart book you have here. Jonathan is a Flutter and Dart developer working, among other things, on text rendering and input for vertical Mongolian script. Online he goes by *Suragch*, a Mongolian word meaning "student", a reminder to never stop learning. In his free time, he enjoys learning about microbiology and the many data structures and algorithms found in nature, a topic that convinced him life shows evidence of design. He's now trying to follow the teachings of Jesus. You can find him on Twitter: @suragch1 (https://twitter.com/suragch1)

About the Editors

Pablo Mateo is the final pass editor for this book. He is Head of the Onboarding & Mobile Center of Excellence at one of the biggest banks in the world and was also the founder and CTO of a technology development company in Madrid. His expertise is focused on web and mobile app development, although he first started as a creative arts director. He was for many years the main professor of the iOS and Android Mobile Development Masters Degree at a well-known technology school in Madrid (CICE). He has a master's degree in Artificial Intelligence & Machine-Learning and a Certificate in Quantum Computing at MIT.

John Hagemann is an editor of this book. He is a government program and policy analyst, technical writer, and editor, and has worked as a journalist and a writing instructor.

Acknowledgments

Content Development

We would like to thank **Kelvin Lau** and **Vincent Ngo** for their work on *Data Structures & Algorithms in Swift*, the Kodeco book that this book is based on. While *Data Structures & Algorithms in Dart* has sought to improve the explanations, illustrations and code wherever possible, this book is heavily indebted to Kevin and Vincent's prior work.

The credit doesn't stop there. *Data Structures & Algorithms in Swift* itself was based on content from the Swift Algorithm Club GitHub repo (https://github.com/kodecocodes/swift-algorithm-club/). Because of that, we would also like to acknowledge **Matthijs Hollemans**, the original creator of the Swift Algorithm Club, as well as other contributors to that repo, including **Donald Pinckney**, **Christian Encarnacion**, **Kevin Randrup**, **Paulo Tanaka**, **Nicolas Ameghino**, **Mike Taghavi** and **Chris Pilcher**.

We would also like to thank the Dart Team at Google for considering the author's questions about the internal workings of Dart, and **Lasse Nielsen** in particular for taking the time and effort to answer those questions.

Finally, we're also grateful to all of the readers who commented on the first edition. Those comments have improved the quality of the current edition.

Introduction

How to Read This Book

The chapters in this book build on each other, so most readers will want to progress through the content in a linear manner.

Most chapters begin by introducing a data structure or algorithm with examples and illustrations. This is to help you gain a high-level conceptual understanding before diving into the code. Adventurous readers may wish to pause at this point and try to implement the data structure or algorithm on their own before looking at how the chapter does it. Even if you're not successful, attempting to solve the problem will almost certainly cause you to have a deeper understanding of the requirements. An alternative strategy is to work through each chapter directly. Then, when finished, delete all of the code you copied and try to reproduce the data structure or algorithm based on your understanding.

You'll find challenge problems at the end of many chapters. These will help to test your understanding of what you learned. Try to solve the challenges yourself before looking at the answers. When you need to look, you can find the solutions at the end of the book or in the supplemental downloadable materials that accompany the book.

This book is split into five main content sections:

Section I: Introduction

The chapters in this short but essential section will provide the foundation and motivation for the study of data structures and algorithms. You'll also get a quick rundown of the Dart core library, which you'll use as a basis for creating your own data structures and algorithms.

Section II: Elementary Data Structures

This section looks at a few important data structures that are not found in the `dart:core` library but form the basis of more advanced algorithms covered in future sections. All of them are collections optimized for and enforcing a particular access pattern.

The `dart:collection` library, which comes with Dart, does contain `LinkedList` and `Queue` classes. However, learning to build these data structures yourself is why you're reading this book, isn't it?

Even with just these basics, you'll begin to start thinking "algorithmically" and seeing the connection between data structures and algorithms.

Section III: Trees

Trees are another way to organize information, introducing the concept of children and parents. You'll take a look at the most common tree types and see how they can be used to solve specific computational problems. Trees are a handy way to organize information when performance is critical. Having them in your tool belt will undoubtedly prove to be useful throughout your career.

Section IV: Sorting Algorithms

Putting lists in order is a classical computational problem. Although you may never need to write your own sorting algorithm, studying this topic has many benefits. This section will teach you about stability, best- and worst-case times, and the all-important technique of divide and conquer.

Studying sorting may seem a bit academic and disconnected from the "real world" of app development, but understanding the tradeoffs for these simple cases will lead you to a better understanding of how to analyze any algorithm.

Section V: Graphs

Graphs are an instrumental data structure that can model a wide range of things: webpages on the internet, the migration patterns of birds, even protons in the nucleus of an atom. This section gets you thinking deeply (and broadly) about using graphs and graph algorithms to solve real-world problems.

Section I: Introduction

The chapters in this short but essential section will provide the foundation and motivation for studying data structures and algorithms. You'll also get a quick rundown of the Dart core library, which you'll use as a basis for creating your own data structures and algorithms.

Chapter 1: Why Learn Data Structures & Algorithms?

The study of data structures is one of efficiency. Given a particular amount of data, what is the best way to store it to achieve a particular goal?

As a programmer, you regularly use a variety of collection types, such as lists, maps and sets. These are data structures that hold a collection of data, each structure having its own performance characteristics.

For example, consider the difference between a list and a set. Both are meant to hold a collection of elements, but searching for an element in a list takes far longer than searching for an element in a set. On the other hand, you can order the elements of a list but you can't order the elements of a set.

Data structures are a well-studied discipline, and the concepts are language agnostic. A data structure from C is functionally and conceptually identical to the same data structure in any other language, such as **Dart**. At the same time, the high-level expressiveness of Dart makes it an ideal choice for learning these core concepts without sacrificing too much performance.

Algorithms, on the other hand, are a set of operations that complete a task. This can be a sorting algorithm that moves data around to put it in order. Or it can be an algorithm that compresses an 8K picture to a manageable size. Algorithms are essential to software, and many have been created to act as building blocks for useful programs.

So why should you learn data structures and algorithms?

Interviews

An important reason to keep your algorithmic skills up to par is to prepare for interviews. Most companies have at least one or two algorithmic questions to test your abilities as an engineer. A strong foundation in data structures and algorithms is the "bar" for many software engineering positions.

Work

Using an appropriate data structure is crucial when working with lots of data, and using the right algorithm plays a significant role in the performance and scalability of your software. Your mobile apps will be more responsive and have better battery life. Your server apps will be able to handle more concurrent requests and use less energy. Algorithms often include proofs of correctness that you can leverage to build better software.

Using the correct data structure also helps to provide context to the reader. As an example, you might come across a `Set` in your code base. Immediately, you can deduce:

- Consumers of the `Set` don't care about the order of the elements, since `Set` is an **unordered** collection.
- `Set` also ensures that there are no duplicate values. You can assume consumers are working with **unique** data.
- `Set` is great for checking for value membership, so it's likely the engineer introduced it for this purpose.

Being familiar with a data structures allows you to extract additional context from the code. This is a powerful skill that will help you understand how a piece of software works.

Self-Improvement

Knowing the strategies used by algorithms to solve tricky problems gives you ideas for improvements that you can make to your code. The Dart core library has a small set of general-purpose collection types; they don't cover every case. And, yet, as you'll see, these primitives can be used as a great starting point for building more complex and special-purpose abstractions. Knowing more data structures than just the common ones gives you a wider range of tools that you can use to build your apps.

The Goal of This Book

This book is meant to be both a reference and an exercise book. If you're familiar with other books from **Kodeco**, you'll feel right at home. Most chapters will include some challenges at the end. The solutions to these challenges appear in the **Challenge Solutions** section at the end of the book.

Do yourself a favor and make a serious attempt at solving each challenge before peeking at the solution.

There are five content sections in this book, each covering a specific theme:

1. Introduction
2. Elementary Data Structures
3. Trees
4. Sorting Algorithms
5. Graphs

It's best to read this book in chronological order, but it also works well as a reference if you have some prior knowledge.

If you're new to the study of algorithms and data structures, you may find some of the material challenging. But, if you stick with it to the end, you'll be well on the way to becoming a Dart data structures and algorithms expert. It's time to get started!

Chapter 2: Complexity

Will it scale?

This age-old question is always asked during the design phase of software development and comes in several flavors. From an architectural standpoint, **scalability** is how easy it is to make changes to your app. From a database standpoint, scalability is about how long it takes to save or retrieve data in the database.

For algorithms, scalability refers to how the algorithm performs in terms of execution time and memory usage as the input size increases.

When you're working with a small amount of data, an expensive algorithm may still feel fast. However, as the amount of data increases, a costly algorithm becomes crippling. So how bad can it get? Understanding how to quantify this is an important skill for you to know.

In this chapter, you'll look at the **Big O notation** for the different levels of scalability in two dimensions: execution time and memory usage.

Time Complexity

For small amounts of data, even the most expensive algorithm can seem fast due to the speed of modern hardware. However, as data increases, the cost of an expensive algorithm becomes increasingly apparent. **Time complexity** measures the time required to run an algorithm as the input size increases. In this section, you'll go through the most common time complexities and learn how to identify them.

Constant Time

A constant-time algorithm has the same running time regardless of the input size. Consider the following:

```
void checkFirst(List<String> names) {
  if (names.isNotEmpty) {
    print(names.first);
  } else {
    print('no names');
  }
}
```

The number of items in `names` has no effect on the running time of this function. Whether the input has 10 items or 10 million items, this function only prints the first element of the list. Here's a visualization of this time complexity in a plot of time versus data size:

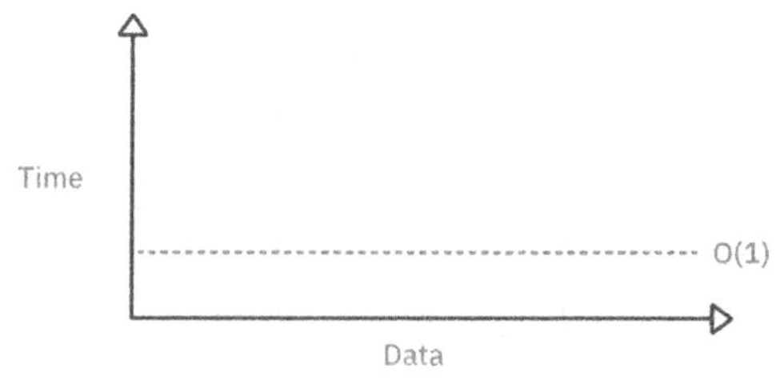

Constant time

As input data increases, the amount of time the algorithm takes does not change.

For brevity, programmers use a way of writing known as **Big O notation** to represent various magnitudes of time complexity. The Big O notation for constant time is **O(1)**.

Linear Time

Consider the following snippet of code:

```
void printNames(List<String> names) {
  for (final name in names) {
    print(name);
  }
}
```

This function prints out all the names in a list. As the input list increases in size, the number of iterations that the `for` loop makes increases by the same amount.

This behavior is known as **linear time** complexity:

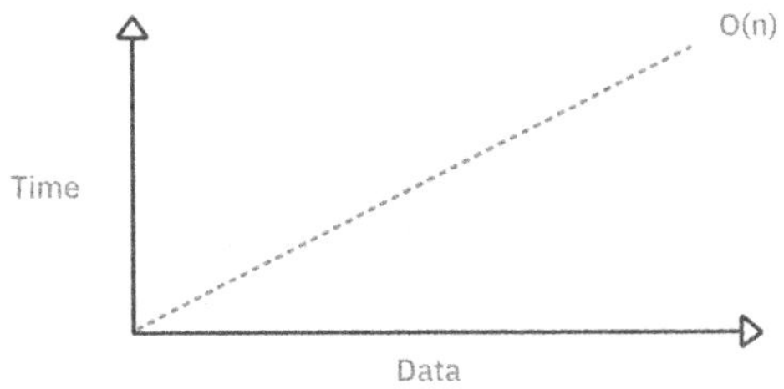

Linear time

Linear time complexity is usually the easiest to understand. As the amount of data increases, the running time increases by the same amount. That's why you have the straight linear graph illustrated above. The Big O notation for linear time is **O(n)**.

> **Note**: What about a function that has two loops over all the data and calls six O(1) methods? Is it O(2n + 6)?
>
> Time complexity only gives a high-level shape of the performance, so loops that happen a fixed number of times are not part of the calculation. All constants are dropped in the final Big O notation. In other words, O(2n + 6) is equal to O(n).
>
> Although not a central concern of this book, optimizing for absolute efficiency can be important. Companies put millions of dollars of R&D into reducing the slope of those constants that Big O notation ignores. For example, a GPU-optimized version of an algorithm might run 100x faster than the naive CPU version while remaining O(n). Although this book will largely ignore that kind of optimization, speedups like this matter.

Quadratic Time

More commonly referred to as **n squared**, this time complexity refers to an algorithm that takes time proportional to the square of the input size. Consider the following code:

```
void printMoreNames(List<String> names) {
  for (final _ in names) {
    for (final name in names) {
      print(name);
    }
  }
}
```

This time, the function prints out all the names in the list for every name in the list. If you have a list with ten pieces of data, it will print the full list of ten names ten times. That's 100 print statements.

Increasing the input size by one, it will print the full list of eleven names eleven times, resulting in 121 print statements. Unlike the previous function, which operates in linear time, the *n* squared algorithm can quickly run out of control as the data size increases.

Here's a graph illustrating this behavior:

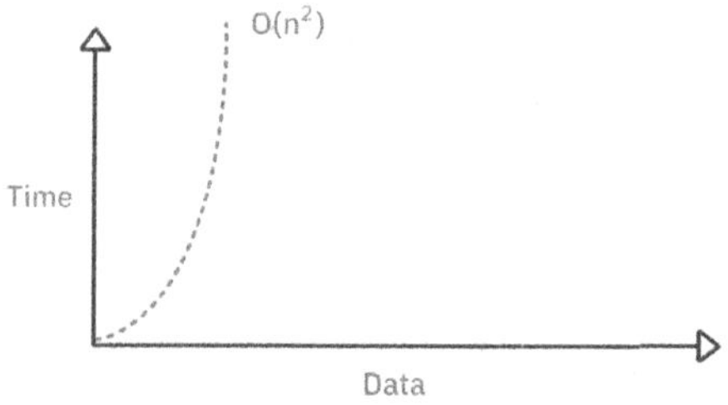

Quadratic time

As the size of the input data increases, the amount of time it takes for the algorithm to run increases drastically. Thus, *n* squared algorithms don't perform well at scale.

The Big O notation for quadratic time is **$O(n^2)$**.

> **Note**: No matter how inefficiently a linear time O(n) algorithm is written, for a sufficiently large *n*, the linear time algorithm will execute faster than a super-optimized quadratic algorithm. Always. Every time.

Logarithmic Time

So far, you've learned about the linear and quadratic time complexities where each element of the input is inspected at least once. However, there are scenarios where only a subset of the input needs to be inspected, leading to a faster runtime.

Algorithms belonging to this time complexity category can leverage some shortcuts by making some assumptions about the input data.

For instance, if you had a *sorted* list of integers, what's the quickest way to find if a particular value exists? A naive solution would be to inspect the list from start to finish before reaching a conclusion. The following is an example of this:

```
const numbers = [1, 3, 56, 66, 68, 80, 99, 105, 450];

bool naiveSearch(int value, List<int> list) {
  for (final element in list) {
    if (element == value) return true;
  }
  return false;
}
```

Since you're inspecting each element once, that would be an O(n) algorithm.

> **Note**: You might be thinking, "Hey, if the value that I'm searching for is at the beginning of the list, then the algorithm can exit early. Isn't that O(1) or at least better than O(n)?"
>
> Big O notation always tells you the **worst-case scenario**. While it's possible that the algorithm above could finish immediately, it's also possible that you would have to check every element. While you might think that looking at the worst case is a pessimistic way to view the world, it's also very helpful because you know it can't get any worse than that. And once you know the worst case, you can try to improve the algorithm.

Linear time is fairly good, but you can do better. Since the input list is sorted, there's an optimization you can make.

If you were checking whether the number 451 existed in the list, the naive algorithm would have to iterate from beginning to end, making a total of nine inspections for the nine values in the list. However, since the list is sorted, you can, right off the bat, drop half of the comparisons necessary by checking the middle value.

The following algorithm shows an example of this:

```
bool betterSearch(int value, List<int> list) {
  int start = 0;
  int end = list.length;

  while (start < end) {
    final size = end - start;
    int middle = start + size ~/ 2;

    if (list[middle] == value) {
      return true;
    } else if (list[middle] < value) {
      start = middle + 1;
    } else {
      end = middle;
    }
  }

  return false;
}
```

The algorithm first checks the middle value to see how it compares with the desired value. If the middle value is less than the desired value, the algorithm won't bother looking at the values on the left half of the list. Since the list is sorted, values to the left of the middle value can only get smaller. In the other case, if the middle value is bigger than the desired value, the algorithm won't look at the right side of the list. This optimization cuts the number of comparisons by half.

The function continues this optimization on every pass of the `while` loop. This algorithm is known as a **binary search**, and you'll learn more about it in Chapter 13, "Binary Search".

An algorithm that can repeatedly drop half of the required comparisons will have **logarithmic time complexity**. Here's a graph depicting how a logarithmic time algorithm behaves:

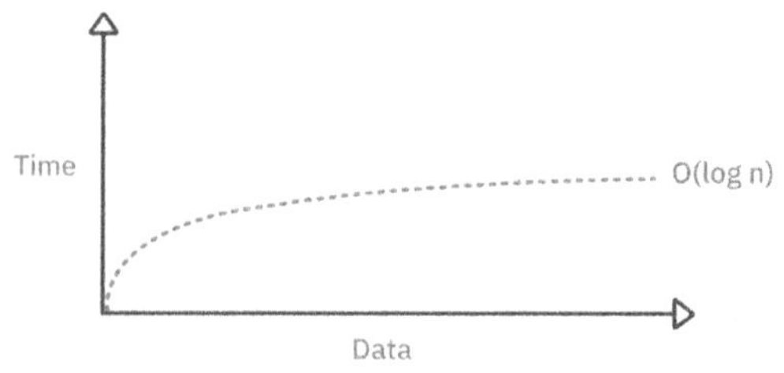

Logarithmic time

As input data increases, the time it takes to execute the algorithm increases at a slow rate. If you look closely, you may notice that the graph seems to exhibit asymptotic behavior. This can be explained by considering the impact of halving the number of comparisons you need to do.

When you have an input size of 100, halving the comparisons means you save 50 comparisons. If the input size is 100,000, halving the comparisons means you save 50,000 comparisons. The more data you have, the more the halving effect scales. Thus, you can see that the graph appears to approach horizontal.

Algorithms in this category are few but extremely powerful in situations that allow for it. The Big O notation for logarithmic time complexity is **O(log n)**.

> **Note**: Is it log base 2, log base 10, or the natural log?
>
> In the above example, log base 2 applies. However, since Big O notation only concerns itself with the shape of the performance, the actual base doesn't matter.

Quasilinear Time

Another common time complexity you'll encounter is **quasilinear time**. Quasilinear time algorithms perform worse than linear time but dramatically better than quadratic time. You can think of *quasi*-linear as "kind of" like linear time for large data sets. An example of a quasilinear time algorithm is Dart's `sort` method.

> **Note**: At the time of this writing, the `List.sort` algorithm in Dart internally uses the quasilinear Dual-Pivot Quicksort algorithm for large lists. However, for lists below a size threshold of 32, it uses an insertion sort.

The Big-O notation for quasilinear time complexity is **O(n log n)**, which is a multiplication of linear and logarithmic time. Here's the graph:

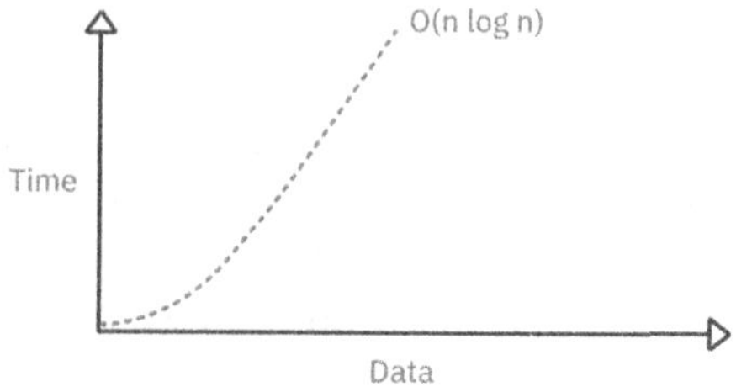

Quasilinear time

Quasilinear time complexity nears a linear slope at higher values. This makes it more resilient to large data sets.

Comparing Time Complexities

Take a look at how the time complexities compare to each other for large data sets:

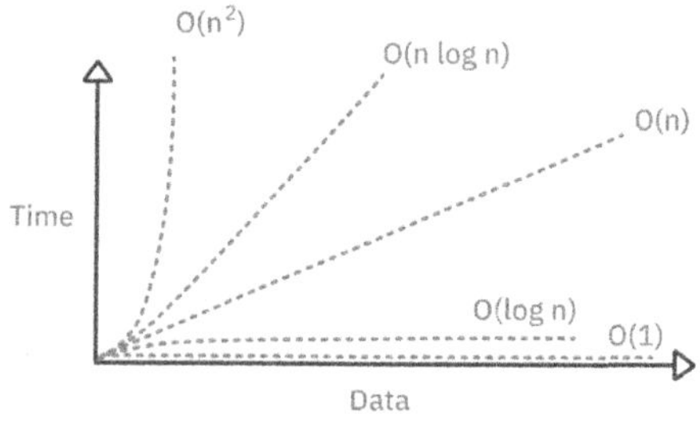

Five major time complexities

Remembering how these curves relate to each other will help you compare the efficiency of various algorithms.

Other Time Complexities

The five time complexities you've encountered so far are the primary ones you'll deal with in this book. Other time complexities do exist but are far less common and tackle more complex problems. These time complexities include:

- **$O(n^k)$**: polynomial time.
- **$O(2^n)$**: exponential time.
- **O(n!)**: factorial time.

And there are many more.

It's important to note that time complexity is a high-level overview of performance, and it doesn't judge the algorithm's speed beyond the general ranking scheme. This means that two algorithms can have the same time complexity, but one may still be much faster than the other. For small data sets, time complexity may not be an accurate measure of actual speed.

For instance, quadratic algorithms such as insertion sort can be faster than quasilinear algorithms such as mergesort if the data set is small. This is because insertion sort doesn't need to allocate extra memory to perform the algorithm, while mergesort does. For small data sets, the memory allocation can be expensive relative to the number of elements the algorithm needs to touch.

Improving Algorithm Performance

Suppose you wrote the following code that finds the sum of numbers from 1 to *n*.

```
int sumFromOneTo(int n) {
  var sum = 0;
  for (var i = 1; i <= n; i++) {
    sum += i;
  }
  return sum;
}

sumFromOneTo(10000);
```

The code loops 10000 times and returns `50005000`. It's O(n) and will take a moment to run as it counts through the loop and prints the results.

If you're curious about how long it takes to run on your machine, you can measure it like so:

```
final start = DateTime.now();
final sum = sumFromOneTo(10000);
final end = DateTime.now();
final time = end.difference(start);
print(sum);
print(time);
```

Try increasing the input value to see how that affects the computation time.

Now try the following implementation:

```
int betterSumFromOneTo(int n) {
  return n * (n + 1) ~/ 2;
}
```

This version of the function uses a trick that Fredrick Gauss noticed in elementary school. Namely, you can compute the sum using simple arithmetic. This final version of the algorithm is O(1) and tough to beat. A constant time algorithm is always preferred. If you ran `betterSumFromOneTo` in a loop, you only end up with linear time. The previous O(n) version was just one outer loop away from slow, quadratic time.

Space Complexity

The time complexity of an algorithm can help predict scalability, but it isn't the only metric. **Space complexity** is a measure of the memory required for an algorithm to run.

Consider the following code:

```
int multiply(int a, int b) {
  return a * b;
}
```

To perform this simple algorithm, Dart needs to allocate space for the two input parameters, `a` and `b`, as well as space for the return value. The actual size that Dart allocates internally depends on the implementation details and where the code is running, but whatever the case, it's still a fixed amount of space. Even for very large input values, the return value will just overflow; it won't take more space. That means the space complexity for this algorithm is **constant**, and so the Big O notation is O(1).

However, now take a look at this example:

```
List<String> fillList(int length) {
  return List.filled(length, 'a');
}
```

This algorithm creates a list filled with the string `'a'`. The larger `length` is, the longer the list will be and thus the more space will be required to store the list in memory. Since the space increases proportionally with the input value, the space complexity of this algorithm is **linear** and the Big O notation is O(n).

With one small change you could make that algorithm have **quadratic** space complexity:

```
List<String> stuffList(int length) {
  return List.filled(length, 'a' * length);
}
```

Not only do larger values for `length` make the list longer, they also increase the size of the string in each element of the list. Specifying 5 for length would create a list of length 5 whose elements are `'aaaaa'`. As with quadratic time complexity, the Big O notation for quadratic space complexity is $O(n^2)$.

Other Notations

So far, you've evaluated algorithms using Big O notation, which tells the worst-case runtime. This is by far the most common measurement that programmers evaluate with. However, other notations exist as well:

- **Big Omega notation** is used to measure the best-case runtime for an algorithm. This isn't as useful as Big O because getting the best case is often untenable.
- **Big Theta notation** is used to measure the runtime for an algorithm that is between the best- and worst-case scenarios.

Become familiar with Big O for now. Later, if you need to learn other notations, you can pick them up.

Key Points

- Time complexity is a measure of the time required to run an algorithm as the input size increases.
- You should know about constant time, logarithmic time, linear time, quadratic time and quasilinear time and be able to order them by cost.
- Space complexity is a measure of the memory required for the algorithm to run.
- Big O notation represents the general form of time and space complexity.
- Time and space complexity are high-level measures of scalability. They don't measure the actual speed of the algorithm itself.
- For small data sets, time complexity is usually irrelevant. A quasilinear algorithm can be slower than a quadratic algorithm.

Chapter 3: Core Data Structures in Dart

The `dart:core` library contains the core components of the Dart language. Inside, you'll find a variety of tools and types to help create your Dart apps. Before you start building your own custom data structures, it's important to understand the primary data structures that come with Dart.

This chapter will focus on the three main data structures the `dart:core` library provides right out of the box: `List`, `Map`, and `Set`.

List

A list is a general-purpose, generic container for storing an ordered collection of elements, and it's commonly used in all sorts of Dart programs. In many other programming languages, this data type is called an **array**.

You can create a list by using a **list literal**, which is a comma-separated list of values surrounded with square brackets. For example:

```
final people = ['Pablo', 'Manda', 'Megan'];
```

Dart defines `List` as an abstract class with methods for accessing and modifying the collection elements by index. Since Dart is platform-independent, how `List` is implemented under the hood depends on the underlying platform, whether that's the Dart VM, or Dart compiled to JavaScript for the web, or native code running directly on your computer.

`List`, like most other Dart collections, is an `Iterable`. This means that you can step through the elements sequentially. All iterables have a `length` getter that returns the number of elements in the collection. While this could take O(n) time for iterables that need to count every element, `List` will efficiently return `length` in O(1) time.

Dart lists can also be growable or fixed-length. When you specify a fixed length for the list, Dart can be more efficient about the space it allocates. However, you won't be able to add or remove elements anymore as you could in a growable list.

As with any data structure, there are certain notable traits that you should be aware of. The first of these is the notion of order.

Order

Elements in a list are explicitly **ordered**. Using the above `people` list as an example, `'Pablo'` comes before `'Manda'`.

All elements in a list have a corresponding **zero-based integer index**. For example, `people` has three indices, one corresponding to each element. You can retrieve the value of an element in the list by writing the following:

```
people[0] // 'Pablo'
people[1] // 'Manda'
people[2] // 'Megan'
```

Order is defined by the `List` data structure and should not be taken for granted. Some data structures, such as `Map`, have a weaker concept of order.

Random-Access

Random-access is a trait that data structures can claim if they can handle element retrieval in a constant amount of time. For example, getting `'Megan'` from the `people` list takes constant time. Again, this performance should not be taken for granted. Other data structures such as linked lists and trees do not have constant time access.

List Performance

Aside from being a random-access collection, other areas of performance will be of interest to you as a developer. Particularly, how well or poorly does the data structure fare when the amount of data it contains needs to grow? For lists, this varies in two aspects.

Insertion Location

The first aspect is where you choose to insert the new element inside the list. The most efficient scenario for adding an element to a list is to add it at the end of the list:

```
people.add('Edith');
print(people); // [Pablo, Manda, Megan, Edith]
```

Inserting `'Edith'` using the `add` method will place the string at the end of the list. This is an **amortized constant-time operation**, meaning the time it takes to perform this operation on average stays the same no matter how large the list becomes. Since Dart lists are backed by a buffer, if you keep adding elements, the buffer will fill up every so often. Then Dart will have to spend some extra time allocating more space for the buffer. That doesn't happen very often, though, so the "amortized" part of *amortized constant-time* means that the occasional complexity bump gets averaged out over time and so the operation is still considered constant-time.

To help illustrate why the insertion location matters, consider the following analogy. You're standing in line for the theater. Someone new comes along to join the lineup. What's the easiest place to add people to the lineup? At the end, of course!

If the newcomer tried to insert themselves into the middle of the line, they would have to convince half the lineup to shuffle back to make room.

And if they were terribly rude, they would try to insert themselves at the head of the line. This is the worst-case scenario because every single person in the lineup would need to shuffle back to make room for this new person in front!

This is exactly how the list works. Inserting new elements anywhere aside from the end of the list will force elements to shuffle backwards to make room for the new element:

```
people.insert(0, 'Ray');
// [Ray, Pablo, Manda, Megan, Edith]
```

If the number of elements in the list doubles, the time required for this `insert` operation will also double.

If inserting elements in front of a collection is a common operation for your program, you may want to consider a different data structure to hold your data.

Capacity

The second factor that determines the speed of insertion is the list's capacity. Underneath the hood, Dart lists are allocated with a predetermined amount of space for its elements. If you try to add new elements to a list that is already at maximum capacity, the list must restructure itself to make room for more elements. This is done by copying all the current elements of the list to a new and bigger container in memory. However, this comes at a cost. Each element of the list has to be visited and copied.

This means that any insertion, even at the end, could take *n* steps to complete if a copy is made. However, Dart employs a strategy that minimizes the times this copying needs to occur. Each time it runs out of storage and needs to copy, it doubles the capacity.

> **Note**: The actual implementation details are determined by where your Dart code is running. For example, in the Dart VM, saying the capacity "doubles" is generally true, but the specific implementation in the internal VM file growable_array.dart is `(old_capacity * 2) | 3`.

Map

A map is a collection that holds **key-value pairs**. For example, here's a map containing users' names and scores:

```
final scores = {'Eric': 9, 'Mark': 12, 'Wayne': 1};
```

The abstract `Map` class itself in Dart doesn't have any guarantees of order, nor can you insert at a specific index. The keys of a map can be of any type, but if you are using your own custom type then that type needs to implement `operator==` and `hashCode`.

Although `Map` itself doesn't guarantee an order, the default Dart implementation of `Map` is `LinkedHashMap`, which, unlike `HashMap`, promises to maintain the insertion order.

You can add a new entry to the map with the following syntax:

```
scores['Andrew'] = 0;
```

Since this is a `LinkedHashMap` under the hood, the new key-value pair will appear at the end of the map:

```
print(scores);
// {Eric: 9, Mark: 12, Wayne: 1, Andrew: 0}
```

That is not the case with `HashMap`, which you can observe if you import `dart:collection`:

```
import 'dart:collection';
```

And then add the following code below what you wrote earlier:

```
final hashMap = HashMap.of(scores);
print(hashMap);
// {Andrew: 0, Eric: 9, Wayne: 1, Mark: 12}
```

Now the order has changed since `HashMap` makes no guarantees about order.

It's possible to traverse through the key-value pairs of a map multiple times. This order, even when undefined as it is with `HashMap`, will be the same every time it's traversed until the collection is mutated.

> **Note**: The `dart:collection` library contains many additional data structures beyond the basic ones found in `dart:core`. By the time you're finished with this book, you'll understand how many of them work and what their performance characteristics and advantages are.

The lack of explicit ordering comes with some redeeming traits, though. Unlike lists, maps don't need to worry about elements shifting around. Inserting into a map always takes a constant amount of time.

Lookup operations are also constant-time. This is significantly faster than searching for a particular element in a list, which requires a walk from the beginning of the list to the insertion point.

Set

A set is a container that holds unique values. Imagine it as a bag that allows you to add items to it but rejects items that have already been added:

```
var bag = {'Candy', 'Juice', 'Gummy'};
bag.add('Candy');
print(bag); // {Candy, Juice, Gummy}
```

Since sets enforce uniqueness, they lend themselves to a variety of interesting applications, such as finding duplicate elements in a collection of values:

```
final myList = [1, 2, 2, 3, 4];
final mySet = <int>{};
for (final item in myList) {
  if (mySet.contains(item)) {
    // mySet already has it, so it's a duplicate
  }
  mySet.add(item);
}
```

Similar to maps, order is generally not an important aspect of sets. That said, Dart's default implementation of `Set` uses `LinkedHashSet`, which, unlike `HashSet`, promises to maintain insertion order.

You won't use sets nearly as often as lists and maps, but they're still common enough to be an essential data structure to keep in your tool belt.

That wraps up this summary of the core data collection structures that Dart provides for you. In the following chapters, you'll use lists, maps and sets to build your own data structures.

Key Points

- Every data structure has advantages and disadvantages. Knowing them is key to writing performant software.
- Functions such as `List.insert` have characteristics that can cripple performance when used haphazardly. If you need to use `insert` frequently with indices near the beginning of the list, you may want to consider a different data structure, such as a linked list.
- `Map` sacrifices the ability to access elements by ordered index but has fast insertion and retrieval.
- `Set` guarantees uniqueness in a collection of values. It's optimized for speed, and like `Map`, abandons the ability to access elements by ordered index.

Where to Go From Here?

Need a more detailed explanation of lists, maps and sets? Check out the "Lists", "Sets" and "Maps" chapters in Dart Apprentice: Fundamentals (https://www.kodeco.com/books/dart-apprentice-fundamentals) from Kodeco.

Section II: Elementary Data Structures

This section looks at a few important data structures that are not found in the `dart:core` library but form the basis of more advanced algorithms covered in future sections. All are collections optimized for and enforcing a particular access pattern.

The `dart:collection` library, which comes with Dart, does contain `LinkedList` and `Queue` classes. However, learning to build these data structures yourself is why you're reading this book, isn't it?

Even with just these basics, you'll begin to start thinking "algorithmically" and see the connection between data structures and algorithms.

Chapter 4: Stacks

Stacks are everywhere. Here are some common examples of things you would stack:

- pancakes
- books
- paper
- cash

The **stack** data structure is identical in concept to a physical stack of objects. When you add an item to a stack, you place it on top of the stack. When you remove an item from a stack, you always remove the topmost item.

Good news: a stack of pancakes with butter on top. Bad news: you have to eat the butter first.

Stack Operations

Stacks are useful and also exceedingly simple. The main goal of building a stack is to enforce how you access your data.

There are only two essential operations for a stack:

- **push**: Add an element to the top of the stack.
- **pop**: Remove the top element of the stack.

Limiting the interface to these two operations means that you can only add or remove elements from one side of the data structure. In computer science, a stack is known as a **LIFO** (last-in-first-out) data structure. Elements that are pushed in last are the first ones to be popped out.

Stacks are used prominently in all disciplines of programming. To list a couple:

- Memory allocation uses stacks at the architectural level. Memory for local variables is also managed using a stack.
- Programming languages that support recursion manage the function calls with a stack. You'll learn more about this in Chapter 7, "Recursion".
- Search and conquer algorithms, such as finding a path out of a maze, use stacks to facilitate backtracking.

Implementation

Open up the **starter** project for this chapter. In the root of the project add a folder named **lib**, and in that folder create a file named **stack.dart**.

> **Note**: If you are using DartPad (https://dartpad.dev) rather than a full IDE, then just create your `Stack` class outside of the `main` function.

Then add the following code to **stack.dart**:

```
class Stack<E> {
  Stack() : _storage = <E>[];
  final List<E> _storage;
}
```

Here, you've defined the backing storage of your Stack. Choosing the right storage type is important. List is an obvious choice since it offers constant time insertions and deletions at one end via add and removeLast. Usage of these two operations will facilitate the LIFO nature of stacks.

For those unfamiliar with **generics**, the E in the code above represents any data type you might want to put in your stack, whether that be String, int, double or your own custom type. While you don't have to use the letter *E*, it's customary to do so when you're representing the *elements* of a collection. To learn more, read the Generics chapter in *Dart Apprentice: Beyond the Basics*.

You'll want to observe the contents of the stack later on, so also override toString inside the class:

```
@override
String toString() {
  return '--- Top ---\n'
      '${_storage.reversed.join('\n')}'
      '\n-----------';
}
```

This will list all of the elements in _storage with the last one at the top.

Push and Pop Operations

Add the following two operations to your Stack:

```
void push(E element) => _storage.add(element);

E pop() => _storage.removeLast();
```

Calling push will add an element to the end of the list while pop will remove the last element of the list and return it.

Open **bin/starter.dart** and import your new stack at the top of the file:

```
import 'package:starter/stack.dart';
```

If you're using your own project, just change **starter** to whatever your project name is.

Then test your stack in the `main` function of **bin/starter.dart**:

```
final stack = Stack<int>();
stack.push(1);
stack.push(2);
stack.push(3);
stack.push(4);
print(stack);

final element = stack.pop();
print('Popped: $element');
```

You should see the following output:

```
--- Top ---
4
3
2
1
-----------
Popped: 4
```

`push` and `pop` both have O(1) time complexity.

Non-Essential Operations

There are a couple of nice-to-have operations that make a stack easier to use.

Adding Getters

In **lib/stack.dart**, add the following to `Stack`:

```
E get peek => _storage.last;

bool get isEmpty => _storage.isEmpty;

bool get isNotEmpty => !isEmpty;
```

`peek` is an operation that is often attributed to the stack interface. The idea of `peek` is to look at the top element of the stack without mutating its contents.

Creating a Stack From an Iterable

You might want to take an existing iterable collection and convert it to a stack so that the access order is guaranteed. Of course it would be possible to loop through the elements and push each one. However, you can add a named constructor that just sets the underlying private storage.

Add the following constructor to your stack implementation:

```
Stack.of(Iterable<E> elements) : _storage =
List<E>.of(elements);
```

Now, run this example in `main`:

```
const list = ['S', 'M', 'O', 'K', 'E'];
final smokeStack = Stack.of(list);
print(smokeStack);
smokeStack.pop();
```

This code creates a stack of strings and pops the top element "E". The Dart compiler infers the element type from the list, so you can use `Stack` instead of the more verbose `Stack<String>`.

Less Is More

Since `Stack` is a collection of elements, you may have wondered about implementing the `Iterable` interface. After all, `List` and `Set` and even the keys and values of a `Map` are all iterable.

However, a stack's purpose is to limit the number of ways to access your data, and adopting interfaces such as `Iterable` would go against this goal by exposing all the elements via the iterator. In this case, less is more!

Stacks are crucial to problems that search trees and graphs. Imagine finding your way through a maze. Each time you come to a decision point of left, right or straight, you can push all possible decisions onto your stack. When you hit a dead end, simply backtrack by popping from the stack and continuing until you escape or hit another dead end. You may want to try your hand at that sometime, but for now, work through the challenges in the following section.

Challenges

A stack is a simple data structure with a surprisingly large number of applications. Try to solve the following challenges using stacks. You can find the answers at the end of the book and in the supplemental materials that accompany the book.

Challenge 1: Reverse a List

Create a function that prints the contents of a list in reverse order.

Challenge 2: Balance the Parentheses

Check for balanced parentheses. Given a string, check if there are `(` and `)` characters, and return `true` if the parentheses in the string are balanced. For example:

```
// 1
h((e))llo(world)() // balanced parentheses

// 2
(hello world // unbalanced parentheses
```

Key Points

- A stack is a LIFO, last-in first-out, data structure.
- Despite being so simple, the stack is a key data structure for many problems.
- The only two essential operations for a stack are `push` for adding elements and `pop` for removing elements.
- `push` and `pop` are both constant-time operations.

Chapter 5: Linked Lists

A linked list is a collection of values arranged in a linear, unidirectional sequence. It has several theoretical advantages over contiguous storage options such as the Dart `List`:

- Constant time insertion and removal from the front of the list.
- Reliable performance characteristics.

A linked list is a chain of **nodes**:

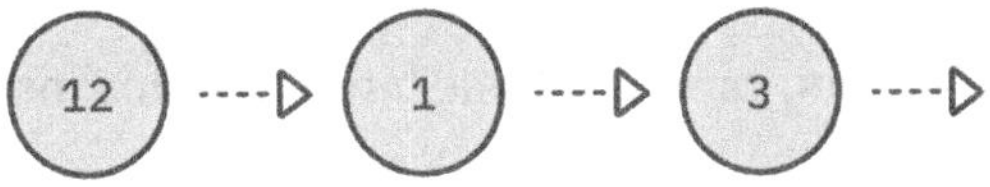

A linked list

Nodes have two responsibilities:

1. Hold a value.
2. Hold a reference to the next node. A `null` reference indicates the end of the list.

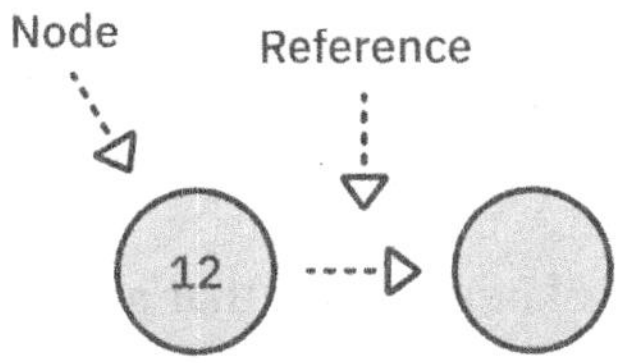

A node holding the value 12

In this chapter, you'll implement a linked list and learn about the common operations associated with it. You'll also learn about the time complexity of each operation.

Open up the **starter** project for this chapter so you can dive into the code.

Node

Create a folder called **lib** in the root of your project. Then add a new file to this folder called **linked_list.dart**. At the top of that file add a class called `Node` with the following code:

```
class Node<T> {
  Node({required this.value, this.next});
  T value;
  Node<T>? next;
}
```

Since `Node` only knows about a single value, `T` is the standard letter people use to mean that the node can hold any *type*. Later when you create a linked list of nodes, you'll use `E` to refer to the type since they are *elements* of the list.

Making Nodes Printable

Override `toString` so that you can print `Node` later. Add this inside your newly created class:

```
@override
String toString() {
  StringBuffer buffer = StringBuffer();
  Node<T>? currentNode = this;
  while (true) {
    buffer.write(currentNode?.value);
    currentNode = currentNode?.next;
    if (currentNode == null) break;
    buffer.write(' -> ');
  }
  return buffer.toString();
}
```

This will follow the sequence of `next` nodes that are connected to the current node and print their values.

Creating a Linked List by Hand

Now it's time to try out your shiny new `Node`! Open **bin/starter.dart** and add the file import:

```
import 'package:starter/linked_list.dart';
```

Change `starter` to whatever your project name is if you aren't using the starter project.

Then add the following code to `main` :

```
final node1 = Node(value: 1);
final node2 = Node(value: 2);
final node3 = Node(value: 3);

node1.next = node2;
node2.next = node3;

print(node1);
```

You've just created three nodes and connected them:

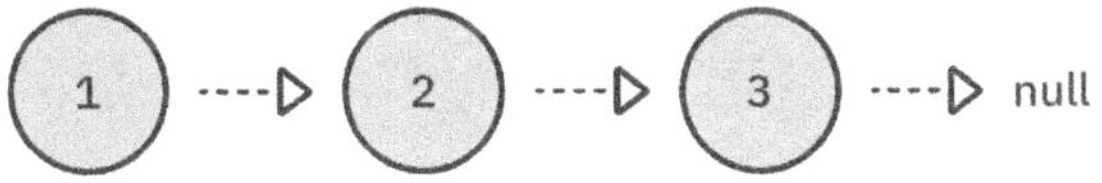

A linked list containing values 1, 2, and 3

Run the code, and you'll see the following output in the console:

```
1 -> 2 -> 3
```

The current method of building lists leaves a lot to be desired. You can easily see that building long lists this way is impractical. A common way to alleviate this problem is to build a `LinkedList` that manages the `Node` objects. You'll do just that!

LinkedList

A linked list has the concept of a **head** and **tail**, which refer to the first and last nodes of the list respectively:

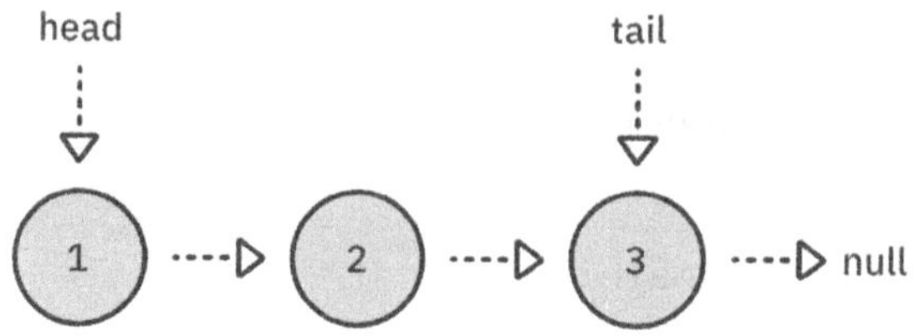

The head and tail of the list

Implement these characteristics by adding the following class below `Node` in **linked_list.dart**:

```
class LinkedList<E> {
  Node<E>? head;
  Node<E>? tail;

  bool get isEmpty => head == null;

  @override
  String toString() {
    if (isEmpty) return 'Empty list';
    return head.toString();
  }
}
```

You know the list is empty if the head is `null`. Also, since you already designed `Node` to print any nodes that follow it, you can print the entire linked list just by calling `head.toString`.

Adding Values to a List

Since you're building a manager for `Node` objects, you must provide a way to add values. There are three ways to add values to a linked list, each having its own unique performance characteristics:

1. **`push`**: Adds a value at the front of the list.
2. **`append`**: Adds a value at the end of the list.
3. **`insertAfter`**: Adds a value after a particular node in the list.

You'll implement each of these in the following sections and analyze their performance characteristics.

Pushing to the Front of a List

Adding a value at the front of the list is known as a **push** operation. This is also known as **head-first insertion**. The code for it is refreshingly simple.

Add the following method to `LinkedList`:

```
void push(E value) {
  head = Node(value: value, next: head);
  tail ??= head;
}
```

You create a new node and point to the node that used to be `head`. Then you set this new node as `head`. In the case in which you're pushing into an empty list, the new node is both the `head` and `tail` of the list.

Go back to **bin/starter.dart** and replace the contents of `main` with the following code, and then run the program:

```
final list = LinkedList<int>();
list.push(3);
list.push(2);
list.push(1);

print(list);
```

Your console output should show this:

```
1 -> 2 -> 3
```

That was much easier than building the list by chaining nodes together by hand!

Appending to the End of a List

The next operation you'll look at is `append`. This is meant to add a value at the end of the list, and it's known as **tail-end insertion**.

In `LinkedList`, add the following code just below `push`:

```
void append(E value) {
  // 1
  if (isEmpty) {
    push(value);
    return;
  }

  // 2
  tail!.next = Node(value: value);

  // 3
  tail = tail!.next;
}
```

This code is relatively straightforward:

1. Like before, if the list is empty, you'll need to update both `head` and `tail` to the new node. Since `append` on an empty list is functionally identical to `push`, you simply invoke `push` to do the work for you.
2. In all other cases, you create a new node *after* the tail node. `tail` is guaranteed to be non-null since you push in the `isEmpty` case.
3. Since this is tail-end insertion, your new node is also the new tail of the list.

Test it out by replacing the contents of `main` with the following:

```
final list = LinkedList<int>();
list.append(1);
list.append(2);
list.append(3);

print(list);
```

Run that, and you should see the following output in the console:

```
1 -> 2 -> 3
```

Inserting in Middle of a List

The third and final operation for adding values is `insertAfter`. This operation inserts a value after a particular node in the list, and requires two steps:

1. Finding a particular node in the list.
2. Inserting the new node after it.

First, you'll implement the code to find the node you want to insert a value after.

In `LinkedList`, add the following code just below `append`:

```
Node<E>? nodeAt(int index) {
  // 1
  var currentNode = head;
  var currentIndex = 0;

  // 2
  while (currentNode != null && currentIndex < index) {
    currentNode = currentNode.next;
    currentIndex++;
  }
  return currentNode;
}
```

`nodeAt` will try to retrieve a node in the list based on the given index. Since you can only access the nodes of the list from the `head` node, you'll have to make an iterative traversal. Here's the play-by-play:

1. You create a new reference to `head` and set up a counter to keep track of where you are in the list.
2. Using a `while` loop, you move the reference down the list until you've reached the desired index. Empty lists or out-of-bounds indexes will result in a `null` return value.

Now you need to insert the new node.

Add the following method just below `nodeAt`:

```
Node<E> insertAfter(Node<E> node, E value) {
  // 1
  if (tail == node) {
    append(value);
    return tail!;
  }

  // 2
  node.next = Node(value: value, next: node.next);
  return node.next!;
}
```

Here's what you've done:

1. In the case where this method is called with the `tail` node, you'll call the functionally equivalent append method. This will take care of updating `tail`.
2. Otherwise, you simply link up the new node with the rest of the list and return the new node.

Test your `insert` method out by replacing the body of `main` with the following:

```
final list = LinkedList<int>();
list.push(3);
list.push(2);
list.push(1);

print('Before: $list');

var middleNode = list.nodeAt(1)!;
list.insertAfter(middleNode, 42);

print('After:  $list');
```

Run that, and you should see the following output:

```
Before: 1 -> 2 -> 3
After:  1 -> 2 -> 42 -> 3
```

You successfully inserted a node with a value of 42 after the middle node.

You might think it's a little strange to insert a value *after* the node at some index, since with normal lists you insert a value *at* some index. The reason it's like this for the linked list data structure, though, is because as long as you have a reference to a node, it's very fast, O(1) time complexity, to insert another node after the known one. However, there's no way to insert *before* a given node (thus replacing its index position) without knowing the node before it. And this requires the much slower task of iterating through the list.

Performance

Whew! You've made good progress so far. To recap, you've implemented the three operations that add values to a linked list and a method to find a node at a particular index.

	push	append	insertAfter	nodeAt
Behavior	insert at head	insert at tail	insert after a node	returns a node at given index
Time complexity	O(1)	O(1)	O(1)	O(i), where i is the given index

Next, you'll focus on the opposite action: removal operations.

Removing Values From a List

There are three main operations for removing nodes:

1. **`pop`**: Removes the value at the front of the list.

2. **`removeLast`**: Removes the value at the end of the list.

3. **`removeAfter`**: Removes the value after a particular node in the list.

You'll implement all three and analyze their performance characteristics.

Popping From the Front of a List

Removing a value at the front of a linked list is often referred to as **pop**. This operation is almost as simple as `push`, so dive right in.

Add the following method to `LinkedList`:

```
E? pop() {
  final value = head?.value;
  head = head?.next;
  if (isEmpty) {
    tail = null;
  }
  return value;
}
```

By moving the `head` down a node, you've effectively removed the first node of the list. If the list becomes empty, you set `tail` to `null`. `pop` returns the value that was removed from the list. This value is nullable, since the list may be empty.

Test it out by replacing the contents of `main` with the following:

```
final list = LinkedList<int>();
list.push(3);
list.push(2);
list.push(1);

print('Before: $list');

final poppedValue = list.pop();

print('After:  $list');
print('Popped value: $poppedValue');
```

Run that, and you'll see the following result:

```
Before: 1 -> 2 -> 3
After:  2 -> 3
Popped value: 1
```

Removing From the End of a List

Removing the last node of the list is somewhat inconvenient. Although you have a reference to the `tail` node, you can't chop it off without getting the reference to the node before it. Thus, you'll have to do an arduous traversal.

Add the following code just below pop:

```
E? removeLast() {
  // 1
  if (head?.next == null) return pop();

  // 2
  var current = head;
  while (current!.next != tail) {
    current = current.next;
  }

  // 3
  final value = tail?.value;
  tail = current;
  tail?.next = null;
  return value;
}
```

Note the following points about the numbered sections above:

1. If the list only consists of one node, `removeLast` is functionally equivalent to pop. Since pop will handle updating the head and `tail` references, you'll just delegate this work. pop will also handle the case of an empty list.

2. You start at the beginning and keep searching the nodes until `current.next` is `tail`. This signifies that `current` is the node right before `tail`.

3. You collect the return value from the tail and after that rewire the node before the `tail` to be the new `tail`.

Test out your new functionality in `main`:

```
final list = LinkedList<int>();
list.push(3);
list.push(2);
list.push(1);

print('Before: $list');

final removedValue = list.removeLast();

print('After:  $list');
print('Removed value: $removedValue');
```

Run that, and you should see the following in the console:

```
Before: 1 -> 2 -> 3
After:  1 -> 2
Removed value: 3
```

`removeLast` requires you to traverse all the way down the list. This makes for an *O(n)* operation, which is relatively expensive.

Removing a Value From the Middle of a List

The final remove operation is removing a node at a particular point in the list. This is achieved much like `insertAfter`. You'll first find the node immediately before the node you wish to remove and then unlink it.

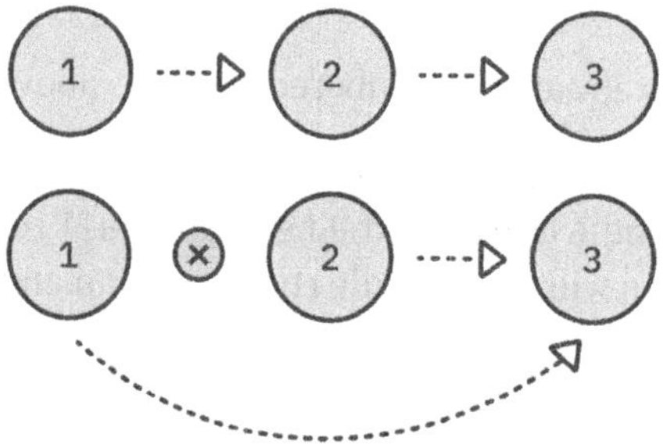

Removing the middle node

Add the following to your `LinkedList`:

```
E? removeAfter(Node<E> node) {
  final value = node.next?.value;
  if (node.next == tail) {
    tail = node;
  }
  node.next = node.next?.next;
  return value;
}
```

You drop the next node from the list by resetting the link of the given node to the next-*next* node, in effect skipping the one that used to come after. Special care needs to be taken if the removed node is the tail node since the tail reference will need to be updated.

Head back to main to try it out. You know the drill:

```
final list = LinkedList<int>();
list.push(3);
list.push(2);
list.push(1);

print('Before: $list');

final firstNode = list.nodeAt(0);
final removedValue = list.removeAfter(firstNode!);

print('After:  $list');
print('Removed value: $removedValue');
```

You should see the following output in the console:

```
Before: 1 -> 2 -> 3
After:  1 -> 3
Removed value: 2
```

Try adding more elements and play around with the value of the node index. Similar to insertAfter, the time complexity of this operation is O(1), but it requires you to have a reference to a particular node beforehand.

Performance

You've hit another checkpoint! To recap, you've implemented the three operations that remove values from a linked list:

	pop	removeLast	removeAfter
Behavior	remove at head	remove at tail	remove the next node
Time complexity	O(1)	O(n)	O(1)

At this point, you've defined an interface for a linked list that most programmers around the world can relate to. However, there's work to be done to adhere to Dart semantics. In the next part of the chapter, you'll focus on making the interface more Dart-like.

Making a List Iterable

With most Dart collections, you can iterate through them using a `for` loop. For example, here is a basic implementation of looping through a standard list:

```
final numbers = [1, 2, 3];
for (final number in numbers) {
  print(number);
}
```

However, if you were to try to do that with your `LinkedList` implementation, you'd get an error. You can try by running the following code in `main`:

```
final list = LinkedList<int>();
list.push(3);
list.push(2);
list.push(1);

for (final element in list) {
  print(element);
}
```

The error reads:

```
The type 'LinkedList<int>' used in the 'for' loop must implement
Iterable.
```

The reason that you can loop through various collections in Dart is because they implement the `Iterable` interface. You can do the same to make `LinkedList` iterable.

Add `extends Iterable<E>` to `LinkedList` so that the first line of the class looks as follows:

```
class LinkedList<E> extends Iterable<E> {
```

`Iterable` requires an iterator, so create the missing override:

```
@override
// TODO: implement iterator
Iterator<E> get iterator => throw UnimplementedError();
```

After you've finished making the iterator, you'll come back and update this getter.

Since Iterable also includes isEmpty, add the @override annotation above your isEmpty getter. It should look like so now:

```
@override
bool get isEmpty => head == null;
```

Note: Rather than extending Iterable, you could have also implemented it. However, the abstract Iterable class contains a lot of default logic that you would have to rewrite yourself if you had used the implement keyword. By using extends, you only need to implement iterator.

What's an Iterator?

An iterator tells an iterable class how to move through its elements. To make an iterator, you create a class that implements the Iterator interface. This abstract class has the following simple form:

```
abstract interface class Iterator<E> {
  E get current;
  bool moveNext();
}
```

You don't need to write that yourself. It's already included in Dart. Here's what the parts mean:

- current refers to the current element in the collection as you are iterating through it. According to Iterator semantics, current is undefined until you've called moveNext at least once.
- moveNext updates the new value of current, so it's your job here to point to whatever item is next in the list. Returning false from this method means that you've reached the end of the list. After that point, you should consider current undefined again.

Creating an Iterator

Now that you know what an iterator is, you can make one yourself. Create the following incomplete class below `LinkedList`:

```
class _LinkedListIterator<E> implements Iterator<E> {
  _LinkedListIterator(LinkedList<E> list) : _list = list;
  final LinkedList<E> _list;
}
```

You pass in a reference to the linked list so that the iterator has something to work with.

Since you implemented `Iterator`, you still need to add the required `current` getter and `moveNext` method.

Implementing current

First add the following code for `current`:

```
Node<E>? _currentNode;

@override
E get current => _currentNode!.value;
```

Someone looping through your `LinkedList` probably doesn't care about the concept of nodes. They just want the values, so when you return `current` you extract the value from the current node, which you are storing as a separate private variable named `_currentNode`. Note that accessing `current` when `_currentNode` is `null` will cause a crash. As long as you implement `moveNext` correctly and people follow `Iterator` semantics, though, this will never happen.

Implementing moveNext

Add the missing `moveNext` method now:

```
bool _firstPass = true;

@override
bool moveNext() {
  // 1
  if (_list.isEmpty) return false;

  // 2
  if (_firstPass) {
    _currentNode = _list.head;
```

```
    _firstPass = false;
  } else {
    _currentNode = _currentNode?.next;
  }

  // 3
  return _currentNode != null;
}
```

Here's what you did:

1. If the list is empty, then there's no need to go any further. Let the iterable know there are no more items in this collection by returning `false`.
2. Since `_currentNode` is `null` to start with, you need to set it to head on the first pass. After that just point it to the next node in the chain.
3. Returning `true` lets the iterable know there are still more elements, but when the current node is `null`, you know you've reached the end of the list.

Looping Through a List

Now that your iterator is finished, you can use it in your `LinkedList`. Replace the unimplemented `iterator` getter that you added earlier to `LinkedList` with the following:

```
@override
Iterator<E> get iterator => _LinkedListIterator(this);
```

Now you're ready to see if it works. Rerun the same code that you unsuccessfully tried earlier:

```
final list = LinkedList<int>();
list.push(3);
list.push(2);
list.push(1);

for (final element in list) {
  print(element);
}
```

This time it works! It prints out the following values as expected:

```
1
2
3
```

Looping through a collection is not the only benefit of implementing `Iterable`. You now have access to all sorts of methods like `where`, `map`, `contains`, and `elementAt`. Just keep in mind that these are O(n) operations, though. Even the innocuous-looking `length` requires iterating through the whole list to calculate.

> **Note**: The `dart:collection` library also contains a class named `LinkedList`. It only accepts elements of type `LinkedListEntry`, though, so it isn't as flexible as yours was for making a list of arbitrary values. Additionally, the Dart version is a doubly linked list (linking to previous as well as next elements), whereas yours was a singly linked list. If you want to use a standard Dart collection that allows adding and removing at the ends in constant or amortized constant time, check out the `Queue` class.

Challenges

These challenges will serve to solidify your knowledge of data structures. You can find the answers at the end of the book and in the supplemental materials.

Challenge 1: Find the Middle Node

Create a function that finds the middle node of a linked list. For example:

```
1 -> 2 -> 3 -> 4 -> null
// middle is 3

1 -> 2 -> 3 -> null
// middle is 2
```

Challenge 2: Reverse a Linked List

Create a function that reverses a linked list. You do this by manipulating the nodes so that they're linked in the other direction. For example:

```
// before
1 -> 2 -> 3 -> null

// after
3 -> 2 -> 1 -> null
```

Challenge 3: Remove All Occurrences

Create a function that removes all occurrences of a specific element from a linked list. The implementation is similar to the `removeAfter` method that you implemented earlier. For example:

```
// original list
1 -> 3 -> 3 -> 3 -> 4

// list after removing all occurrences of 3
1 -> 4
```

Key Points

- Linked lists are linear and unidirectional. As soon as you move a reference from one node to another, you can't go back.
- Linked lists have O(1) time complexity for head first insertions, whereas standard lists have O(n) time complexity for head-first insertions.
- Implementing the Dart `Iterable` interface allows you to loop through the elements of a collection as well as offering a host of other helpful methods.

Where to Go From Here?

The nodes in this chapter only pointed to the next node in the list. This type of linked list is called a **singly linked list**. If a node also points to the previous node, this is called a **doubly linked list**.

A doubly linked list has some performance benefits over singly linked lists. For example, deleting from the end of the list or inserting before a given node are both O(1) operations. The downside is that the logic is a little more complex, and the nodes require a little more memory.

If you'd like to try your hand at creating your own doubly linked list, you can compare your solution to the `DoublyLinkedList` implementation in the **challenge** folder of the supplemental materials for this chapter.

Chapter 6: Queues

Everyone is familiar with waiting in line. Whether you are in line to buy tickets to your favorite movie or waiting for a printer to print a file, these real-life scenarios mimic the **queue** data structure.

Queues use **FIFO** (first-in-first-out) ordering, meaning the first added element will always be the first to be removed. Queues are handy when you need to maintain the order of your elements to process later.

In this chapter, you'll learn all the common operations of a queue, go over various ways to implement a queue, and look at the time complexity of each approach.

Common Operations

The following interface defines what a queue needs to do:

```
abstract interface class Queue<E> {
  bool enqueue(E element);
  E? dequeue();
  bool get isEmpty;
  E? get peek;
}
```

These are the meanings of the core operations:

- **enqueue**: Insert an element at the back of the queue. Return `true` if the operation was successful.
- **dequeue**: Remove the element at the front of the queue and return it.
- **isEmpty**: Check if the queue is empty.
- **peek**: Return the element at the front of the queue without removing it.

Notice that the queue only cares about removal from the front and insertion at the back. You don't need to know what the contents are in between. If you did, you would probably just use a list.

Go ahead and open the **starter** project. Add a file called **queue.dart** to the **lib** folder. Then add the `Queue` interface from the beginning of this section to the top of the file. You'll use this interface later in the chapter when implementing a queue.

> **Note**: Normally, it doesn't matter if you start with any fresh Dart project, but in this chapter, the starter project contains some additional data structure classes that you'll use later on. So you'll have an easier time if you actually do use the starter project. If you're using DartPad, you'll need to copy those classes to the bottom of the code window.

Example of a Queue

The easiest way to understand how a queue works is to see an example. Imagine a group of people waiting in line to buy a movie ticket. The queue currently holds Ray, Brian, Sam and Mic:

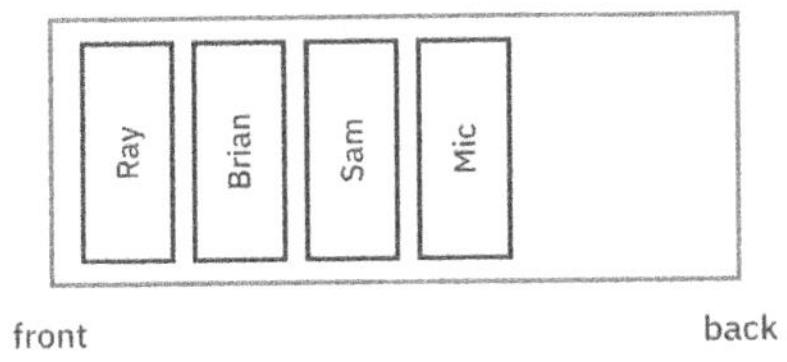

Once Ray has received his ticket, he moves out of the line. By calling `dequeue`, Ray is removed from the *front* of the queue:

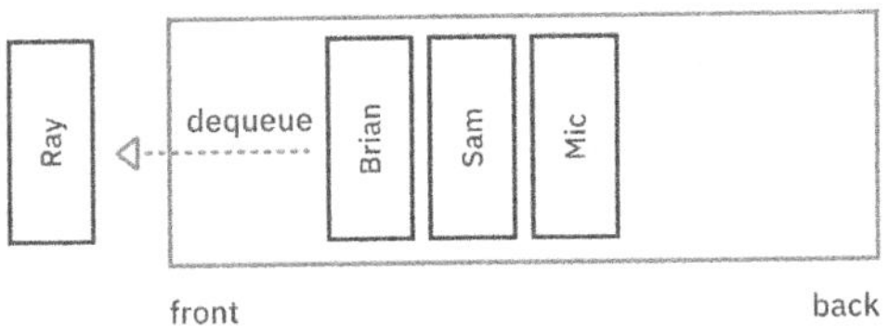

Calling `peek` will return Brian since he is now at the front of the line:

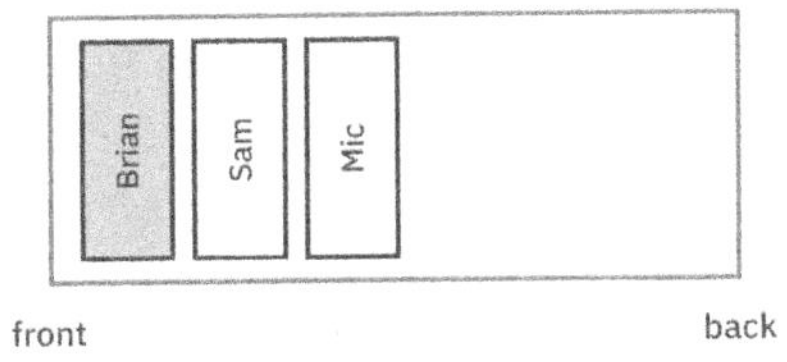

Now comes Vicki, who just joined the line to buy a ticket. By calling `enqueue('Vicki')`, Vicki gets added to the *back* of the queue:

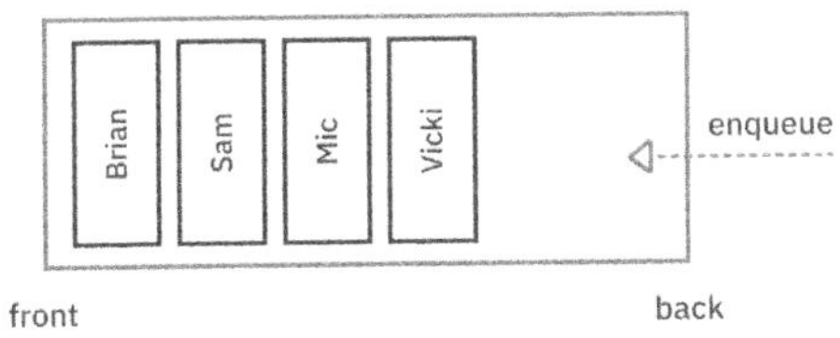

In the following sections, you'll learn to create a queue using four different internal data structures:

- List
- Linked list
- Ring buffer
- Two stacks

List-Based Implementation

The Dart core library comes with a set of highly optimized data structures that you can use to build higher-level abstractions. One of them that you're already familiar with is `List`, the data structure that stores a contiguous, ordered collection of elements. In this section, you'll use a list to create a queue.

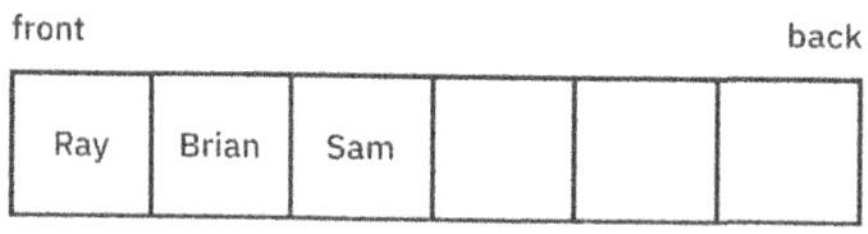

A simple Dart list can be used to model the queue.

In **lib/queue.dart**, add the following code below your `Queue` interface:

```
class QueueList<E> implements Queue<E> {
  final _list = <E>[];

  @override
  bool enqueue(E element) => throw UnimplementedError();

  @override
  E? dequeue() => throw UnimplementedError();

  @override
  bool get isEmpty => throw UnimplementedError();

  @override
  E? get peek => throw UnimplementedError();
}
```

This sets up a private list to hold the elements of the queue. You've also added the methods required by the `Queue` interface that you defined earlier. Trying to access them now would throw an `UnimplementedError`, but you'll implement them in the following sections.

Leveraging Lists

Replace `isEmpty` and `peek` in your `QueueList` with the following:

```
@override
bool get isEmpty => _list.isEmpty;

@override
E? get peek => (isEmpty) ? null : _list.first;
```

Using the features of `List`, you get the following for free:

1. Check if the queue is empty.
2. Return the element at the front of the queue, or `null` if the queue is empty.

These operations are both O(1).

Enqueue

Enqueuing an element at the back of the queue is easy. Just add an element to the list. Replace `enqueue` with the following:

```
@override
bool enqueue(E element) {
  _list.add(element);
  return true;
}
```

Enqueuing an element is, on average, an O(1) operation. This is because the list has empty space at the back.

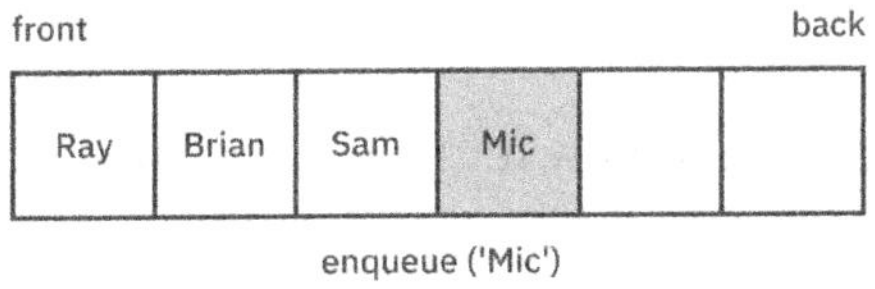

In the example above, notice that, once you add Mic, the list has two empty spaces.

After adding multiple elements, the list will eventually be full:

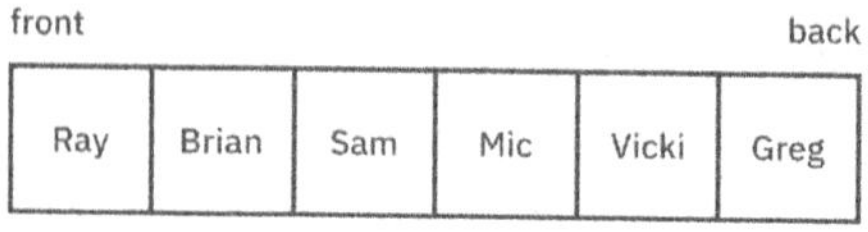

When you want to use more than the allocated space, the list must resize to make additional room:

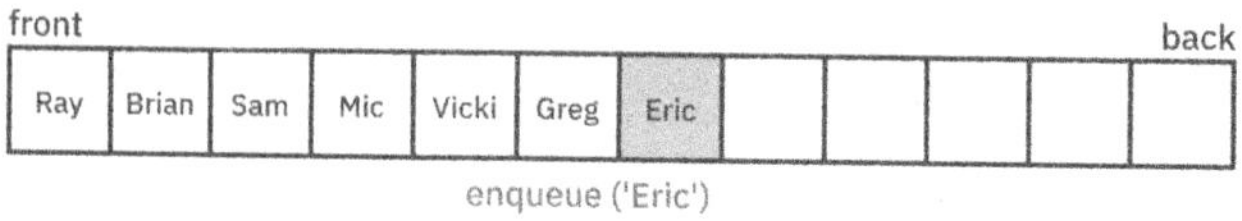

As a review of what you learned in an earlier chapter, appending to a list is an O(1) operation even though sizing is an O(n) operation. Resizing, after all, requires the list to allocate new memory and copy all existing data over to the new list. The key is that this doesn't happen very often. This is because the capacity doubles each time it runs out of space. As a result, if you work out the **amortized cost** of the operation (the average cost), enqueuing is only O(1). That said, the worst-case performance is O(n) when the copy is performed.

Dequeue

Removing an item from the front requires a bit more work. Replace `dequeue` with the following:

```
@override
E? dequeue() => (isEmpty) ? null : _list.removeAt(0);
```

If the queue is empty, `dequeue` simply returns `null`. If not, it removes the element from the front of the list and returns it.

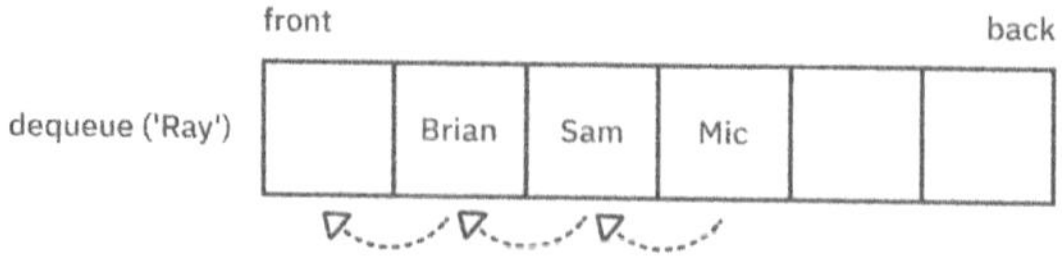

Removing an element from the beginning of a list is always a linear-time operation because it requires all the remaining elements in the list to be shifted in memory.

Testing the List-Based Implementation

Add a new method to override `toString` in `QueueList` so that you can see the results of your operations:

```
@override
String toString() => _list.toString();
```

Then open **bin/starter.dart** and add the following code to `main`:

```
final queue = QueueList<String>();
queue.enqueue('Ray');
queue.enqueue('Brian');
queue.enqueue('Eric');
print(queue);

queue.dequeue();
print(queue);

queue.peek;
print(queue);
```

You'll need to import your **queue.dart** file:

```
import 'package:starter/queue.dart';
```

Change **starter** to whatever your project name is if you're using something else besides the starter project that came with this book.

Run the code, and you should see the following in the console:

```
[Ray, Brian, Eric]
[Brian, Eric]
[Brian, Eric]
```

This code puts Ray, Brian and Eric in the queue, then removes Ray and peeks at Brian but doesn't remove him.

Performance

Here's a summary of the algorithmic and storage complexity of the list-based queue implementation:

List-Based Queue

Operations	Average case	Worst case
enqueue	O(1)	O(n)
dequeue	O(n)	O(n)
Space Complexity	O(n)	O(n)

You've seen how easy it is to implement a list-based queue by leveraging a Dart `List`. Enqueue is, on average, very fast, thanks to the O(1) `add` operation. There are some shortcomings to the implementation, though. Removing an item from the front of the queue can be inefficient, as removal causes all elements to shift by one. This makes a difference for very large queues. Once the list gets full, it has to resize and may have unused space. This could increase your memory footprint over time.

Is it possible to address these shortcomings? Compare this one to the linked-list-based implementation in the next section.

Linked List Implementation

In the previous chapter, you built a linked list. You'll use that now to implement a queue. Open the **lib** folder you'll find a copy of the **linked_list.dart** file that contains your `LinkedList`.

Start by adding a generic `QueueLinkedList` to **queue.dart** as shown below.

First, import **linked_list.dart** at the top of the file:

```
import 'linked_list.dart';
```

Then, add the following code after the QueueList class.

```
class QueueLinkedList<E> implements Queue<E> {
  final _list = LinkedList<E>();

  @override
  bool enqueue(E element) => throw UnimplementedError();

  @override
  E? dequeue() => throw UnimplementedError();

  @override
  bool get isEmpty => throw UnimplementedError();

  @override
  E? get peek => throw UnimplementedError();
}
```

This implementation is similar to QueueList, but instead of using List, the internal data structure is LinkedList.

Next, you'll start implementing the methods of the Queue interface.

Enqueue

To add an element to the back of the queue, simply replace enqueue with the following:

```
@override
bool enqueue(E element) {
  _list.append(element);
  return true;
}
```

Behind the scenes, the linked list will update the tail node's next reference to the new node. This is an O(1) operation.

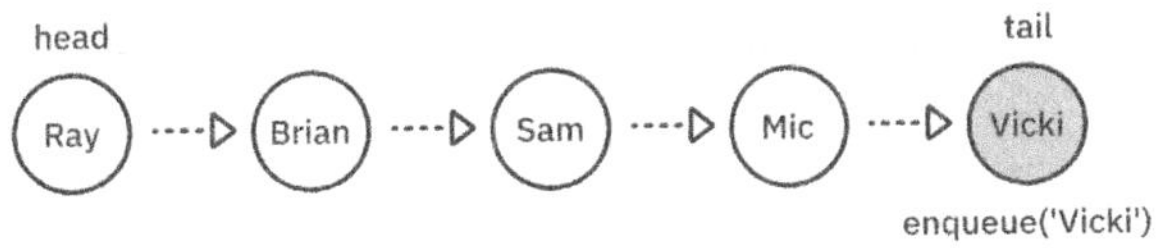

Dequeue

To remove an element from the queue, replace dequeue with the following:

```
@override
E? dequeue() => _list.pop();
```

pop does exactly what you want dequeue to do, so you can use it directly.

Removing from the front of a linked list is also an O(1) operation. Compared to the List implementation, you don't have to shift elements one by one. Instead, as shown in the diagram below, you simply update the pointer for the head node of the linked list:

Checking the State of a Queue

Similar to the List implementation, you can implement peek and isEmpty using the properties of LinkedList.

Replace isEmpty and peek with the following:

```
@override
bool get isEmpty => _list.isEmpty;

@override
E? get peek => _list.head?.value;
```

Testing the Linked-List-Based Implementation

Override toString in QueueLinkedList so that you can see the results of your operations:

```
@override
String toString() => _list.toString();
```

Then replace the contents of `main` with the following code:

```
final queue = QueueLinkedList<String>();
queue.enqueue('Ray');
queue.enqueue('Brian');
queue.enqueue('Eric');
print(queue); // Ray -> Brian -> Eric

queue.dequeue();
print(queue); // Brian -> Eric

queue.peek;
print(queue); // Brian -> Eric
```

Run the code, and you'll see similar results as your `QueueList` implementation:

```
Ray -> Brian -> Eric
Brian -> Eric
Brian -> Eric
```

Performance

Here is a summary of the algorithmic and storage complexity of the linked-list-based queue implementation.

Linked-List Based Queue

Operations	Average case	Worst case
enqueue	O(1)	O(1)
dequeue	O(1)	O(1)
Space Complexity	O(n)	O(n)

One of the main problems with `QueueList` was that dequeuing an item took linear time. With the linked list implementation, you reduced it to a constant operation, O(1). All you needed to do was update the head pointer.

The main weakness with `QueueLinkedList` is not apparent from the table. Despite O(1) performance, it suffers from high overhead. Each element has to have extra storage for the next node pointer. Moreover, every time you create a new element, it requires a relatively expensive dynamic allocation of memory for the new node. By contrast, `QueueList` does bulk allocation, which is faster.

Can you eliminate allocation overhead and maintain O(1) dequeues? If you don't have to worry about your queue ever growing beyond a maximum fixed size, then the answer is yes! What you are looking for is a **ring buffer**. For example, you might have a game of Monopoly with four players. You can use a ring-buffer-based queue to track whose turn is coming up next. You'll take a look at the ring buffer implementation next.

Ring Buffer Implementation

A ring buffer, also known as a **circular buffer**, is a fixed-size list. This data structure strategically wraps around to the beginning when there are no more items to remove at the end.

Example

What follows is a simple example of how a queue can be implemented using a ring buffer:

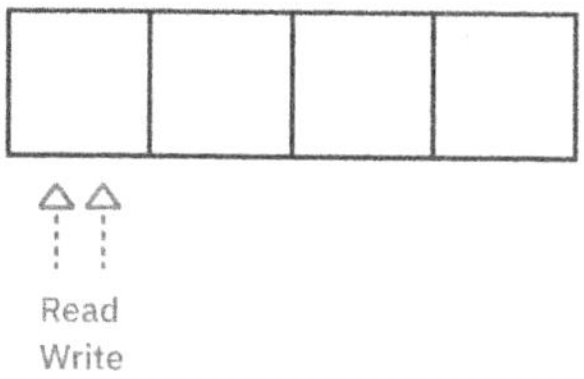

You first create a ring buffer with a fixed size of **4**. The ring buffer has two pointers that keep track of two things:

1. The **read** pointer keeps track of the front of the queue.
2. The **write** pointer keeps track of the next available slot so that you can overwriteexisting elements that have already been read.

The image below shows the **read** and **write** pointers after you enqueue an item:

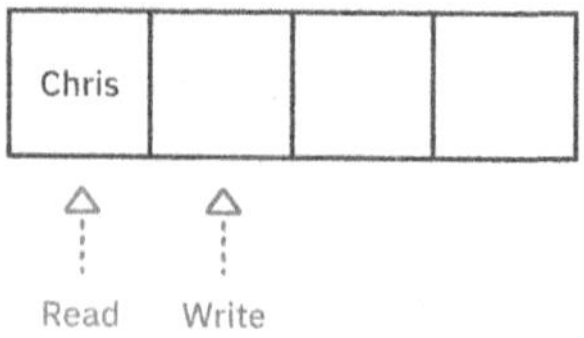

Each time you add an item to the queue, the **write** pointer increments by one. Here is what it looks like after adding a few more elements:

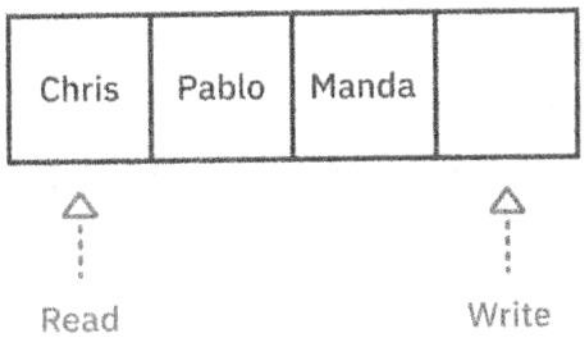

Notice that the **write** pointer moved two more spots and is ahead of the **read** pointer. This means that the queue is not empty.

Next, dequeue two items:

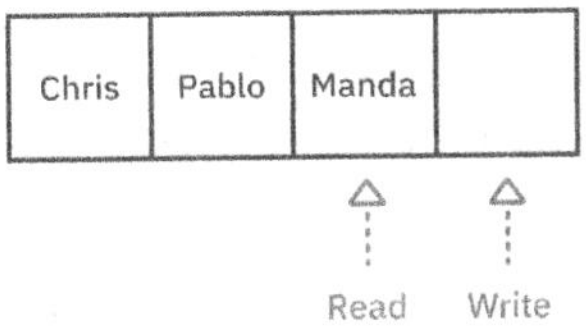

Dequeuing is the equivalent of reading a ring buffer. Notice how the read pointer moved twice.

Now, enqueue one more item:

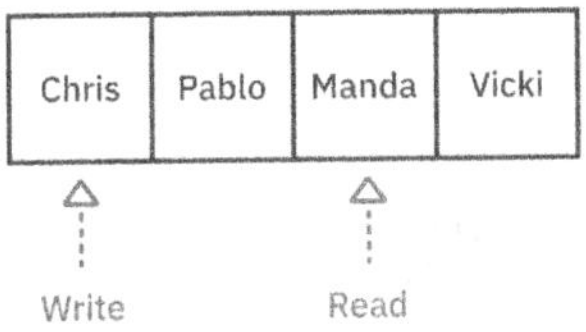

Since the write pointer reached the end, it simply wraps around to the starting index again. This is why the data structure is known as a circular buffer.

Finally, dequeue the two remaining items:

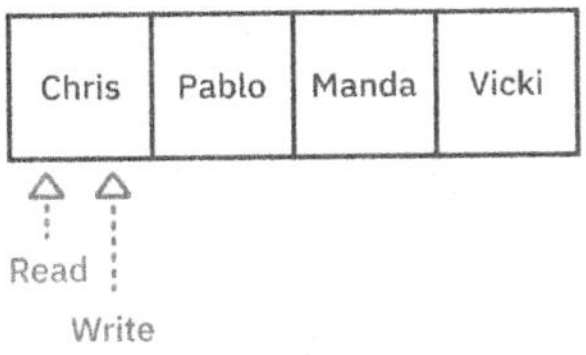

The read pointer wraps to the beginning, as well. Whenever the read and write pointers are at the same index, that means the queue is empty.

> **Note**: You might wonder what happens if you enqueue too many items and the write pointer loops around and catches up with the read pointer. One option is to throw an error. Alternatively, you could overwrite the unread data and push the read pointer ahead of the write pointer. The ring buffer in the starter project implements the first option, but you could modify it for the second option if losing data at the front of the queue is acceptable in your application.

Implementation

Now that you have a better understanding of how ring buffers can be used to make a queue, it's time to implement one!

You'll find a file called **ring_buffer.dart** in the **lib** folder of the **starter** project. This file includes the `RingBuffer` implementation that you'll use in the next section.

> **For the adventurous**: If you'd like a little extra challenge before proceeding, try to implement a ring buffer yourself based on the description above. Check the source code in the starter project if you get stuck.

Add a generic `QueueRingBuffer` to **queue.dart** as shown below:

```
import 'ring_buffer.dart';

class QueueRingBuffer<E> implements Queue<E> {
  QueueRingBuffer(int length)
    : _ringBuffer = RingBuffer<E>(length);

  final RingBuffer<E> _ringBuffer;

  @override
  bool enqueue(E element) => throw UnimplementedError();

  @override
  E? dequeue() => throw UnimplementedError();

  @override
  bool get isEmpty => _ringBuffer.isEmpty;

  @override
  E? get peek => _ringBuffer.peek;
}
```

There are a couple of points to pay attention to:

- You must include a `length` parameter since the ring buffer has a fixed size.
- `isEmpty` and `peek` are already implemented. Both of these are O(1) operations.

You'll implement `enqueue` and `dequeue` in the following sections.

Enqueue

Replace `enqueue` with the method below:

```
@override
bool enqueue(E element) {
  if (_ringBuffer.isFull) {
    return false;
  }
  _ringBuffer.write(element);
  return true;
}
```

To append an element to the queue, you simply call `write` on the `_ringBuffer`. This increments the write pointer by one.

Since the queue has a fixed size, you must now return `true` or `false` to indicate whether the element has been successfully added. `enqueue` is still an O(1) operation.

Dequeue

Next replace `dequeue` with the following:

```
@override
E? dequeue() => _ringBuffer.read();
```

To remove an item from the front of the queue, you simply call `read` on the `_ringBuffer`. Behind the scenes, it checks if the ring buffer is empty and, if so, returns `null`. If not, it returns the item at the read index of the buffer and then increments the index by one.

Testing the Ring-Buffer-Based Implementation

Override `toString` in `QueueRingBuffer` so that you can see the results of your operations:

```
@override
String toString() => _ringBuffer.toString();
```

This creates a string representation of `Queue` by delegating to the underlying ring buffer.

That's all there is to it! Test your ring-buffer-based queue by running the following code in `main`:

```
final queue = QueueRingBuffer<String>(10);
queue.enqueue("Ray");
queue.enqueue("Brian");
queue.enqueue("Eric");
print(queue); // [Ray, Brian, Eric]

queue.dequeue();
print(queue); // [Brian, Eric]

queue.peek;
print(queue); // [Brian, Eric]
```

This test code works like the previous examples, dequeuing Ray and peeking at Brian.

Performance

How does the ring-buffer implementation compare? Have a look at a summary of the algorithmic and storage complexity.

Ring-Buffer Based Queue

Operations	Average case	Worst case
enqueue	O(1)	O(1)
dequeue	O(1)	O(1)
Space Complexity	O(n)	O(n)

The ring-buffer-based queue has the same time complexity for enqueue and dequeue as the linked-list implementation. The space complexity for a ring-buffer-based queue, while still O(n), doesn't require new memory allocation internally when enqueuing new elements like the linked-list implementation does. However, the ring buffer has a fixed size, which means that enqueue can fail.

So far, you've seen three implementations of a queue: a simple list, a linked list and a ring buffer. These were all useful in their own ways, but next you'll make a queue implemented with two stacks. Its spatial locality is superior to the linked list, and it also doesn't need a fixed size like a ring buffer.

Double-Stack Implementation

Add a generic `QueueStack` to **queue.dart** as shown below:

```
class QueueStack<E> implements Queue<E> {
  final _leftStack = <E>[];
  final _rightStack = <E>[];

  @override
  bool enqueue(E element) => throw UnimplementedError();

  @override
  E? dequeue() => throw UnimplementedError();

  @override
  bool get isEmpty => throw UnimplementedError();

  @override
  E? get peek => throw UnimplementedError();
}
```

You're using lists rather than the `Stack` class you made in Chapter 4, "Stacks". The reason for this is that you're going to leverage a few functions of `List` that your `Stack` doesn't currently have: `first`, `last` and `reverse`.

The idea behind using two stacks is simple. Whenever you enqueue an element, it goes in the **right** stack.

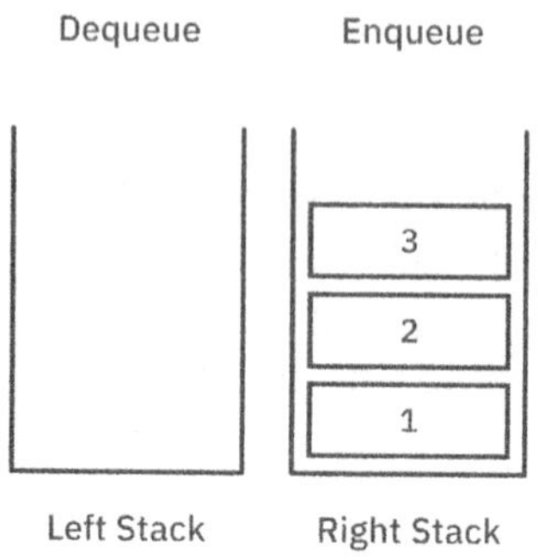

When you need to dequeue an element, reverse the right stack, place it in the **left** stack, and remove the top element.

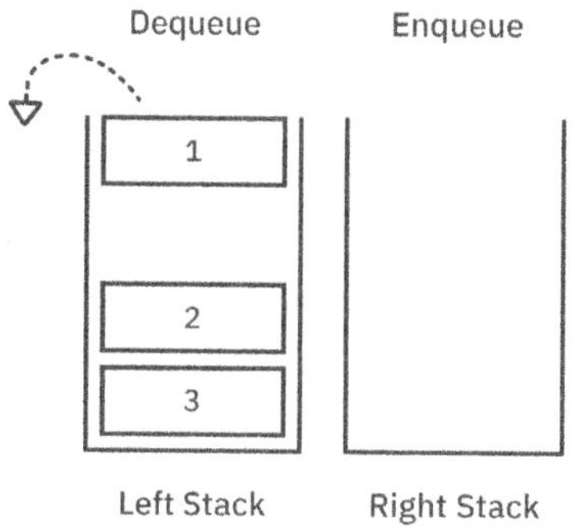

This reversing operation is only required when the left stack is empty, making most enqueue and dequeue operations constant-time.

Leveraging Lists

Implement the common features of a queue, starting with the following:

```
@override
bool get isEmpty => _leftStack.isEmpty && _rightStack.isEmpty;
```

To check if the queue is empty, simply check that both the left and right stacks are empty. This means that no elements are left to dequeue and no new elements have been enqueued.

Next, replace peek with the following:

```
@override
E? get peek => _leftStack.isNotEmpty
    ? _leftStack.last
    : _rightStack.first;
```

You know that peeking looks at the top element. If the left stack is not empty, the element on top of this stack is at the front of the queue. If the left stack is empty, the right stack will be reversed and placed in the left stack. In this case, the element at the bottom of the right stack is next in the queue.

Note that the two properties `isEmpty` and `peek` are still O(1) operations.

Enqueue

Next replace `enqueue` with the method below:

```
@override
bool enqueue(E element) {
  _rightStack.add(element);
  return true;
}
```

Recall that the **right** stack is used to enqueue elements.

You simply push to the stack by appending it to the list. From implementing the `QueueList` previously, you know that adding an element is an O(1) operation.

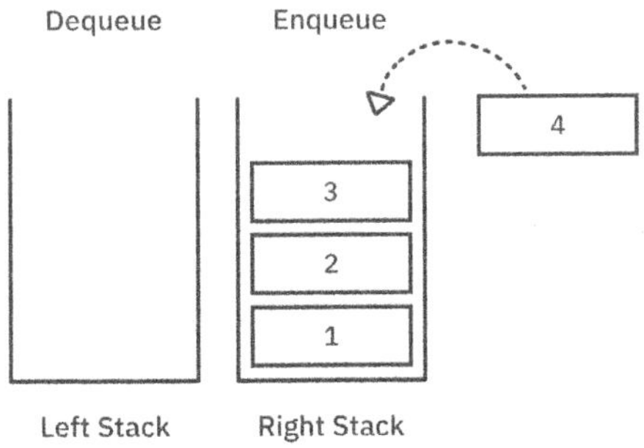

Dequeue

Removing an item in a two-stack-based implementation of a queue is tricky. Add the following method:

```
@override
E? dequeue() {
  if (_leftStack.isEmpty) {
    // 1
    _leftStack.addAll(_rightStack.reversed);
    // 2
    _rightStack.clear();
  }
  if (_leftStack.isEmpty) return null;
  // 3
  return _leftStack.removeLast();
}
```

The following explanations refer to the numbered comments in the code above:

1. If the left stack is empty, set it as the reverse of the right stack:

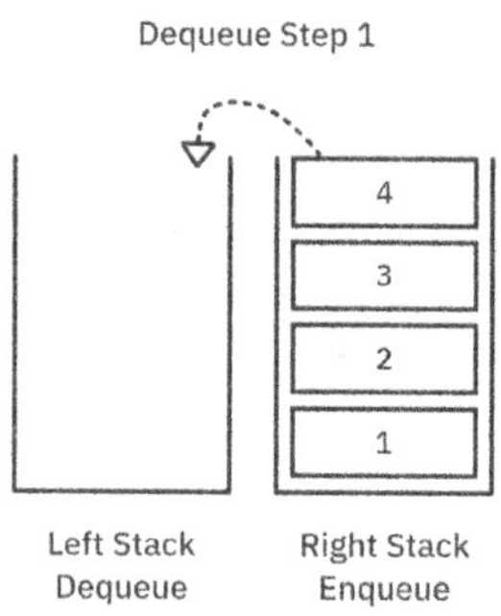

2. Invalidate your right stack. Since you have transferred everything to the left, just clear the right:

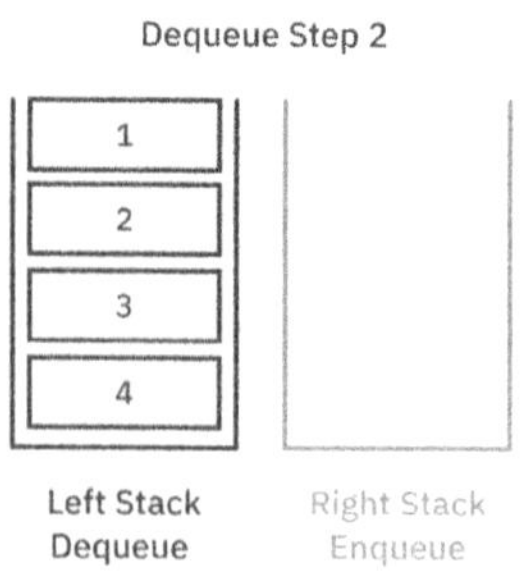

3. Remove the last element from the left stack:

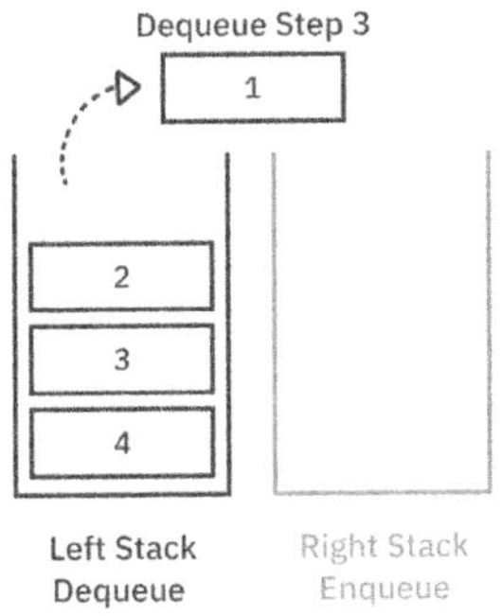

Remember, you only transfer the elements in the right stack when the left stack is empty!

> **Note**: Yes, reversing the contents of a list and adding them to another list is an O(n) operation. However, the overall dequeue cost is still amortized O(1). Imagine having a large number of items in both the left and right stacks. The reverse copy is only required infrequently when the left stack becomes empty.

Testing the Double-Stack-Based Implementation

As usual, override `toString` in `QueueStack` so that you can print the results:

```
@override
String toString() {
  final combined = [
    ..._leftStack.reversed,
    ..._rightStack,
  ].join(', ');
  return '[$combined]';
}
```

Here, you simply combine the reverse of the left stack with the right stack using the spread operator.

Try out the double-stack implementation:

```
final queue = QueueStack<String>();
queue.enqueue("Ray");
queue.enqueue("Brian");
queue.enqueue("Eric");
print(queue); // [Ray, Brian, Eric]

queue.dequeue();
print(queue); // [Brian, Eric]

queue.peek;
print(queue); // [Brian, Eric]
```

Just like all of the examples before, this code enqueues Ray, Brian and Eric, dequeues Ray and then peeks at Brian.

Performance

Here is a summary of the algorithmic and storage complexity of your two-stack-based implementation.

Double Stack Based Queue

Operations	Average case	Worst case
enqueue	O(1)	O(n)
dequeue	O(1)	O(n)
Space Complexity	O(n)	O(n)

Compared to the list-based implementation, by leveraging two stacks, you were able to transform dequeue into an amortized O(1) operation.

Moreover, your two-stack implementation is fully dynamic and doesn't have the fixed size restriction that your ring-buffer-based queue implementation has. Worst-case performance is O(n) when the right queue needs to be reversed or runs out of capacity. Running out of capacity doesn't happen very often thanks to the fact that Dart doubles the capacity every time.

Finally, it beats the linked list in terms of spatial locality. This is because list elements are next to each other in memory blocks. So a large number of elements will be loaded in a cache on first access. Even though a list requires O(n) for simple copy operations, it's a very fast O(n) happening close to memory bandwidth.

Compare the two images below:

A list has its data stored contiguously in memory.

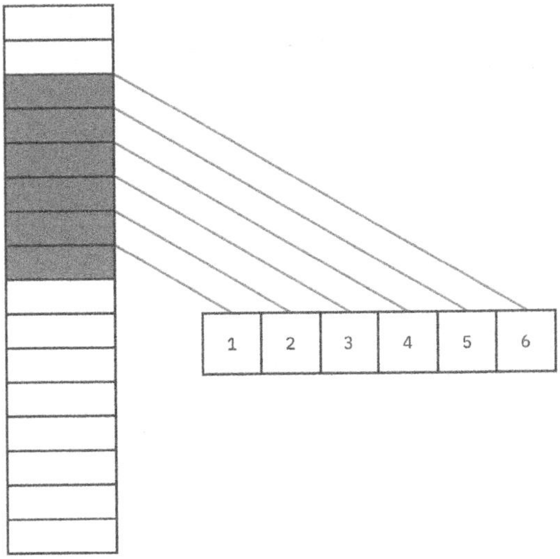

The data for a linked list, on the other hand, could be all over the place. This non-locality could lead to more cache misses, increasing access time.

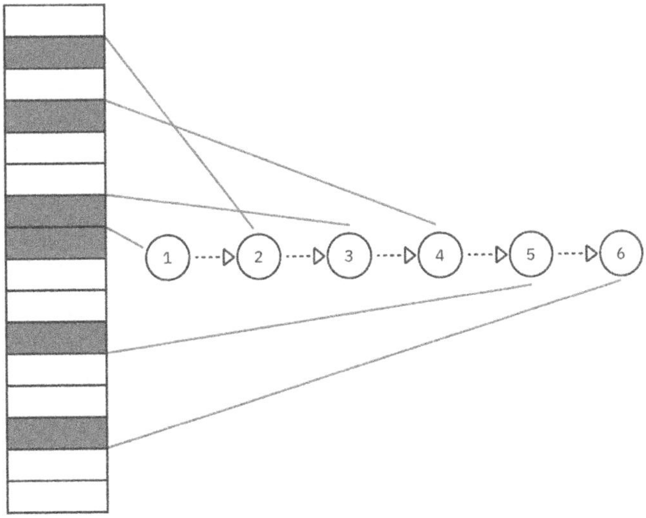

Challenges

Think you have a handle on queues? In this section, you'll explore four different problems related to queues. They'll serve to solidify your fundamental knowledge of data structures in general. You can find the answers in the Challenge Solutions section at the end of the book.

Challenge 1: Stack vs. Queue

Explain the difference between a stack and a queue. Provide two real-life examples for each data structure.

Challenge 2: Step-by-Step Diagrams

Given the following queue where the left is the front of the queue and the right is the back:

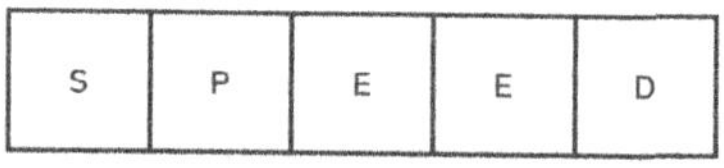

Provide step-by-step diagrams showing how the following series of commands affects the queue internally:

```
queue.enqueue('D');
queue.enqueue('A');
queue.dequeue();
queue.enqueue('R');
queue.dequeue();
queue.dequeue();
queue.enqueue('T');
```

Do this for each of the following queue implementations:

1. List
2. Linked list
3. Ring buffer
4. Double stack

Assume that the list and ring buffer have an initial size of 5.

Challenge 3: Whose Turn Is It?

Imagine that you are playing a game of Monopoly with your friends. The problem is that everyone always forgets whose turn it is! Create a Monopoly organizer that always tells you whose turn it is. Below is an extension method that you can implement:

```
extension BoardGameManager<E> on QueueRingBuffer {
  E? nextPlayer() {
    // TODO
  }
}
```

Challenge 4: Double-Ended Queue

A doubled-ended queue — a.k.a. **deque** — is, as its name suggests, a queue where elements can be added or removed from the front or back.

- A queue (FIFO order) allows you to add elements to the back and remove from the front.
- A stack (LIFO order) allows you to add elements to the back, and remove from the back.

Deque can be considered both a queue and a stack at the same time.

Your challenge is to build a deque. Below is a simple `Deque` interface to help you build your data structure. The enum `Direction` describes whether you are adding or removing an element from the front or back of the deque. You can use any data structure you prefer to construct a `Deque`.

```
enum Direction {
  front,
  back,
}

abstract interface class Deque<E> {
  bool get isEmpty;
  E? peek(Direction from);
  bool enqueue(E element, Direction to);
  E? dequeue(Direction from);
}
```

Key Points

- Queue takes a FIFO strategy: an element added first must also be removed first.
- Enqueue adds an element to the back of the queue.
- Dequeue removes the element at the front of the queue.
- Elements in a list are laid out in contiguous memory blocks, whereas elements in a linked list are more scattered with the potential for cache misses.
- A ring-buffer-based implementation is good for queues with a fixed size.
- Compared to a single list-based implementation, leveraging two stacks improves the dequeue time complexity to an amortized O(1) operation.
- The double-stack implementation beats out linked-list in terms of spatial locality.

Section III: Trees

Trees are another way to organize information, introducing the concept of children and parents. You'll take a look at the most common tree types and see how they can be used to solve specific computational problems. Trees are a handy way to organize information when performance is critical. Having them in your tool belt will undoubtedly be useful throughout your career.

To start your study of trees, you'll learn about an important concept called recursion, a technique that makes it much easier to visit all of the branches and nodes of a tree-like data structure.

Chapter 7: Recursion

You probably heard this joke in third grade:

- Pete and Repeat were in a boat. Pete fell out. Who's left?
- Repeat.
- Pete and Repeat were in a boat. Pete fell out. Who's left?
- Repeat.

... and on it went until someone got tired.

This is an example of an infinite loop. A related term is **recursion**, describing something that "occurs again."

In language, a recursive definition points back to itself. For example, programmers have taken a particular liking to recursive acronyms:

- **YAML**: YAML Ain't Markup Language.
- **GNU**: GNU's Not Unix!
- **gRPC**: gRPC Remote Procedure Calls.

There are also recursive patterns in nature. For example, a tree has branches, which divide into smaller branches, which divide into still smaller branches. River systems and blood vessels also show this tree-like branching pattern into ever-smaller parts.

Computing has borrowed the tree metaphor, and in this chapter, you'll learn how the technique called recursion can be a powerful tool to help you visit all the nodes of a tree-like data structure.

Recursion in Computing

In programming, **recursion** is when a function calls itself. Here's an example:

```
void tellJoke() {
  print("Pete and Repeat were in a boat. Pete fell out. Who's
left?");
  print('Repeat');
  tellJoke();
}
```

`tellJoke` calls itself from inside the function. And because there's nothing to stop it, it'll continue to do so seemingly forever. This is known as **infinite recursion**.

Run that code from `main` like so:

```
void main() {
  tellJoke();
}
```

Rather than continuing forever, though, the program will soon stop with the following error:

```
Unhandled exception:
Stack Overflow
```

Stack Overflow? Isn't that the name of that website?

Yes, that's where the site got its name. The real question is: If you ask a question about a stack overflow on Stack Overflow, is that recursion? Or maybe reading a chapter about stack overflows that asks you about asking stack overflow questions on Stack Overflow is. Or if you ask your friend ... never mind — that could go on forever, or at least until your mind overflows.

You'll come back to the stack overflow error later in the chapter.

Recursion vs Iteration

Rewrite the previous joke as a loop:

```
void tellJoke() {
  while (true) {
    print("Pete and Repeat were in a boat. Pete fell out. Who's left?");
    print('Repeat');
  }
}
```

You don't need to bother running that infinite loop. It won't crash. It'll just lock up your computer.

Another word to describe looping is **iteration**. Recursion and iteration are two different means of repeating a task. You can write any recursive function as an iterative function and any iterative function as a recursive function.

The Base Case

Infinite loops and infinite recursion aren't very useful by themselves. That's why you use `for` loops and why `while` loops typically have a test case or a means of breaking out of the loop:

```
int i = 0;
while (true) {
  print('Knock knock');
  print("Who's there?");
  if (i == 5) break;
  print('Banana');
  print('Banana who?');
  i++;
}
print('Orange');
print('Orange who?');
print("Orange you glad I didn't say banana again?");
```

The loop above breaks out of the iteration on the sixth loop.

Like iteration, recursive functions also need a way to know when to stop calling themselves. This signal to stop is known as the **base case**.

To see this in action, write a recursive function that counts to 10 and then stops:

```
void countToTenRecursively([int i = 1]) {
  // 1
  if (i > 10) return;
  print('$i Mississippi');
  // 2
  countToTenRecursively(i + 1);
}
```

Here are some notes on the numbered comments:

1. **Base case**: If `i` is greater than `10`, the function will immediately return. This will prevent the function from calling itself anymore.
2. **Recursive case**: The function calls itself with one higher value for `i` than the last call was. `i` defaults to `1` in the beginning, but on the second time through, it's `2`, then `3` and so on through `10`.

> **Note**: In case you weren't one of them, some school children use "Mississippi" when counting seconds in games like Hide and Seek. Modify the code above with `async` and `await Future.delayed(Duration(seconds: 1))` to make it more realistic if you prefer.

Exercises

Solve the following exercises both iteratively and recursively:

1. Count by fives to 100. (5, 10, 15, ..., 100)
2. Print all the square integers from 1 to 100. (1, 4, 9, 16, ..., 100)

When Recursion Is Useful

Although you can solve certain problems both recursively and iteratively, sometimes one way makes more sense. The following problem will show that.

Encountering a Tree-Like Data Structure

Say a particular rabbit has three baby rabbits, and each of those bunnies grows up to have its own babies. The image below shows their family tree:

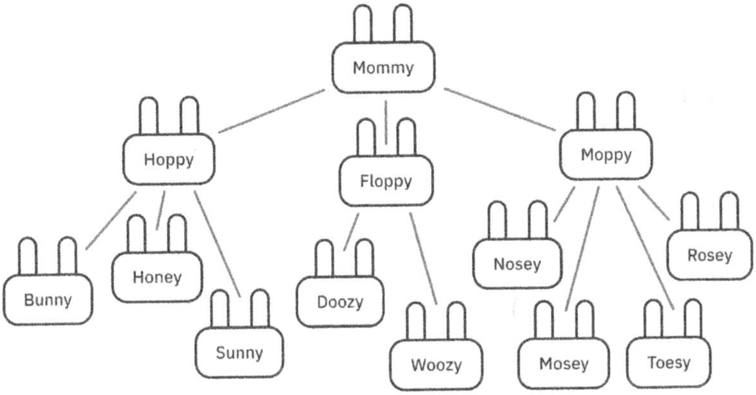

Bunny family tree

In code, define your `Rabbit` class like so:

```
class Rabbit {
  Rabbit(this.name, {this.babies});
  final String name;
  final List<Rabbit>? babies;
}
```

Then, build the family tree from the previous image like this:

```
final family = Rabbit(
  'Mommy',
  babies: [
    Rabbit(
      'Hoppy',
      babies: [
        Rabbit('Bunny'),
        Rabbit('Honey'),
        Rabbit('Sunny'),
      ],
    ),
    Rabbit(
      'Moppy',
      babies: [
        Rabbit('Doozy'),
        Rabbit('Woozy'),
      ],
    ),
    Rabbit(
      'Floppy',
      babies: [
        Rabbit('Nosey'),
        Rabbit('Mosey'),
        Rabbit('Toesy'),
        Rabbit('Rosey'),
      ],
    ),
  ],
);
```

Now, if you wanted to print the name of each rabbit in the family, how would you do it? Could you do it with a loop? Take a minute to think about it.

Visiting the Members

If you have a linear collection like a list, queue or any other data structure you've studied thus far in the book, it's relatively simple to loop over the members. But when you have a branching data structure like the rabbit family tree, it's not so easy to visit each member using a loop.

Recursion comes to the rescue, though!

Write the following recursive function:

```
void printName(Rabbit rabbit) {
  // 1
  print(rabbit.name);
  // 2
  final babies = rabbit.babies;
  if (babies == null) return;
  // 3
  for (final baby in babies) {
    printName(baby);
  }
}
```

Here's what's happening in the numbered comments:

1. You start by printing the given rabbit's name. This is the main task you want to accomplish for each rabbit.
2. This is the base case. If a rabbit has no babies, you don't need to continue.
3. Call `printName` for each baby a rabbit has. This is the recursive case. After reaching the end of the `for` loop, you stop recursing. This is a second base case.

Add the following line at the bottom of your `main` function:

```
printName(family);
```

`family` here is Mommy rabbit with all the babies and grandbabies.

Run that to see the result:

```
Mommy
Hoppy
Bunny
Honey
Sunny
Floppy
Doozy
Woozy
Moppy
Nosey
Mosey
Toesy
Rosey
```

Carefully observe the order. It might help to refer back to the image.

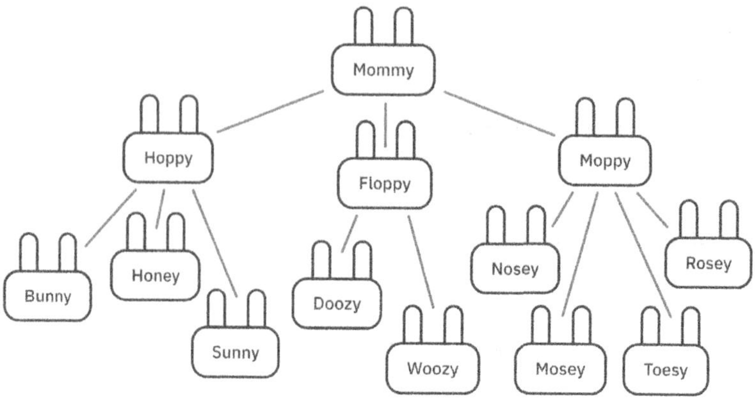

Bunny family tree

- You started with Mommy rabbit.
- Next, you took the first baby, named Hoppy.
- Then, before taking any of the sibling bunnies (Floppy or Moppy), you took the first baby of Hoppy. That bunny (named Bunny, coincidentally) didn't have any babies, so you met the base case. Then, you took Hoppy's next baby, which was Honey, the sibling of Bunny. Honey also had no babies, so you went on to Sunny.
- That was all of Hoppy's babies, so you met another base case. But you continue to recurse over Mommy's other babies by going on to Floppy and its babies.
- And so it continues until you visit all of the rabbits.

Using a Debugger to Observe Program Flow

To get a feel for how recursion works, it's important to take the time to step over the logic in the same way the program does it. The debugger is useful for this.

Add a breakpoint in front of `printName(family);`.

Then, rerun your program in debug mode.

In VS Code, press the **Step Into** button repeatedly for each line:

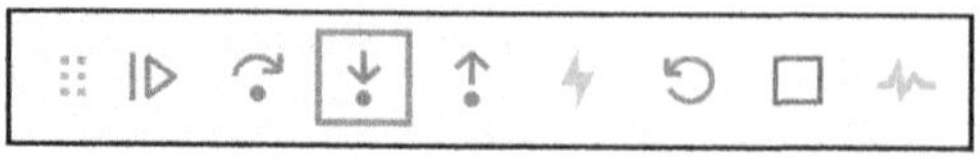

Now, watch the logic play out:

- Note when you reach the base case.
- Note when the `for` loop finishes and you complete the function normally.

Now, repeat the procedure, but this time pay attention to the **Call Stack** window in the **Run and Debug** panel in VS Code. Note how when you go deeper into a recursive function, another `printName` is added to the call stack:

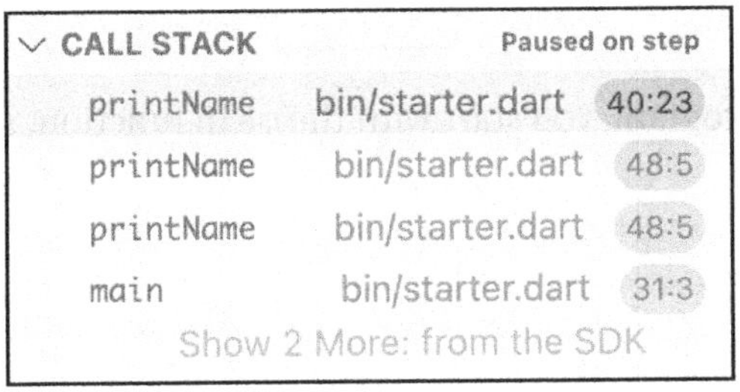

This is key to how recursion works, which you'll read about in the next section.

How Recursion Works

In Chapter 4, "Stacks", you learned about the stack data structure. Well, Dart uses this data structure internally to implement recursion. This internal stack is known as the **call stack**. When one function calls another, Dart pushes the new function onto the call stack. Each function on the stack is known as a **stack frame**.

When a function completes, Dart pops it off the top of the call stack. Because Dart saves the function states in the stack frames, the previous function continues from where it had left off.

The images in the following section will show how Dart pushes and pops functions to and from the call stack.

Visualizing the Call Stack

At first, the call stack is empty:

When you run your program, you start with the `main` function, so Dart pushes `main` to the call stack:

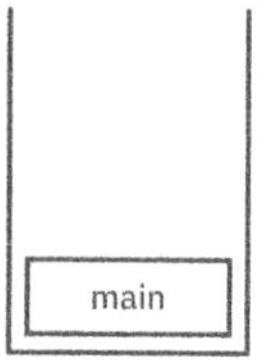

When you enter `printName` the first time, Dart pushes it to the stack. Because Mommy is at the top of `family`, this is Mommy's stack frame:

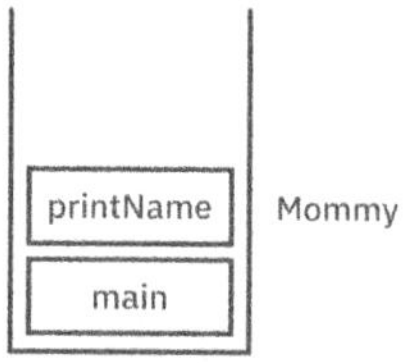

Mommy's first baby is Hoppy, so as you recursively call `printName` for each baby, Hoppy is first. Dart adds `printName` for Hoppy to the call stack:

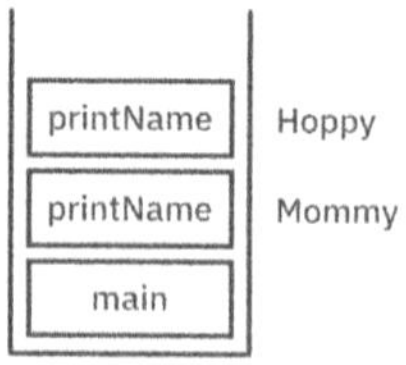

Hoppy also has babies, so the recursion continues. You call `printName` for Hoppy's first baby, Bunny, and Dart adds this function to the stack:

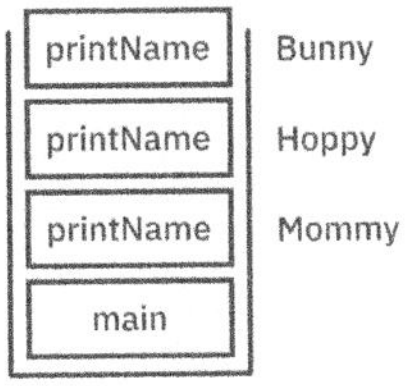

Bunny has no babies, so you've reached the base case. You exit Bunny's `printName` function, so Dart pops it off the stack. Now, you're back inside the Hoppy `printName` function:

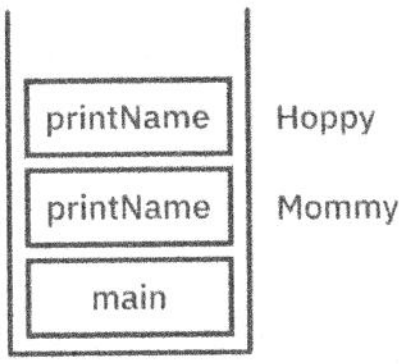

The stack frame stored the execution state of Hoppy's `printName` function, so you continue from where you had left off because you were looping through all of Hoppy's babies. The next one after Bunny is Honey. You call Honey's `printName` function, and Dart pushes it to the call stack:

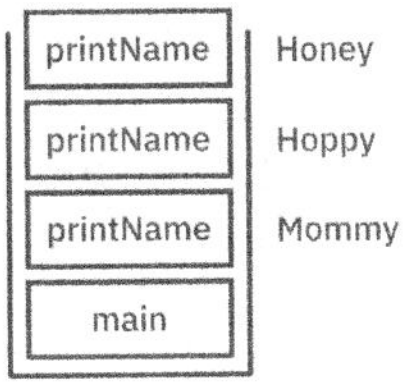

Honey doesn't have any babies either, so Dart pops its stack frame off the call stack:

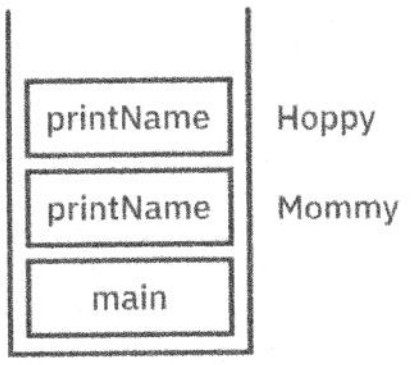

Back in Hoppy's `printName` function, you've now iterated to the last baby, Sunny. Call its `printName`, and Dart pushes it to the call stack:

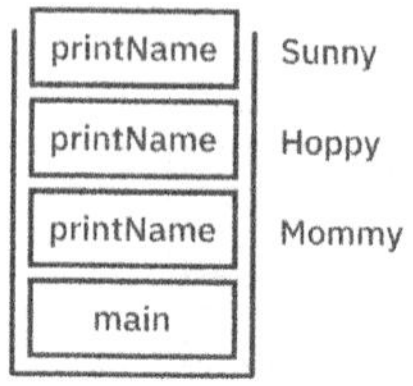

Sunny has no babies, so Dart pops its `printName` from the call stack:

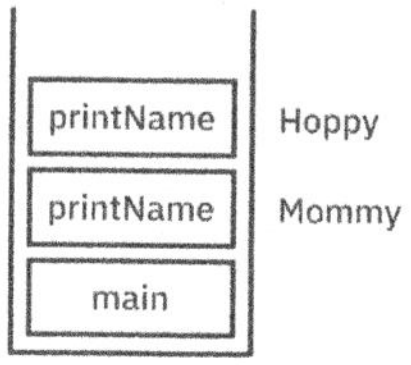

You've also finished iterating through Hoppy's babies, so its `printName` function finishes normally. Dart pops it off the stack:

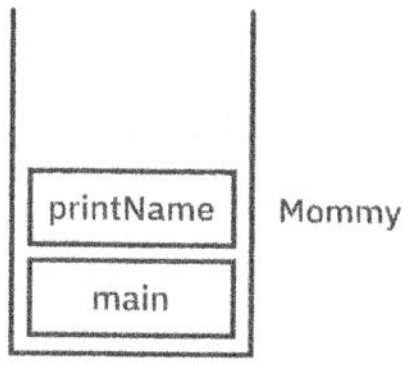

Mommy's `printName` function was also in the middle of looping through its babies. Because the state is saved in the stack frame, Dart knows the next baby after Hoppy is Floppy.

The same process continues for Floppy's babies and Moppy's babies. Finally, when you've finished recursing through all Mommy's babies, this `printName` function finishes, and Dart can pop it off the stack:

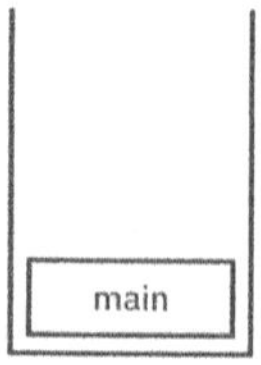

The `main` function also completes now, so Dart pops it off the stack. The call stack is empty, and your program is complete:

Replacing Recursion With a Loop and a Stack

As the chapter mentioned earlier, you can convert any recursive function to an iterative one. Sometimes, though, you need an extra data structure to do so. You learned how Dart implements recursion using an internal stack. You can do the same thing by hand with your stack.

You'll find the **stack.dart** file you created in Chapter 4, "Stacks", in the **lib** folder of your **starter** project. Open the file with your `main` function and import your stack:

```
import 'package:starter/stack.dart';
```

Then, write the following code:

```
void printNamesIteratively(Rabbit rabbit) {
  // 1
  final stack = Stack<Rabbit>();
  stack.push(rabbit);
  // 2
  while (stack.isNotEmpty) {
    // 3
    Rabbit current = stack.pop();
    print(current.name);
    // 4
    final babies = current.babies;
    if (babies == null) continue;
    // 5
    for (final baby in babies.reversed) {
      stack.push(baby);
    }
  }
}
```

Here's what's happening:

1. You initialize the stack by pushing the first rabbit. In this case, that will be Mommy.

2. As long as there's a rabbit on the stack, you keep popping and pushing.
3. Rather than waiting to handle all the babies first, this algorithm pops a rabbit off the stack before moving on to its babies.
4. If no babies exist, you backtrack and pop the next rabbit off the stack.
5. If a rabbit does have babies, though, you queue them up for future handling by pushing them to the stack. There isn't any special requirement to use `babies.reversed` rather than just `babies`. Either way, you visit each rabbit once. The only reason this function used `reversed` was to mimic the same order Dart gave in the recursive version.

Call your function at the bottom of `main` like so:

```
printNamesIteratively(family);
```

Run that, and it'll print the rabbit names in the same order as before:

```
Mommy
Hoppy
Bunny
Honey
Sunny
Floppy
Doozy
Woozy
Moppy
Nosey
Mosey
Toesy
Rosey
```

The key takeaway is that you can use iteration and a stack to accomplish the same thing as recursion. There's nothing magical about recursion.

> **Note**: You can also use a queue rather than a stack when iterating over a tree-like data structure. The main difference is the order in which you visit the elements. You'll learn more about this in a future chapter.

Now that you understand how recursion works, it's time to come back to the question of the stack overflow error you saw at the beginning of the chapter.

What Is a Stack Overflow?

When a recursive function keeps calling itself, Dart keeps adding the function state to the call stack. Each stack frame on the stack takes a bit of the memory the system has allocated to your program. Eventually, that memory runs out, and you have a stack overflow.

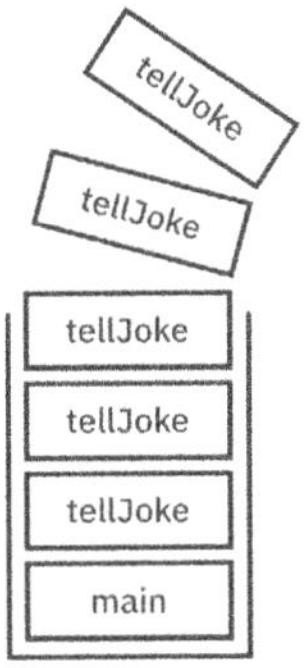

Stack overflow

When Not to Use Recursion

An oft-used example when teaching recursion is the Fibonacci sequence. For a refresher, the Fibonacci sequence is 0, 1, 1, 2, 3, 5, 8, 13, ... Besides the first two, every number in the sequence is the sum of the two before it.

Unoptimized Recursive Fibonacci Function

You can find the value of the *n*th number in the sequence using a recursive function like so:

```
int fibonacci(int n) {
  if (n <= 1) return n;
  return fibonacci(n - 1) + fibonacci(n - 2);
}
```

The base case is when *n* is less than or equal to one, which means you've reached the beginning of the sequence. The recursive case takes the two previous values before *n* and adds them to find *n*.

The code is very compact and looks quite elegant. The problem is it's inefficient. To see why, add a print statement to the beginning of `fibonacci`:

```
print('fibonacci($n)');
```

Then, run the following from `main`:

```
final value = fibonacci(5);
print('value: $value');
```

Here is the printout:

```
fibonacci(5)
fibonacci(4)
fibonacci(3)
fibonacci(2)
fibonacci(1)
fibonacci(0)
fibonacci(1)
fibonacci(2)
fibonacci(1)
fibonacci(0)
fibonacci(3)
fibonacci(2)
fibonacci(1)
fibonacci(0)
fibonacci(1)
value: 5
```

For every function call, you make two more recursive calls. Here's the same information in visual form:

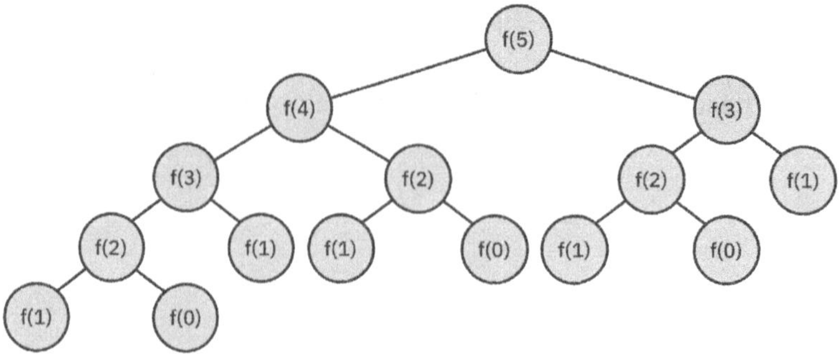

You're repeating a lot of work. For example, look for `f(3)`, and it's there twice. Look for `f(2)`, and you see it three times. You did the work to calculate `fibonacci(3)` and `fibonacci(2)` once. Repeating that work is a complete waste of time. Because the amount of work nearly doubles for every increase in *n*, the time complexity of this algorithm is O(2^n). This is known as **exponential time complexity**.

> **Note**: O(2^n) is much worse than O(n^2), which is only quadratic complexity. Take *n* to be 30, for example. Thirty squared is merely 900. Two to the 30th power, though, is 1,073,741,824. Much worse!

Optimizing With Memoization

A major optimization technique in this sort of scenario is to store the computed values and just look them up when needed. This is known as **memoization**.

> **Note**: You pronounce the *-ization* part of memoization the same as in *memorization*, but say "memo" first. That's /ˌmɛmoʊaɪˈzeɪʃən/, if you're familiar with the phonetic alphabet.

Replace your inefficient `fibonacci` function with the following optimized one:

```
int fibonacci(int n, [Map<int, int>? memo]) {
  print('fibonacci($n)');
  memo ??= {};
  if (n <= 1) return n;
  if (!memo.containsKey(n)) {
    memo[n] = fibonacci(n - 1, memo) + fibonacci(n - 2, memo);
  }
  return memo[n]!;
}
```

This time you used a map called `memo` to cache the Fibonacci values you've already calculated. Now, you only need to perform the recursive calls when `memo` doesn't contain the value. This saves a lot of work.

Run the code again, and this time you see the shortened output:

```
fibonacci(5)
fibonacci(4)
fibonacci(3)
fibonacci(2)
fibonacci(1)
```

```
fibonacci(0)
fibonacci(1)
fibonacci(2)
fibonacci(3)
value: 5
```

Graphically, that looks like so:

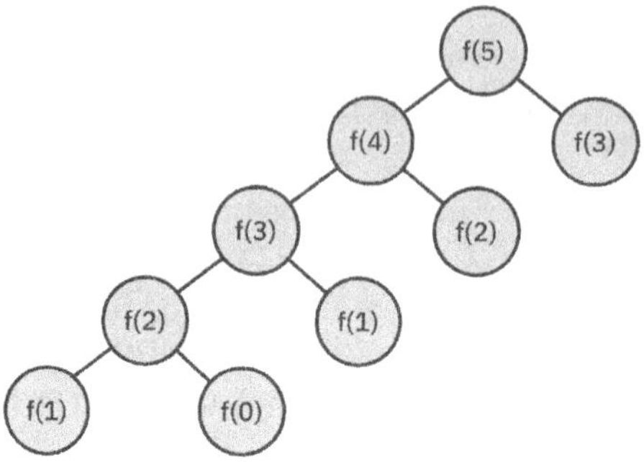

Your time complexity has turned into a much more acceptable O(n).

Preferring Iteration

Memoization is good, and it has its place, but this is a situation where there's no need to use recursion at all. Why not use simple iteration?

Replace `fibonacci` with the following iterative version:

```
int fibonacci(int n) {
  if (n <= 1) return n;

  int first = 1;
  int second = 1;

  for (int i = 3; i <= n; i++) {
    int temp = first + second;
    first = second;
    second = temp;
  }

  return second;
}
```

This time, you used a simple `for` loop to calculate the successive Fibonacci values. The time complexity is still linear, like your memoized version, but this version is easier to reason about because you don't have to worry about recursion or memoization.

Choosing Between Recursion and Iteration

So when do you need to use recursion, and when can you just use iteration?

Think back to the rabbit example earlier in the chapter. The branching nature of the problem made it difficult to use a simple loop. It was still possible but required the help of a stack.

When learning about recursion, I found Al Sweigart's advice helpful in the talk Recursion for Beginners: A Beginner's Guide to Recursion (bit.ly/40c2AoC). The general rule of thumb is to use recursion whenever the following two conditions are true:

1. You have a tree-like data structure.
2. You need to backtrack to visit different branches of the tree.

The rest of the time, iteration with a simple loop is probably all you need.

The rabbit family had a tree-like data structure, and visiting each of the babies in different branches of the tree required backtracking. That made it a good candidate for recursion. Comparing the recursive and iterative approaches, it was easier to use recursion than to manage iteration with the help of a stack.

On the other hand, calculating the Fibonacci sequence, counting to 10 and finding the squared integers from 1 to 100 can all be accomplished with a simple loop. You don't even need a helper stack. If you can solve a problem using simple iteration, go for it! Don't use recursion just because you know how.

In the first edition of this book, I implemented the `toString` method of `LinkedList` recursively in Chapter 5, "Linked Lists." But while writing this chapter for the book's second edition, I realized a linked list is not very tree-like. Also, you don't need to backtrack to visit every list member. Because of that, I rewrote `toString` using a loop. That also meant I could delay this new recursion chapter until the Trees section, where it belongs.

This chapter has given you an informal introduction to trees. In the following chapters, you'll learn a lot more. Recursion will be an important tool to help you along the way.

Challenges

Here are a few challenges to test your understanding of what you learned in this chapter. You can find the answers in the Challenge Solutions section and in the supplementary materials that accompany the book.

Challenge 1: Would You Rather

Based on the advice at the end of the chapter, would it likely be easier to use iteration or recursion for the following problems:

1. Printing all the file names on your hard drive.
2. Calculating *n* factorial.
3. Tracking a person's matrilineal line (mother's mother's mother) in a family tree.
4. Parsing JSON.

Challenge 2: How Many

Using the `Rabbit` class and `family` object you wrote earlier in the chapter, create a function that returns the total number of family members.

The function signature looks like so:

```
int countSize(Rabbit family)
```

Challenge 3: Even Faster

Use memoization to convert your iterative `fibonacci` function from O(n) to amortized O(1), assuming the function will be called many times.

Key Points

- A recursive function is a function that calls itself.
- The base case is the condition when recursion stops.
- Dart implements recursion with a call stack, which uses the stack data structure internally.
- Each function on the call stack is known as a stack frame.
- A stack overflow error occurs when recursion continues unchecked and fills the call stack beyond its memory limit.
- Memoization refers to caching the results of expensive function calls, which improves efficiency.
- Any recursive function can be converted to an iterative function, though potentially needing a helper data structure like a stack or queue.
- Recursion is useful if your problem has a tree-like data structure and requires backtracking. Otherwise, iteration is likely better.

Chapter 8: Trees

The **tree** is a data structure of profound importance. It's used to tackle many recurring challenges in software development, such as:

- Representing hierarchical relationships.
- Managing sorted data.
- Facilitating fast lookup operations.

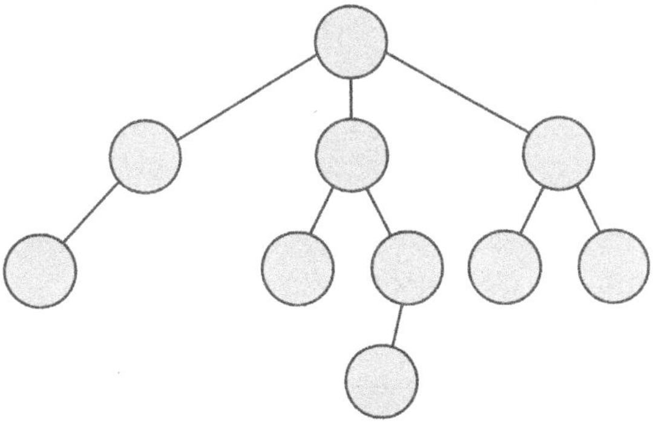

A tree

There are many types of trees, and they come in various shapes and sizes. In this chapter, you'll learn the basics of using and implementing a tree.

Terminology

Many terms are associated with trees, and here are some you should know right off the bat.

Node

Like the linked list, trees are made up of **nodes**.

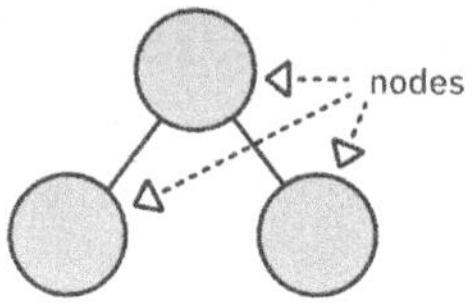

Each node can carry some data and keeps track of its **children**.

Parent and Child

Trees are viewed starting from the top and branching towards the bottom, just like a real tree. Well, OK, exactly the opposite of a real tree. :]

Every node except the topmost one is connected to exactly one node above it. That node is called a **parent** node. The nodes connected directly below a parent are called **child** nodes. In a tree, every child has exactly one parent. That's what makes a tree a tree.

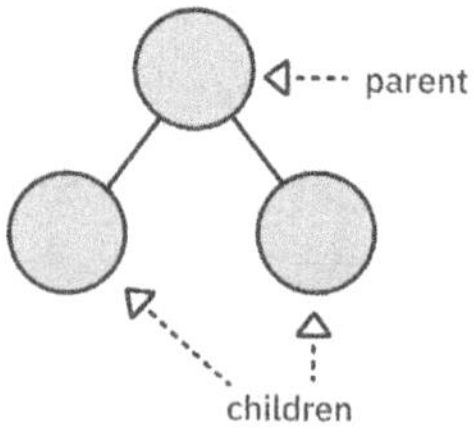

In the last chapter, you saw this parent-child relationship with the rabbit family. Mommy was the parent of Hoppy, Floppy and Moppy. At the same time, Hoppy, Floppy and Moppy were child nodes of Mommy and also parent nodes of their own babies:

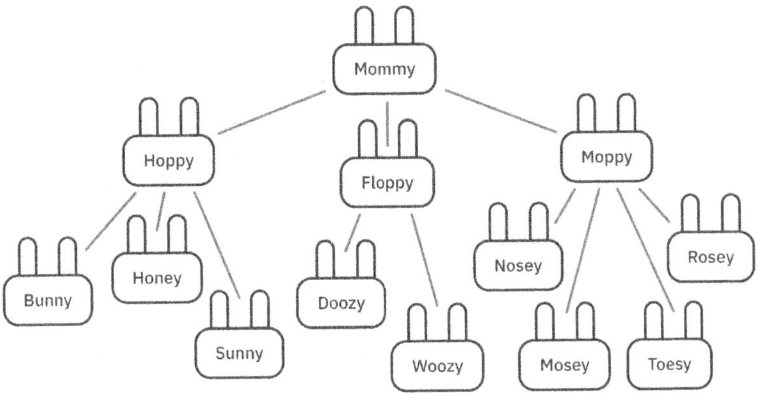

Root

The topmost node in the tree is called the **root** of the tree. It is the only node that has no parent:

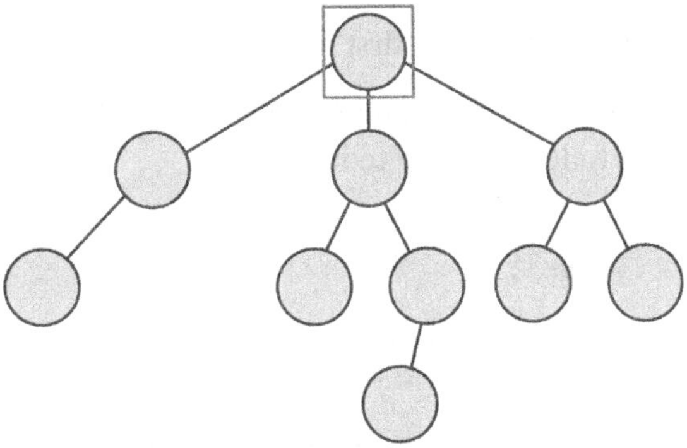

In the rabbit family, Mommy was the root node.

Leaf

A node is a **leaf** if it has no children:

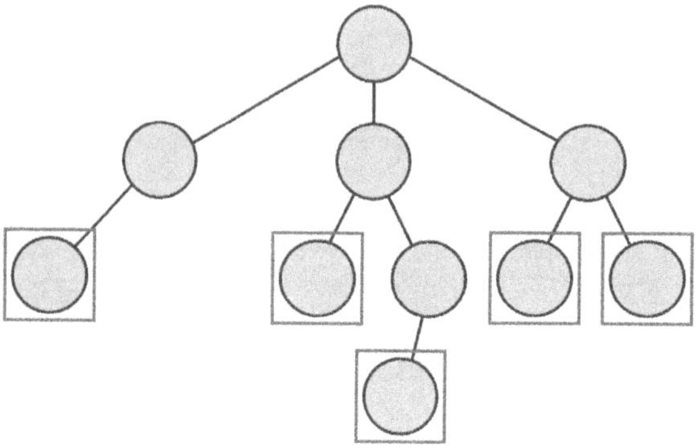

In the rabbit family, Bunny, Honey, Sunny, Doosy, Woosy, Nosey, Mosey, Toesy, and Rosey were all leaf nodes.

You'll run into more terms later on, but these should be enough to get you started.

Implementation

Since a tree is made up of nodes, your first task is to make a `TreeNode` class.

Open up the **starter** project for this chapter. Create a new file called **tree.dart** in the **lib** folder. Then add the following code to it:

```
class TreeNode<T> {
  TreeNode(this.value);
  T value;
  List<TreeNode<T>> children = [];
}
```

Like a linked-list node, each `TreeNode` stores a `value`. However, since tree nodes can point to multiple other nodes, you use a list to hold references to all the `children`.

Next, add the following method inside `TreeNode`:

```
void add(TreeNode<T> child) {
  children.add(child);
}
```

This method adds a child node to a node.

Time to give it a whirl. Open **bin/starter.dart** and replace the file contents with the following code::

```
import 'package:starter/tree.dart';

void main() {
  final beverages = TreeNode('Beverages');
  final hot = TreeNode('Hot');
  final cold = TreeNode('Cold');
  beverages.add(hot);
  beverages.add(cold);
}
```

Hierarchical structures are natural candidates for tree structures, so here you've defined three different nodes and organized them into a logical hierarchy. This arrangement corresponds to the following structure:

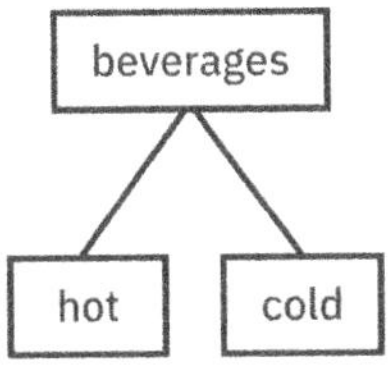

Traversal Algorithms

Iterating through *linear* collections such as lists or linked lists is straightforward. Linear collections have a clear start and end:

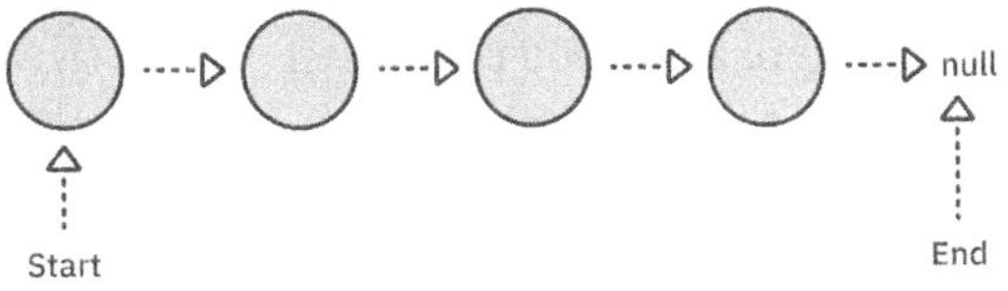

Iterating through trees is a bit more complicated:

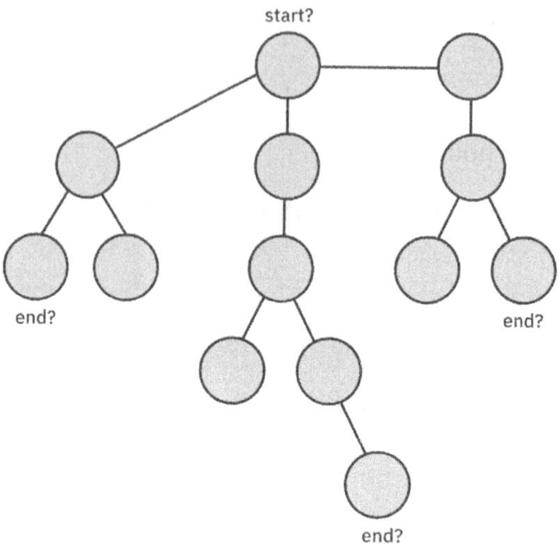

Should nodes on the left have precedence? How should the depth of a node relate to its precedence? Your traversal strategy depends on the problem that you're trying to solve. There are multiple strategies for different trees and different problems. In the next section, you'll look at **depth-first traversal**, a technique that starts at the root and visits nodes as deep as it can before backtracking.

Depth-First Traversal

Add the following method to `TreeNode` in **lib/tree.dart**:

```
void forEachDepthFirst(void Function(TreeNode<T> node)
performAction) {
  performAction(this);
  for (final child in children) {
    child.forEachDepthFirst(performAction);
  }
}
```

This code uses **recursion** to visit the next node. As you learned in the previous chapter, recursive code is where a method calls itself. It's particularly useful for visiting all of the members of a tree data structure.

This time you allow the caller to pass in an anonymous function named `performAction` that will be called once for every node. Then you visit all of the current node's children and call their `forEachDepthFirst` methods. Eventually, you reach leaf nodes without any children and so the recursive function calls don't go on forever. This is the **base case**.

Time to test it out. Add the following top-level function below `main` in **bin/starter.dart**:

```
TreeNode<String> makeBeverageTree() {
  final tree = TreeNode('beverages');
  final hot = TreeNode('hot');
  final cold = TreeNode('cold');
  final tea = TreeNode('tea');
  final coffee = TreeNode('coffee');
  final chocolate = TreeNode('cocoa');
  final blackTea = TreeNode('black');
  final greenTea = TreeNode('green');
  final chaiTea = TreeNode('chai');
  final soda = TreeNode('soda');
  final milk = TreeNode('milk');
  final gingerAle = TreeNode('ginger ale');
  final bitterLemon = TreeNode('bitter lemon');

  tree.add(hot);
  tree.add(cold);

  hot.add(tea);
  hot.add(coffee);
  hot.add(chocolate);

  cold.add(soda);
  cold.add(milk);

  tea.add(blackTea);
  tea.add(greenTea);
  tea.add(chaiTea);

  soda.add(gingerAle);
  soda.add(bitterLemon);

  return tree;
}
```

That function creates the following tree:

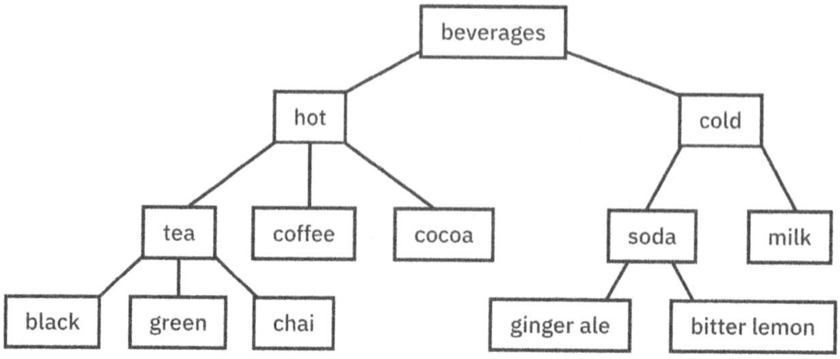

Replace the contents of `main` with the following:

```
final tree = makeBeverageTree();
tree.forEachDepthFirst((node) => print(node.value));
```

Running that produces the following depth-first output:

```
beverages
hot
tea
black
green
chai
coffee
cocoa
cold
soda
ginger ale
bitter lemon
milk
```

The astute reader will notice that the order of this depth-first traversal is the same as when you visited all of the members of the rabbit family in Chapter 7, "Recursion."

In the next section, you'll look at **level-order traversal**, a technique that visits each node of the tree based on the depth of the nodes.

Level-Order Traversal

A tree can be divided into levels based on the distance of the nodes from the root. The root itself is level 0, nodes that are direct children of the root are level 1, the children of these children are level 2, and on it goes. Here's what that looks like in image form:

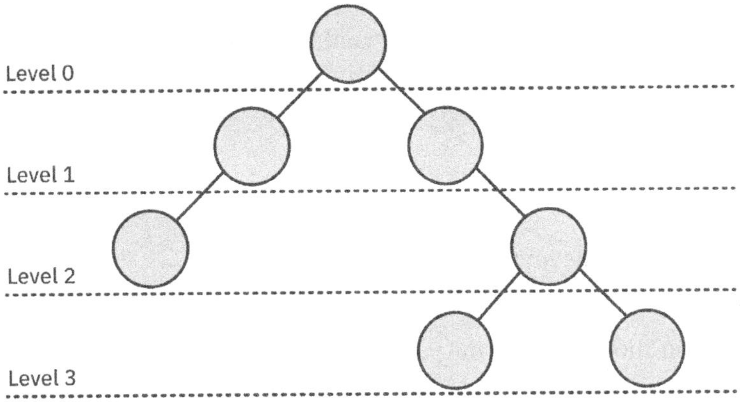

A level-order traversal means that you visit all of the nodes at an upper level before visiting any of the nodes at the next level down.

You can accomplish this by using a queue. The double-stack queue you made in Chapter 6 already exists in the **lib** folder of the **starter** project, so import it at the top of **lib/tree.dart**:

```
import 'queue.dart';
```

Then add the following method to `TreeNode`:

```
void forEachLevelOrder(void Function(TreeNode<T> node)
performAction) {
  final queue = QueueStack<TreeNode<T>>();
  performAction(this);
  children.forEach(queue.enqueue);
  var node = queue.dequeue();
  while (node != null) {
    performAction(node);
    node.children.forEach(queue.enqueue);
    node = queue.dequeue();
  }
}
```

Note the following points:

- The queue ensures that the nodes are visited in the right level-order. A simple recursion, which implicitly uses a stack, would not have worked!
- `QueueStack` is one of the queue implementations you made in the last chapter. You could also use `Queue` from the `dart:collection` library, but you would need to adjust the code somewhat since the Dart `Queue` uses different method names.
- You first enqueue the root node (level 0) and then add the children (level 1). The `while` loop subsequently enqueues all of the children on the next level down. Since a queue is first-in-first-out, this will result in each level dequeuing in order from top to bottom.

Head back to `main` and replace its content with the following:

```
final tree = makeBeverageTree();
tree.forEachLevelOrder((node) => print(node.value));
```

Run that, and you should see the output below:

```
beverages
hot
cold
tea
coffee
cocoa
soda
milk
black
green
chai
ginger ale
bitter lemon
```

Compare that to the beverage hierarchy again. This time the beverages were printed according to their level in the tree:

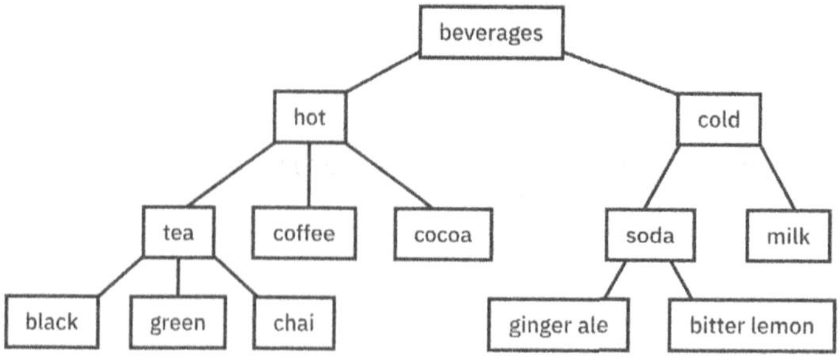

Search

You already have two methods that iterate through all the nodes, so building a search algorithm shouldn't take long. Write the following at the bottom of `TreeNode`:

```
TreeNode<T>? search(T value) {
  TreeNode<T>? result;
  forEachLevelOrder((node) {
    if (node.value == value) {
      result = node;
    }
  });
  return result;
}
```

You iterate through each node and check if its value is the same as what you're searching for. If so, you return it as the result, but return `null` if not.

Head back to `main` to test the code. Replace the function body with the following:

```
final tree = makeBeverageTree();

final searchResult1 = tree.search('ginger ale');
print(searchResult1?.value); // ginger ale

final searchResult2 = tree.search('water');
print(searchResult2?.value); // null
```

Run that, and you'll see the first search founds a match while the second doesn't.

Here, you used your level-order traversal algorithm. Since it visits all of the nodes, if there are multiple matches, the last match will win. This means you'll get different objects back depending on what traversal method you use.

This chapter was a general introduction to trees and tree traversal algorithms. In the next few chapters, you'll learn about more specialized types of trees.

Challenges

The following challenges will help to strengthen your understanding of the tree data structure. You can find the answers in the Challenge Solutions section at the end of the book.

Challenge 1: Print a Tree in Level Order

Print all the values in a tree in order based on their level. Nodes in the same level should be printed on the same line. For example, consider the following tree:

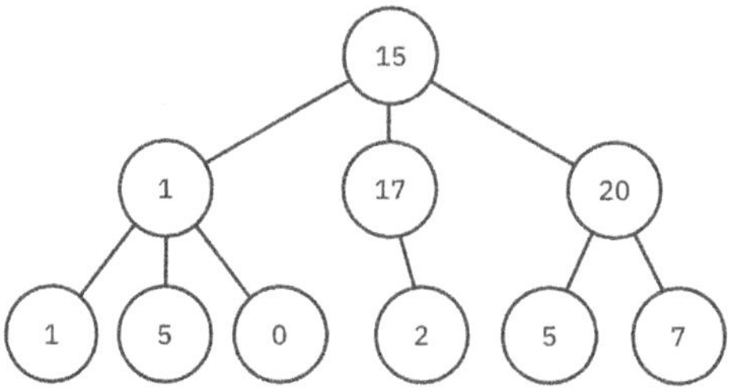

Your algorithm should print the following:

```
15
1 17 20
1 5 0 2 5 7
```

Challenge 2: Widget Tree

Flutter calls the nodes in its user-facing UI tree **widgets**. You can make a mini-version of the same thing.

Create three separate nodes with the following names and types:

- **`Column`**: a tree node that takes multiple children.
- **`Padding`**: a tree node that takes a single child.
- **`Text`**: a tree leaf node.

Use your widget nodes to build a simple widget tree.

Key Points

- Trees share some similarities to linked lists, but, whereas linked-list nodes may only link to one successor node, a tree node can connect to many child nodes.
- Every tree node, except for the root node, has exactly one parent node.
- A root node has no parent nodes.
- Leaf nodes have no child nodes.
- Visiting all the nodes of a tree is called traversal.
- In depth-first traversal, you start at the root and visit the first child of every node as far as you can before backtracking and going on to the child in another branch. You can accomplish this with recursion or a stack.
- In level-order traversal, you start at the root and visit all of its immediate children before going on to the next level of children. You can accomplish this with a queue.

Chapter 9: Binary Trees

In the previous chapter, you looked at a basic tree where each node can have many children. A **binary tree** is a tree where each node has at most **two** children, often referred to as the **left** and **right** children:

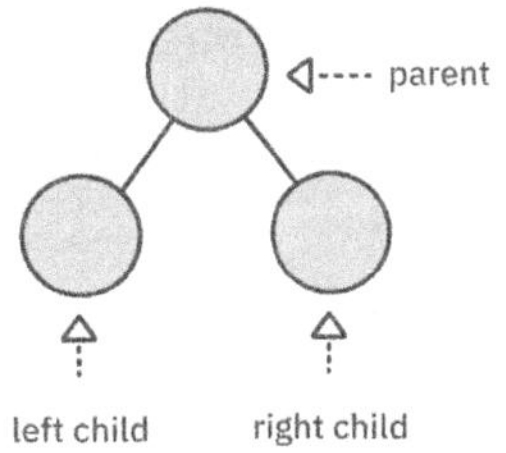

Binary trees serve as the basis for many tree structures and algorithms. In this chapter, you'll build a binary tree and learn about the three most important tree traversal algorithms.

Implementation

Create a folder called **lib** in the root of your **starter** project and, in that folder, create a file named **binary_node.dart**. Then add the following code:

```
class BinaryNode<T> {
  BinaryNode(this.value);
  T value;
  BinaryNode<T>? leftChild;
  BinaryNode<T>? rightChild;
}
```

Rather than maintaining a list of child nodes as you did with `TreeNode` in the previous chapter, you can directly reference `leftChild` and `rightChild`. They're nullable since not every node will have children.

Now open **bin/starter.dart** and import your new class:

```
import 'package:starter/binary_node.dart';
```

Add the following top-level function below `main`:

```
BinaryNode<int> createBinaryTree() {
  final zero = BinaryNode(0);
  final one = BinaryNode(1);
  final five = BinaryNode(5);
  final seven = BinaryNode(7);
  final eight = BinaryNode(8);
  final nine = BinaryNode(9);

  seven.leftChild = one;
  one.leftChild = zero;
  one.rightChild = five;
  seven.rightChild = nine;
  nine.leftChild = eight;

  return seven;
}
```

This defines the following tree:

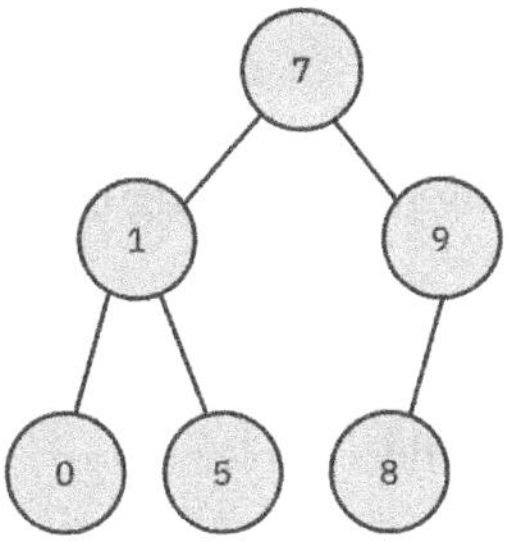

Building a Diagram

Building a mental model of a data structure can be quite helpful in learning how it works. To that end, you'll implement a reusable algorithm that helps visualize a binary tree in the console.

Open **lib/binary_node.dart** and add the following two methods to the bottom of `BinaryNode`:

```
@override
String toString() {
  return _diagram(this);
}

String _diagram(
  BinaryNode<T>? node, [
  String top = '',
  String root = '',
  String bottom = '',
]) {
  if (node == null) {
    return '$root null\n';
  }
  if (node.leftChild == null && node.rightChild == null) {
    return '$root ${node.value}\n';
  }
  final a = _diagram(
    node.rightChild,
    '$top ',
    '$top┌──',
    '$top│ ',
  );
  final b = '$root${node.value}\n';
  final c = _diagram(
    node.leftChild,
    '$bottom│ ',
    '$bottom└──',
```

```
    '$bottom ',
  );
  return '$a$b$c';
}
```

This will recursively create a string representing the binary tree.

> **Note**: This algorithm is based on an implementation by Károly Lőrentey in his book *Optimizing Collections*, available from https://www.objc.io/books/optimizing-collections/.

Try it out by opening **bin/starter.dart** and running the following in `main`:

```
final tree = createBinaryTree();
print(tree);
```

You should see the following console output:

```
  ┌── null
 ┌──9
 │ └── 8
7
 │ ┌── 5
 └──1
  └── 0
```

You'll use this diagraming method for other binary trees in this book.

Traversal Algorithms

Previously, you looked at a **level-order** traversal of a tree. With a few tweaks, you could make that algorithm work for binary trees as well. However, instead of re-implementing level-order traversal, you'll look at three traversal algorithms for binary trees: **in-order**, **pre-order** and **post-order** traversals.

In-Order Traversal

An in-order traversal visits the nodes of a binary tree in the following order, starting from the root node:

1. If the current node has a left child, recursively visit this child first.
2. Then visit the node itself.
3. If the current node has a right child, recursively visit this child.

Here's what an in-order traversal looks like for your example tree:

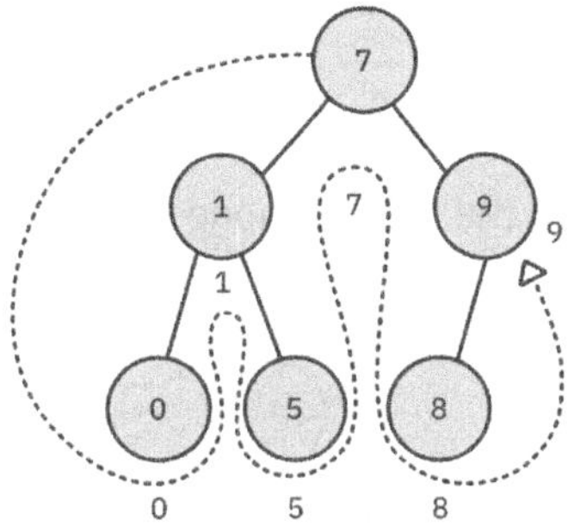

0, 1, 5, 7, 8, 9

You may have noticed that this prints the example tree in ascending order. If the tree nodes are structured in a certain way, in-order traversal visits them in ascending order! Binary search trees take advantage of this, and you'll learn more about them in the next chapter.

Add the following code to `BinaryNode` in **lib/binary_node.dart**:

```
void traverseInOrder(void Function(T value) action) {
  leftChild?.traverseInOrder(action);
  action(value);
  rightChild?.traverseInOrder(action);
}
```

Following the above-mentioned rules, you first traverse to the leftmost node before visiting the value. You then traverse to the rightmost node.

Head back to `main` and replace its content to test this out:

```
final tree = createBinaryTree();
tree.traverseInOrder(print);
```

Run that, and you should see the following in the console:

```
0
1
5
7
8
9
```

Pre-Order Traversal

Pre-order traversal always visits the current node first, then recursively visits the left and right child:

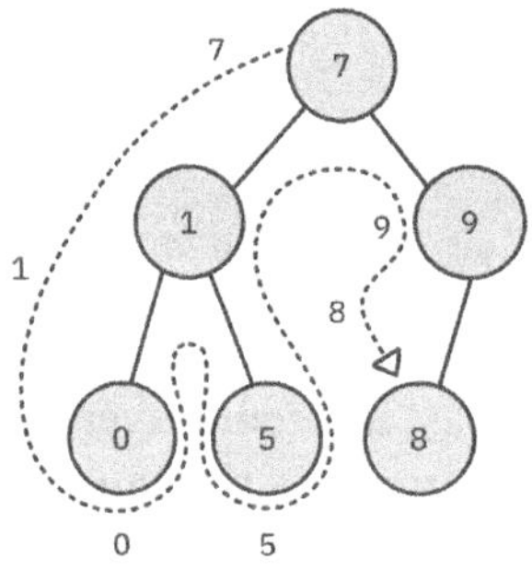

7, 1, 0, 5, 9, 8

Write the following to `BinaryNode` just below your in-order traversal method:

```
void traversePreOrder(void Function(T value) action) {
  action(value);
  leftChild?.traversePreOrder(action);
  rightChild?.traversePreOrder(action);
}
```

You call `action` *before* recursively traversing the children, hence the "pre" of pre-order traversal.

Test it out back in `main` with the following code:

```
final tree = createBinaryTree();
tree.traversePreOrder(print);
```

You should see the following output in the console:

```
7
1
0
5
9
8
```

Post-Order Traversal

Post-order traversal only visits the current node after the left and right child have been visited recursively.

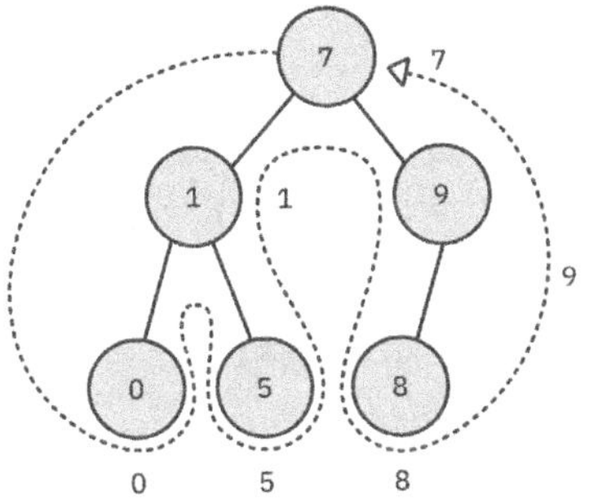

0, 5, 1, 8, 9, 7

In other words, given any node, you'll visit its children before visiting itself. An interesting consequence of this is that the root node is always visited last.

Back inside `BinaryNode`, write the following below `traversePreOrder`:

```
void traversePostOrder(void Function(T value) action) {
  leftChild?.traversePostOrder(action);
  rightChild?.traversePostOrder(action);
  action(value);
}
```

Note that you perform `action` *after* the recursive traversal calls.

Go back to `main` to try it out:

```
final tree = createBinaryTree();
tree.traversePostOrder(print);
```

You should see the following in the console:

```
0
5
1
8
9
7
```

Comparison

Take a moment to review the differences between those three traversal algorithms:

```
void traverseInOrder(void Function(T value) action) {
  leftChild?.traverseInOrder(action);
  action(value);
  rightChild?.traverseInOrder(action);
}

void traversePreOrder(void Function(T value) action) {
  action(value);
  leftChild?.traversePreOrder(action);
  rightChild?.traversePreOrder(action);
}

void traversePostOrder(void Function(T value) action) {
  leftChild?.traversePostOrder(action);
  rightChild?.traversePostOrder(action);
  action(value);
}
```

The methods all contained the same lines of code but executed them in varying order. The list below summarizes that order:

- `traverseInOrder`: left → action → right
- `traversePreOrder`: action → left → right
- `traversePostOrder`: left → right → action

The difference is only in where the action takes place.

Each one of these traversal algorithms has a time and space complexity of O(n).

You saw that in-order traversal can be used to visit the nodes in ascending order. Binary trees can enforce this behavior by adhering to certain rules during insertion. In the next chapter, you'll look at a binary tree with stricter semantics: the binary search tree.

Challenges

Binary trees are a surprisingly popular topic in algorithm interviews. Questions on the binary tree not only require a good foundation of how traversals work, but can also test your understanding of recursive backtracking, so it's good to test what you've learned in this chapter.

Challenge 1: Height of a Tree

Given a binary tree, find the height of the tree. The **height** of the binary tree is determined by the distance between the root and the furthest leaf. The height of a binary tree with a single node is zero since the single node is both the root and the furthest leaf.

Challenge 2: Serialization

A common task in software development is representing a complex object using another data type. This process is known as **serialization** and allows custom types to be used in systems that only support a closed set of data types. An example of serialization is JSON.

Your task is to devise a way to serialize a binary tree into a list, and a way to deserialize the list back into the same binary tree.

To clarify this problem, consider the following binary tree:

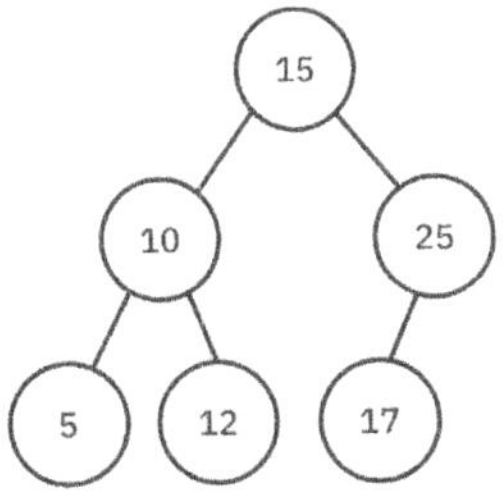

A particular algorithm may output the serialization as follows:

```
[15, 10, 5, null, null, 12, null, null, 25, 17, null, null,
null]
```

The deserialization process should transform the list back into the same binary tree. Note that there are many ways to perform serialization. You may choose any way you wish.

Key Points

- A binary tree is a tree where each node has at most two children, often referred to as the left child and right child.
- Tree traversal algorithms visit each node in the tree once.
- In-order traversal recursively visits the left child first, then the current parent node, and finally the right child.
- Pre-order traversal visits the parent node first, followed by the child nodes.
- Post-order traversal visits the child nodes before the parent node.

Chapter 10: Binary Search Trees

A **binary search tree**, or **BST**, is a data structure that facilitates fast lookup, insert and removal operations. Consider the following decision tree where picking a side forfeits all the possibilities of the other side, cutting the problem in half:

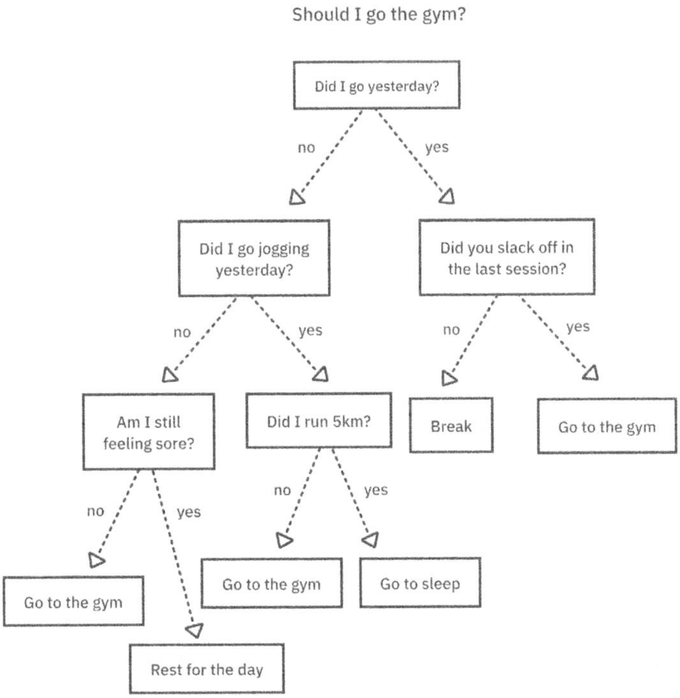

Once choose a branch, there is no looking back. You keep going until you make a final decision at a leaf node. Binary trees let you do the same thing. Specifically, a binary search tree imposes two rules on the binary tree you saw in the previous chapter:

- The value of a left child must be *less than* the value of its parent.
- Consequently, the value of a right child must be *greater than or equal to* the value of its parent.

Binary search trees use these properties to save you from performing unnecessary checking. As a result, lookup, insert and removal have an average time complexity of O(log n), which is considerably faster than linear data structures such as lists and linked lists.

In this chapter, you'll learn about the benefits of BST relative to a list and, as usual, implement the data structure from scratch.

List vs. BST

To illustrate the power of using BST, you'll look at some common operations and compare the performance of lists against the binary search tree.

Consider the following two collections:

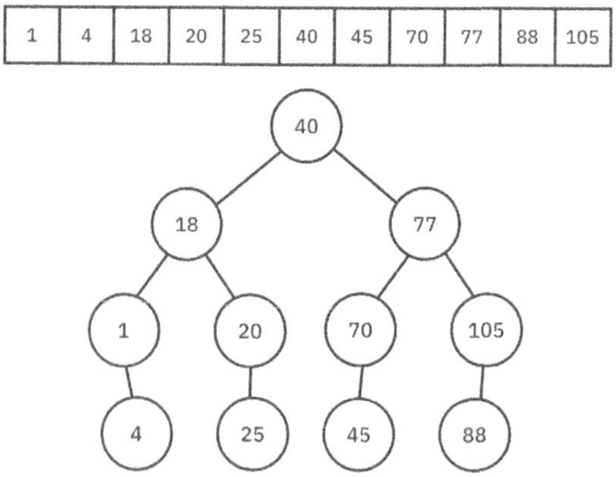

Lookup

There's only one way to do element lookups for an unsorted list. You need to check every element in the list from the start:

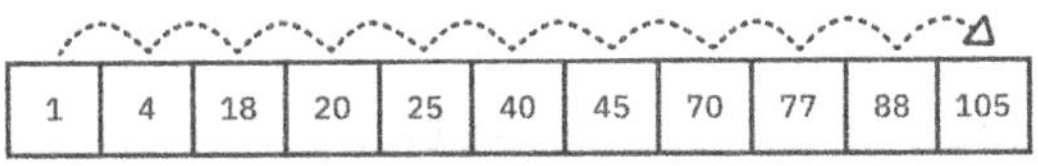

Searching for 105

That's why `list.contains` is an O(n) operation.

> **Note**: If a list is *sorted*, as the one in the diagram above is, you can use a binary search to lookup a value in O(log n) time. You'll come back to this topic in Chapter 13, "Binary Search."

Now consider the case for binary search trees:

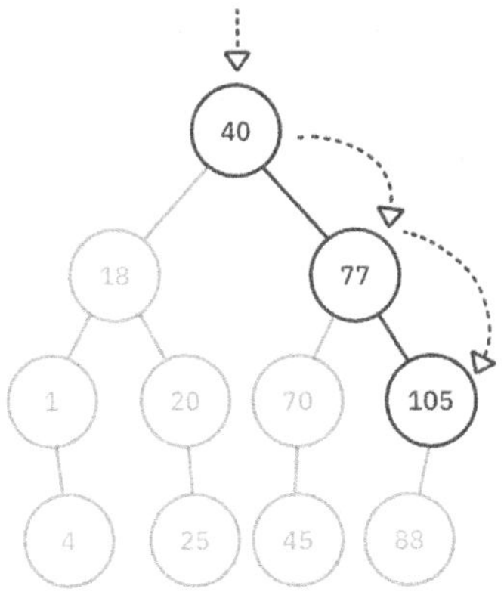

Searching for 105

Every time the search algorithm visits a node in the BST, it can safely make these two assumptions:

- If the search value is **less than** the current value, it must be in the **left** subtree.
- If the search value is **greater than** the current value, it must be in the **right** subtree.

By leveraging the rules of the BST, you can avoid unnecessary checks and cut the search space in half every time you make a decision. That's why element lookup in BST is an O(log n) operation.

Insertion

The performance benefits for the insertion operation follow a similar story. Assume you want to insert **0** into a collection. Inserting at the front of the list causes all other elements to shift backwards by one position. It's like butting in line. Everyone in the line behind your chosen spot needs to make space for you by shuffling back:

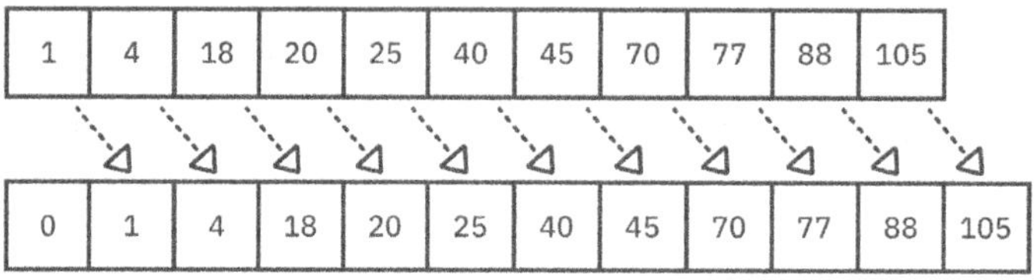

Inserting 0 in sorted order

Inserting into a list has a time complexity of O(n).

Insertion into a binary search tree is much faster. By leveraging the rules of BST, you only need to make three traversals in the example below to find the location for the insertion, and you don't have to shuffle all the elements around!

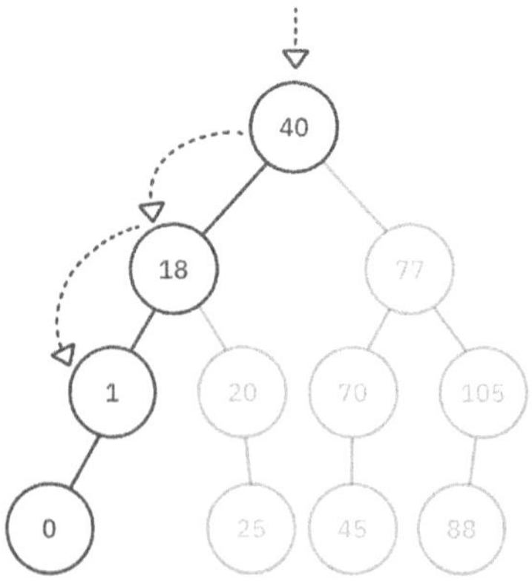

Inserting elements in BST is an O(log n) operation.

Removal

Similar to insertion, removing an element in a list also triggers a shuffling of elements:

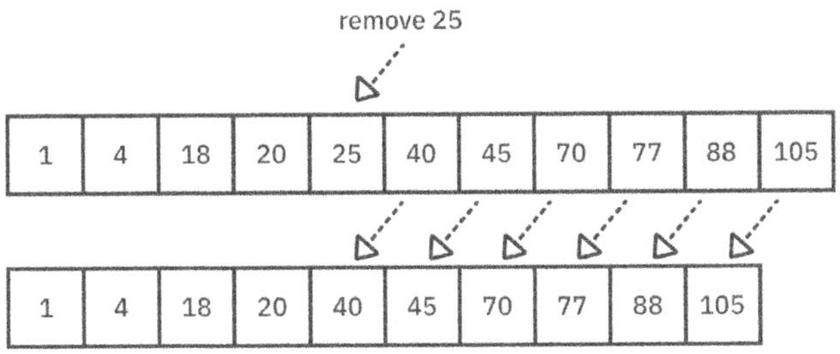

Removing 25 from the list

This behavior also goes along with the lineup analogy. If you leave the middle of the line, everyone behind you needs to shuffle forward to take up the empty space.

Here's what removing a value from a binary search tree looks like. You just hop down the tree until you find the value and then you delete that node:

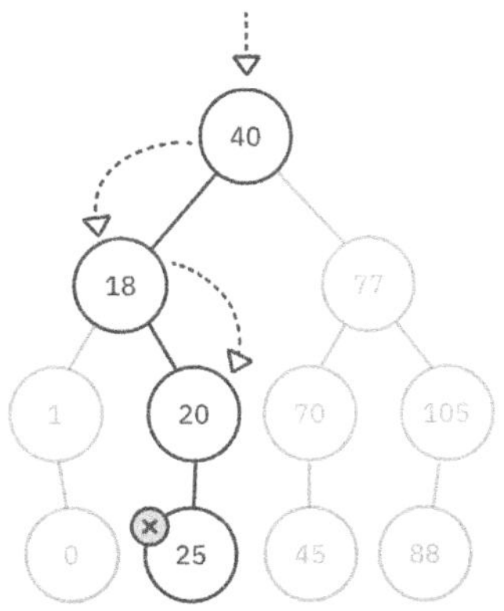

Nice and easy! There are complications to manage when the node you're removing has children, but you'll look into that later. Even with those complications, removing an element from a BST is still an O(log n) operation.

Binary search trees drastically reduce the number of steps for add, remove and lookup operations. Now that you understand the benefits of using a binary search tree, you can move on to the actual implementation.

Implementation

Open up the **starter** project for this chapter. In the **lib** folder, you'll find **binary_node.dart** with the `BinaryNode` type you created in the previous chapter. Create a new file named **binary_search_tree.dart** in the same folder and add the following code to it:

```
import 'binary_node.dart';

class BinarySearchTree<E extends Comparable<E>> {
  BinaryNode<E>? root;

  @override
  String toString() => root.toString();
}
```

By definition, binary search trees can only hold `Comparable` values.

Inserting Elements

In accordance with BST rules, nodes of the left child must contain values less than the current node. Nodes of the right child must contain values greater than or equal to the current node. You'll implement the `insert` method while respecting these rules.

Adding an Insert Method

Add the following to `BinarySearchTree`:

```
void insert(E value) {
  root = _insertAt(root, value);
}

BinaryNode<E> _insertAt(BinaryNode<E>? node, E value) {
  // 1
  if (node == null) {
    return BinaryNode(value);
  }
  // 2
  if (value.compareTo(node.value) < 0) {
    node.leftChild = _insertAt(node.leftChild, value);
  } else {
    node.rightChild = _insertAt(node.rightChild, value);
  }
  // 3
  return node;
}
```

You expose `insert` to users, while using `_insertAt` as a private helper method:

1. This is a recursive method, so it requires a base case for terminating recursion. If the current node is `null`, you've found the insertion point and you return the new `BinaryNode`.
2. Because element types are comparable, you can perform a comparison. This `if` statement controls which way the next `_insertAt` call should traverse. If the new value is less than the current value, that is, if `compareTo` returns a negative number, you'll look for an insertion point on the *left* child. If the new value is greater than or equal to the current value, you'll turn to the *right* child.
3. Return the current node. This makes assignments of the form `node = _insertAt(node, value)` possible since `_insertAt` will either create `node`, if it was `null`, or return `node`, if it was not `null`.

Testing it Out

Open **bin/starter.dart** and replace the contents with the following:

```
import 'package:starter/binary_search_tree.dart';

void main() {
  final tree = BinarySearchTree<num>();
  for (var i = 0; i < 5; i++) {
    tree.insert(i);
  }
  print(tree);
}
```

You need to mark the type as `num` rather than `int` because `num` implements `Comparable` while `int` doesn't.

Run the code above and you should see the following output:

```
    ┌── 4
   ┌──3
   │ └── null
  ┌──2
  │ └── null
 ┌──1
 │ └── null
0
└── null
```

Balanced vs. Unbalanced Trees

The previous tree looks a bit **unbalanced**, but it does follow the rules. However, this tree layout has undesirable consequences. When working with trees, you always want to achieve a **balanced** format:

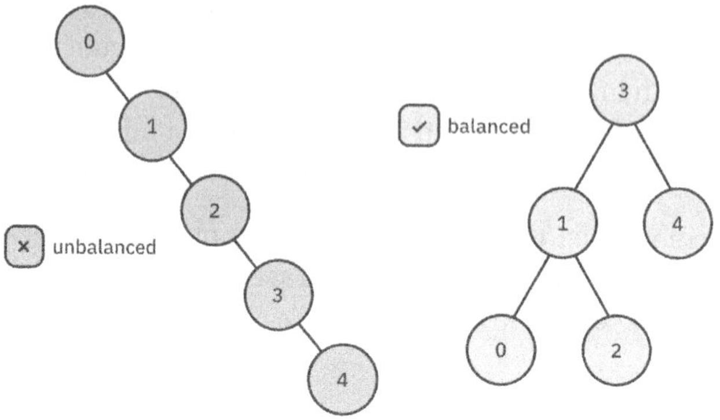

An unbalanced tree affects performance. If you insert **5** into the unbalanced tree you've created, it becomes an O(n) operation:

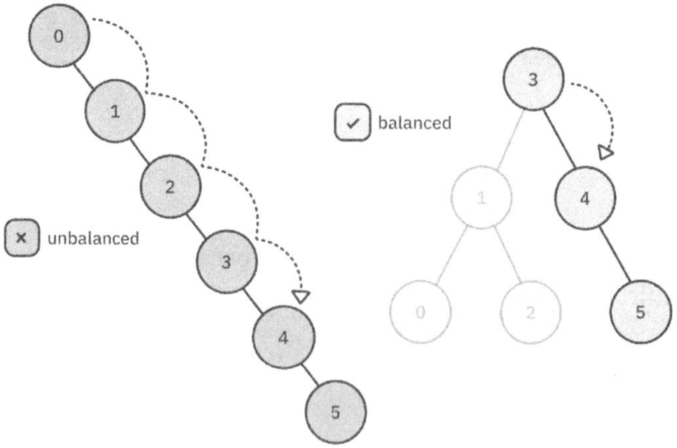

You can create structures known as **self-balancing trees** that use clever techniques to maintain a balanced structure, but you'll have to wait for those details until Chapter 11, "AVL Trees." For now, you'll build a sample tree with a bit of care to keep it from becoming unbalanced.

Building a Balanced Tree

Add the following function below `main`:

```
BinarySearchTree<int> buildExampleTree() {
  var tree = BinarySearchTree<num>();
  tree.insert(3);
  tree.insert(1);
  tree.insert(4);
  tree.insert(0);
  tree.insert(2);
  tree.insert(5);
  return tree;
}
```

Replace the contents of `main` with the following:

```
final tree = buildExampleTree();
print(tree);
```

Run the code. You should see the following in the console:

```
  ┌── 5
 ┌──4
 │ └── null
3
 │ ┌── 2
 └──1
  └── 0
```

Much nicer!

Finding Elements

Finding an element in a binary search tree requires you to traverse through its nodes. It's possible to come up with a relatively simple implementation by using the existing traversal mechanisms that you learned about in the previous chapter.

Add the following method to `BinarySearchTree`:

```
bool contains(E value) {
  if (root == null) return false;
  var found = false;
  root!.traverseInOrder((other) {
    if (value == other) {
      found = true;
    }
  });
  return found;
}
```

Next, head back to `main` to test this out:

```
final tree = buildExampleTree();
if (tree.contains(5)) {
  print("Found 5!");
} else {
  print("Couldn't find 5");
}
```

You should see the following in the console:

```
Found 5!
```

In-order traversal has a time complexity of O(n). Thus, this implementation of `contains` has the same time complexity as an exhaustive search through an unsorted list.

You can do better.

Optimizing contains

Relying on the properties of BST can help you avoid needless comparisons. Back in `BinarySearchTree`, replace `contains` with the following:

```
bool contains(E value) {
  // 1
  var current = root;
  // 2
  while (current != null) {
    // 3
    if (current.value == value) {
      return true;
    }
    // 4
    if (value.compareTo(current.value) < 0) {
      current = current.leftChild;
    } else {
      current = current.rightChild;
    }
  }
  return false;
}
```

The numbered comments refer to the following explanations:

1. Set `current` to the `root` node.
2. As long as `current` isn't `null`, you'll keep branching through the tree.
3. If the current node's `value` equals what you're trying to find, return `true`.
4. Otherwise, decide whether you're going to check the left or the right child.

This implementation of `contains` is an O(log n) operation in a balanced binary search tree.

Removing Elements

Removing elements is a little more tricky because you need to handle a few different scenarios.

Removing a Leaf Node

Removing a leaf node is straightforward. Simply detach the leaf node:

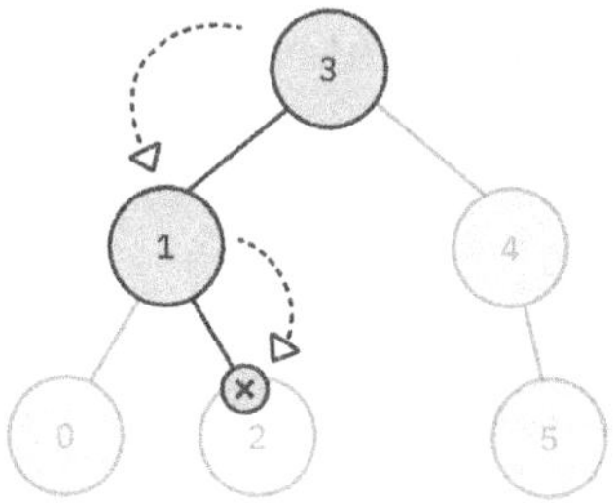

removing 2

For non-leaf nodes, however, there are extra steps you must take.

Removing Nodes With One Child

When removing nodes with *one* child, you'll need to reconnect that child with the rest of the tree:

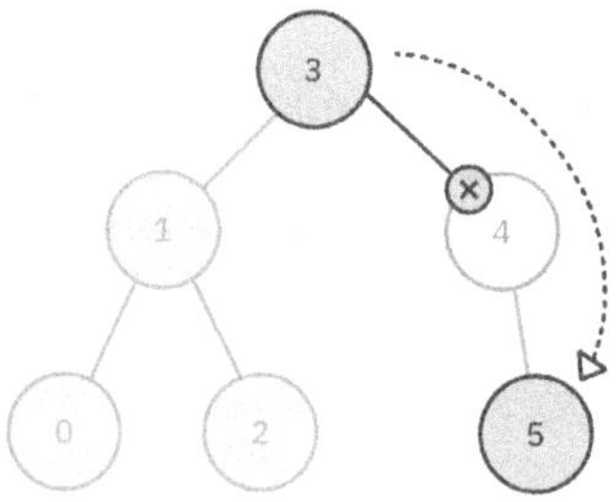

removing 4, which has one child

Removing Nodes With Two Children

Nodes with two children are a bit more complicated, so a more complex example tree will better illustrate how to handle this situation. Assume that you have the following tree and that you want to remove the value **25**:

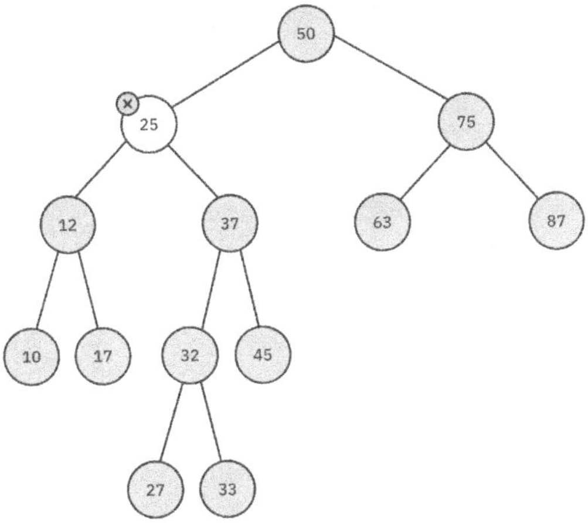

Simply deleting the node presents a dilemma. You have two child nodes (**12** and **37**) to reconnect, but the parent node only has space for one child:

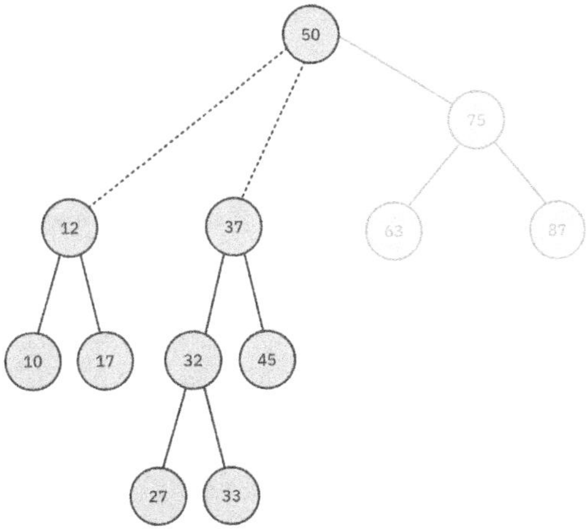

To solve this problem, you'll implement a clever workaround. When removing a node with two children, replace the value you want to remove with the smallest value in the node's *right* subtree. Based on the principles of BST, this is in the *leftmost* node of the right subtree. In the example, that means you'll replace **25** with **27**:

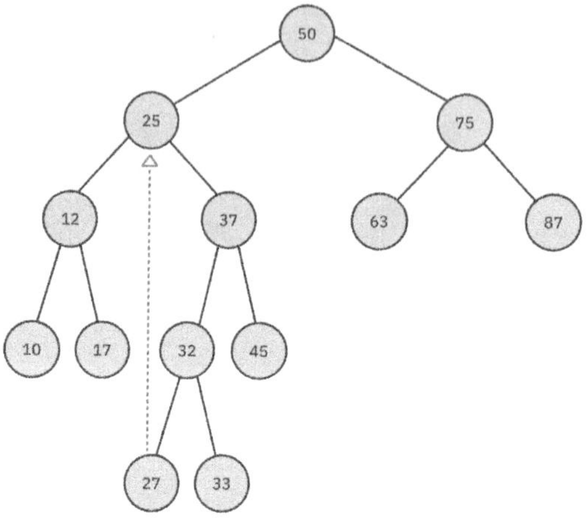

It's important to note that this will produce a **valid** binary search tree. Because the new value was the smallest in the right subtree, all values in the right subtree will still be greater than or equal to the new value. And because the new value came from the right subtree, all values in the left subtree will be less than the new value.

After performing the replacement, you can simply remove the node you copied from, just a leaf node.

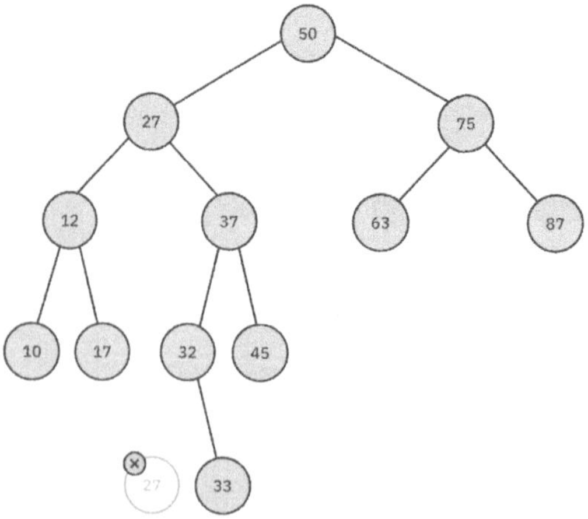

This will take care of removing nodes with two children.

Finding the Minimum Node in a Subtree

Open up **binary_search_tree.dart**. You'll implement the `remove` method in just a minute, but first add the following helper extension at the bottom of the file:

```
extension _MinFinder<E> on BinaryNode<E> {
  BinaryNode<E> get min => leftChild?.min ?? this;
}
```

If `leftChild` exists for a particular node, then by definition, it has a lower value than the node itself. Recursively calling `min` on `BinaryNode` will then tell you the minimum node in a subtree.

Implementing remove

Now add these two methods to `BinarySearchTree`:

```
void remove(E value) {
  root = _remove(root, value);
}

BinaryNode<E>? _remove(BinaryNode<E>? node, E value) {
  if (node == null) return null;

  if (value == node.value) {
    // more to come
  } else if (value.compareTo(node.value) < 0) {
    node.leftChild = _remove(node.leftChild, value);
  } else {
    node.rightChild = _remove(node.rightChild, value);
  }
  return node;
}
```

This should look familiar to you. You're using the same recursive setup with a private helper method as you did for `insert`. The method isn't quite finished yet, though. Once you've found the node that you want to remove, you still need to separately handle the removal cases for (1) a leaf node, (2) a node with one child, and (3) a node with two children.

Handling the Removal Cases

Replace the `// more to come` comment above with the following code:

```
// 1
if (node.leftChild == null && node.rightChild == null) {
  return null;
}
// 2
if (node.leftChild == null) {
  return node.rightChild;
}
if (node.rightChild == null) {
  return node.leftChild;
}
// 3
node.value = node.rightChild!.min.value;
node.rightChild = _remove(node.rightChild, node.value);
```

1. If the node is a leaf node, you simply return `null`, thereby removing the current node.

2. If the node has no *left* child, you return `node.rightChild` to reconnect the right subtree. If the node has no *right* child, you return `node.leftChild` to reconnect the left subtree.

3. This is the case in which the node to be removed has both a left and right child. You replace the node's value with the smallest value from the right subtree. You then call `remove` on the right child to remove this swapped value.

Testing it Out

Head back to `main` and test `remove` by writing the following:

```
final tree = buildExampleTree();
print('Tree before removal:');
print(tree);
tree.remove(3);
print('Tree after removing root:');
print(tree);
```

You should see the output below in the console:

```
Tree before removal:
  ┌── 5
 ┌──4
 │ └── null
3
 │ ┌── 2
 └──1
  └── 0

Tree after removing root:
┌── 5
4
│ ┌── 2
└──1
 └── 0
```

Successfully implemented!

In the next chapter you'll learn how to create a self-balancing binary search tree called an AVL tree.

Challenges

Think you've gotten the hang of binary search trees? Try out these three challenges to lock the concepts down. As usual, you can find the answers in the Challenge Solutions section at the end of the book.

Challenge 1: Binary Tree or Binary Search Tree?

Write a function that checks if a binary tree is a binary search tree.

Challenge 2: Equality

Given two binary trees, how would you test if they are equal or not?

Challenge 3: Is it a Subtree?

Create a method that checks if the current tree contains all the elements of another tree.

Key Points

- The binary search tree (BST) is a powerful data structure for holding sorted data.
- Elements of the binary search tree must be comparable.
- The time complexity for `insert`, `remove` and `contains` methods in a BST is O(log n).
- Performance will degrade to O(n) as the tree becomes unbalanced. This is undesirable, but self-balancing trees such as the AVL tree can overcome the problem.

Chapter 11: AVL Trees

In the previous chapter, you learned about the O(log n) performance characteristics of the binary search tree. However, you also learned that *unbalanced* trees can deteriorate the performance of the tree, all the way down to O(n). In 1962, Georgy Adelson-Velsky and Evgenii Landis came up with the first **self-balancing** binary search tree: The **AVL Tree**. In this chapter, you'll dig deeper into how the balance of a binary search tree can impact performance. Then you'll implement the AVL tree from scratch!

Understanding Balance

A balanced tree is the key to optimizing the performance of the binary search tree. In this section, you'll learn about the three main states of balance: perfectly balanced, balanced and unbalanced.

Perfect Balance

The ideal form of a binary search tree is the **perfectly balanced** state. In technical terms, this means every level of the tree is filled with nodes, from top to bottom.

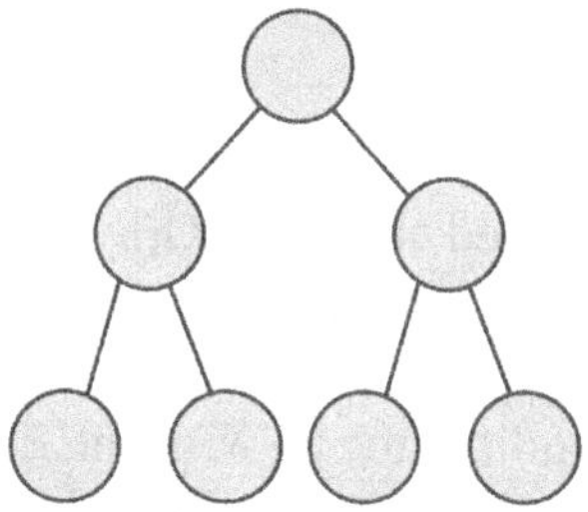

Perfectly balanced tree

Not only is the tree perfectly symmetrical, but the nodes at the bottom level are also completely filled. This is the requirement for being perfectly balanced.

"Good-enough" Balance

Although achieving perfect balance is ideal, it's rarely possible. A perfectly balanced tree must contain the exact number of nodes to fill every level to the bottom, so it can only be perfect with a particular number of elements.

For example, a tree with 1, 3 or 7 nodes can be perfectly balanced, but a tree with 2, 4, 5 or 6 cannot be perfectly balanced since the last level of the tree will not be filled.

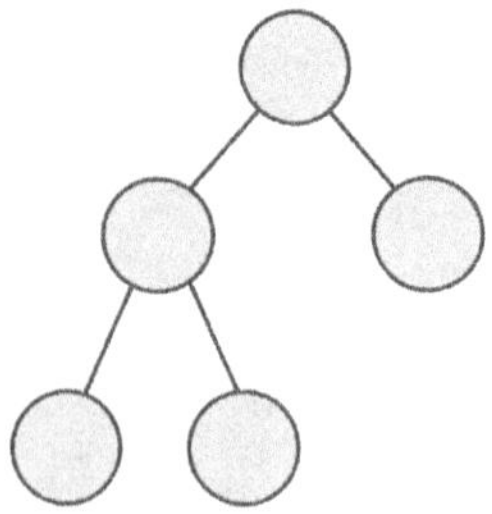

Balanced tree

A tree is **balanced** as long as the heights of both child branches of any particular node differ by no more than one. In practice, that usually means every level of the tree must be filled, except for the bottom level. For most binary trees, this is the best you can do.

Unbalanced

Finally, there's the **unbalanced** state. Binary search trees in this state suffer from various levels of performance loss, depending on the degree of imbalance.

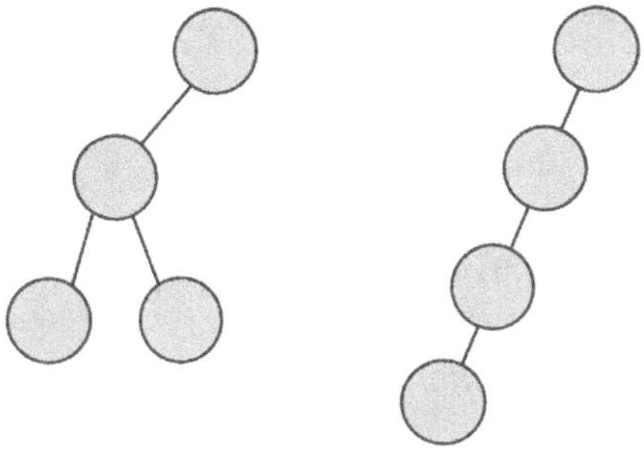

Unbalanced trees

Keeping the tree balanced gives the find, insert and remove operations an O(log n) time complexity. AVL trees maintain balance by adjusting the structure of the tree when the tree becomes unbalanced. You'll learn how this works as you progress through the chapter.

Implementation

Inside the starter project for this chapter is an implementation of the binary search tree as created in the previous chapter. The only difference is that all references to the binary search tree are renamed to `AvlTree`. Similarly, the binary node is renamed to `AvlNode`.

Binary search trees and AVL trees share much of the same implementation. In fact, all that you'll add is the balancing component. Open the **starter** project to begin.

Measuring Balance

To keep a binary tree balanced, you'll need a way to measure the balance of the tree. The AVL tree achieves this with a `height` property in each node. In tree-speak, the **height** of a node is the *longest* distance from the current node to a leaf node:

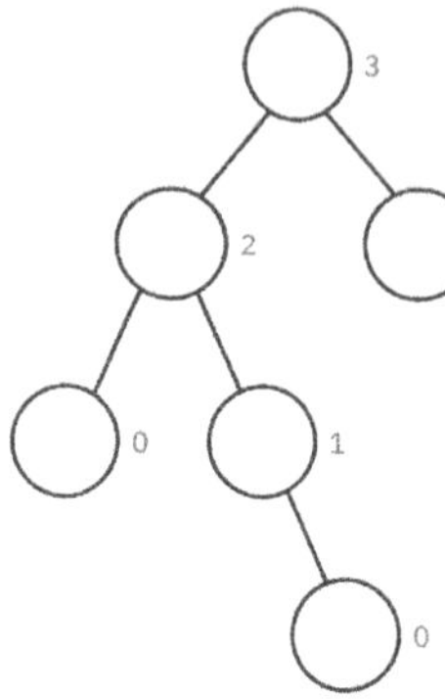

Nodes marked with heights

Open the **lib** folder and add the following property to `AvlNode` in **avl_node.dart**:

```
int height = 0;
```

You'll use the relative heights of a node's children to determine whether a particular node is balanced. The height of the left and right children of each node must differ at most by 1. This number is known as the **balance factor**.

Write the following just below the `height` property of `AvlNode`:

```
int get balanceFactor => leftHeight - rightHeight;

int get leftHeight => leftChild?.height ?? -1;

int get rightHeight => rightChild?.height ?? -1;
```

The `balanceFactor` computes the height difference between the left and right child. If a particular child is `null`, its height is considered to be -1.

Here's an example of an AVL tree. The diagram shows a balanced tree — all levels except the bottom one are filled. The numbers to the right of the node represent the `height` of each node, while the numbers to the left represent the `balanceFactor`.

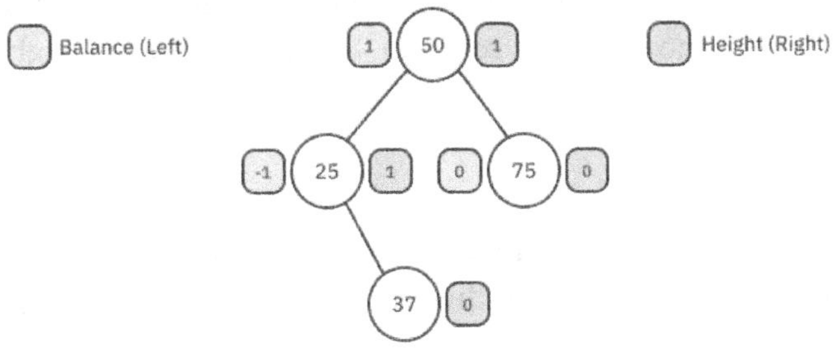

AVL tree with balance factors and heights

Here's an updated diagram with **40** inserted. Inserting **40** into the tree turns it into an unbalanced tree. Notice how the `balanceFactor` changes:

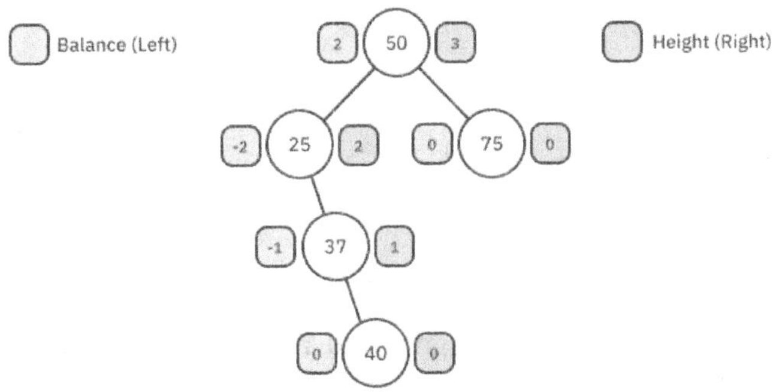

Unbalanced tree

A `balanceFactor` of **2** or **-2** or something more extreme indicates an unbalanced tree. By checking after each insertion or deletion, though, you can guarantee that it's never more extreme than a magnitude of two.

Although more than one node may have a bad balancing factor, you only need to perform the balancing procedure on the bottommost node containing the invalid balance factor. For example, in the figure above both **50** and **25** have a balance factor with a magnitude of **2**. However, you only need to perform the balancing procedure on the lower node, that is, the one containing **25**.

This is where rotations come in.

Rotations

The procedures used to balance a binary search tree are known as **rotations**. There are four rotations in total, one for each of the four different ways that a tree can be unbalanced. These are known as **left** rotation, **left-right** rotation, **right** rotation and **right-left** rotation.

Left Rotation

The imbalance caused by inserting **40** into the tree can be solved by a **left rotation**. A generic left rotation of node **X** looks like this:

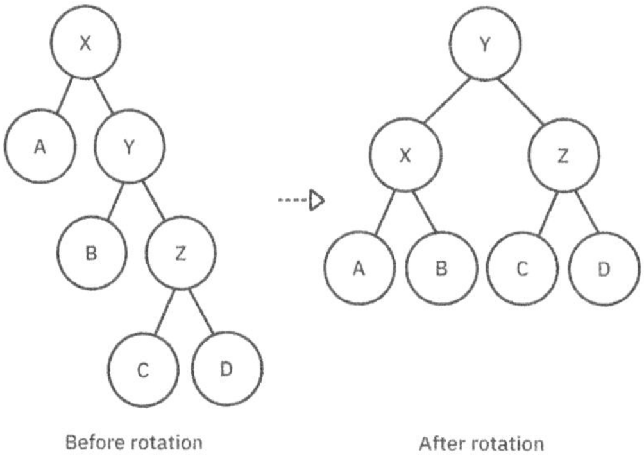

Left rotation applied on node X

When you do a left rotation on **X**, its right child **Y** becomes the **pivot** and moves up a level. Since **X** is rotating down to be **Y**'s new left child, **Y**'s old left child **B** becomes **X**'s right child.

There are two takeaways from this before-and-after comparison:

- In-order traversal for these nodes remains the same.
- The *depth* of the tree is reduced by one level after the rotation.

Open **lib/avl_tree.dart** and add the `dart:math` library to the top of the file:

```
import 'dart:math' as math;
```

Then add the following method to `AvlTree` below the `_insertAt` method:

```
AvlNode<E> leftRotate(AvlNode<E> node) {
  // 1
  final pivot = node.rightChild!;
  // 2
  node.rightChild = pivot.leftChild;
  // 3
  pivot.leftChild = node;
  // 4
  node.height = 1 +
      math.max(
        node.leftHeight,
        node.rightHeight,
      );
  pivot.height = 1 +
      math.max(
        pivot.leftHeight,
        pivot.rightHeight,
      );
  // 5
  return pivot;
}
```

Here are the steps needed to perform a left rotation:

1. The right child is chosen as the **pivot** point. This node will replace the rotated node as the root of the subtree. That means the pivot node will move up a level.
2. The node to be rotated will become the left child of the pivot. It moves down a level. This means that the current left child of the pivot must be moved elsewhere.
3. The pivot's `leftChild` can now be set to the rotated node.
4. You update the heights of the rotated node and the pivot.
5. Finally, you return the pivot so that it can replace the rotated node in the tree.

Here are the before-and-after effects of the left rotation of **25** from the previous example:

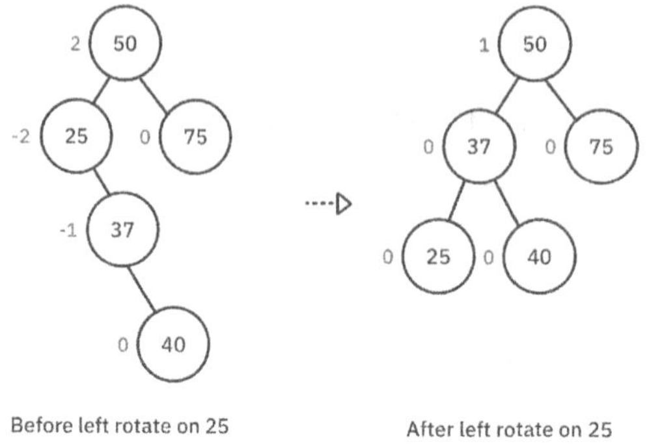

Right Rotation

Right rotation is the symmetric opposite of left rotation. When a series of left children is causing an imbalance, it's time for a right rotation.

A generic right rotation of node **X** looks like this:

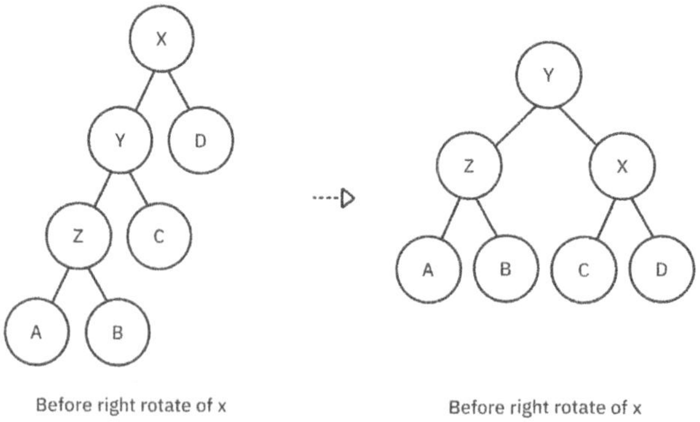

Right rotation applied on node X

When performing a right rotation on **X**, its left child **Y** becomes the **pivot** and moves up a level. Since **X** is rotating down to become **Y**'s new right child, **Y**'s old right child **C** becomes **X**'s left child. The tree is balanced and the properties of the binary search tree are still intact.

To implement this, add the following code just after `leftRotate`:

```
AvlNode<E> rightRotate(AvlNode<E> node) {
  final pivot = node.leftChild!;
  node.leftChild = pivot.rightChild;
  pivot.rightChild = node;
  node.height = 1 +
      math.max(
        node.leftHeight,
        node.rightHeight,
      );
  pivot.height = 1 +
      math.max(
        pivot.leftHeight,
        pivot.rightHeight,
      );
  return pivot;
}
```

This algorithm is nearly identical to the implementation of `leftRotate`, except the references to the left and right children are swapped.

Right-Left Rotation

You may have noticed that the left and right rotations balance nodes that are all left children or all right children. Consider the case in which **36** is inserted into the original example tree.

The tree now requires a right-left rotation:

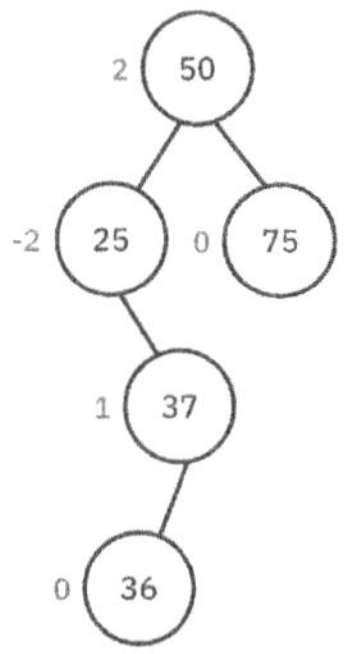

Inserted 36 as left child of 37

Doing a left rotation, in this case, won't result in a balanced tree. The way to handle cases like this is to perform a right rotation on the right child *before* doing the left rotation. Here's what the procedure looks like:

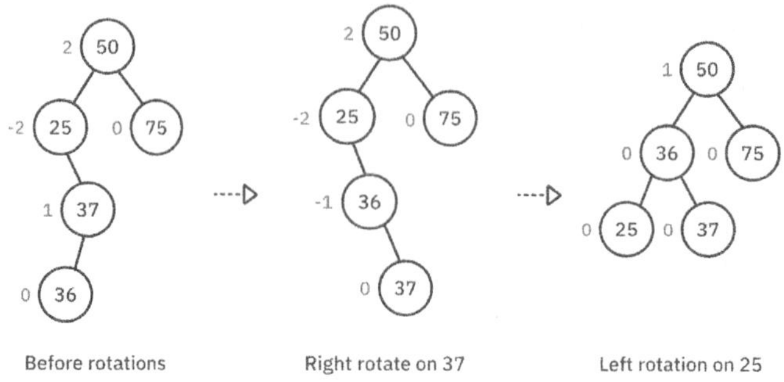

Right-left rotation

1. You apply a right rotation to **37**.
2. Now that nodes **25**, **36** and **37** are all right children, you can apply a left rotation to balance the tree.

Add the following code just after `rightRotate`:

```
AvlNode<E> rightLeftRotate(AvlNode<E> node) {
  if (node.rightChild == null) {
    return node;
  }
  node.rightChild = rightRotate(node.rightChild!);
  return leftRotate(node);
}
```

Don't worry just yet about when to call this. You'll get to that in a second. You first need to handle the last case, left-right rotation.

Left-Right Rotation

Left-right rotation is the symmetric opposite of the right-left rotation. Here's an example:

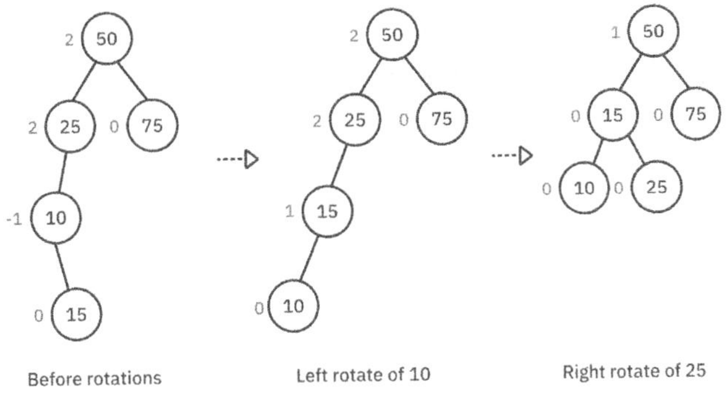

Left-right rotation

1. You apply a left rotation to node **10**.
2. Now that nodes **25, 15** and **10** are all left children; you can apply a right rotation to balance the tree.

Add the following code just after `rightLeftRotate`:

```
AvlNode<E> leftRightRotate(AvlNode<E> node) {
  if (node.leftChild == null) {
    return node;
  }
  node.leftChild = leftRotate(node.leftChild!);
  return rightRotate(node);
}
```

That's it for rotations. Now you just need to apply them at the correct time.

Balance

The next task is to design a method that uses `balanceFactor` to decide whether a node requires balancing or not. Write the following method below `leftRightRotate`:

```
AvlNode<E> balanced(AvlNode<E> node) {
  switch (node.balanceFactor) {
    case 2:
    // ...
    case -2:
    // ...
    default:
      return node;
  }
}
```

There are three cases to consider.

1. A `balanceFactor` of **2** suggests that the left child is "heavier" (contains more nodes) than the right child. This means that you want to use either right or left-right rotations.
2. A `balanceFactor` of **-2** suggests that the right child is heavier than the left child. This means that you want to use either left or right-left rotations.
3. The default case suggests that the particular node is balanced. There's nothing to do here except to return the node.

The sign of the child's `balanceFactor` can be used to determine if a single or double rotation is required:

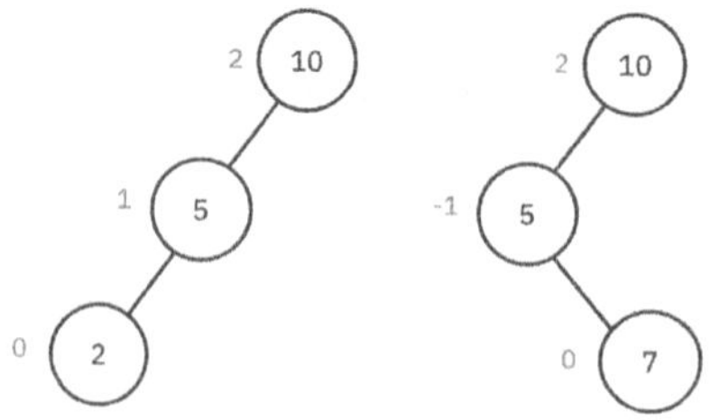

Right rotate, or left-right rotate?

Replace balanced with the following:

```
AvlNode<E> balanced(AvlNode<E> node) {
  switch (node.balanceFactor) {
    case 2:
      final left = node.leftChild;
      if (left != null && left.balanceFactor == -1) {
        return leftRightRotate(node);
      } else {
        return rightRotate(node);
      }
    case -2:
      final right = node.rightChild;
      if (right != null && right.balanceFactor == 1) {
        return rightLeftRotate(node);
      } else {
        return leftRotate(node);
      }
    default:
      return node;
  }
}
```

balanced inspects the balanceFactor to determine the proper course of action. All that's left is to call balanced at the proper time.

Revisiting Insertion

You've already done the majority of the work. The remainder is fairly straightforward. Replace _insertAt with the following:

```
AvlNode<E> _insertAt(AvlNode<E>? node, E value) {
  if (node == null) {
    return AvlNode(value);
  }
  if (value.compareTo(node.value) < 0) {
    node.leftChild = _insertAt(node.leftChild, value);
  } else {
    node.rightChild = _insertAt(node.rightChild, value);
  }
  // new code
  final balancedNode = balanced(node);
  balancedNode.height = 1 +
      math.max(
        balancedNode.leftHeight,
        balancedNode.rightHeight,
      );
  return balancedNode;
}
```

Instead of returning the node directly after inserting, you pass it into `balanced`. Passing it ensures every node in the call stack is checked for balancing issues. You also update the node's `height`.

That's all there is to it! Open **bin/starter.dart** and replace the contents of the file with the following:

```
import 'package:starter/avl_tree.dart';

void main() {
  final tree = AvlTree<num>();
  for (var i = 0; i < 15; i++) {
    tree.insert(i);
  }
  print(tree);
}
```

Run that, and you should see the following output in the console:

```
   ┌── 14
  ┌──13
  │ └── 12
 ┌──11
 │ │ ┌── 10
 │ └──9
 │   └── 8
7
 │   ┌── 6
 │ ┌──5
 │ │ └── 4
 └──3
   │ ┌── 2
   └──1
     └── 0
```

Take a moment to appreciate the uniform spread of the nodes. If the rotations weren't applied, this would have become a long, unbalanced link of right children.

Revisiting Remove

Retrofitting the `remove` operation for self-balancing is just as easy as fixing `insert`. In `AvlTree`, find `_remove` and replace the final `return node;` statement with the following:

```
final balancedNode = balanced(node);
balancedNode.height = 1 +
    math.max(
      balancedNode.leftHeight,
      balancedNode.rightHeight,
    );
return balancedNode;
```

Head back to **starter.dart** and replace the body of `main` with the following code:

```
final tree = AvlTree<num>();
tree.insert(15);
tree.insert(10);
tree.insert(16);
tree.insert(18);
print(tree);
tree.remove(10);
print(tree);
```

Run that, and you should see the following console output:

```
  ┌── 18
 ┌──16
 │ └── null
15
└── 10

┌── 18
16
└── 15
```

Removing **10** caused a left rotation on **15**. Feel free to try out a few more test cases of your own.

Whew! The AVL tree is the culmination of your search for the ultimate binary search tree. The self-balancing property guarantees that the `insert` and `remove` operations function at optimal performance with an O(log n) time complexity.

Challenges

Here are three challenges that revolve around AVL trees. Solve these to make sure you have the concepts down. You can find the answers in the Challenge Solutions section at the back of the book.

Challenge 1: Number of Leaves

How many *leaf* nodes are there in a perfectly balanced tree of height 3? What about a perfectly balanced tree of height `h`?

Challenge 2: Number of Nodes

How many *nodes* are there in a perfectly balanced tree of height 3? What about a perfectly balanced tree of height `h`?

Challenge 3: A Tree Traversal Interface

Since there are many variants of binary trees, it makes sense to group shared functionality in an interface. The traversal methods are a good candidate for this.

Create a `TraversableBinaryNode` abstract class that provides a default implementation of the traversal methods so that conforming types get these methods for free. Have `AvlNode` extend this.

Key Points

- A self-balancing tree avoids performance degradation by performing a balancing procedure whenever you add or remove elements in the tree.
- AVL trees preserve balance by readjusting parts of the tree when the tree is no longer balanced.
- Balance is achieved by four types of tree rotations on node insertion and removal: right rotation, left rotation, right-left rotation and left-right rotation.

Where to Go From Here?

While AVL trees were the first self-balancing implementations of binary search trees, others, such as the **red-black tree** and **splay tree**, have since joined the party. If you're interested, look them up. You might even try porting a version from another language into Dart. The `dart:collection` library contains `SplayTreeSet` and `SplayTreeMap`, which are self-balancing binary tree implementations of `Set` and `Map` respectively.

Chapter 12: Tries

The **trie**, pronounced “try”, is a tree that specializes in storing data that can be represented as a collection, such as English words:

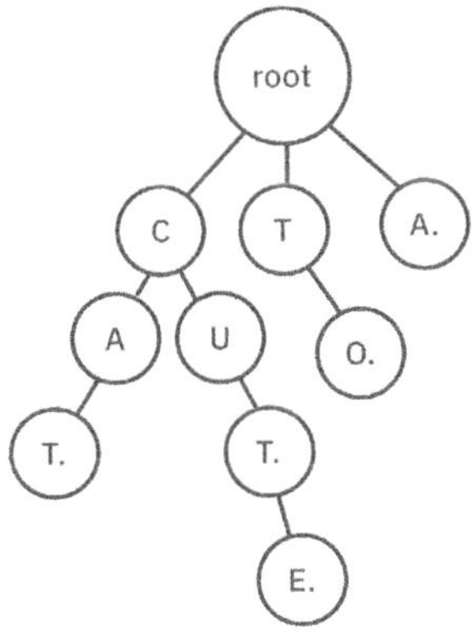

A trie containing the words CAT, CUT, CUTE, TO and A

Each string character maps to a node where the last node is terminating. These are marked in the diagram above with a dot. The benefits of a trie are best illustrated by looking at it in the context of prefix matching.

In this chapter, you'll first compare the performance of a trie to a list. Then you'll implement the trie from scratch!

List vs. Trie

You're given a collection of strings. How would you build a component that handles prefix matching? Here's one way:

```
class EnglishDictionary {
  final List<String> words = [];

  List<String> lookup(String prefix) {
    return words.where((word) {
      return word.startsWith(prefix);
    }).toList();
  }
}
```

`lookup` will go through the collection of strings and return those that match the prefix.

This algorithm is reasonable if the number of elements in the `words` list is small. But if you're dealing with more than a few thousand words, the time it takes to go through the `words` list will be unacceptable. The time complexity of `lookup` is $O(k \times n)$, where *k* is the longest string in the collection, and *n* is the number of words you need to check.

Imagine the number of words Google needs to parse

The trie data structure has excellent performance characteristics for this problem. Since it's a tree with nodes that support multiple children, each node can represent a single character.

You form a word by tracing the collection of characters from the root to a node with a special indicator — a terminator — represented by a black dot. An interesting characteristic of the trie is that multiple words can share the same characters.

To illustrate the performance benefits of the trie, consider the following example in which you need to find the words with the prefix CU. First, you travel to the node containing C. That quickly excludes other branches of the trie from the search operation:

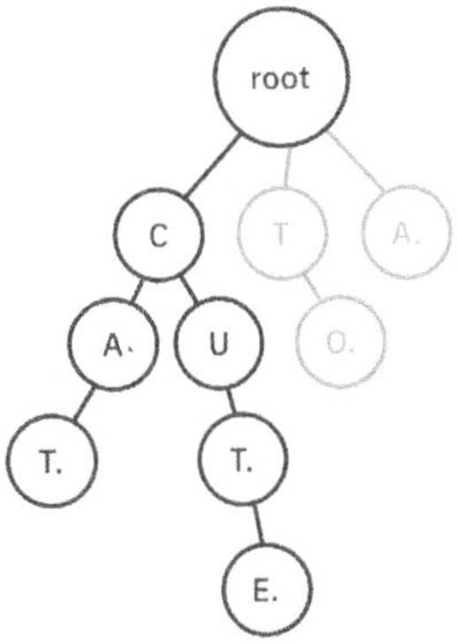

Next, you need to find the words with the next letter, U. You traverse to the U node:

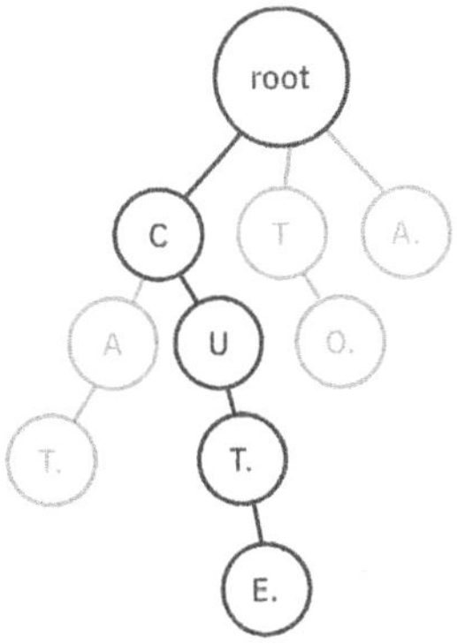

Since that's the end of your prefix, the trie would return all collections formed by the chain of nodes from the U node. In this case, the words CUT and CUTE would be returned.

Imagine if this trie contained hundreds of thousands of words. The number of comparisons you can avoid by employing a trie is substantial.

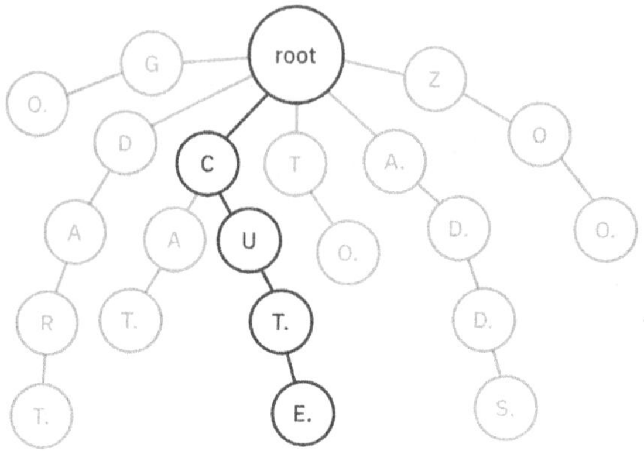

Implementation

As always, open up the **starter** project for this chapter.

TrieNode

You'll begin by creating the node for the trie. Create a **lib** folder in the root of your project and add a file to it named **trie_node.dart**. Add the following to the file:

```
class TrieNode<T> {
  TrieNode({this.key, this.parent});
  // 1
  T? key;
  // 2
  TrieNode<T>? parent;
  // 3
  Map<T, TrieNode<T>?> children = {};
  // 4
  bool isTerminating = false;
}
```

This interface is slightly different compared to the other nodes you've encountered:

1. key holds the data for the node. This is nullable because the root node of the trie has no key. The reason it's called a *key* is because you use it in a map of key-value pairs to store children nodes.

2. `TrieNode` holds a reference to its parent. This reference simplifies the `remove` method later on.

3. In binary search trees, nodes have a left and right child. In a trie, a node needs to hold multiple different elements. The `children` map accomplishes that.

4. `isTerminating` acts as a marker for the end of a collection.

> **Note**: A parent `TrieNode` holds a reference to its children and the children hold a reference to the parent. You might wonder if this creates a circular reference problem where the memory is never released. Languages like Swift that use reference counting for memory management need to be especially careful about this. Dart, on the other hand, frees up the memory from old unused objects with a garbage collector, which is able to handle the `parent-children` circular references in the code above. Garbage collection works not by counting references to individual objects but by checking if objects are reachable from certain root objects.

Trie

Next, you'll create the trie itself, which will manage the nodes. Since strings are one of the most common uses for tries, this chapter will walk you through building a `String`-based trie. In Challenge 2 at the end of the chapter, you'll create a generic trie that can handle any iterable collection.

In the **lib** folder, create a new file named **string_trie.dart**. Add the following to the file:

```
import 'trie_node.dart';

class StringTrie {
  TrieNode<int> root = TrieNode(key: null, parent: null);
}
```

Here are a couple of points to note:

- In Dart, a `String` is a collection of UTF-16 code units, so that's why the type for `TrieNode` is `int` rather than `String`.

- The `key` and `parent` of a trie's `root` node are always `null`.

Next, you'll implement four operations for the trie: `insert`, `contains`, `remove` and `matchPrefix`.

Insert

Tries work on collections internally, so you'll need to take whatever string is inserted and convert its code units into `TrieNode` keys.

Add the following method to `StringTrie`:

```
void insert(String text) {
  // 1
  var current = root;
  // 2
  for (var codeUnit in text.codeUnits) {
    current.children[codeUnit] ??= TrieNode(
      key: codeUnit,
      parent: current,
    );
    current = current.children[codeUnit]!;
  }
  // 3
  current.isTerminating = true;
}
```

Here's what's going on:

1. `current` keeps track of your traversal progress, which starts with the `root` node.
2. The trie stores each code unit in a separate node. You first check if the node exists in the `children` map. If it doesn't, you create a new node. During each loop, you move `current` to the next node.
3. After the `for` loop completes, `current` references the node at the end of the collection, that is, the last code unit in the string. You mark that node as the terminating node.

The time complexity for this algorithm is O(k), where *k* is the number of code units you're trying to insert. This cost is because you need to traverse through or create a new node for each code unit.

Contains

`contains` is very similar to `insert`. Add the following method to `StringTrie`:

```
bool contains(String text) {
  var current = root;
  for (var codeUnit in text.codeUnits) {
    final child = current.children[codeUnit];
    if (child == null) {
      return false;
    }
    current = child;
  }
  return current.isTerminating;
}
```

You check every code unit to see if it's in the tree. When you reach the last one, it must be terminating. If not, the collection wasn't added, and what you've found is a subset of a larger collection.

Like `insert`, the time complexity of `contains` is O(k), where *k* is the length of the string you're using for the search. This time complexity comes from traversing through *k* nodes to determine whether the code unit collection is in the trie.

To test out `insert` and `contains`, head over to **bin/starter.dart** and replace the contents of the file with the following code:

```
import 'package:starter/string_trie.dart';

void main() {
  final trie = StringTrie();
  trie.insert("cute");
  if (trie.contains("cute")) {
    print("cute is in the trie");
  }
}
```

Run that, and you should see the following console output:

```
cute is in the trie
```

Remove

Removing a node from the trie is a bit more tricky. You need to be particularly careful since multiple collections can share nodes.

Go back to **lib/string_trie.dart** and write the following method just below `contains`:

```
void remove(String text) {
  // 1
  var current = root;
  for (final codeUnit in text.codeUnits) {
    final child = current.children[codeUnit];
    if (child == null) {
      return;
    }
    current = child;
  }
  if (!current.isTerminating) {
    return;
  }
  // 2
  current.isTerminating = false;
  // 3
  while (current.parent != null &&
         current.children.isEmpty &&
         !current.isTerminating) {
    current.parent!.children[current.key!] = null;
    current = current.parent!;
  }
}
```

Taking it comment-by-comment:

1. You check if the code unit collection you want to remove is part of the trie and point `current` to the last node of the collection. If you don't find your search string or the final node isn't marked as terminating, that means the collection isn't in the trie and you can abort.

2. You set `isTerminating` to `false` so the current node can be removed by the loop in the next step.

3. This is the tricky part. Since nodes can be shared, you don't want to remove code units that belong to another collection. If there are no other children in the current node, it means that other collections don't depend on the current node. You also check to see if the current node is terminating. If it is, then it belongs to another collection. As long as `current` satisfies these conditions, you continually backtrack through the `parent` property and remove the nodes.

The time complexity of this algorithm is O(k), where *k* represents the number of code units in the string you're trying to remove.

Head back to **bin/starter.dart** and replace the contents of `main` with the following:

```
final trie = StringTrie();
trie.insert('cut');
trie.insert('cute');

assert(trie.contains('cut'));
print('"cut" is in the trie');
assert(trie.contains('cute'));
print('"cute" is in the trie');

print('\n--- Removing "cut" ---');
trie.remove('cut');
assert(!trie.contains('cut'));
assert(trie.contains('cute'));
print('"cute" is still in the trie');
```

Run that, and you should see the following output added to the console:

```
"cut" is in the trie
"cute" is in the trie

--- Removing "cut" ---
"cute" is still in the trie
```

Prefix Matching

The most iconic algorithm for a trie is the prefix-matching algorithm. Write the following at the bottom of `StringTrie`:

```
List<String> matchPrefix(String prefix) {
  // 1
  var current = root;
  for (final codeUnit in prefix.codeUnits) {
    final child = current.children[codeUnit];
    if (child == null) {
      return [];
    }
    current = child;
  }
  // 2 (to be implemented shortly)
  return _moreMatches(prefix, current);
}
```

Here's what's happening:

1. You start by verifying that the trie contains the prefix. If not, you return an empty list.

2. After you've found the node that marks the end of the prefix, you call a recursive helper method named `_moreMatches` to find all the sequences after the `current` node.

Next, add the code for the helper method after the `matchPrefix` method:

```
List<String> _moreMatches(String prefix, TrieNode<int> node) {
  // 1
  List<String> results = [];
  if (node.isTerminating) {
    results.add(prefix);
  }
  // 2
  for (final child in node.children.values) {
    final codeUnit = child!.key!;
    results.addAll(
      _moreMatches(
        '$prefix${String.fromCharCode(codeUnit)}',
        child,
      ),
    );
  }
  return results;
}
```

This method performs the following tasks:

1. You create a list to hold the results. If the current node is a terminating one, you add what you've got to the results.

2. Next, you need to check the current node's children. For every child node, you recursively call `_moreMatches` to seek out other terminating nodes.

`matchPrefix` has a time complexity of $O(k \times m)$, where *k* represents the longest collection matching the prefix and *m* represents the number of collections that match the prefix. Recall that lists have a time complexity of $O(k \times n)$, where *n* is the number of elements in the *entire* collection. For large sets of data in which each collection is uniformly distributed, tries perform far better than using lists for prefix matching.

Time to take the method for a spin. Navigate back to `main` and run the following:

```
final trie = StringTrie();
trie.insert('car');
trie.insert('card');
trie.insert('care');
trie.insert('cared');
trie.insert('cars');
trie.insert('carbs');
trie.insert('carapace');
trie.insert('cargo');

print('Collections starting with "car"');
final prefixedWithCar = trie.matchPrefix('car');
print(prefixedWithCar);

print('\nCollections starting with "care"');
final prefixedWithCare = trie.matchPrefix('care');
print(prefixedWithCare);
```

You should see the output below in the console:

```
Collections starting with "car"
[car, card, care, cared, cars, carbs, carapace, cargo]

Collections starting with "care"
[care, cared]
```

Challenges

How was this chapter for you? Are you ready to take it a bit further? The following challenges will ask you to add functionality to and generalize what you've already accomplished. Check out the Challenge Solutions section or the supplemental materials that come with the book if you need any help.

Challenge 1: Additional Properties

The current implementation of `StringTrie` is missing some notable operations. Your task for this challenge is to augment the current implementation of the trie by adding the following:

1. An `allStrings` property that returns all the collections in the trie.
2. A `count` property that tells you how many strings are currently in the trie.
3. An `isEmpty` property that returns `true` if the trie is empty, `false` otherwise.

Challenge 2: Generic Trie

The trie data structure can be used beyond strings. Make a new class named `Trie` that handles any iterable collection. Implement the `insert`, `contains` and `remove` methods.

Key Points

- Tries provide great performance metrics for prefix matching.
- Tries are relatively memory efficient since individual nodes can be shared between many different values. For example, "car," "carbs," and "care" can share the first three letters of the word.

Chapter 13: Binary Search

Binary search is one of the most efficient searching algorithms with a time complexity of O(log n). You've already implemented a binary search once using a binary search tree. In this chapter, you'll reimplement binary search on a sorted list.

Two conditions need to be met for the type of binary search that this chapter describes:

- The collection must be sorted.
- The underlying collection must be able to perform random index lookup in constant time.

As long as the elements are sorted, a Dart `List` meets both requirements.

Linear Search vs. Binary Search

The benefits of binary search are best illustrated by comparing it with linear search. Dart's `List` type uses a linear search to implement its `indexOf` method. It traverses through the whole collection until it finds the first element:

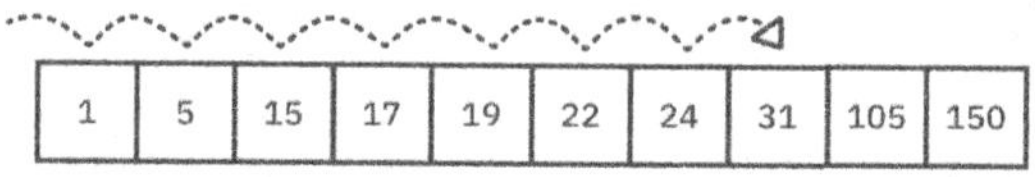

Linear search for the value 31

Binary search handles things differently by taking advantage of the fact that the collection is already sorted. Here's an example of applying binary search to find the value **31**:

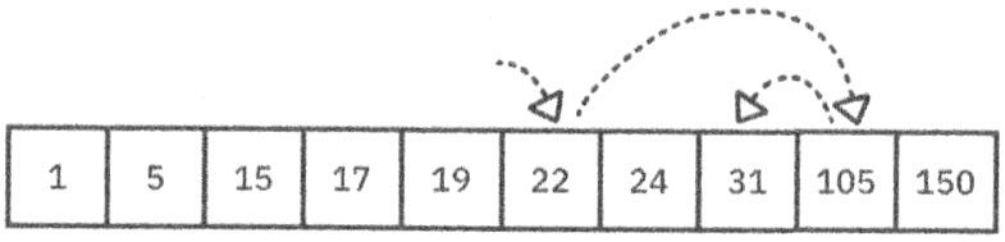

Binary search for the value 31

Instead of eight steps to find 31, it only takes three. Here's how it works:

Step 1: Find the Middle Index

The first step is to find the middle index of the collection.

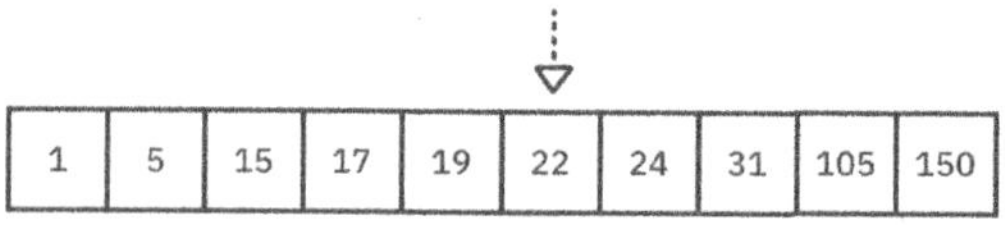

Step 2: Check the Element at the Middle Index

The next step is to check the element stored at the middle index. If it matches the value you're looking for, return the index. Otherwise, continue to Step 3.

Step 3: Split and Repeat

The final step is to cut the list in half and start over. This time, you'll only consider the elements exclusively to the *left* or to the *right* of the middle index, depending on the value you're searching for. If the value you're searching for is less than the middle value, you search the left subsequence. If it's greater than the middle value, you search the right subsequence.

Each step effectively removes half of the comparisons you would otherwise need to perform.

In the example where you're looking for the value **31** (which is greater than the middle element **22**), you apply binary search on the right subsequence:

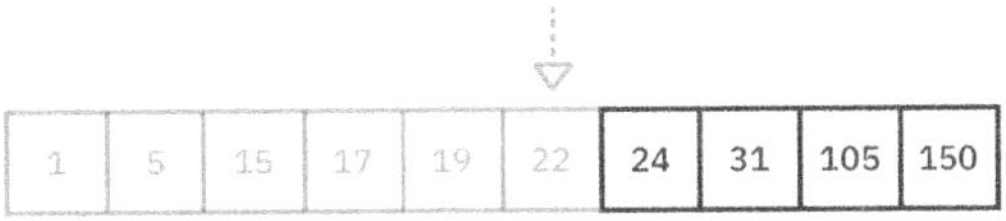

You continue these three steps until you can no longer split up the collection into left and right halves or until you find the value inside the collection.

Binary search achieves an O(log n) time complexity this way.

Implementation

Open the **starter** project for this chapter. Create a new **lib** folder in the root of your project. Then add a new file to it called **binary_search.dart**.

Adding an Extension on List

Add the following `List` extension to **binary_search.dart**:

```
extension SortedList<E extends Comparable<E>> on List<E> {
  int? binarySearch(E value) {
    // more to come
  }
}
```

Here are a couple of comments:

- You use `List` since it allows random access to any element by index.
- Since you need to be able to compare elements, the value type must be `Comparable`. As mentioned in an earlier chapter, users will need to specify `List<num>` for integers rather than `List<int>` since only `num` directly implements `Comparable`.
- `binarySearch` returns the `int` index of the search value if it's in the list, or `null` if it's not.

Writing the Algorithm

Next, fill in the logic for `binarySearch` by replacing `// more to come` in the code above with the following:

```
// 1
var start = 0;
var end = length;
// 2
while (start < end) {
  // 3
  final size = end - start;
  final middle = start + size ~/ 2;
  // 4
  if (this[middle] == value) {
    return middle;
  // 5
  } else if (this[middle].compareTo(value) < 0) {
    start = middle + 1;
  } else {
    end = middle;
  }
}
// 6
return null;
```

Here are the steps:

1. `start` and `end` are the indexes of the range within the list that you're checking. As is common for range indices, `start` is inclusive and `end` is exclusive. That is, the end index is one greater than the index it refers to. This makes it play well with `length` since the length of a zero-based list is always one greater than the last index.

2. `start` and `end` will keep getting progressively closer to each other on each iteration of the loop. If they meet, you're finished searching.
3. Next, you find the middle index of the range.
4. You then compare the value at this index with the value you're searching for. If the values match, you return the middle index.
5. If not, you update the range to either the right or left half of the collection.
6. If the `while` loop exits without finding a match, the value wasn't in the list.

Testing it Out

That wraps up the implementation of binary search! Open **bin/starter.dart** to test it out. Replace the contents of the file with the following:

```
import 'package:starter/binary_search.dart';

void main() {
  final list = <num>[1, 5, 15, 17, 19, 22, 24, 31, 105, 150];

  final search31 = list.indexOf(31);
  final binarySearch31 = list.binarySearch(31);

  print('indexOf: $search31');
  print('binarySearch: $binarySearch31');
}
```

Run that, and you should see the following output in the console:

```
indexOf: 7
binarySearch: 7
```

7 is the index of the value **31** that you were looking for. Both search methods returned the same result. However, `binarySearch` has a fast logarithmic time complexity while `indexOf` has a slower linear complexity. `binarySearch` assumes that the list is sorted. If it's not, `binarySearch` won't work. `indexOf` can't make that assumption, so it has to use a slower algorithm.

Binary search is a powerful algorithm to learn and comes up often in programming interviews. Whenever you read something along the lines of "Given a sorted list...", consider using the binary search algorithm. Also, if you're given a problem that looks like it's going to be $O(n^2)$ to search, consider doing some up-front sorting so you can use a binary search to reduce it down to the cost of the sort at $O(n \log n)$.

> **Note**: You'll learn more about sorting and the time complexity of sorting algorithms in Section IV, "Sorting Algorithms."

Challenges

Try out the challenges below to further strengthen your understanding of binary searches. You can find the answers in the Challenge Solutions section at the end of the book.

Challenge 1: Binary Search as a Free Function

In this chapter, you implemented binary search as an extension of `List`. Since binary search only works on sorted lists, exposing `binarySearch` for every list (including unsorted ones) opens it up to being misused.

Your challenge is to implement binary search as a free function.

Challenge 2: Recursive Search

Since a sorted list isn't a tree-like data structure, you didn't need to use recursion to perform the binary search. But that doesn't mean you can't. Just for fun, write `binarySearch` as a recursive function.

Challenge 3: Searching for a Range

Write a function that searches a sorted list and finds the range of indices for a particular element. You can start by creating a class named `Range` that holds the start and end indices.

For example:

```
final list = [1, 2, 3, 3, 3, 4, 5, 5];
final range = findRange(list, value: 3);
```

`findRange` should return `Range(2, 5)` since those are the start and end indices for the value `3`.

Key Points

- Binary search is only a valid algorithm on *sorted* collections.
- Binary search guesses the middle value in a list. If it's wrong, it continues cutting the list in half and guessing the middle value until it finds the value or discovers it doesn't exist.
- Sometimes it may be beneficial to sort a collection to leverage the binary search capability for looking up elements.
- The `indexOf` method on `List` uses a linear search with O(n) time complexity. Binary search has O(log n) time complexity, which scales much better for large data sets if you do repeated lookups.

Chapter 14: Heaps

Heaps are another classical tree-based data structure with special properties to quickly fetch the largest or smallest element.

In this chapter, you'll focus on creating and manipulating heaps. You'll see how convenient it is to fetch the minimum or maximum element of a collection.

What's a Heap?

A **heap** is a complete binary tree, also known as a **binary heap**, that can be constructed using a list.

> **Note**: Don't confuse these heaps with memory heaps. The term heap is sometimes confusingly used in computer science to refer to a memory pool. Memory heaps are a different concept and not what you're studying here.

Heaps come in two flavors:

1. **Max-heap**, in which elements with a **higher** value have a higher priority.
2. **Min-heap**, in which elements with a **lower** value have a higher priority.

The Heap Property

A heap has an essential characteristic that must always be satisfied. This characteristic is known as the **heap property**:

- In a max-heap, parent nodes must always contain a value that is *greater than or equal to* the value in its children. The root node will always contain the highest value.
- In a min-heap, parent nodes must always contain a value that is *less than or equal to* the value in its children. The root node will always contain the lowest value.

The image below on the left is a max-heap with **10** as the maximum value. Every node in the heap has values *greater* than the nodes below it. The image on the right is a min-heap. Since **1** is the minimum value, it's on the top of the heap. Every node in this heap has values *less* than those below it.

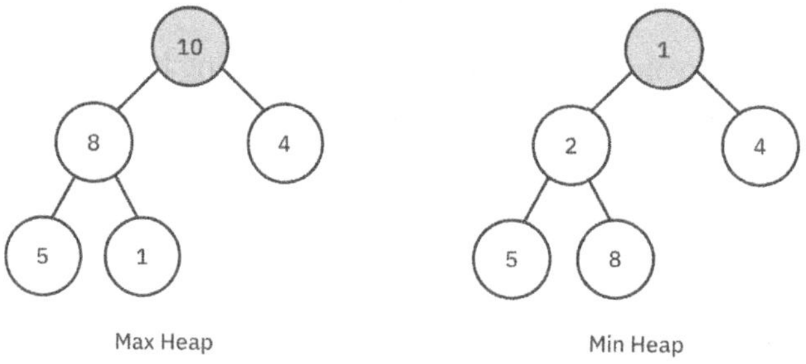

Note that, unlike a binary search tree, it's not a requirement of the heap property that the left or right child needs to be greater. For that reason, a heap is only a partially sorted tree.

The Shape Property

Another essential aspect of a heap is its **shape property**. There can't be any holes in a heap. A heap must be a **complete binary tree**. This means that every level must be filled except for the last level. Additionally, when adding elements to the last level, you must add them from left to right.

In the diagram below, you can see that the first two levels are filled. The last level, Level 3, isn't full yet, but the nodes that are there are located on the left.

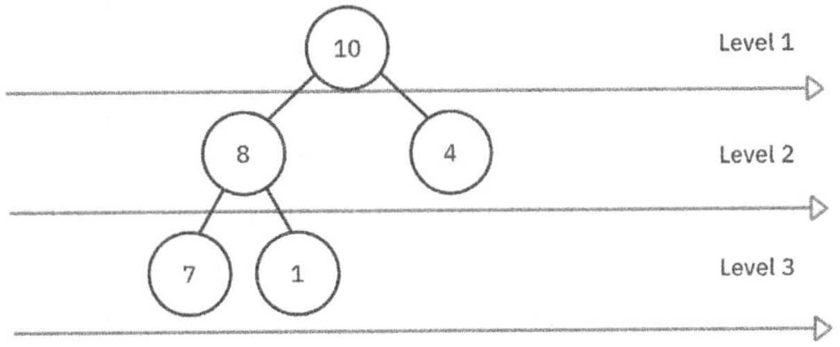

Heap Applications

Some practical applications of a heap include:

- Calculating the minimum or maximum element of a collection.
- Implementing the heapsort algorithm.
- Constructing a priority queue.
- Building graph algorithms that use a priority queue, like Dijkstra's algorithm.

> **Note**: You'll learn about priority queues in Chapter 15, heapsort in Chapter 19, and Dijkstra's algorithm in Chapter 24.

Fitting a Binary Tree Into a List

Trees hold nodes that store references to their children. In the case of a binary tree, these are references to a left and right child. Heaps are binary trees, but they are implemented with a simple list.

Using a list might seem like an unusual way to build a tree, but one of the benefits of this heap implementation is efficient time and space complexity since the elements in a heap are all stored together in memory. You'll see later on that swapping elements will play a big part in heap operations. This manipulation is easier to do with a list than it is with an ordinary binary tree.

Take a look at the following image to see how you can represent a heap using a list. The numbers inside the circular nodes represent the values in the list, while the numbers outside the nodes represent the indices of the list. Note how index **0** is at the top of the heap, indices **1** and **2** are for the left and right children in Level 2, indices **3** to **6** form Level 3, and finally index **7** is in the partially filled Level 4.

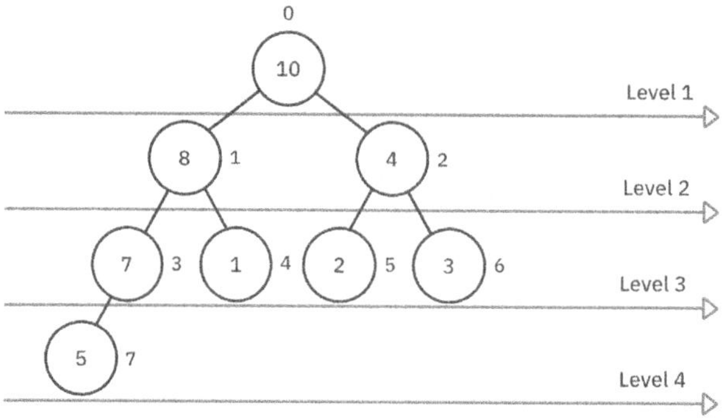

To represent the heap above as a list, you iterate through each element level-by-level from left to right. Your traversal looks something like this:

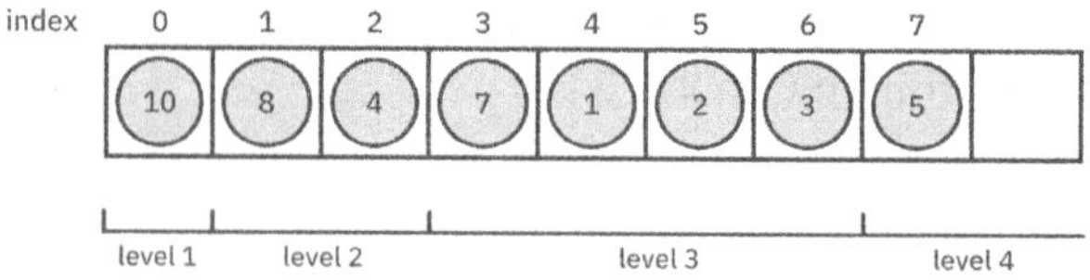

Every level gets twice as many indices allocated to it as the level before.

Accessing Nodes

It's now easy to access any node in the heap. Instead of traversing down the left or right branch, you access a node in your list using simple formulas.

Given a node at a zero-based index `i`:

- The **left child** of this node is at index `2i + 1`.
- The **right child** of this node is at index `2i + 2`.

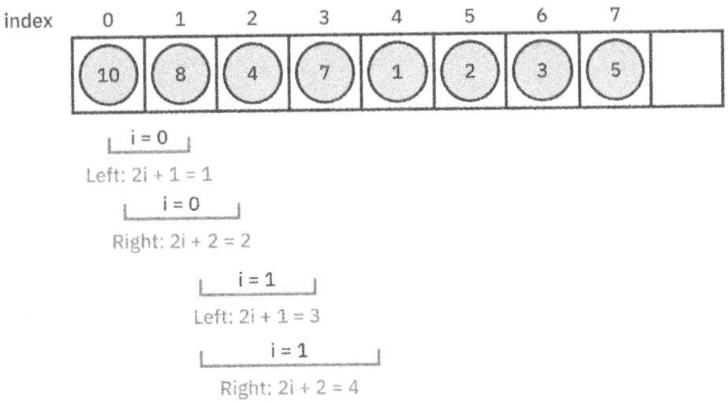

If you want to obtain the index of a parent node, you can use either of the formulas above and solve for `i`.

Given a node at index `i`:

- The **parent** of this node is at index `(i - 1) ~/ 2`.

That works for both left and right children since the ~/ integer division operator drops any fractional value.

Accessing a particular node in an actual binary tree requires traversing the tree from the root, which is an O(log n) operation. That same operation is just O(1) in a random-access data structure such as a list.

Implementation

Open the **starter** project for this chapter and add a **lib** folder to the root of the project. Inside that folder create a file named **heap.dart**.

Adding a Constructor

Since there are both max-heaps and min-heaps, start by adding the following enum to **heap.dart**:

```
enum Priority { max, min }
```

You'll provide `Priority` as a constructor parameter to specify the priority type when you create a heap.

Below `Priority` create a class named `Heap` with the following basic implementation:

```
class Heap<E extends Comparable<E>> {
  Heap({List<E>? elements, this.priority = Priority.max}) {
    this.elements = (elements == null) ? [] : elements;
  }

  late final List<E> elements;
  final Priority priority;
}
```

This setup offers a few features:

- The default is a max-heap, but users can also choose to create a min-heap.
- You can optionally specify a list of elements to initialize your heap with. Later in the chapter, you'll add a method to sort them.
- Since elements of a heap need to be sortable, the element type extends `Comparable`.

Providing Basic Properties

Add the following properties to Heap:

```
bool get isEmpty => elements.isEmpty;

int get size => elements.length;

E? get peek => (isEmpty) ? null : elements.first;
```

Calling peek will give you the maximum value in the collection for a max-heap, or the minimum value in the collection for a min-heap. This is an O(1) operation.

Preparing Helper Methods

Any complex task can be broken down into simpler steps. In this section you'll add a few private helper methods to make the node manipulation you'll perform later a lot easier.

Accessing Parent and Child Indices

You've already learned the formulas for accessing the indices of the children or parent of a given node. Add the Dart implementation of those formulas to Heap:

```
int _leftChildIndex(int parentIndex) {
  return 2 * parentIndex + 1;
}

int _rightChildIndex(int parentIndex) {
  return 2 * parentIndex + 2;
}

int _parentIndex(int childIndex) {
  return (childIndex - 1) ~/ 2;
}
```

Selecting a Priority

When you made the Heap constructor, you allowed the user to pass in a max or min priority. Add the following two helper methods that will make use of that property:

```
bool _firstHasHigherPriority(E valueA, E valueB) {
  if (priority == Priority.max) {
    return valueA.compareTo(valueB) > 0;
  }
  return valueA.compareTo(valueB) < 0;
}

int _higherPriority(int indexA, int indexB) {
  if (indexA >= elements.length) return indexB;
  final valueA = elements[indexA];
  final valueB = elements[indexB];
  final isFirst = _firstHasHigherPriority(valueA, valueB);
  return (isFirst) ? indexA : indexB;
}
```

Both methods compare two inputs and return a value to indicate the one with the greater priority. However, the first method compares any two values while the second method compares the values at two specific indices in the list.

Again, in a max-heap, the *higher* value has a greater priority, while in a min-heap, the *lower* value has a greater priority. Centralizing that decision here means that none of the code in the rest of the class knows whether it's in a min-heap or max-heap. It just asks for the results of the priority comparison and goes on with its business.

Swapping Values

You'll add `insert` and `remove` methods to the class in just a bit. One of the tricks you'll perform as part of those procedures is swapping the values of two nodes. Add a helper method to Heap for that:

```
void _swapValues(int indexA, int indexB) {
  final temp = elements[indexA];
  elements[indexA] = elements[indexB];
  elements[indexB] = temp;
}
```

Now that you've got your helpers, you're ready to start the real magic!

Inserting Into a Heap

Say you start with the max-heap shown in the image below:

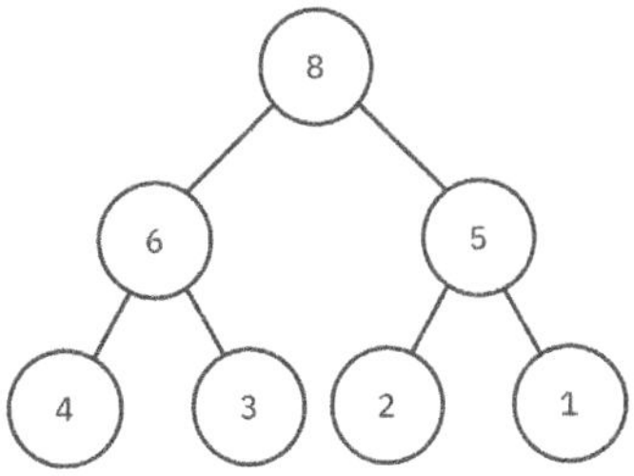

If you want to insert the value **7**, you start by adding it to the end of the heap. Internally, that means you're appending it to the end of the list:

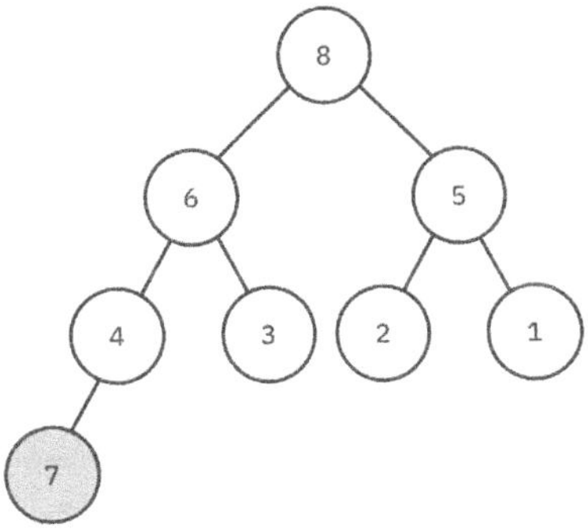

The problem, though, is that this is a max-heap, and the **7** violates the rules of a max-heap. It needs to be on a higher priority level.

The procedure for moving a node to a higher level is called **sifting up**. What you do is compare the node in question to its parent. If the node is larger, then you swap the value with that of its parent. You continue swapping with the next parent up until the value is no longer larger than its parent. At that point, the sifting is finished and order has returned to the universe...or at least to your heap anyway.

Take a look at this in action in the following image. First you compare **7** with its parent **4**. Since this is a max-heap and **7** is larger than **4**, you need to swap the values:

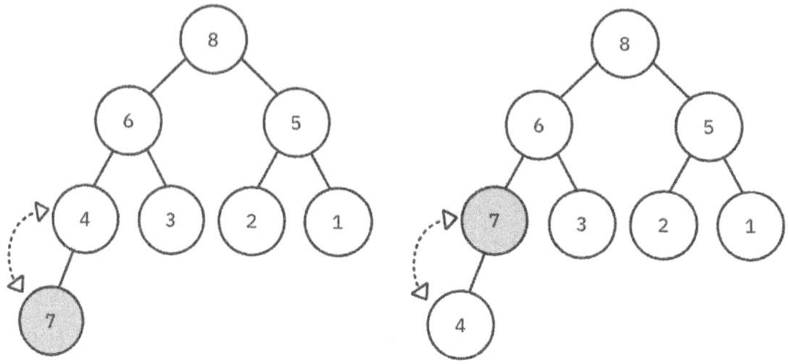

The next parent up is **6**. Since **7** is also larger than **6**, swap those two values:

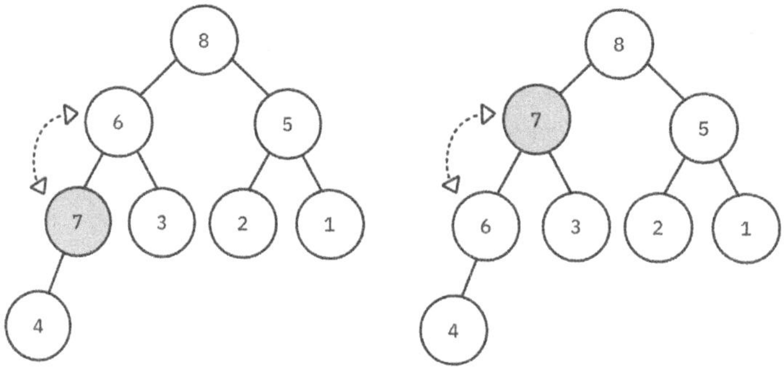

The final parent is **8**, but since **8** is larger than **7**, you leave the **7** where it is. The sifting is finished.

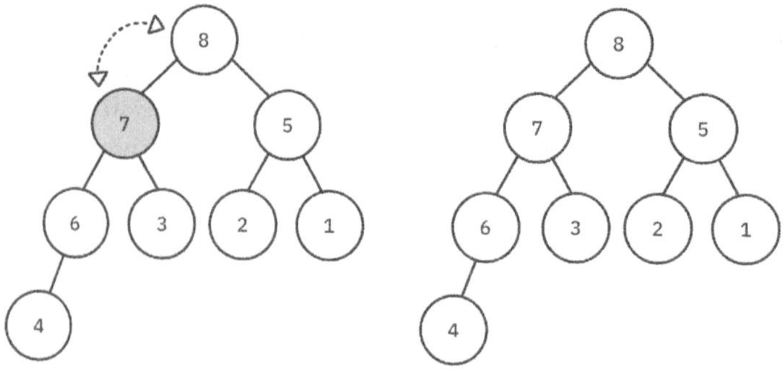

Your heap now satisfies the max-heap property.

Implementing insert

Now that you've got the theory, it's time to implement it in code. Add the following two methods to Heap:

```
void insert(E value) {
  // 1
  elements.add(value);
  // 2
  _siftUp(elements.length - 1);
}

void _siftUp(int index) {
  var child = index;
  var parent = _parentIndex(child);
  // 3
  while (child > 0 && child == _higherPriority(child, parent)) {
    _swapValues(child, parent);
    child = parent;
    parent = _parentIndex(child);
  }
}
```

The implementation is pretty straightforward:

1. First, you add the value that you want to insert to the end of the `elements` list.
2. Then, you start the sifting procedure using the index of the value you just added.
3. As long as that value has a higher priority than its parent, then you keep swapping it with the next parent value. Since you're only concerned about priority, this will sift larger values up in a max-heap and smaller values up in a min-heap.

The overall complexity of `insert` is O(log n). Adding an element to a list takes only O(1) while sifting elements up in a heap takes O(log n).

That's all there is to inserting an element in a heap.

Making the Heap Printable

It's time to try out your handiwork, but before you do, override the `toString` method of Heap so that it's a little easier to observe what's happening:

```
@override
String toString() => elements.toString();
```

That will show the raw list, which is good enough for now, but feel free to implement something that looks more like a binary tree.

Testing Insertion Out

Replace the contents of **bin/starter.dart** with the following code:

```
import 'package:starter/heap.dart';

void main() {
  final heap = Heap<num>();
  heap.insert(8);
  heap.insert(6);
  heap.insert(5);
  heap.insert(4);
  heap.insert(3);
  heap.insert(2);
  heap.insert(1);
  print(heap);
}
```

These inserts don't require sifting since you inserted them in max-heap order.

Run that, and you should see the output below in the console:

```
[8, 6, 5, 4, 3, 2, 1]
```

This list corresponds to the image you saw earlier:

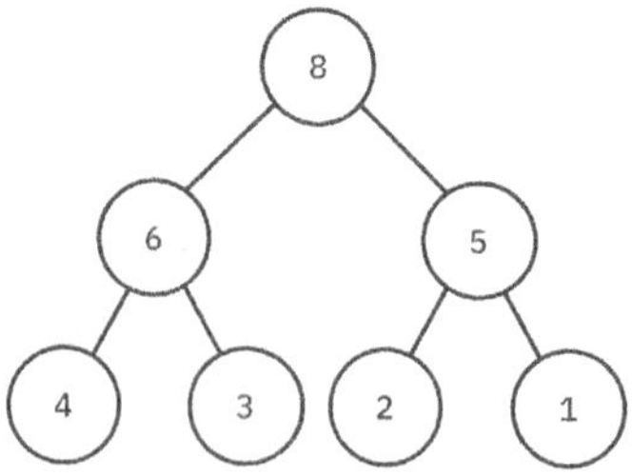

Now add the following two lines at the bottom of `main` and run the code again:

```
heap.insert(7);
print(heap);
```

This time adding the **7** does require the internal sifting. Run the code again and the final line in the console output will be the following:

```
[8, 7, 5, 6, 3, 2, 1, 4]
```

Your code moved **7** to its appropriate location. The list above corresponds with the following heap:

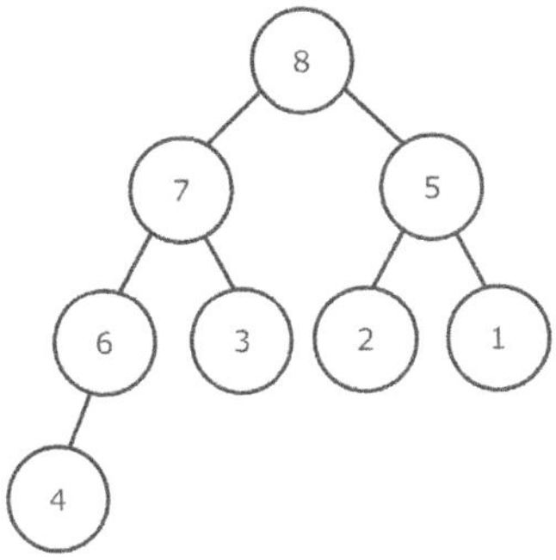

Success!

Removing From a Heap

A basic remove operation removes the root node from the heap.

Take the following max-heap as an example. The root node you want to remove has a value of **10**.

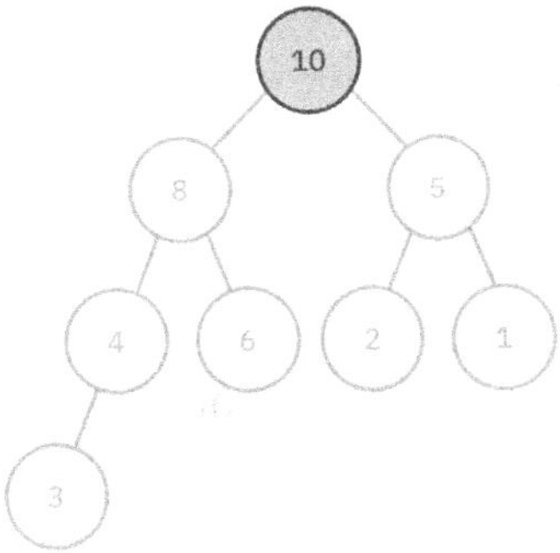

In order to perform the remove operation, you must first swap the **root** node with the **last** element in the heap. In this case, since the last node has a value of **3**, you swap the **10** and the **3**.

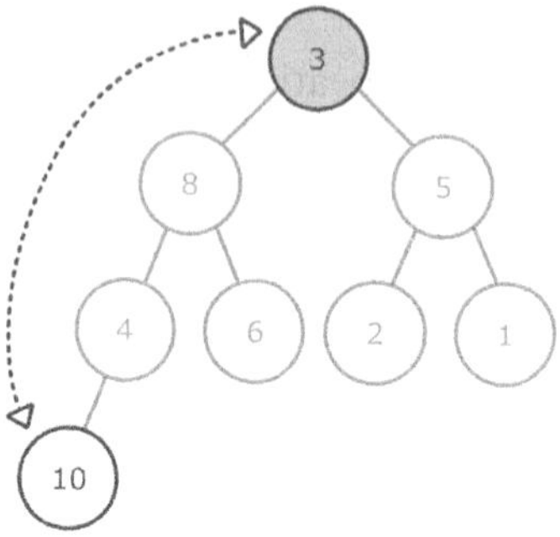

Once you've swapped the two elements, you can remove the last one:

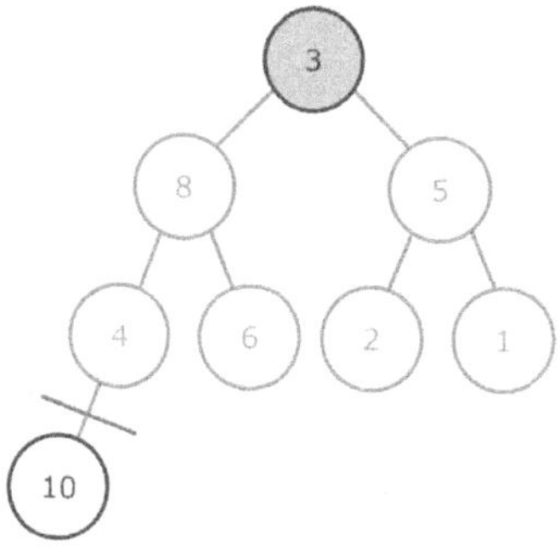

Now, you must check the max-heap's integrity. Ask yourself, "Is it still a max-heap?" Remember, the rule for a max-heap is that the value of every parent node must be larger than or equal to the values of its children. If not, you must **sift down**.

To sift down, start from the current value and check its left and right child. If one of the children has a value that's greater than the current value, you swap it with the parent. If both children have a greater value, you swap the parent with the larger of the two children. You continue to sift down until the node's value is no longer larger than the values of its children.

In this case, both **8** and **5** are greater than **3**, so you choose the larger left child **8** and swap it with the **3**:

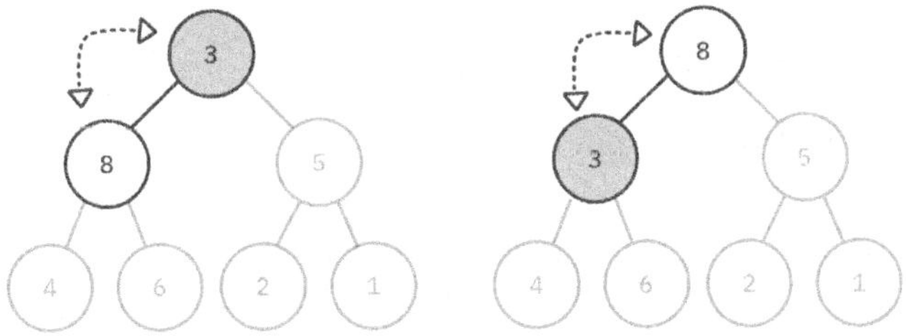

Now compare the **3** with its two new children, **4** and **6**. Since **6** is the largest, swap the **3** with that one.

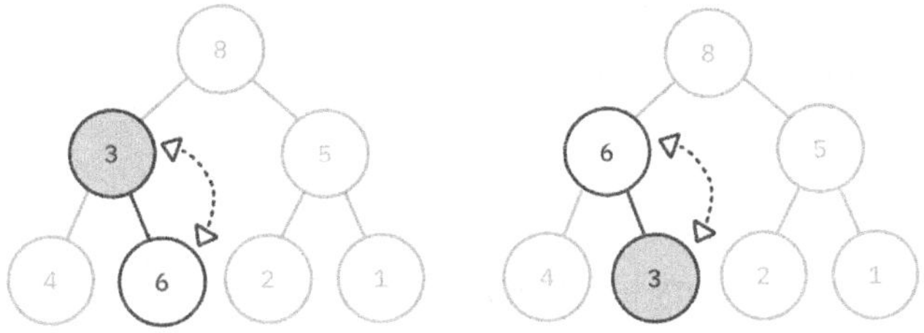

Once you reach the end, you're done, and the max-heap property has been restored!

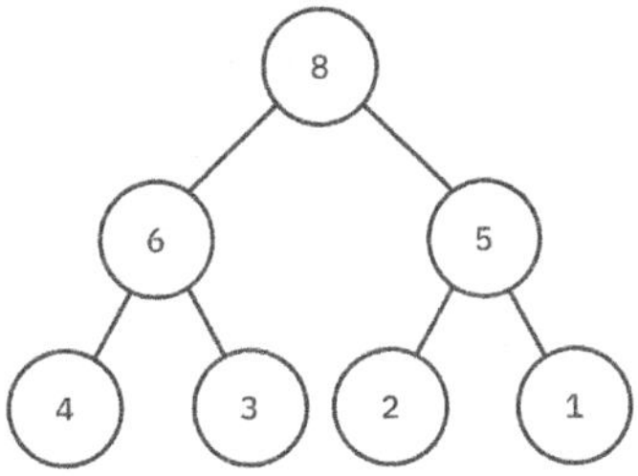

Implementing a Down Sift

Go back to **lib/heap.dart** and add a method to `Heap` to handle sifting down:

```
void _siftDown(int index) {
  // 1
  var parent = index;
  while (true) {
    // 2
    final left = _leftChildIndex(parent);
    final right = _rightChildIndex(parent);
    // 3
    var chosen = _higherPriority(left, parent);
    // 4
    chosen = _higherPriority(right, chosen);
    // 5
    if (chosen == parent) return;
    // 6
    _swapValues(parent, chosen);
    parent = chosen;
  }
}
```

`_siftDown` accepts an arbitrary index. The node in this index will always be treated as the parent node. Here's how the method works:

1. Store the `parent` index to keep track of where you are in the traversal.
2. Find the indices of the parent's left and right children.
3. The `chosen` variable keeps track of which index to swap with the parent. If there's a left child, and it has a higher priority than its parent, make it the chosen one.
4. If there's a right child, and it has an even greater priority, it will become the chosen one instead.
5. If `chosen` is still `parent`, then no more sifting is required.
6. Otherwise, swap `chosen` with `parent`, set it as the new parent, and continue sifting.

Implementing remove

Now that you have a way to sift down, add the `remove` method to `Heap`:

```
E? remove() {
  if (isEmpty) return null;
  // 1
  _swapValues(0, elements.length - 1);
  // 2
  final value = elements.removeLast();
  // 3
  _siftDown(0);
  return value;
}
```

Here's how this method works:

1. Swap the root with the last element in the heap.
2. Before removing it from the list, save a copy to return the value at the end of the method.
3. The heap may not be a max- or min-heap anymore, so you must perform a down sift to make sure it conforms to the rules.

The overall complexity of `remove` is O(log n). Swapping elements in a list is only O(1) while sifting elements down in a heap takes O(log n) time.

Testing remove

Go back to **bin/starter.dart** and replace the body of `main` with the following:

```
final heap = Heap<num>();
heap.insert(10);
heap.insert(8);
heap.insert(5);
heap.insert(4);
heap.insert(6);
heap.insert(2);
heap.insert(1);
heap.insert(3);

final root = heap.remove();
print(root);
print(heap);
```

Run that, to see the results below:

```
10
[8, 6, 5, 4, 3, 2, 1]
```

This removes **10** from the top of the heap and then performs a down sift that results in **8** being the new root.

You're now able to remove the root element, but what if you want to delete any arbitrary element from the heap? You'll handle that next.

Removing From an Arbitrary Index

Add the following method to `Heap`:

```
E? removeAt(int index) {
  final lastIndex = elements.length - 1;
  // 1
  if (index < 0 || index > lastIndex) {
    return null;
  }
  // 2
  if (index == lastIndex) {
    return elements.removeLast();
  }
  // 3
  _swapValues(index, lastIndex);
  final value = elements.removeLast();
  // 4
  _siftDown(index);
  _siftUp(index);
  return value;
}
```

To remove an arbitrary element from the heap, you need an index. Given that, here's what happens next:

1. Check to see if the index is within the bounds of the list. If not, return `null`.
2. If you're removing the last element in the heap, you don't need to do anything special. Simply remove it and return the value.
3. If you're not removing the last element, first swap the element with the last element. Then, remove the last element, saving its value to return at the end.
4. Perform a down sift and an up sift to adjust the heap.

But — why do you have to perform *both* a down sift *and* an up sift?

Assume you're trying to remove **5** from the max-heap below. You swap **5** with the last element, which is **8**. You now need to perform an *up* sift to satisfy the max-heap property:

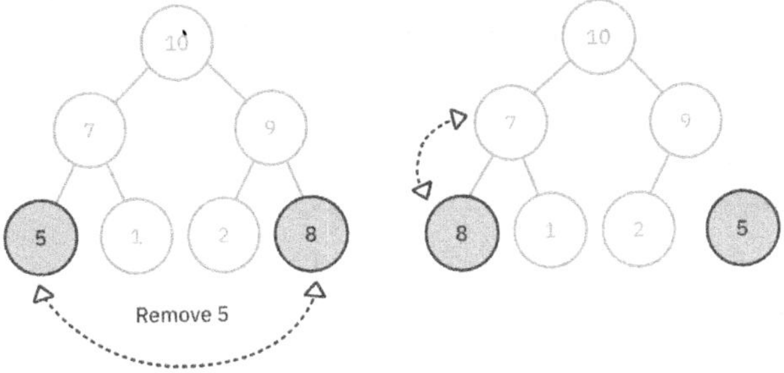

Shifting up case

Now, assume you are trying to remove **7** from the heap below. You swap **7** with the last element, **1**. In this case, you need to perform a *down* sift to satisfy the max-heap property.

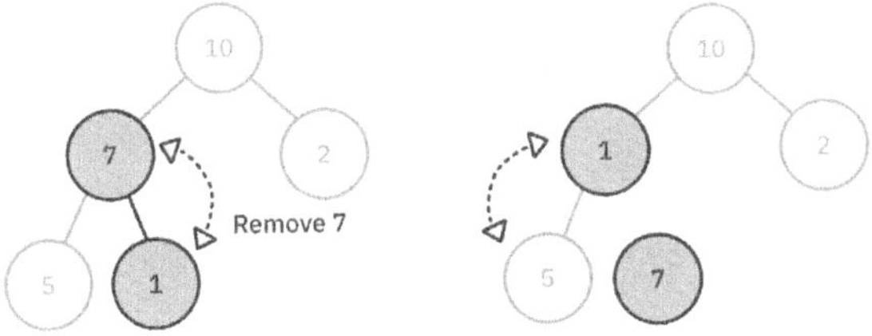

Shifting down case

Calling `_siftDown` and `_siftUp` ensures that both of these situations are handled.

Testing removeAt

The code that follows demonstrates the example from the previous image:

```
final heap = Heap<num>();
heap.insert(10);
heap.insert(7); // remove this
heap.insert(2);
heap.insert(5);
heap.insert(1);

final index = 1;
heap.removeAt(index);
print(heap);
```

Internally, the value **7** is at index **1**. Run that in `main` to see that `removeAt` successfully sifts the necessary nodes to give the following heap:

```
[10, 5, 2, 1]
```

Removing an arbitrary element from a heap is an O(log n) operation. However, it also requires knowing the index of the element you want to delete. How do you find that index?

Searching for an Element in a Heap

To find the index of the element you wish to delete, you need to perform a search on the heap. Unfortunately, heaps are not designed for fast searches. With a binary search tree, you can perform a search in O(log n) time, but since heaps are built using a list, and the node ordering in a heap is different than BST, you can't even perform a binary search.

Searching for an element in a heap is, in the worst-case, an O(n) operation since you may have to check every element in the list. However, you can optimize the search by taking advantage of the heap's max or min priority.

Add the following recursive function to `Heap`:

```
int indexOf(E value, {int index = 0}) {
  // 1
  if (index >= elements.length) {
    return -1;
  }
  // 2
  if (_firstHasHigherPriority(value, elements[index])) {
    return -1;
  }
  // 3
  if (value == elements[index]) {
    return index;
  }
  // 4
  final left = indexOf(value, index: _leftChildIndex(index));
  if (left != -1) return left;
  return indexOf(value, index: _rightChildIndex(index));
}
```

Here's what's happening:

1. If the index is too big, the search fails. Return `-1`. Alternatively, you could rewrite the method to return `null`, but `-1` is what `List` uses in its `indexOf` method.
2. This step is the optimization part. Check to see if the value you're looking for has a higher priority than the current node at your recursive traversal of the tree. If it does, the value you're looking for cannot possibly be lower in the heap. For example, if you're looking for **10** in a max-heap, but the current node has a value of **9**, there's no use checking all the nodes below **9** because they're just going to be even lower.
3. If the value you're looking for equals the value at `index`, you found it. Return `index`.
4. Recursively search for the value starting from the left child and then on to the right child. If both searches fail, the whole search fails. Return `-1`.

Testing it Out

Go back to **bin/starter.dart** and replace the body of `main` with the following:

```
final heap = Heap<num>();
heap.insert(10);
heap.insert(7);
heap.insert(2);
heap.insert(5);
heap.insert(1);
print(heap);

final index = heap.indexOf(7);
print(index);
```

This code attempts to find the index of the value **7**.

Run the code, and you should see the output below:

```
[10, 7, 2, 5, 1]
1
```

The index was correctly recognized as **1**.

Accepting a List in the Constructor

You may recall that when you made the `Heap` constructor, it took a list of elements as an optional parameter. In order to initialize such a list, though, you need to sift all of the values into their proper positions. Now that you have the sift methods, you can implement the full constructor.

Replace the current `Heap` constructor with the following one:

```
Heap({List<E>? elements, this.priority = Priority.max}) {
  this.elements = (elements == null) ? [] : elements;
  _buildHeap();
}

void _buildHeap() {
  if (isEmpty) return;
  final start = elements.length ~/ 2 - 1;
  for (var i = start; i >= 0; i--) {
    _siftDown(i);
  }
}
```

If a non-empty list is provided, you use that as the initial elements for the heap. You loop through the list backwards, starting from the first non-leaf node, and sift all parent nodes down. You loop through only half of the elements because there's no point in sifting **leaf** nodes down, only parent nodes.

> **Note**: You might wonder whether you could start at the front of the list and call `_siftUp` on every element. Well, you'd be right. You *could* do that. However, it wouldn't be as efficient. Since the top of the heap has only one node, you'd have to do more work to sift *every* other node toward this position. And when sifting is required, the nodes are more likely to have to travel further. The bottom of the heap, on the other hand, holds half of the nodes already, and it doesn't take so much work to sift the relatively fewer number of nodes above them down.
>
> In Big O notation, although a single up or down sift is O(log n), building a heap using the up-sift algorithm has a time complexity of O(n log n), while building it with the down-sift algorithm has a time complexity of only O(n). Read stackoverflow.com/a/18742428 for a more in-depth explanation.

Testing it Out

Time to try your new constructor out. Add the following to `main`:

```
var heap = Heap<num>(elements: [1, 12, 3, 4, 1, 6, 8, 7]);
print(heap);

while (!heap.isEmpty) {
  print(heap.remove());
}
```

The constructor creates a max-heap from the elements of the list. Then the `while` loop repeatedly removes the largest element until none are left. Run that, and you should see the following output:

```
[12, 7, 8, 4, 1, 6, 3, 1]
12
8
7
6
4
3
1
1
```

Try it again but this time make it a min-heap. Replace the first line in the code block above with the following:

```
var heap = Heap<num>(
  elements: [1, 12, 3, 4, 1, 6, 8, 7],
  priority: Priority.min,
);
```

This time you should see the opposite result:

```
[1, 1, 3, 4, 12, 6, 8, 7]
1
1
3
4
6
7
8
12
```

Challenges

Think you have a handle on heaps? Try out the following challenges. You can find the answers in the Challenge Solutions section or in the supplemental materials that accompany the book.

Challenge 1: Find the Nth Smallest Number

Write a function to find the *n*th smallest number in an unsorted list. For example, given the following list:

```
final numbers = [3, 10, 18, 5, 21, 100];
```

If `n = 3`, the result should be `10`.

Challenge 2: Step-by-Step Diagram

Given the following unsorted list, visually construct a min-heap. Provide a step-by-step diagram of how the min-heap is formed.

```
[21, 10, 18, 5, 3, 100, 1]
```

Challenge 3: Combining Two Heaps

Write a method that combines two heaps.

Challenge 4: Is it a Min-Heap?

Write a function to check if a given list is a min-heap.

Key Points

- The heap data structure is good for maintaining the highest- or lowest-priority element.
- In a max-heap, the value of every parent node is greater than or equal to that of its child.
- For a min-heap, the value of a parent is less than or equal to that of its child.
- Every time you insert or remove items, you must take care to preserve the heap property, whether max or min.
- There can't be any holes in a heap. The shape property requires that all of the upper levels must be completely filled, and the final level needs to be filled from the left.
- Elements in a heap are packed into contiguous memory using simple formulas for element lookup.
- Here is a summary of the algorithmic complexity of the heap operations you implemented in this chapter:

Heap Data Structure

Operations	Time Complexity
remove	O(log n)
insert	O(log n)
search	O(n)
peek	O(1)

Heap operation time complexity

Chapter 15: Priority Queues

Queues are simply lists that maintain the order of elements using *first-in-first-out* (FIFO) ordering. A priority queue is another version of a queue in which elements are dequeued in priority order instead of FIFO order.

A priority queue can be either of these two:

1. **Max-priority**, in which the element at the front is always the largest.
2. **Min-priority**, where the element at the front is always the smallest.

You'll notice the similarity here to the heap data structure that you made in the last chapter. In fact, in this chapter you'll implement a priority queue using a heap. A priority queue creates a layer of abstraction by focusing on the key operations of a queue and leaving out the additional functionality provided by a heap. This makes the priority queue's intent clear and concise. Its only job is to enqueue and dequeue elements, nothing else. Simplicity for the win!

Applications

Some practical applications of a priority queue include:

- **Dijkstra's algorithm**, which uses a priority queue to calculate the minimum cost.
- **A* pathfinding algorithm**, which uses a priority queue to track the unexplored routes that will produce the path with the shortest length.
- **Heapsort**, which can be implemented using a priority queue.

- **Huffman coding** that builds a compression tree. A min-priority queue is used to repeatedly find two nodes with the smallest frequency that do not yet have a parent node.

These are just some of the use cases, but priority queues have many more applications as well.

Common Operations

In Chapter 6, "Queues", you established the following interface for queues:

```
abstract interface class Queue<E> {
  bool enqueue(E element);
  E? dequeue();
  bool get isEmpty;
  E? get peek;
}
```

A priority queue has the same operations as a regular queue, so only the implementation will differ:

- **enqueue**: Inserts an element into the queue, and returns `true` if the operation was successful.
- **dequeue**: Removes the element with the highest priority and returns it. Returns `null` if the queue was empty.
- **isEmpty**: Checks if the queue is empty.
- **peek**: Returns the element with the highest priority without removing it. Returns `null` if the queue was empty.

Implementation

You can create a priority queue in the following ways:

1. **Sorted list**: This is useful to obtain the maximum or minimum value of an element in O(1) time. However, insertion is slow and will require O(n) time since you have to first search for the insertion location and then shift every element after that location.

2. **Balanced binary search tree**: This is useful in creating a double-ended priority queue, which features getting both the minimum and maximum value in O(log n) time. Insertion is better than a sorted list, also O(log n).

3. **Heap**: This is a natural choice for a priority queue. A heap is more efficient than a sorted list because a heap only needs to be partially sorted. Inserting and removing from a heap are O(log n) while simply querying the highest priority value is O(1).

You'll implement a priority queue in this chapter using a heap. However, check out Challenge 2 in which you'll reimplement a priority queue using a list.

Getting Started

Here's how to use a heap to create a priority queue.

Open up the **starter** project. In the **lib** folder, you'll find the following files:

1. **heap.dart**: Contains the heap data structure from the previous chapter.

2. **queue.dart**: Contains the interface that defines a queue.

Create a new file in the **lib** folder called **priority_queue.dart** and add the following code to it:

```
import 'heap.dart';
import 'queue.dart';

// 1
export 'heap.dart' show Priority;

// 2
class PriorityQueue<E extends Comparable<E>> implements Queue<E>
{

  PriorityQueue({
    List<E>? elements,
    Priority priority = Priority.max,
  }) {
    // 3
    _heap = Heap<E>(elements: elements, priority: priority);
  }

  late Heap<E> _heap;

  // more to come
}
```

Here are some notes corresponding to the commented numbers:

1. When you use your priority queue in the future to implement Dijkstra's algorithm, exporting `Priority` here will save you from having to import **heap.dart** separately.
2. `PriorityQueue` will conform to the `Queue` protocol. The generic type `E` must extend `Comparable` since you need to sort the elements.
3. You'll use this heap to implement the priority queue. By passing an appropriate `Priority` type into the constructor, `PriorityQueue` can be used to create either min- or max-priority queues.

Implementing the Queue Interface

To implement the `Queue` interface, add the following to `PriorityQueue`:

```
@override
bool get isEmpty => _heap.isEmpty;

@override
E? get peek => _heap.peek;

// 1
@override
bool enqueue(E element) {
  _heap.insert(element);
  return true;
}

// 2
@override
E? dequeue() => _heap.remove();
```

The heap data structure makes it easy to implement a priority queue.

1. You implement enqueue by calling `insert` on the heap. From the previous chapter, you should recall that when you insert, the heap will sift up to validate itself. The overall complexity of enqueue is O(log n).
2. By calling dequeue, you remove the root element from the heap by replacing it with the last heap element and then sifting down to validate the heap. The overall complexity of dequeue is also O(log n).

Testing it Out

Go to **bin/starter.dart** and replace the contents of the file with the following code:

```
import 'package:starter/priority_queue.dart';

void main() {
  var priorityQueue = PriorityQueue<num>(
    elements: [1, 12, 3, 4, 1, 6, 8, 7],
  );
  while (!priorityQueue.isEmpty) {
    print(priorityQueue.dequeue()!);
  }
}
```

Your priority queue has the same interface as a regular queue. Since you didn't change the default priority, the code above creates a max-priority queue.

Run the code, and you'll see the following numbers are printed to the console in descending order:

```
12
8
7
6
4
3
1
1
```

That's all there is to making a priority queue with a heap! Ready to try some challenges?

Challenges

The first challenge below will test your ability to apply the data structure to a practical problem, while the second challenge will give you some more practice implementing a priority queue. As always, you can find the answers in the Challenge Solutions section at the end of the book.

Challenge 1: Prioritize a Waitlist

Your favorite concert was sold out. Fortunately, there's a waitlist for people who still want to go! However, ticket sales will first prioritize someone with a military background, followed by seniority.

Use a priority queue to prioritize the order of people on the waitlist. Start by making a `Person` class that you can instantiate like so:

```
final person = Person(name: 'Josh', age: 21, isMilitary: true);
```

Challenge 2: List-Based Priority Queue

You've learned how to construct a priority queue by implementing the `Queue` interface with an internal heap data structure. Now your challenge is to do it again, but this time with a `List`.

Key Points

- A priority queue is often used to retrieve elements in priority order.
- A max-priority queue prioritizes the largest elements, while a min-priority queue, the smallest.
- Wrapping a heap with a queue interface allows you to focus on the key operations of a queue while ignoring unneeded heap operations.

Section IV: Sorting Algorithms

Putting lists in order is a classical computational problem. Although you may never need to write your own sorting algorithm, studying this topic has many benefits. This section will teach you about stability, best- and worst-case times, and the all-important technique of divide and conquer.

Studying sorting may seem a bit academic and disconnected from the "real world" of app development, but understanding the tradeoffs for these simple cases will lead you to a better understanding of how to analyze any algorithm.

Chapter 16: O(n^2) Sorting Algorithms

O(n^2) time complexity isn't great performance, but the sorting algorithms in this category are easy to understand and useful in some scenarios. One advantage of these algorithms is that they have constant O(1) space complexity, making them attractive for certain applications where memory is limited. For small data sets, these sorting algorithms compare very favorably against more complex sorts.

In this chapter, you'll learn about the following sorting algorithms:

- Bubble sort
- Selection sort
- Insertion sort

All of these are **comparison-based** sorting methods since they rely on comparisons to order the elements. You can measure a sorting technique's general performance by counting the number of times the sorting algorithm compares elements.

Bubble Sort

One of the most straightforward sorts is the **bubble sort**, which repeatedly compares adjacent values and swaps them, if needed, to perform the sort. Therefore, the larger values in the set will "bubble up" to the end of the collection.

Example

Consider the following hand of cards. The order is `[9, 4, 10, 3]`:

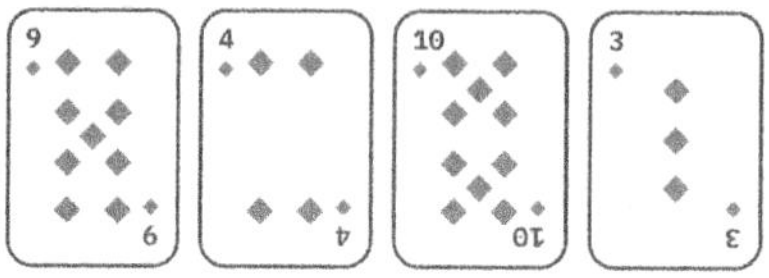

In the first pass of the bubble-sort algorithm, you start at the beginning of the collection. Compare the first two elements: **9** and **4**. Since **9** is larger than **4**, these values need to be swapped. The collection then becomes `[4, 9, 10, 3]`:

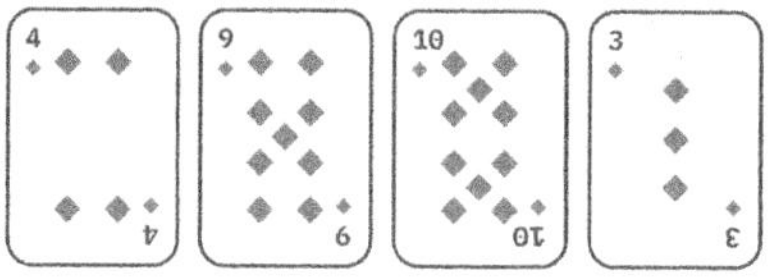

Move to the next index in the collection to compare **9** and **10**. These are already in order, so move to the next index in the collection to compare **10** and **3**. Since **10** is larger, these values need to be swapped. The collection then becomes `[4, 9, 3, 10]`:

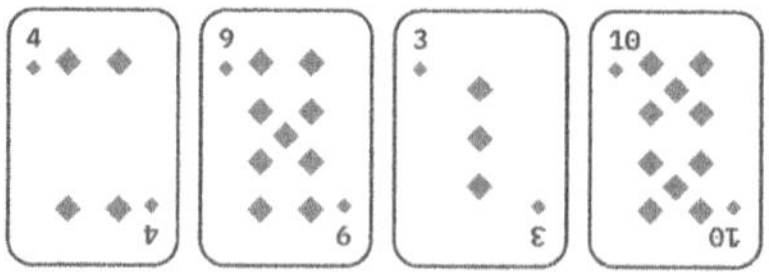

This completes the first pass. However, a single algorithm pass will seldom result in a complete ordering. It certainly didn't for this example. It will, however, cause the largest value — **10** in this case — to bubble up to the end of the collection. Subsequent passes through the collection will do the same with the next highest numbers.

For the second pass, go back to the beginning of the collection and compare **4** and **9**. These are already in order so there's no need to swap anything. Go on to the next index and compare **9** and **3**. Since **9** is larger, swap them. Now the collection becomes `[4, 3, 9, 10]`:

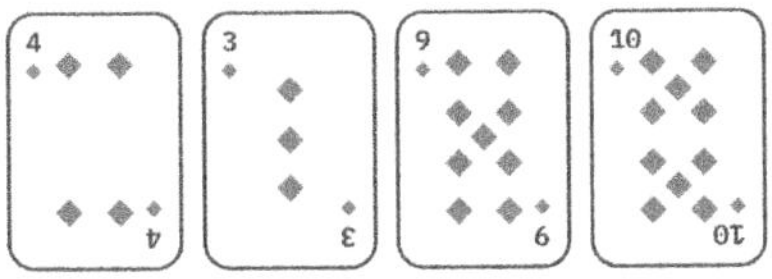

There's no need to compare **9** and **10** since the first pass already guaranteed that **10** is the largest value. Likewise, the second pass guaranteed that **9** is the second-largest value.

Time for the third pass. Go back to the beginning of the collection and compare **4** and **3**. Since **4** is larger, swap them. This gives you `[3, 4, 9, 10]`:

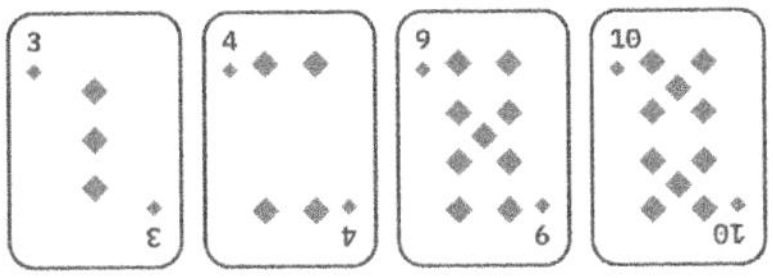

Now the list is completely sorted. No need to keep comparing the **4** with any other cards since those were already sorted in the earlier passes.

Here's a summary:

- Since there were four elements in the collection, you performed three passes. To generalize that, for a collection of length *n*, you need to do at most *n* - 1 passes. This is the worst case. If any single pass doesn't require a swap, that means the list is sorted and bubble sort can terminate early.
- The number of comparisons in each pass is one less than the pass before. In the example above, you made three comparisons in the first pass, two comparisons in the second pass and one comparison in the last pass. This is because each pass moves the largest value to the end, so it isn't necessary to compare those sorted values again.

Implementation

Open up the **starter** project for this chapter and create a **lib** folder in the root of the project.

Adding a Swap Extension to List

All sorting algorithms in this chapter will require swapping values between two indices in a list. To make that more convenient, you can add an extension to `List` itself.

Create a new file called **swap.dart** in the **lib** folder. Then add the following extension:

```
extension SwappableList<E> on List<E> {
  void swap(int indexA, int indexB) {
    final temp = this[indexA];
    this[indexA] = this[indexB];
    this[indexB] = temp;
  }
}
```

Implementing Bubble Swap

Now create a new file in **lib** named **bubble_sort.dart**. Write the following inside the file:

```
import 'swap.dart';

void bubbleSort<E extends Comparable<E>>(List<E> list) {
  // 1
  for (var end = list.length - 1; end > 0; end--) {
    var swapped = false;
    // 2
    for (var current = 0; current < end; current++) {
      if (list[current].compareTo(list[current + 1]) > 0) {
        list.swap(current, current + 1);
        swapped = true;
      }
    }
    // 3
    if (!swapped) return;
  }
}
```

Here's the play-by-play:

1. The outer `for` loop counts the passes. A single pass bubbles the largest value to the end of the collection. Every pass needs to compare one less value than in the previous pass, so you shorten the list by one with each pass.
2. The inner `for` loop handles the work of a single pass. It moves through the indices, comparing adjacent values and swapping them if the first value is larger than the second.
3. If no values were swapped during a pass, the collection must be sorted, and you can exit early.

Testing it Out

Head back to **bin/starter.dart** and replace the contents of the file with the following:

```
import 'package:starter/bubble_sort.dart';

void main() {
  final list = <num>[9, 4, 10, 3];
  print('Original: $list');
  bubbleSort(list);
  print('Bubble sorted: $list');
}
```

Run that, and you should see the output below:

```
Original: [9, 4, 10, 3]
Bubble sorted: [3, 4, 9, 10]
```

Bubble sort has a *best* time complexity of O(n) if it's already sorted, and a *worst* and *average* time complexity of O(n^2), making it one of the *least* appealing sorts in the known universe.

> **Note**: Bubble sort may be slow, but there are slower ones still. How about if you keep randomly shuffling the elements of the list until you finally get a list that just happens to be sorted? This "algorithm" is known as **bogosort**. It has an average time complexity of O($n \times n!$), and factorial time complexities are much worse than quadratic ones.

Selection Sort

Selection sort follows the basic idea of bubble sort but improves this algorithm by reducing the number of `swap` operations. Selection sort will only swap at the end of each pass. You'll see how that works in the following example.

Example

During each pass, selection sort will find the lowest unsorted value and swap it into place.

Assume you have the following hand of cards represented by the list `[9, 4, 10, 3]`:

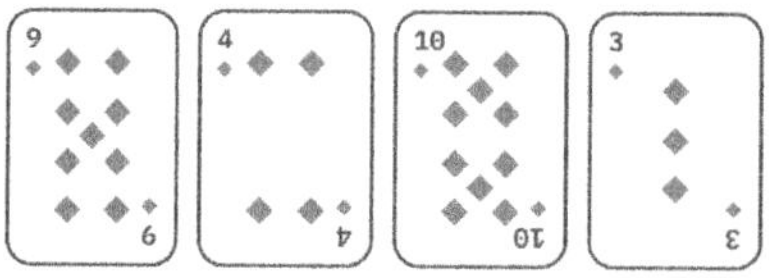

In the first pass, selection sort starts at the beginning of the collection and sees the **9**. So far that's the lowest value. The index moves to **4**. This is lower than **9**, so **4** becomes the new lowest value. Then index moves on to **10**. That's not lower than **4**, so the index moves on to **3**. Three is lower than **4**, so **3** is the new lowest value.

Since you've reached the end of the list, you swap the lowest value **3** with the first card in the pass, which was **9**. Now you have `[3, 4, 10, 9]`:

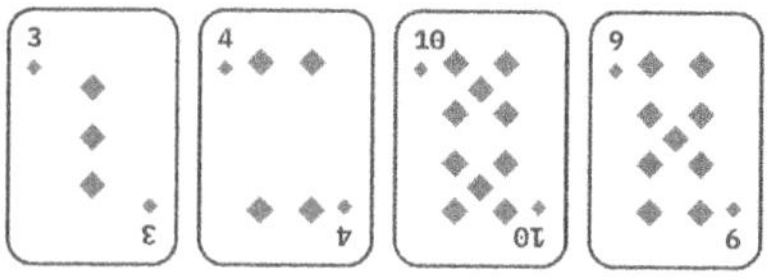

Time for the second pass. You can skip card **3** since it's already sorted. Start with **4**. Compare **4** to **10** and then to **9**, but **4** remains the lowest value in this pass. Since it's already in the right location, you don't need to swap anything.

For the third pass, start with **10**. Ten starts as the lowest value, but after you compare it to **9**, you find that **9** is lower. There isn't anything else to compare, so swap the lowest value **9** with the first value **10**. That finishes up pass three with `[3, 4, 9, 10]`, and the list is sorted:

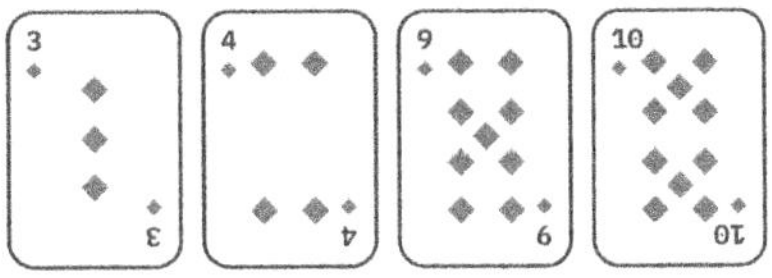

Implementation

Now that you know on a mental level how selection sort works, have a go at implementing it in Dart.

Create a new file named **selection_sort.dart** in the **lib** folder. Then add the following code inside the file:

```
import 'swap.dart';

void selectionSort<E extends Comparable<E>>(List<E> list) {
  // 1
  for (var start = 0; start < list.length - 1; start++) {
    var lowest = start;
    // 2
    for (var next = start + 1; next < list.length; next++) {
      if (list[next].compareTo(list[lowest]) < 0) {
        lowest = next;
      }
    }
    // 3
    if (lowest != start) {
      list.swap(lowest, start);
    }
  }
}
```

Here's what's going on:

1. The outer `for` loop represents the passes, where `start` is the index the current pass should begin at. Since the lowest value is moved to `start` at the end of every pass, `start` increments by one each time.
2. In every pass, you go through the remainder of the collection to find the element with the lowest value.
3. If a lower value was found, then swap it with the value at the `start` index.

Testing it Out

Back in **bin/starter.dart**, replace the contents of the file with the following code:

```
import 'package:starter/selection_sort.dart';

void main() {
  final list = <num>[9, 4, 10, 3];
  print('Original: $list');
  selectionSort(list);
  print('Selection sorted: $list');
}
```

Run that, and you should see the following output in your console:

```
Original: [9, 4, 10, 3]
Selection sorted: [3, 4, 9, 10]
```

Selection sort has a *best*, *worst* and *average* time complexity of $O(n^2)$, which is fairly dismal. It's a simple one to understand, though, and it does perform better than bubble sort!

Insertion Sort

Insertion sort is a more useful algorithm. Like bubble sort and selection sort, insertion sort has an average time complexity of $O(n^2)$, but the performance of insertion sort can vary. The more the data is already sorted, the less work it needs to do. Insertion sort has a best time complexity of $O(n)$ if the data is already sorted.

Dart itself uses the insertion sort. For lists with 32 or fewer elements, the `List.sort` method defaults to an insertion sort. Only for larger collections does Dart make use of a different sorting algorithm.

Example

The idea of insertion sort is similar to how many people sort a hand of cards. You start with the card at one end and then go through the unsorted cards one at a time, taking each one as you come to it and inserting it in the correct location among your previously sorted cards.

Consider the following hand of `[9, 4, 10, 3]`:

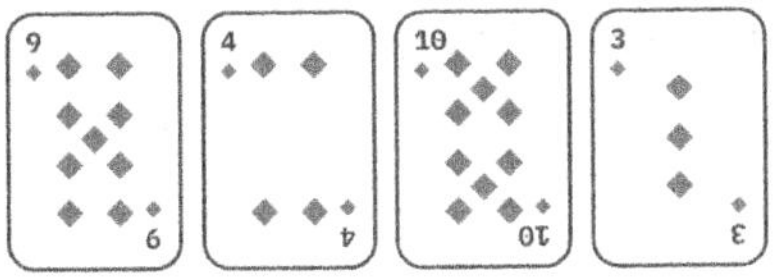

Insertion sort will start at the left where the **9** is. The next card is **4**, which is smaller than **9**, so you swap the **4** and the **9**, giving you `[4, 9, 10, 3]`. This is the first pass. The first two cards are now sorted:

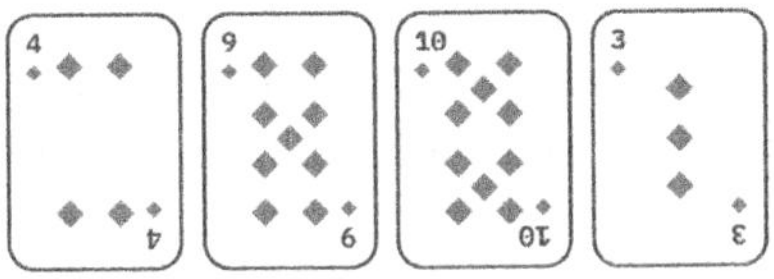

For the second pass, you take the third card, **10**. You need to insert it in the right location, so you begin by comparing **10** with the previous card, **9**. Well, what do you know? Ten is bigger so it's already in the right location. You can skip the rest of the comparisons in this pass. This shows how insertion sort can save time when some elements are already sorted.

For the third pass, you need to insert the fourth card, **3**, in its proper location. Begin by comparing **3** with the previous card, which is **10**. Since **10** is larger, swap them. Now, you've got `[4, 9, 3, 10]`:

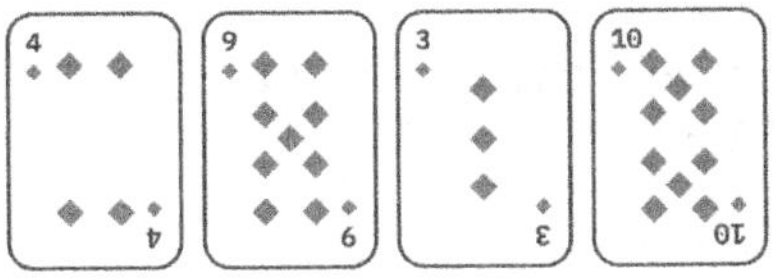

Keep going. Compare the **3** to the next card to the left, **9**. Since **9** is larger, swap **9** and **3**, leaving you `[4, 3, 9, 10]`:

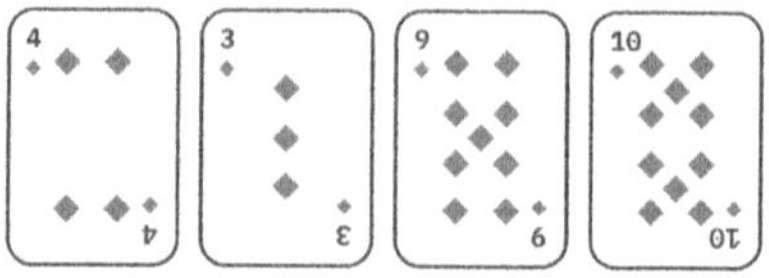

You're not done yet. The **3** needs to keep shifting left until it's in its correct sort order. So compare **3** with the next card to the left, which is **4**. Four is also larger, so swap them to give you `[3, 4, 9, 10]`:

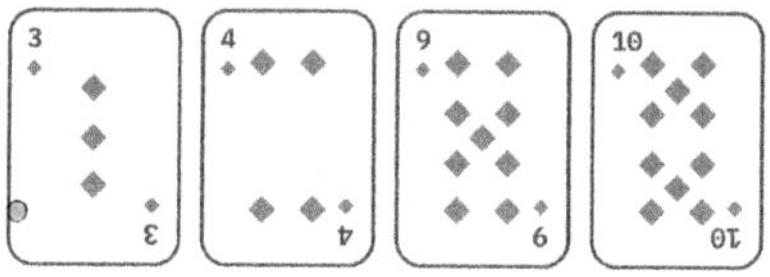

The third pass is now finished, and you've got a sorted hand.

It's worth pointing out that the best-case scenario for insertion sort occurs when the sequence of values is already in sorted order and no left shifting is necessary.

Implementation

Create a new file named **insertion_sort.dart** in the **lib** folder. Add the following code inside the file:

```
import 'swap.dart';

void insertionSort<E extends Comparable<E>>(List<E> list) {
  // 1
  for (var current = 1; current < list.length; current++) {
    // 2
    for (var shifting = current; shifting > 0; shifting--) {
      // 3
      if (list[shifting].compareTo(list[shifting - 1]) < 0) {
        list.swap(shifting, shifting - 1);
      } else {
        break;
      }
    }
  }
}
```

Here's what you have:

1. Insertion sort requires you to iterate from left to right once, which is the job of this outer `for` loop. At the beginning of the loop, `current` is the index of the element you want to sort in this pass.
2. Here, you run backwards from the `current` index so you can shift left as needed.
3. Keep shifting the element left as long as necessary. As soon as the element is in position, break the inner loop and start with the next element.

Testing it Out

Head back to **bin/starter.dart** and replace the code there with the following:

```
import 'package:starter/insertion_sort.dart';

void main() {
  var list = <num>[9, 4, 10, 3];
  print('Original: $list');
  insertionSort(list);
  print('Insertion sorted: $list');
}
```

Run that, and you should see the following console output:

```
Original: [9, 4, 10, 3]
Insertion sorted: [3, 4, 9, 10]
```

Insertion sort is one of the fastest sorting algorithms if the data is already sorted. That might sound obvious, but it isn't true for *all* sorting algorithms. In practice, many data collections will already be largely — if not entirely — sorted, and insertion sort will perform exceptionally well in those scenarios.

Stability

A sorting algorithm is called **stable** if the elements of the same type retain their order after being sorted. For example, say you had an unsorted deck of cards in which the 5 of clubs comes before the 5 of diamonds. If you then sort the cards by number only, the 5 of clubs would still come before the 5 of diamonds in a stable sort. That would not necessarily be true for an unstable sorting algorithm.

Of the three sorting algorithms in this chapter, bubble sort and insertion sort are both stable. Selection sort, on the other hand, is not stable because the swapping used in the algorithm can change the relative position of the cards. Take a few cards and see for yourself!

Most of the time it doesn't matter if a sort is stable or not. However, there are situations when it does matter. For example, say you sort a list of cities from around the world into alphabetical order. If you then sort that same list again by country, the cities within each country will still be in alphabetical order as long as the sort was stable. Using an unstable sort, on the other hand, would result in the cities potentially losing their sort order.

In the following chapters, you'll take a look at sorting algorithms that perform better than $O(n^2)$. Next is a stable sorting algorithm that uses an approach known as **divide and conquer**: merge sort!

Challenges

To really get a grasp on how sorting algorithms work, it helps to think through step by step what's happening. The challenges in this chapter will allow you to do that.

Grab a deck of cards or some paper and a pencil to help yourself out. Sprinkling a few `print` statements in the code might also help.

You can find the answers in the Challenge Solutions section as well as in the supplemental materials that come with the book.

Challenge 1: Bubble Up

Here's a list of randomly distributed elements:

```
[4, 2, 5, 1, 3]
```

Work out by hand the steps that a **bubble sort** would perform on this list.

Challenge 2: Select the Right One

Given the same list as above:

```
[4, 2, 5, 1, 3]
```

Work out by hand the steps that a **selection sort** would perform on this list.

Challenge 3: Insert Here

Again, using the same initial list as in the previous challenges:

```
[4, 2, 5, 1, 3]
```

Work out by hand the steps that an **insertion sort** would take to sort this list.

Challenge 4: Already Sorted

When you have a list that's already sorted like the following:

```
[1, 2, 3, 4, 5]
```

Are bubble sort, selection sort and insertion sort still $O(n^2)$? How do the algorithms take shortcuts to finish more quickly?

Key Points

- $O(n^2)$ algorithms often have a terrible reputation. Still, some of these algorithms have some redeeming qualities. Insertion sort can sort in $O(n)$ time if the collection is already in sorted order and gradually scales down to $O(n^2)$ the more unsorted the collection is.
- Insertion sort is one of the best sorts in situations where you know ahead of time that your data is already mostly sorted.

Chapter 17: Merge Sort

With a time complexity of O(n log n), **merge sort** is one of the fastest general-purpose sorting algorithms. The idea behind merge sort is to **divide and conquer** — to break up a big problem into several smaller, easier-to-solve problems and then combine the solutions into a final result. The merge sort mantra is to split first and merge later.

In this chapter, you'll implement merge sort from scratch. The example below will help you gain an intuitive understanding of how the algorithm works before you write the code.

Example

Assume that you're given a pile of unsorted playing cards:

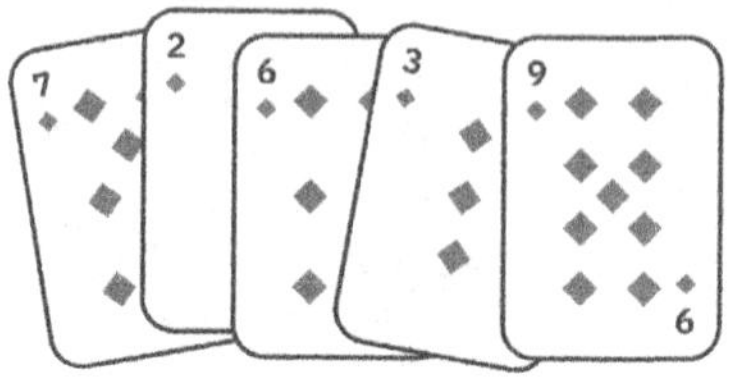

The merge sort algorithm works as follows. First, split the pile in half. You now have two unsorted piles:

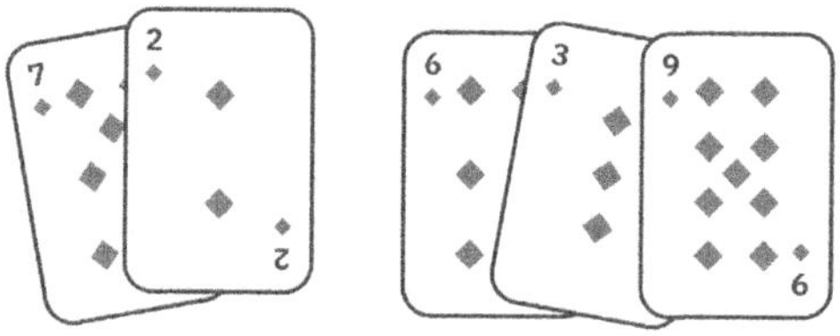

Split those piles again:

You keep splitting until you can't split anymore. In the end, you'll have one (sorted!) card in each pile:

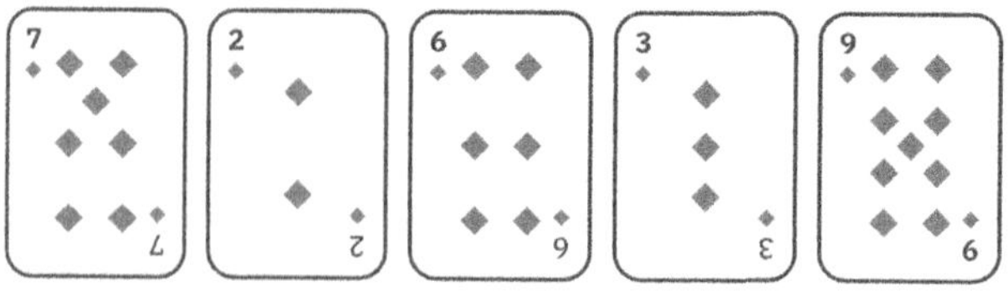

Finally, merge the piles in the reverse order in which you split them. During each merge, you put the contents in sorted order. This process is easy because each pile is already sorted.

Merge **2** with **7** and **3** with **9**:

Merge the **6** into the **3**-**9** pile:

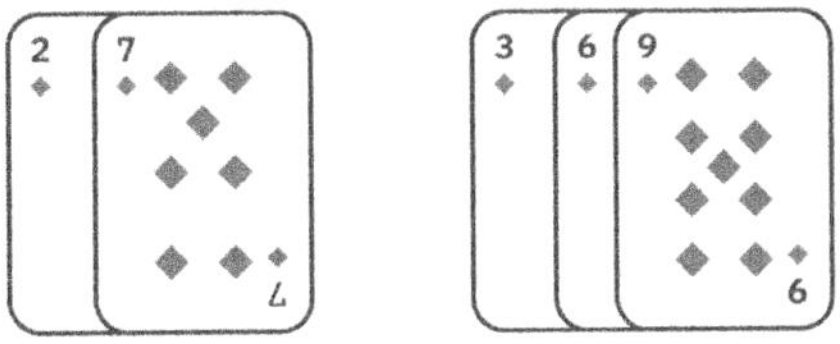

Finally, merge the two piles in order:

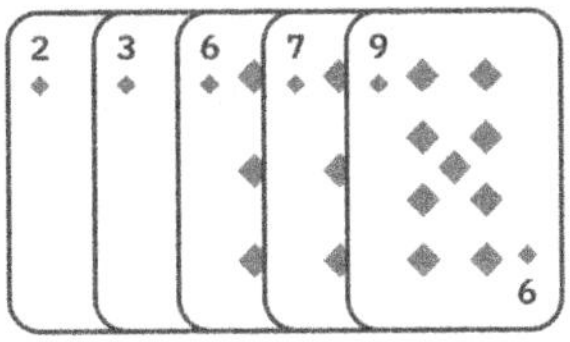

Do you understand the general idea of how merge sort works now? You'll build the algorithm with code next.

Implementation

Open up the **starter** project and create a new **lib** folder in the root of your project. Then create a new file in **lib** named **merge_sort.dart**.

Merging Lists

You'll start by creating a helper function named `_merge`. The sole responsibility of this function is to take in two sorted lists and combine them while retaining the sort order. Add the following to **merge_sort.dart**:

```
List<E> _merge<E extends Comparable<E>>(
  List<E> listA,
  List<E> listB,
) {
  var indexA = 0;
  var indexB = 0;
  final result = <E>[];

  // more to come
}
```

`indexA` and `indexB` track your progress as you parse through the two lists. The `result` list will house the merged list that you're about to make.

Next, add the following `while` loop at the bottom of `_merge`:

```
// 1
while (indexA < listA.length && indexB < listB.length) {
  final valueA = listA[indexA];
  final valueB = listB[indexB];
  // 2
  if (valueA.compareTo(valueB) < 0) {
    result.add(valueA);
    indexA += 1;
  } else if (valueA.compareTo(valueB) > 0) {
    result.add(valueB);
    indexB += 1;
  } else {
    // 3
    result.add(valueA);
    result.add(valueB);
    indexA += 1;
    indexB += 1;
  }
}

// more to come
```

Here's what's happening:

1. Starting from the beginning of `listA` and `listB`, you sequentially compare the values. If you've reached the end of either list, there's nothing else to compare.
2. The smaller of the two values goes into the result list.
3. If the values are equal, add both to the result list.

Finally, add the following code to the bottom of `_merge`:

```
if (indexA < listA.length) {
  result.addAll(listA.getRange(indexA, listA.length));
}

if (indexB < listB.length) {
  result.addAll(listB.getRange(indexB, listB.length));
}

return result;
```

The `while` loop above guarantees that either `left` or `right` is already empty. Since both lists are sorted, this ensures that any leftover elements are greater than or equal to the ones currently in `result`. In this scenario, you can directly add the rest of the elements without comparison.

> **Note**: `getRange` is similar to `sublist` except it doesn't return a new list. It just returns an iterable pointing to the elements of the current list. No need to spend time creating unnecessary objects.

Splitting

Now it's time to create the main `mergeSort` function. Write the following at the top of **merge_sort.dart**, above the `_merge` function:

```
List<E> mergeSort<E extends Comparable<E>>(List<E> list) {
  final middle = list.length ~/ 2;
  final left = list.sublist(0, middle);
  final right = list.sublist(middle);

  // more to come
}
```

Here, you split the list into halves. Splitting once isn't enough, though. You need to keep splitting recursively until you can't split anymore, which is when each subdivision contains just one element.

To do this, replace `mergeSort` with the following:

```
List<E> mergeSort<E extends Comparable<E>>(List<E> list) {
  // 1
  if (list.length < 2) return list;
  // 2
  final middle = list.length ~/ 2;
  final left = mergeSort(list.sublist(0, middle));
  final right = mergeSort(list.sublist(middle));
  // 3
  return _merge(left, right);
}
```

You've made a few changes here:

1. The base case is when the list only has one element.
2. You're now recursively calling `mergeSort` on the left and right halves of the original list. As soon as you've split the list in half, you try to split it again.
3. Complete the `mergeSort` function by calling `_merge`. This will combine the `left` and `right` lists that you split above.

You're finished with the implementation. Time to see it in action.

Testing it Out

Head back to **bin/starter.dart** to test your merge sort:

```
import 'package:starter/merge_sort.dart';

void main() {
  final list = <num>[7, 2, 6, 3, 9];
  final sorted = mergeSort(list);
  print('Original: $list');
  print('Merge sorted: $sorted');
}
```

This outputs:

```
Original: [7, 2, 6, 3, 9]
Merge sorted: [2, 3, 3, 6, 7]
```

Nice! It works.

Performance

The best, worst and average time complexity of merge sort is **quasilinear**, or O(n log n), which isn't too bad.

If you're struggling to understand where *n* log *n* comes from, think about how the recursion works:

- As you recurse, you split a single list into two smaller lists. This means a list of size two will need one recursion level, a list of size four will need two levels, a list of size eight will need three levels, and so on. If you had a list of 1,024 elements, it would take ten levels of recursively splitting in two to get down to 1,024 single element lists. In general, if you have a list of size *n*, the number of recursion levels is $\log_2(n)$.
- The cost of a single recursion is O(n). A single recursion level will merge *n* elements. It doesn't matter if there are many small merges or one large one. The number of elements merged will still be *n* at each level.

This brings the total cost to O(log n) × O(n) = O(n log n).

Bubble sort, selection sort and insertion sort were **in-place algorithms** since they used `swap` to move elements around in an existing list. Merge sort, by contrast, allocates additional memory to do its work. How much? There are $\log_2(n)$ levels of recursion, and at each level, *n* elements are used. That makes the total O(n log n) in space complexity. If you're clever with your bookkeeping, though, you can reduce the memory required to O(n) by discarding the memory that's not actively being used.

Merge sort is also stable. Elements of the same type retain their relative order after being sorted. This will also be true for radix sort in the next chapter, but not for heapsort and quicksort that you'll learn about later.

Merge sort is one of the classic sorting algorithms. It's relatively simple to understand and serves as a great introduction to how divide-and-conquer algorithms work.

Challenges

The following challenges will help to strengthen your understanding of merge sort. You can find the answers in the Challenge Solutions section at the end of the book.

Challenge 1: Mind Merge

Given the following list:

```
[4, 2, 5, 1, 3]
```

Work through the steps merge sort would take. Go slowly enough for your brain to understand what's happening. You'll have the easiest time if you use breakpoints in your IDE or add `print` statements to your code.

Challenge 2: Merge Two Sequences

In this chapter, you created a `_merge` function that merges two sorted lists. The challenge here is to generalize `_merge` so that it takes two *iterables* as inputs rather than lists. Here's the function signature to start off:

```
List<E> _merge<E extends Comparable<E>>(
  Iterable<E> first,
  Iterable<E> second,
)
```

Key Points

- Merge sort is in the category of divide-and-conquer algorithms.
- Merge sort works by splitting the original list into many individual lists of length one. It then merges pairs of lists into larger and larger sorted lists until the entire collection is sorted.
- There are many implementations of merge sort, and you can have different performance characteristics depending on the implementation.
- Merge sort has a time complexity of O(n log n). It does not sort in place, so the space complexity is also O(n log n), but can be O(log n) if optimized.
- Merge sort is a stable sorting algorithm.

Chapter 18: Radix Sort

In this chapter, you'll look at a completely different sorting model. So far, you've been relying on comparisons to determine the sorting order. **Radix sort** is a non-comparative algorithm for sorting integers. The word **radix** means **base**, as in the base of a number system. For example, decimal is base 10, and binary is base 2. You can use any base with a radix sort, but to keep things simple, this chapter will focus on sorting base-10 integers.

Radix sort relies on the position of digits within a number. For example, there are four digits in the number **1772**. The least significant digit is **2** since this is in the *ones* place. The most significant digit is **1** since this is the *thousands*-place value, greater than any other place value in this particular number. The following diagram shows the place values of a four-digit number:

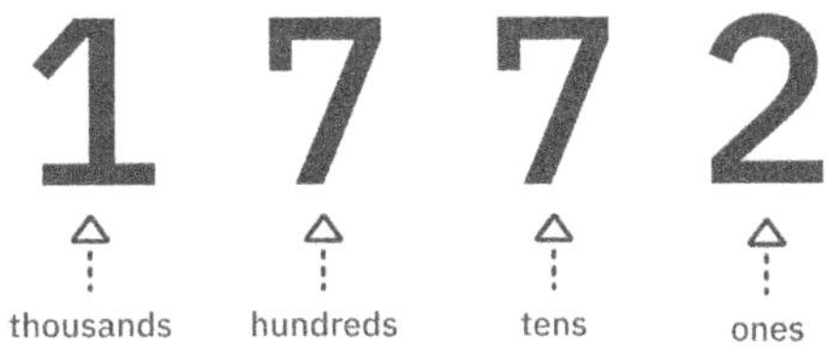

There are multiple implementations of radix sort that focus on different problems. One type sorts by the **least significant digit** (LSD) and another by the **most significant digit** (MSD).

You'll learn about both LSD- and MSD-radix sorting in this chapter.

Sorting by Least Significant Digit

Before you implement a radix sort in code, go through the following example to get an intuitive idea of how the sort works.

Example

An **LSD-radix sort** starts by looking at the least significant digits in a list of numbers. For example, the image below shows the numbers **88**, **410**, **1772** and **20** vertically aligned with a box drawn around the ones place:

```
  8|8|
 41|0|
177|2|
  2|0|
```

You've got one **8** from the final digit of **88**, a **0** from the end of **410**, a **2** from the last digit of **1772** and another **0** from the least significant digit of **20**. A radix sort goes through multiple rounds of sorting, but these final digits are what you'll use to sort the numbers in the first round.

Round One

You start by making ten buckets to sort the numbers into. You can think of this like sorting fruit. You put the apples in the apple bucket, the oranges in the oranges bucket, and the pears in the pear bucket.

> **Note**: You use ten buckets because you're working with decimal numbers. If you were using binary numbers, then you would use two buckets. Or if you were using hexadecimal numbers, then 16 buckets.

With an LSD-radix sort, you put the numbers that end in **0** in the zero bucket, the numbers that end in **1** in the ones bucket, the numbers that end in **2** in the twos bucket, and so on up to the nines bucket. This is known as a **bucket sort**.

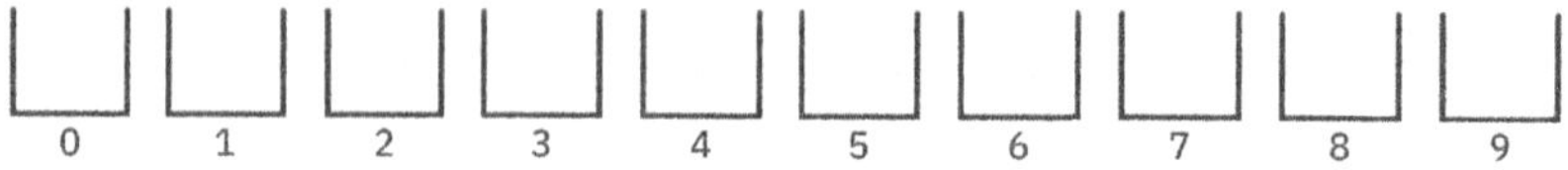

In this case, since **88** ends in **8**, you put it in the eights bucket. Likewise, **410** goes in the zeros bucket since it ends with **0**, and **1772** goes in the twos bucket. Since **20** also ends in **0**, it goes in the zeros bucket along with **410**. The buckets maintain insertion order so **20** is after **410** in the zeros bucket.

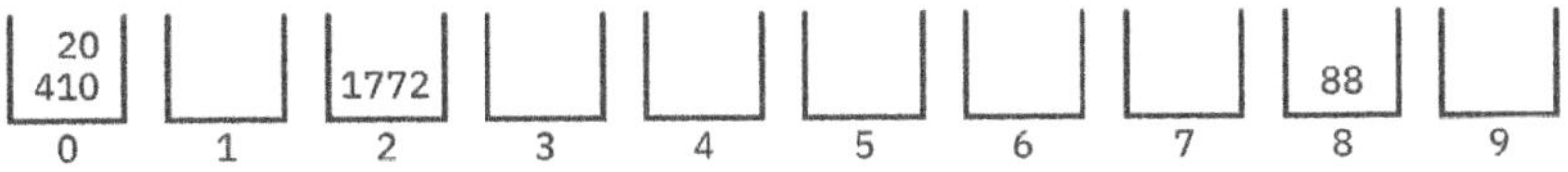

> **Note**: The radix sort algorithm described here is stable since the order within the buckets is maintained. Even though **410** and **20** are different numbers, the **0** digit used for this round of the sort is the same.

If you extract all of the numbers out of the buckets in order now, you have the list **410, 20, 1772, 88**:

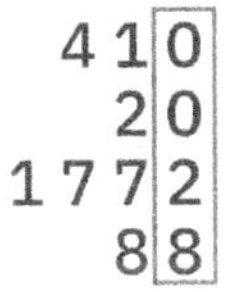

This finishes round one.

Round Two

For round two, you look at the next significant digit, the tens-place value:

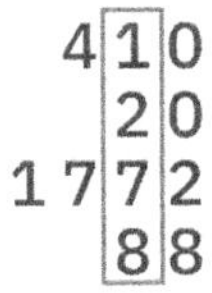

Again, you make ten buckets for the ten digits of base ten:

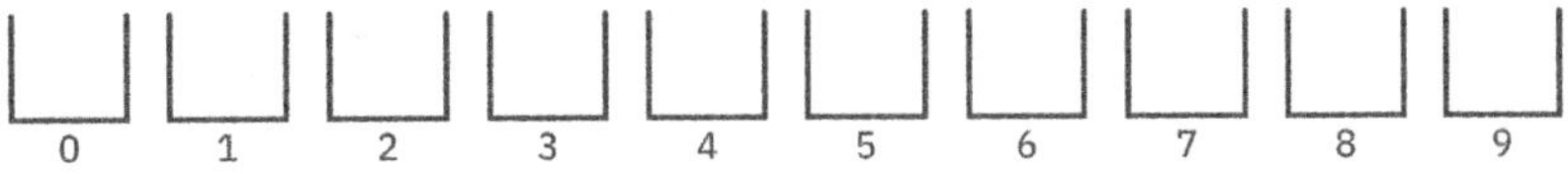

Sort the numbers starting at the beginning of the list. That means **410** is first. Since the second digit of **410** is **1**, it goes in the ones bucket. Likewise, **20** goes in the twos bucket, **1772** goes in the sevens bucket, and **88** goes in the eights bucket:

This time it turns out they are all in different buckets. All that sorting you did in round one was for nothing, but you didn't know that at the time.

Combining the numbers in order, you still have **410, 20, 1772, 88**. The order didn't change.

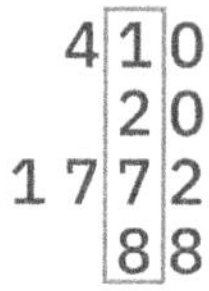

Time for round three now.

Round Three

This time look at the hundreds place. Since **20** and **88** are less than **100**, you can use **0**s for the hundreds place:

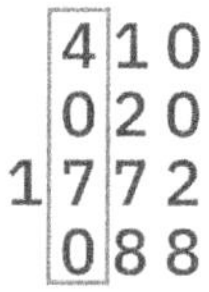

Again, make ten buckets and add the numbers in order according to their hundreds-place digit. Although **20** and **88** are both in the zeros bucket (**020** and **088**), **20** was first in the list, so it also maintains the first position in the bucket.

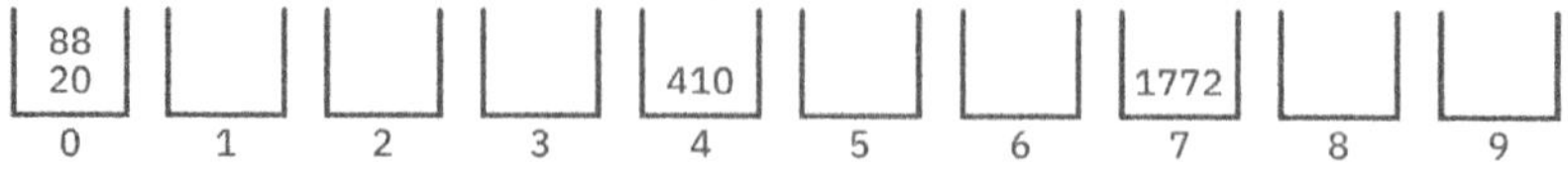

Combine the numbers in order from the buckets, and you have the new order of **20**, **88**, **410**, **1772**:

```
 020
 088
 410
1772
```

The list is already sorted in this case, but radix sort doesn't know that yet. There's still one more round to go.

Round Four

In this radix sort algorithm, there's one round for every significant digit. Since **1722** has four digits, this fourth round will ensure that the thousands-place value is also sorted. Pad any numbers less than one thousand with zeros in front:

```
0020
0088
0410
1772
```

Make your ten buckets again. **20**, **88** and **410** all go in the zeros bucket since they're less than 1000. However, within the bucket, they maintain their previous order:

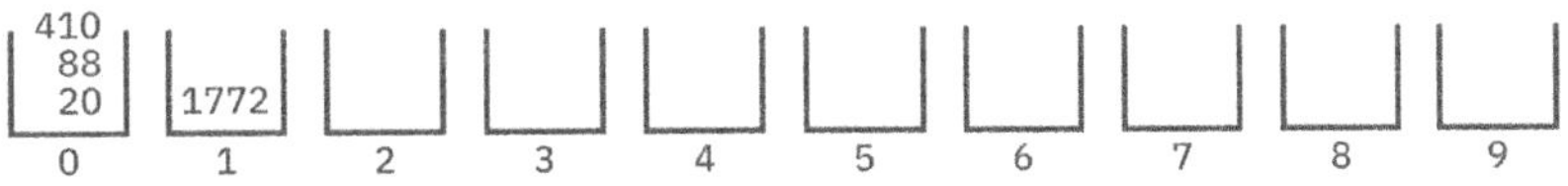

Finally, you can combine the numbers from the buckets in order, and they're indeed sorted as **20**, **88**, **410**, and **1772**:

```
  20
  88
 410
1772
```

The entire list was sorted without any comparisons!

Implementation

To implement LSD-radix sort, you'll use a `while` loop for each round as you step through the place values. Your ten buckets will be ten integer lists.

Open up the **starter** project for this chapter. Create a folder named **lib** in the root of the project. Then create a new file named **radix_sort.dart** in **lib**.

Add the following to the file:

```
extension RadixSort on List<int> {
  void radixSort() {
    const base = 10;
    var done = false;
    // 1
    var place = 1;
    while (!done) {
      done = true;
      // 2
      final buckets = List.generate(base, (_) => <int>[]);
      forEach((number) {
        // 3
        final remainingPart = number ~/ place;
        final digit = remainingPart % base;
        // 4
        buckets[digit].add(number);
        if (remainingPart ~/ base > 0) {
          done = false;
        }
      });
      // 5
      place *= base;
      clear();
      addAll(buckets.expand((element) => element));
    }
  }
}
```

Here are the main points:

1. Loop through each place value, where `place` is first `1`, then `10`, then `100`, and so on through the largest place value in the list.
2. Create your ten buckets. The type for `buckets` is `List<List<int>>`.
3. Find the significant digit of the current `number`.
4. Put `number` in the appropriate bucket.
5. Take the numbers from the buckets in their new order and put them back in the original list. Since `buckets` is a list of lists, `expand` helps you flatten them back into a single-dimensional list.

With that, you've implemented your first non-comparative sorting algorithm.

Testing it Out

Head back to **bin/start.dart** and replace the contents of the file with the following code:

```
import 'package:starter/radix_sort.dart';

void main() {
  final list = [88, 410, 1772, 20];
  print("Original list: $list");
  list.radixSort();
  print("Radix sorted: $list");
}
```

Run that, and you should see the following console output:

```
Original: [88, 410, 1772, 20]
Radix sorted: [20, 88, 410, 1772]
```

Radix sort is one of the fastest sorting algorithms. The average time complexity of this LSD-radix sort is $O(k \times n)$, where *k* is the number of significant digits in the largest number, and *n* is the number of integers in the list.

Sorting by Most Significant Digit

The MSD-radix sort uses the *most* significant digit to sort a list. You might think that's a little strange when you look at a list of numbers sorted in this way:

```
  13
1345
 459
  46
 500
 999
```

What, **459** comes *after* **1345**? Yes, it does. The reason is that the most significant digit of **459** is **4**, which comes after **1**, the most significant digit of **1345**.

Although MSD sorting might look strange for numbers, it makes a lot more sense when you're sorting words:

```
ad
adept
done
do
eel
zoo
```

You don't want the short words sorted before the long words. You want them sorted in alphabetical order, or if you use the more technical term, **lexicographical order**.

> **Note**: Some implementations of lexicographical ordering do sort shorter elements before longer ones, regardless of the elements' initial values. This chapter will not.

A key point about words, at least English words, is that they're a sequence of letters. And when you have a sequence of letters, you can treat them like a sequence of digits. That means you can use the MSD-radix sort for lexicographical ordering of a list of words. For the sake of simplicity, though, the following example will use numbers to show you how MSD-radix sort works.

Example

Start with the following unsorted list:

```
[46, 500, 459, 1345, 13, 999]
```

Beginning the Sort

As with LSD-radix sort, you first create ten buckets. However, this time you add the numbers to the buckets according to their *most* significant digit, that is, the first digit on their left:

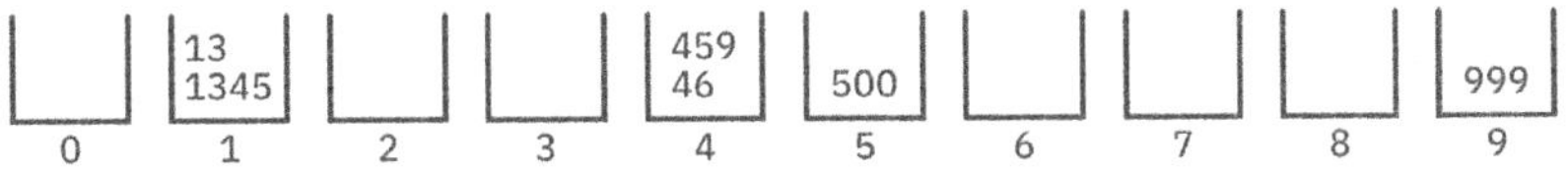

If the values all had the same number of digits, you could proceed as you did with the LSD-radix sort, looping round after round. However, the values don't have the same number of digits. Imagine a list with mostly small numbers but a few really large numbers. It would be inefficient to keep looping over all of the short numbers. That kind of thing can easily happen with lists of strings, for example.

So, instead of doing a full bucket sort for every digit, you'll do a recursive bucket sort. That means if any buckets in a particular round have more than one number, you'll recursively perform another bucket sort on that bucket.

Recursively Sorting 1345 and 13

In the previous image, the ones bucket and the fours bucket both have more than one element. Start with the ones bucket, which contains **1345** and **13**. Take those numbers and perform another bucket sort, this time on the *second* most significant digit:

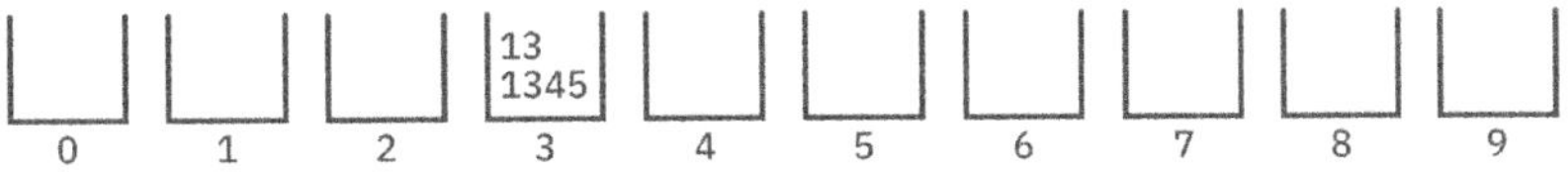

1345 and **13** are still together because the second digit for both of them is **3**.

Perform another bucket sort on the next digit. Since the next digit of **1345** is **4**, it goes in the fours bucket. The number 13 doesn't have a third digit, so there is no place to put it. You can't put it in the zeros bucket because then how would you distinguish 13 and 130? Instead, you'll put it in a special priority bucket. It gets sorted before any of the other buckets.

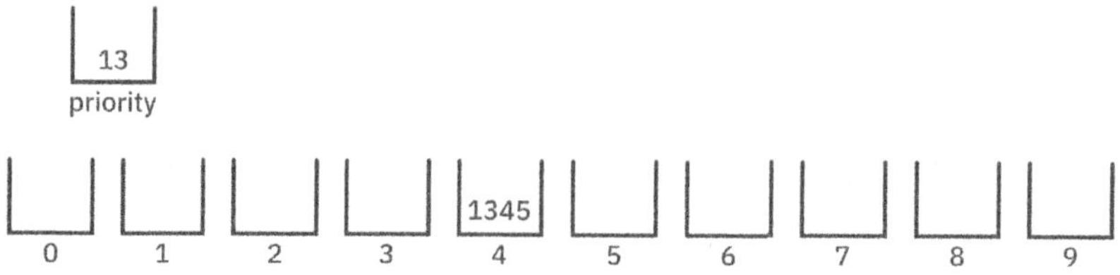

There's nothing more to sort in this recursive branch, so pop back out a few levels, returning the sorted list `[13, 1345]`.

Recursively Sorting 46 and 459

Now you need to do the same thing with **46** and **459**. Perform a bucket sort on the second digit. That gives the following:

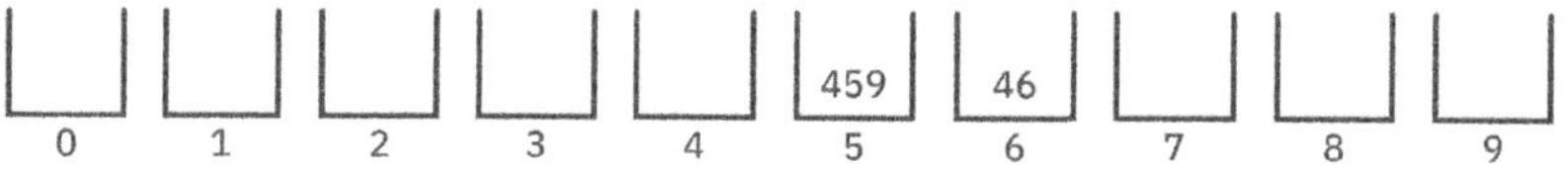

Since none of the buckets has more than one item, you can stop this branch of the recursion here and return the sorted sublist `[459, 46]`.

Combining All the Buckets

There were no other buckets with more than one number from the original round, so you're finished. Combine all of the buckets and sorted sublists into the final sorted result of `[13, 1345, 459, 46, 500, 999]`:

```
13
1345
459
46
500
999
```

Hopefully, you have a better intuitive grasp of how MSD-radix sort works now. You'll implement this algorithm in the next section.

Implementation

To start off, you'll write a few helper methods.

Getting the Number of Digits

Open **lib/radix_sort.dart** again and add the following `int` extension to the file:

```
extension Digits on int {
  static const _base = 10;

  int digits() {
    var count = 0;
    var number = this;
    while (number != 0) {
      count += 1;
      number ~/= _base;
    }
    return count;
  }
}
```

This helper method tells you how many digits are in a particular integer. Since there isn't a `length` property on the `int` type, you count how many times you have to divide by `10` before you get `0`.

Go back to **bin/starter.dart** and run the following in `main` to try out a few examples:

```
print(13.digits());    // 2
print(999.digits());   // 3
print(1345.digits());  // 4
```

Finding the Digit at Some Position

Add the following import to **lib/radix_sort.dart**:

```
import 'dart:math';
```

Then add the following additional method to the `Digits` extension on `int`:

```
int? digitAt(int position) {
  if (position >= digits()) {
    return null;
  }
  var number = this;
  while (number ~/ pow(_base, position + 1) != 0) {
    number ~/= _base;
  }
  return number % _base;
}
```

`digitAt` returns the digit at a given position. Like with lists, the leftmost position is zero. Thus, the digit for position zero of the value **1345** is **1**. The digit for position three is **5**. Since there are only four digits, the digit for position five will return `null`.

The implementation of `digitAt` works by repeatedly chopping a digit off the end of the number until the requested digit is at the end. It's then extracted using the remainder operator.

Test your new `int` extension out in **bin/starter.dart** with the following code:

```
print(1345.digitAt(0)); // 1
print(1345.digitAt(1)); // 3
print(1345.digitAt(2)); // 4
print(1345.digitAt(3)); // 5
print(1345.digitAt(4)); // null
print(1345.digitAt(5)); // null
```

Finding the Max Digits in the List

Go back to **lib/radix_sort.dart** and add a new `List` extension with the following method:

```
extension MsdRadixSort on List<int> {
  int maxDigits() {
    if (isEmpty) return 0;
    return reduce(max).digits();
  }

  // more to come
}
```

The `reduce` method belongs to `List`. It uses an input function to reduce the entire list to a single value. In this case, the function is `max` from the `dart:math` library. So `reduce(max)` gives you the maximum value in the list, and `digits` tells you the number of digits in that integer.

Test in out in `main` like so:

```
final list = [46, 500, 459, 1345, 13, 999];
print(list.maxDigits()); // 4
```

The result is **4** since the largest number, **1345**, has four digits.

Now you're ready to write the actual sort implementation.

Adding the Recursive Sort Methods

Go back to the `MsdRadixSort` extension on `List` in **lib/radix_sort.dart**. You're going to add two more methods to this extension. One will be public and the other a private recursive helper method.

First, add the public `lexicographicalSort` extension method to `MsdRadixSort`:

```
void lexicographicalSort() {
  final sorted = _msdRadixSorted(this, 0);
  clear();
  addAll(sorted);
}

// more to come
```

This method wraps a currently unimplemented recursive helper method that does the real work of sorting the list.

Next, add that helper method after `lexicographicalSort`:

```
// 1
List<int> _msdRadixSorted(List<int> list, int position) {
  // 2
  if (list.length < 2 || position >= list.maxDigits()) {
    return list;
  }
  // 3
  final buckets = List.generate(10, (_) => <int>[]);
  // 4
  var priorityBucket = <int>[];

  // more to come
}
```

Here's where the real work starts happening:

1. The `list` that you pass to this recursive method will be the full list on the first round (when `position` is `0`), but after that, it'll be the smaller bucket lists. If writing private MSD recursive methods was on *your* bucket list, you can cross it off now.
2. As with all recursive operations, you need to set a terminating condition that stops the recursion. Recursion should halt if there's only one element in the list or if you've exceeded the max number of digits.
3. Similar to the LSD-radix sort, you instantiate a two-dimensional list for the buckets.
4. The `priorityBucket` is a special bucket that stores values with fewer digits than the current position. Values that go in `priorityBucket` will be ordered first.

Continue by adding the following `for` loop at the bottom of `_msdRadixSorted`:

```
for (var number in list) {
  final digit = number.digitAt(position);
  if (digit == null) {
    priorityBucket.add(number);
    continue;
  }
  buckets[digit].add(number);
}

// more to come
```

For every number in the list, you find the digit at the current position and use it to place the number in the appropriate bucket.

Finally, finish off `_msdRadixSorted` by adding the following code at the bottom of the method:

```
// 1
final bucketOrder = buckets.reduce((result, bucket) {
  if (bucket.isEmpty) return result;
  // 2
  final sorted = _msdRadixSorted(bucket, position + 1);
  return result..addAll(sorted);
});
// 3
return priorityBucket..addAll(bucketOrder);
```

This bit of code is perhaps the hardest to understand because it includes both an anonymous function and a recursive method. It's not so terrible when you grasp the parts, though:

1. The higher-order method `reduce` takes a collection and reduces it to a single value. Since your collection here is a list of lists, `reduce` will give you a single list. The values in that list will be numbers in the order they came from the buckets. `reduce` works by keeping a running `result` list which you can add to based on the current `bucket` that you're iterating to. If `reduce` and its anonymous function are too confusing, you could rewrite them as a `for` loop.

2. For every non-empty bucket you come to, recursively sort that bucket at the next digit position.

3. Everything in the priority bucket goes first, but then add any other values that were in the other buckets to the end of the list.

That was a bit more involved than LSD-radix sort, wasn't it? You're done now, though, so it's time to try it out!

Testing it Out

Open **bin/starter.dart** again and run the following code in `main`:

```
final list = [46, 500, 459, 1345, 13, 999];
list.lexicographicalSort();
print(list);
```

You should see the output below in the console:

```
[13, 1345, 459, 46, 500, 999]
```

And that's what you want if you're asking for the lexicographical order!

Challenges

The challenges below will help strengthen your understanding of radix sorts. You can find the answers in the Challenge Solutions section or in the supplementary materials that accompany this book.

Challenge 1: What Are in the Buckets?

Add a `print` statement to your `radixSort` implementation to tell you what's in the buckets after each round of sorting.

Do the same for each recursion of `lexicographicalSort`.

Use the following list for both sorts:

```
var list = [46, 500, 459, 1345, 13, 999];
```

Challenge 2: Unique Characters

Write a function that returns the total number of unique characters used in a list of words.

You can use the following list:

```
final words = ['done', 'ad', 'eel', 'zoo', 'adept', 'do'];
```

If you had a bucket for each unique character, how many buckets would you need?

Challenge 3: Optimization

Given the following list:

```
[88, 410, 1772, 20, 123456789876543210]
```

Your current implementation of `radixSort` would take 18 rounds, 14 of which are completely unnecessary. How could you optimize radix sort for cases where a single number is much larger than the others?

Key Points

- Unlike the other sorting algorithms you've implemented in previous chapters, radix sort doesn't rely on comparing two values. It leverages bucket sort, which is a way to sort numbers by their digits.
- The word radix means base, as in base-10 or base-2 numbering systems. The internal bucket sort will use the same number of buckets as the base.
- Radix sort can be one of the fastest sorting algorithms for sorting values with positional notation.
- A least-significant-digit (LSD) radix sort begins sorting with the rightmost digit.
- Another way to implement radix sort is the most-significant-digit (MSD) form. This form sorts by prioritizing the leftmost digits over the lesser ones to the right. It's best illustrated by the sorting behavior of the `String` type.

Chapter 19: Heapsort

Heapsort is a comparison-based algorithm that sorts a list in ascending order using a heap. This chapter builds on the heap concepts presented in Chapter 14, "Heaps".

Heapsort takes advantage of a heap being, by definition, a partially sorted binary tree with the following qualities:

1. In a **max-heap**, all parent nodes are larger than or equal to their children.
2. In a **min-heap**, all parent nodes are smaller than or equal to their children.

The diagram below shows a max- and min-heap with parent node values highlighted:

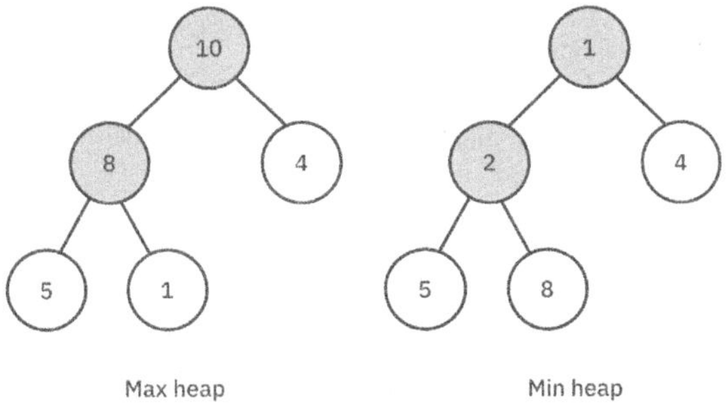

Once you have a heap, the sorting algorithm repeatedly removes the highest priority value from the top of the heap.

Example

A concrete example of how heapsort works will help to make things more clear.

Building a Heap

The first step in a heapsort algorithm is to create a heap from an unsorted list.

Here's the unsorted list that this example will begin with:

6	12	2	26	8	18	21	9	5

To sort from lowest to highest, the heapsort algorithm that this example will use needs a max-heap. This conversion is done by sifting all the parent nodes down so they end up in the right spot. If you need to review how creating a heap works, look back at Chapter 14, "Heaps". The resulting max-heap is shown below:

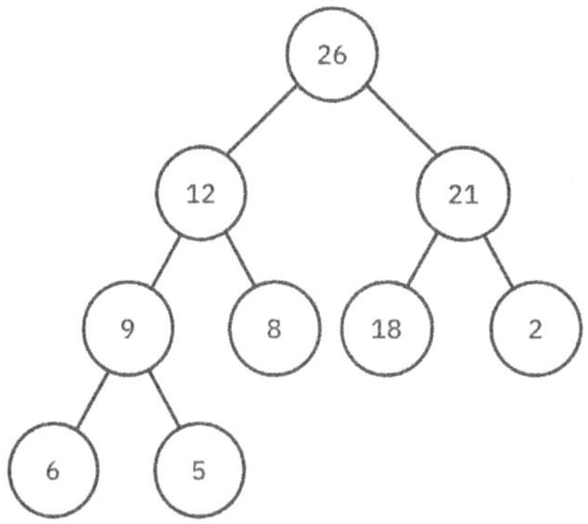

This corresponds with the following list:

26	12	21	9	8	18	2	6	5

Because the time complexity of a single down-sift operation is O(log n), the total time complexity of building a heap is O(n log n).

Sorting the List

Once you have a heap, you can go on to use its properties to sort the list in ascending order.

Because the largest element in a max-heap is always at the root, you start by swapping the first element at index **0** with the last element at index **n - 1**. After the swap, the last element of the list is in the correct spot but invalidates the heap.

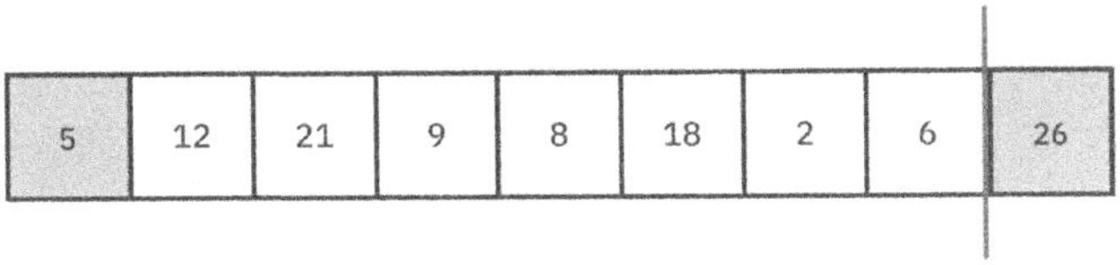

Thus, the next step is to sift the new root node **5** down until it lands in its correct position. You need to exclude the last element of the list from your heap since you no longer consider it part of the heap but of the sorted list. As a result of sifting **5** down, the second largest element **21** becomes the new root.

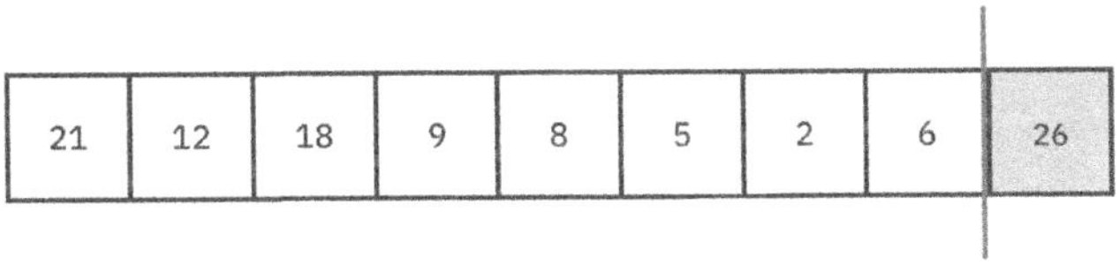

You can now repeat the previous steps. Swap **21** with the last element **6**, and move the end of the heap up by one:

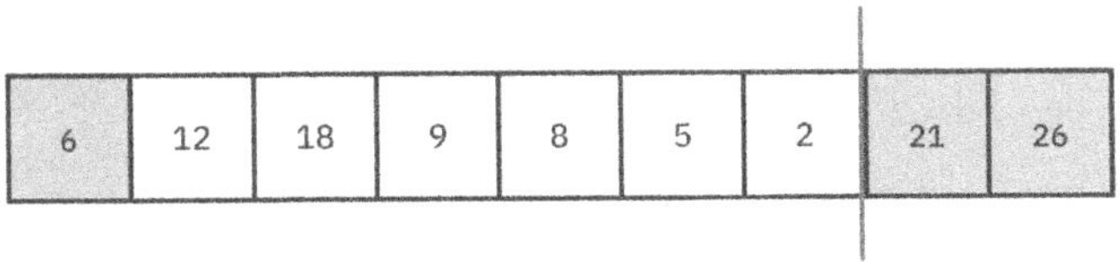

Then sift **6** down, and **18** will rise to the top:

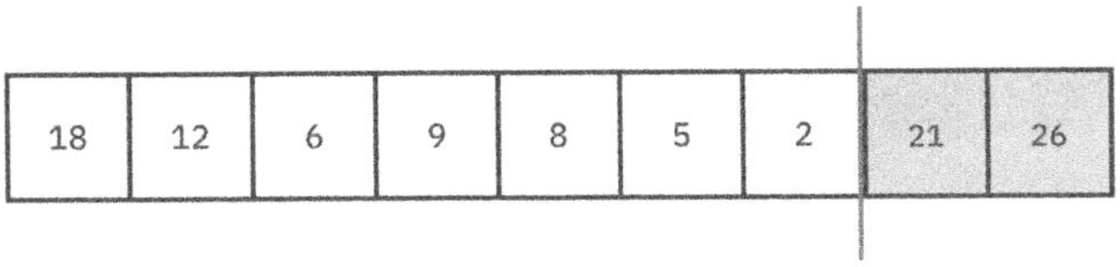

Are you starting to see a pattern? As you swap the first and last elements, the larger elements make their way to the back of the list in the correct order. You repeat the swapping and sifting steps until you reach a heap of size 1. The list is then fully sorted.

After swapping **18** and **2**, move the end of the heap up. Then sift the **2** down:

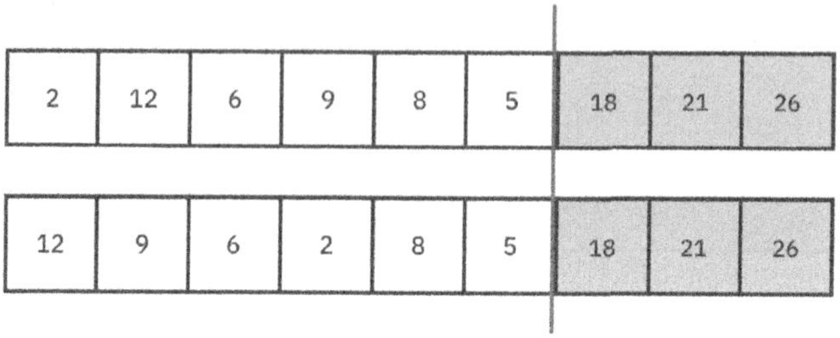

Swap the **12** and **5**. Move the end of the heap up. Sift the **5** down:

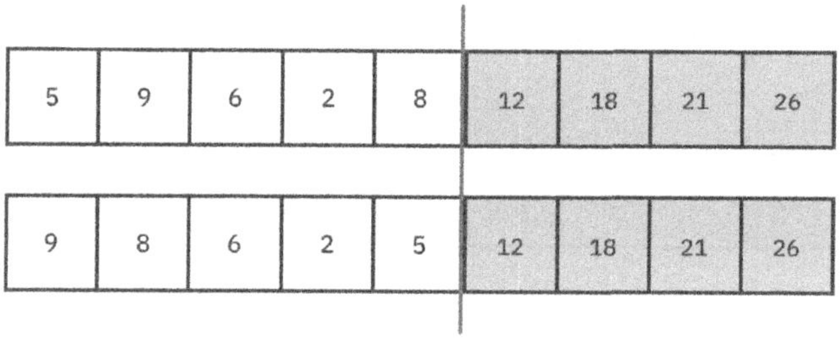

Swap the **9** and **5**. Move the end of the heap up. Sift the **5** down:

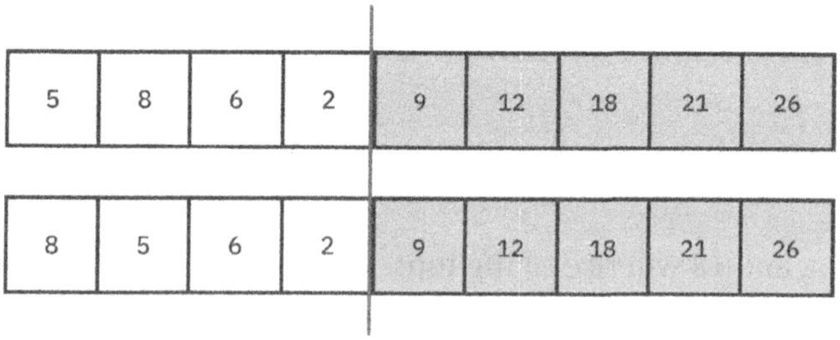

Swap the **8** and **2**. Move the end of the heap up. Sift the **2** down:

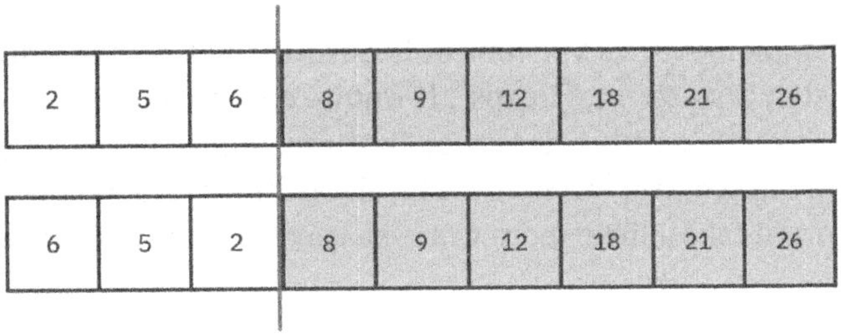

Swap the **6** and **2**. Move the end of the heap up. Sift the **2** down:

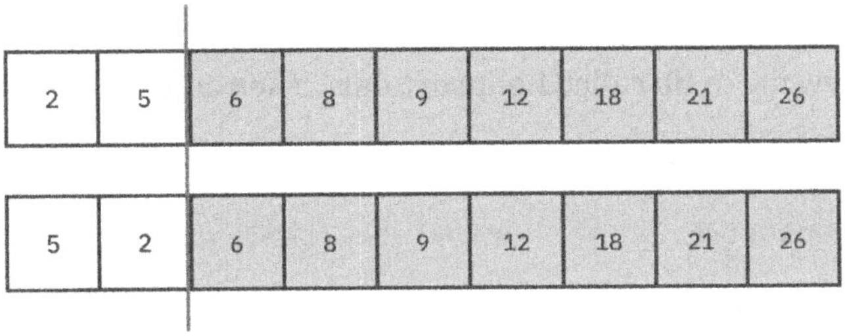

Swap the **5** and **2**. Move the end of the heap up. No need to sift the **2**:

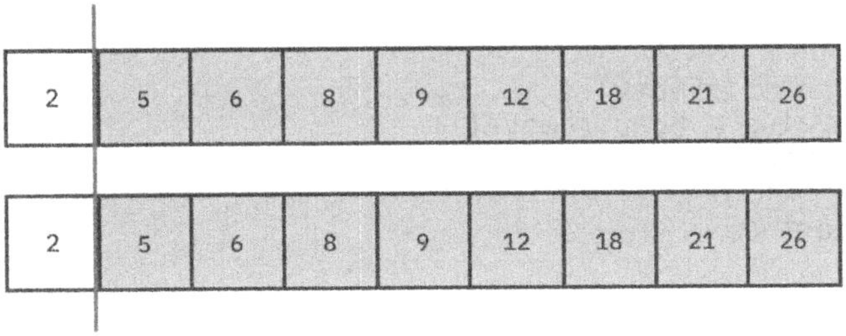

Move the end of the heap up, and you're finished:

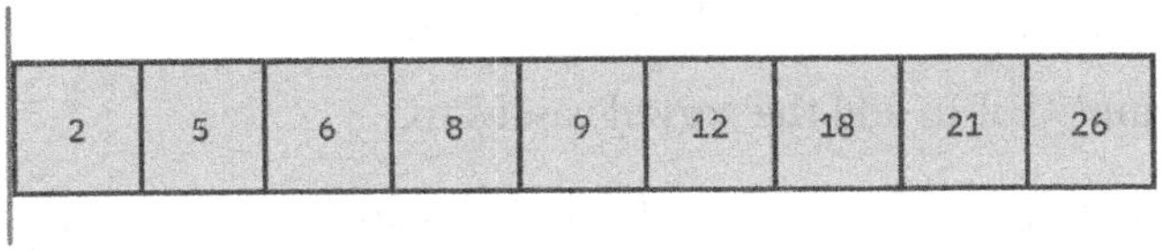

This sorting process is very similar to selection sort from Chapter 16, "O(n^2) Sorting Algorithms."

Implementation

You're going to implement two versions of heapsort. The first one will use the `Heap` class you created in Chapter 14, "Heaps". It's quite easy to implement. However, it won't follow the exact algorithm described in the example above. For your second implementation, though, you *will* follow this algorithm. Although the second implementation will take a little more work, space efficiency will improve.

Using Your Heap Class

Open the **starter** project for this chapter. In **lib/heap.dart**, you'll find the `Heap` class you created in Chapter 14.

Now create a new file in **lib** called **heapsort.dart**. Then add the following code:

```
import 'heap.dart';

List<E> heapsort<E extends Comparable<E>>(List<E> list) {
  // 1
  final heap = Heap<E>(
    elements: list.toList(),
    priority: Priority.min,
  );
  // 2
  final sorted = <E>[];
  // 3
  while (!heap.isEmpty) {
    final value = heap.remove();
    sorted.add(value!);
  }
  return sorted;
}
```

That's it for the entire implementation of heapsort! Nice, huh? The simplicity is because the heavy lifting is done by the `Heap` class. Here's what's going on:

1. First, add a copy of the input list to a heap. `Heap` sorts this into a min-heap.
2. Create an empty list to add the sorted values to.
3. Keep removing the minimum value from the heap until it's empty. Since you're adding to the end of the list, `sorted` will be sorted.

Time to test it out. Open **bin/starter.dart** and replace the contents of the file with the following code:

```dart
import 'package:starter/heapsort.dart';

void main() {
  final sorted = heapsort<num>([6, 12, 2, 26, 8, 18, 21, 9, 5]);
  print(sorted);
}
```

Run the code, and it should print the ordered list you see below:

```
[2, 5, 6, 8, 9, 12, 18, 21, 26]
```

Although you have a properly sorted list, this algorithm didn't behave like the description in the example section. The diagrams there showed an in-place sort within a single list. However, the `heapsort` function you made just now used two additional lists, one inside the heap and another to store the sorted results. It also used a min-heap rather than a max-heap.

Sorting in Place

In this section, you'll rewrite `heapsort` without using the `Heap` class. The sort will take an input list and mutate that list in place in the manner described in the example section.

Creating an Extension

Since you want to mutate the list itself, you can create an extension method on `List`. Add the following code at the bottom of **lib/heapsort.dart**:

```dart
extension Heapsort<E extends Comparable<E>> on List<E> {
  // more to come
}
```

Preparing Private Helper Methods

Before implementing the main sort method, you need to add a few other helper methods. They're just a copy-and-paste of what you wrote earlier when you made the `Heap` class.

Add the following methods to the `Heapsort` extension body:

```
int _leftChildIndex(int parentIndex) {
  return 2 * parentIndex + 1;
}

int _rightChildIndex(int parentIndex) {
  return 2 * parentIndex + 2;
}

void _swapValues(int indexA, int indexB) {
  final temp = this[indexA];
  this[indexA] = this[indexB];
  this[indexB] = temp;
}
```

These will allow you to find the heap node's left or right child index and also swap values between nodes. If you're unfamiliar with how any of these work, go back and review Chapter 14, "Heaps".

Modifying the Sift Method

You also need a method to help you sift the root index down. This one is a little different than the one in `Heap`. Add the following code to `Heapsort` extension:

```
// 1
void _siftDown({required int start, required int end}) {
  var parent = start;
  while (true) {
    final left = _leftChildIndex(parent);
    final right = _rightChildIndex(parent);
    var chosen = parent;
    // 2
    if (left < end &&
        this[left].compareTo(this[chosen]) > 0) {
      chosen = left;
    }
    // 3
    if (right < end &&
        this[right].compareTo(this[chosen]) > 0) {
      chosen = right;
    }
    if (chosen == parent) return;
    _swapValues(parent, chosen);
    parent = chosen;
  }
}
```

Like before, `_siftDown` swaps a parent value with its left or right child if one of them is larger and continues to do so until the parent finds its correct place in the heap.

However, this time there are a few minor differences:

1. `start` is the index of the node that you want to sift down within the heap. end marks the end of the heap. This will allow you to resize your heap while maintaining the list size.
2. Check if the left child is within the bounds of the heap and is larger than the parent. This implementation assumes a max-heap.
3. Do the same for the right child.

Adding the Main Extension Method

Now you're finally ready to perform the actual in-place heapsort. Add the following method to the `Heapsort` extension:

```
void heapsortInPlace() {
  if (isEmpty) return;
  // 1
  final start = length ~/ 2 - 1;
  for (var i = start; i >= 0; i--) {
    _siftDown(start: i, end: length);
  }
  // 2
  for (var end = length - 1; end > 0; end--) {
    _swapValues(0, end);
    _siftDown(start: 0, end: end);
  }
}
```

These are the two main tasks of heapsort:

1. Turn the list into a max-heap. Some people call this task **heapify**.
2. Sort the list in ascending order. You do that by swapping the max value, which is at the front of the list, with a smaller value at the end of the heap. Sift that smaller value down to its proper location and then repeat, each time moving the heap's end index up by one to preserve the sorted values at the end of the list.

Testing it Out

To check that your in-place heapsort works, head back to **bin/starter.dart** and replace the contents of `main` with the following code:

```
final list = <num>[6, 12, 2, 26, 8, 18, 21, 9, 5];
print(list);
list.heapsortInPlace();
print(list);
```

Run that, and you should see the following output:

```
[6, 12, 2, 26, 8, 18, 21, 9, 5]
[2, 5, 6, 8, 9, 12, 18, 21, 26]
```

It works!

Performance

The performance of heapsort is O(n log n) for its best, worst and average cases. This uniformity in performance is because you have to traverse the whole list once, and every time you swap elements, you must perform a down-sift, which is an O(log n) operation.

The space complexity of your first implementation, `heapsort`, was linear since you needed the extra list copies. However, your second implementation, `heapsortInPlace`, had a constant O(1) space complexity.

Heapsort isn't a stable sort because it depends on how the elements are put into the heap. If you were heapsorting a deck of cards by their rank, for example, you might see their suite change order compared to the original deck.

Challenges

Here are a couple of small challenges to test your knowledge of heapsort. You can find the answers in the Challenge Solutions section as well as in the supplementary materials that accompany the book.

Challenge 1: Theory

When performing heapsort in ascending order, which of these starting lists requires the fewest comparisons?

- `[1, 2, 3, 4, 5]`
- `[5, 4, 3, 2, 1]`

You can assume that the implementation uses a max-heap.

Challenge 2: Descending Order

The current implementations of heapsort in this chapter sort the elements in *ascending* order. How would you sort in *descending* order?

Key Points

- Heapsort leverages the heap data structure to sort elements in a list.
- The algorithm works by moving the values from the top of the heap to an ordered list. This can be performed in place if you use an index to separate the end of the heap from the sorted list elements.

Chapter 20: Quicksort

Quicksort is another comparison-based sorting algorithm. Much like merge sort, it uses the same strategy of **divide and conquer**. One important feature of quicksort is choosing a **pivot** value. The pivot divides the list into three partitions: values less than the pivot, values equal to the pivot, and values greater than the pivot. In the example below, the pivot is **8**, while the partition on the left has values less than **8** and the partition on the right has values greater than **8**:

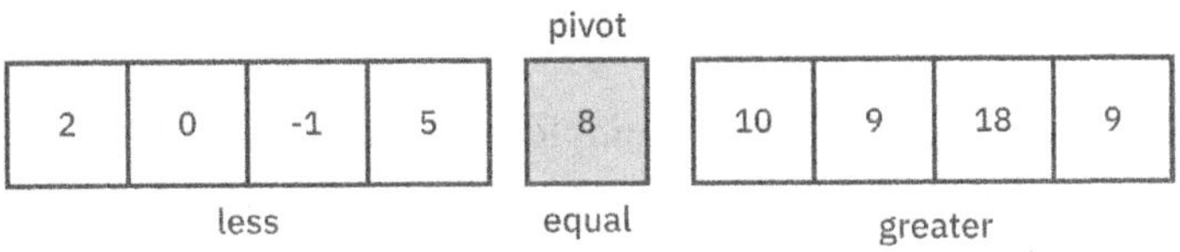

Quicksort continues to recursively divide each partition until there's only a single element in each one. At this point, the list is sorted.

The quicksort algorithm isn't stable. That is, two elements of the same value may have different final locations depending on their initial positions. For example, if you're only sorting by numerical value, a nine of clubs might come before a nine of hearts one time, but after it another time.

In this chapter, you'll implement quicksort and look at various partitioning strategies to get the most out of this sorting algorithm.

Example

Before implementing quicksort, here's a step-by-step example of how the quicksort algorithm works.

Start with the following unsorted list:

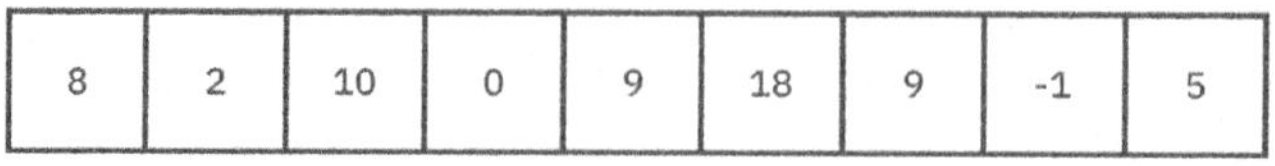

The first step is to choose a pivot value. It can be any value from the list. In this case, just take the first value, which is **8**:

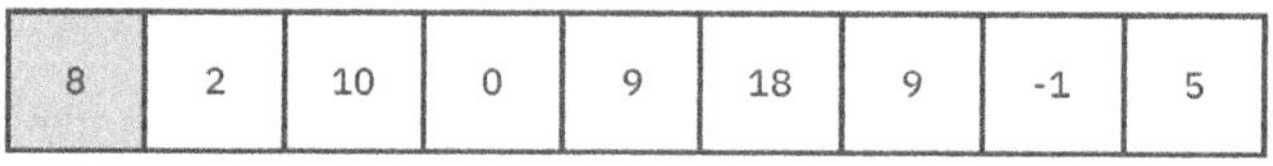

Once you have a pivot value, you can partition the elements of the list into three sublists. Put the values *smaller* than **8** in the left sublist and the values *larger* than **8** in the right sublist. The value 8 itself is in its own sublist:

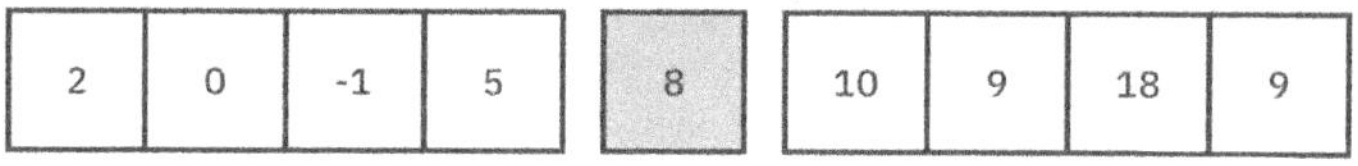

Notice that the three partitions aren't completely sorted yet. Quicksort will recursively divide these partitions into even smaller ones. The recursion will only halt when all partitions have either zero or one element.

In the left sublist from above, choose **2** for the pivot value, and partition the sublist:

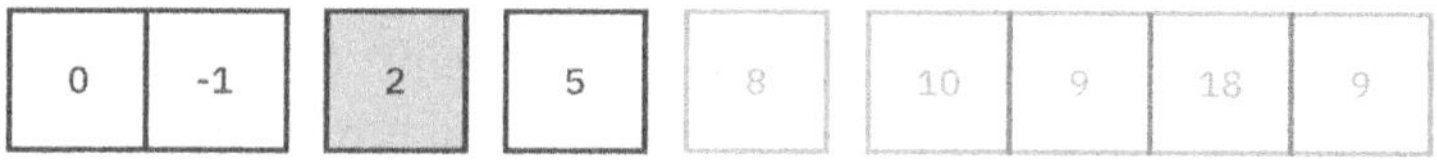

The values **0** and **-1** are still in a sublist with more than one element, so they need to be partitioned, too. Choose **0** for the pivot:

Everything on the left is partitioned now, so go back to the sublist on the right. Choose **10** for the pivot value, and partition the sublist:

You need to keep going until every sublist has less than two elements, so that includes the two **9**s in the left sublist above. Partition them:

And the list is now sorted:

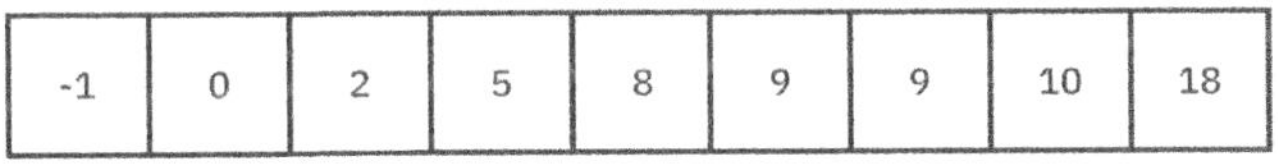

In the next sections, you'll look at a few different ways to implement quicksort, but they'll generally follow the pattern you observed above.

Naïve Implementation

Open up the **starter** project. In the project root, create a **lib** folder. Then create a new file there named **quicksort.dart**. Finally, add the following code to the file:

```
List<E> quicksortNaive<E extends Comparable<E>>(
  List<E> list,
) {
  // 1
  if (list.length < 2) return list;
  // 2
  final pivot = list[0];
  // 3
  final less = list.where(
    (value) => value.compareTo(pivot) < 0,
  );
  final equal = list.where(
    (value) => value.compareTo(pivot) == 0,
  );
  final greater = list.where(
    (value) => value.compareTo(pivot) > 0,
  );
  // 4
  return [
    ...quicksortNaive(less.toList()),
    ...equal,
    ...quicksortNaive(greater.toList()),
  ];
}
```

The implementation above recursively filters the list into three sublists:

1. There must be more than one element in the list. If not, you can consider the list sorted.
2. Pick the first element in the list as your pivot value.
3. Using the pivot, split the original list into three partitions. Elements less than, equal to, or greater than the pivot go into different sublists.
4. Recursively sort the partitions and then combine them.

To try it out, open **bin/starter.dart** and replace the contents of the file with the code below:

```
import 'package:starter/quicksort.dart';

void main() {
  final list = <num>[8, 2, 10, 0, 9, 18, 9, -1, 5];
  final sorted = quicksortNaive(list);
  print(sorted);
}
```

Run that, and you should see the following sorted list printed in the console:

```
[-1, 0, 2, 5, 8, 9, 9, 10, 18]
```

While this naïve implementation is relatively easy to understand, it raises some issues and questions:

- Calling `where` three times on the same list isn't time-efficient.
- Creating a new list for every partition isn't space-efficient. Could you possibly sort in place?
- Is picking the first element the best pivot strategy? What pivot strategy should you adopt?

Partitioning Strategies

In this section, you'll look at partitioning strategies to make this quicksort implementation more efficient.

All of these strategies will sort in place by swapping values, so you'll need a `swap` helper method. Add the following extension to **lib/quicksort.dart**:

```
extension Swappable<E> on List<E> {
  void swap(int indexA, int indexB) {
    if (indexA == indexB) return;
    final temp = this[indexA];
    this[indexA] = this[indexB];
    this[indexB] = temp;
  }
}
```

This will allow you to use `list.swap` to exchange the values at two different indices.

Lomuto's Algorithm

Lomuto's partitioning algorithm always chooses the *last* element as the pivot value. The algorithm then partially sorts the list by putting lower values before the pivot and higher ones after it. Finally, Lomuto returns the index of the pivot location within the list.

Example

In the following list, the pivot value is **5** since this is the last value in the list. You then set a **pivot index** pointing to the beginning of the list. This index is where the pivot will go after the partitioning is over. You also use the index ***i*** to iterate through the list.

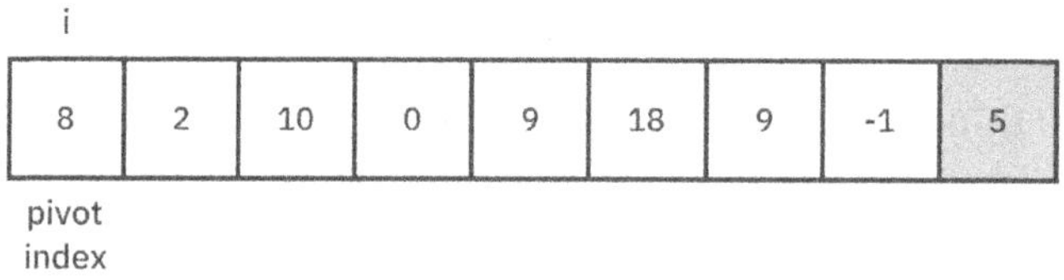

Keep increasing ***i*** until it reaches a value less than or equal to the pivot value **5**. That would be **2**:

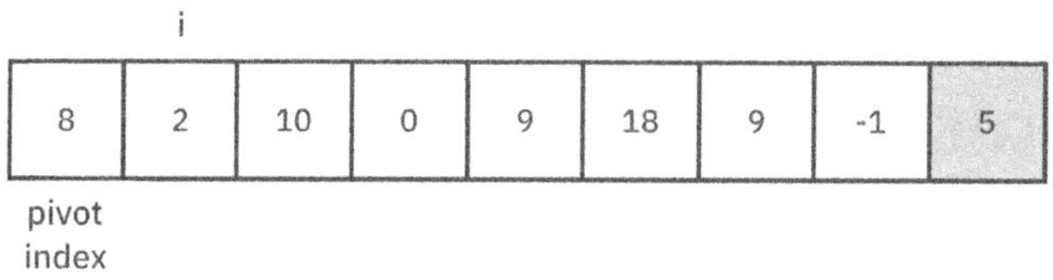

Then swap the values at ***i*** and the pivot index, that is, **2** and **8**:

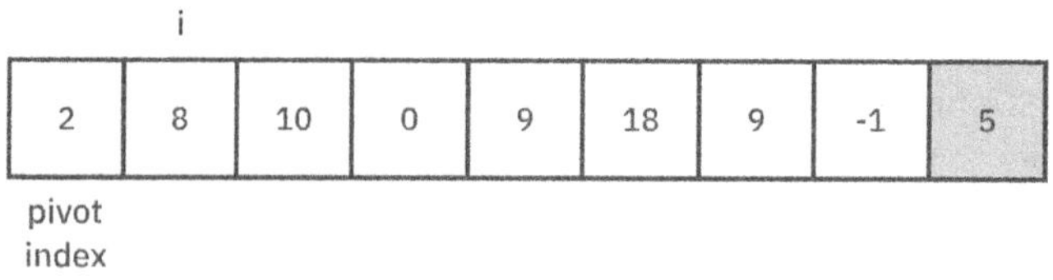

Move the pivot index up by one. Then keep iterating ***i*** until you get to another value less than or equal to **5**. That happens at **0**:

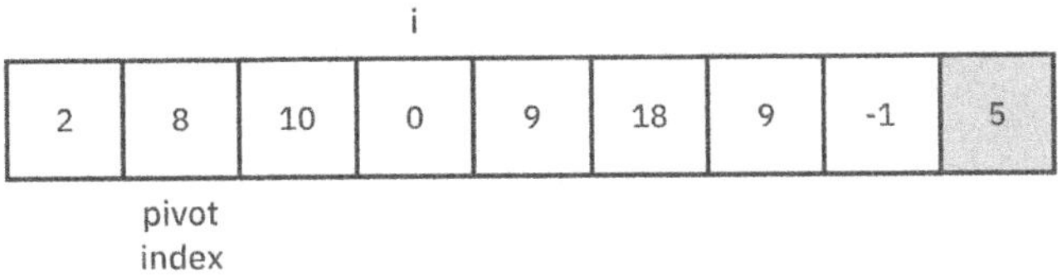

Swap the **8** and **0**:

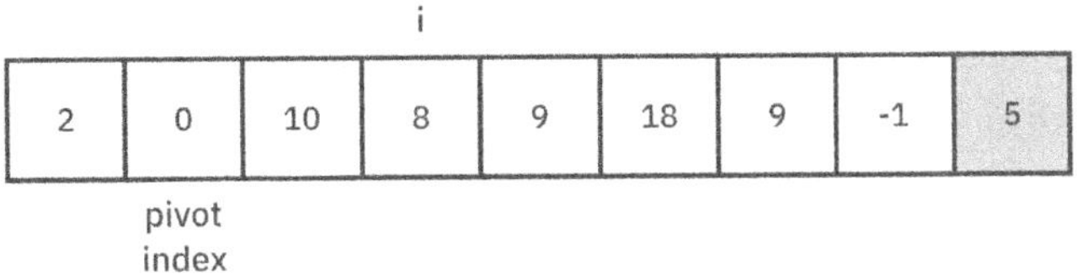

Advance the pivot index by one, and advance ***i*** until the next value is less than or equal to **5**. That would be **-1**:

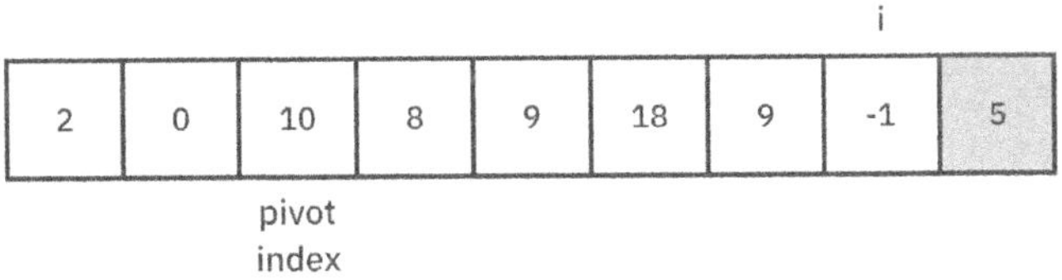

Swap **10** and **-1**:

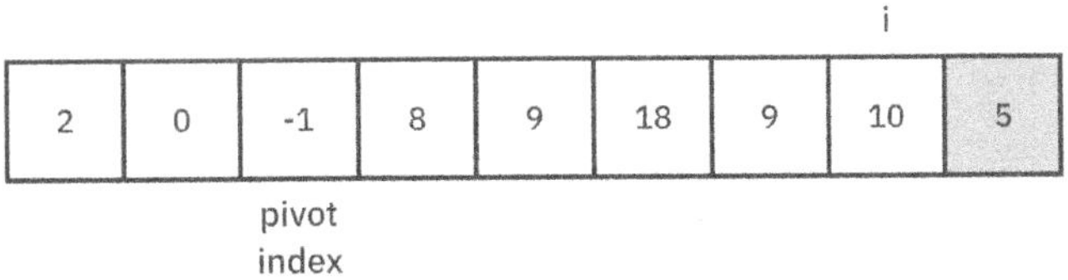

i is finished with its work. Advance the pivot index:

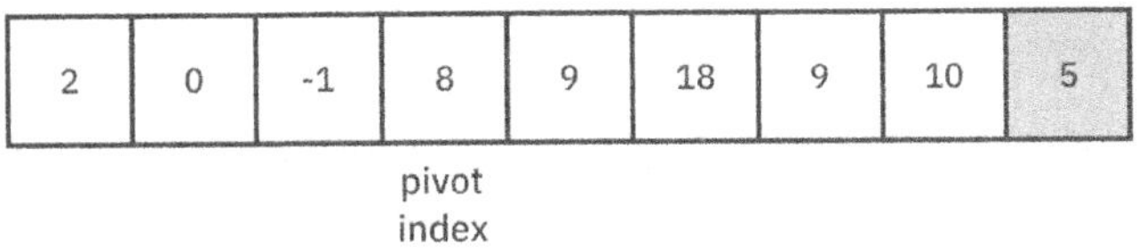

The last step is to swap the pivot with the value at the pivot index:

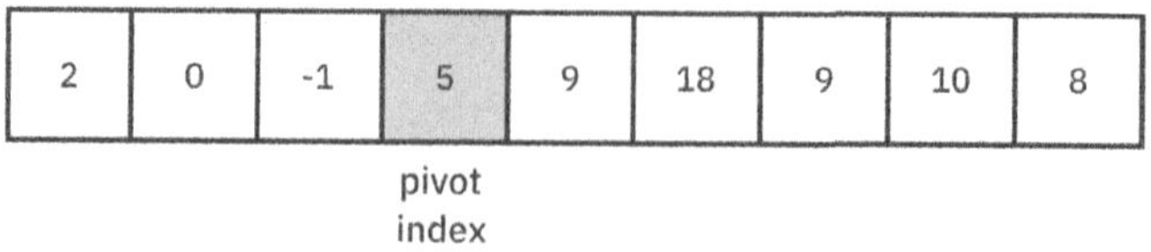

The list is now partitioned. Smaller values are to the left of **5**, and larger values are to the right.

Implementation

Add the Lomuto partitioning function to **lib/quicksort.dart**:

```
// 1
int _partitionLomuto<E extends Comparable<E>>(
  List<E> list,
  int low,
  int high,
) {
  // 2
  final pivot = list[high];
  // 3
  var pivotIndex = low;
  for (int i = low; i < high; i++) {
    if (list[i].compareTo(pivot) <= 0) {
      list.swap(pivotIndex, i);
      pivotIndex += 1;
    }
  }
  // 4
  list.swap(pivotIndex, high);
  return pivotIndex;
}
```

Here are the highlights:

1. `low` and `high` are the index values of the range that you want to partition within the list. This range will get smaller and smaller with every recursion.
2. Lomuto always chooses the last element as the pivot.
3. `pivotIndex` will keep track of where the pivot value needs to go later. As you loop through the elements, swap any value less than or equal to the pivot with the value at the `pivotIndex`. Then advance `pivotIndex`.
4. Once done with the loop, swap the value at `pivotIndex` with the pivot. The pivot always sits between the **less** and **greater** partitions.

That function only partitioned a single sublist. You still need to use recursion to implement the final sort. Add the following function to **quicksort.dart**:

```
void quicksortLomuto<E extends Comparable<E>>(
  List<E> list,
  int low,
  int high,
) {
  if (low >= high) return;
  final pivotIndex = _partitionLomuto(list, low, high);
  quicksortLomuto(list, low, pivotIndex - 1);
  quicksortLomuto(list, pivotIndex + 1, high);
}
```

Here, you apply Lomuto's algorithm to partition the list into two regions. Then, you recursively sort these regions. The recursion ends once a region has less than two elements.

Testing it Out

You can try out Lomuto's quicksort by returning to **bin/start.dart** and replacing the contents of `main` with the following code:

```
final list = <num>[8, 2, 10, 0, 9, 18, 9, -1, 5];
quicksortLomuto(list, 0, list.length - 1);
print(list);
```

Run this to see the same result as before:

```
[-1, 0, 2, 5, 8, 9, 9, 10, 18]
```

In the naïve implementation of quicksort, you created three new lists and filtered the unsorted list three times. Lomuto's algorithm performs the partitioning in place. That's much more efficient!

Hoare's Partitioning

Hoare's partitioning algorithm always chooses the *first* element as the pivot value. Then it uses two pointers moving toward the middle from both ends. When the pointers reach values on the wrong side of the pivot, the values are swapped to the correct side.

Example

As before, start with the following unsorted list:

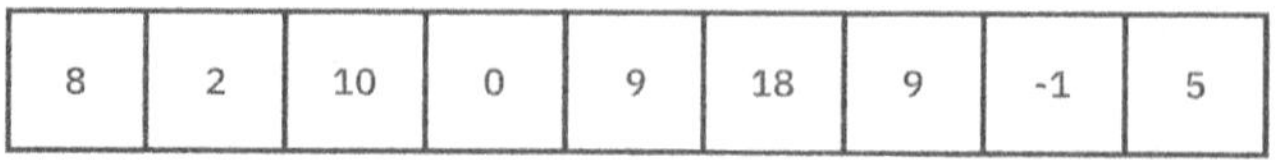

Since Hoare's algorithm chooses the first element, **8** is the pivot value. The left pointer also starts here. The right pointer starts at the right:

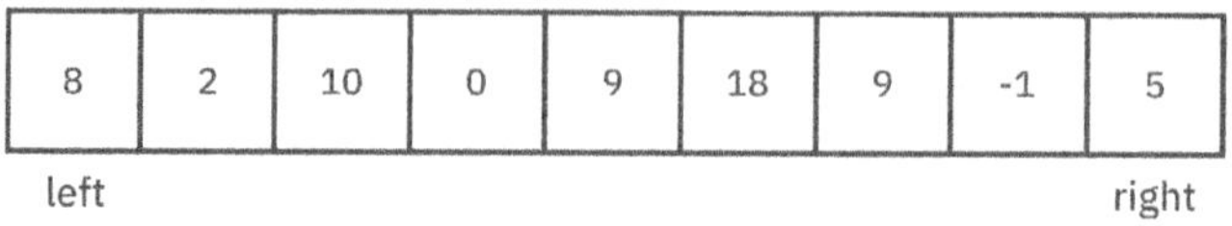

5 is less than the pivot **8**, so it should be on the left. Swap **5** and **8**:

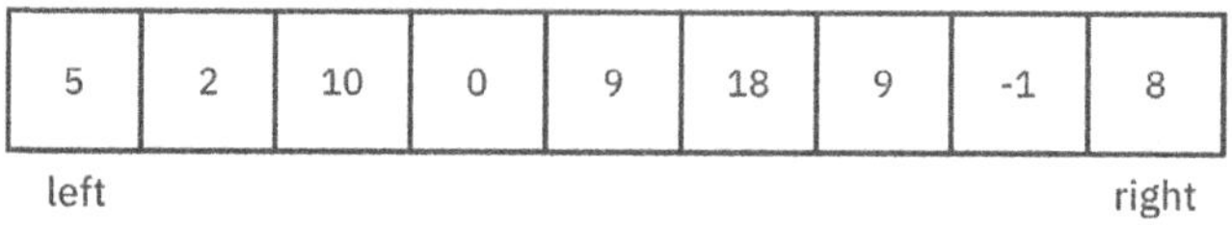

You can move the left pointer to the right until it gets to a value larger than **8**. That would be **10**. Likewise, move the right pointer to the left until it gets to a value smaller than **8**. That would be **-1**:

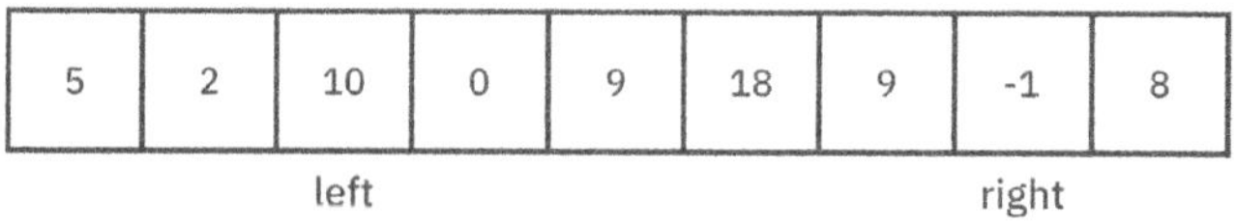

Swap **10** and **-1** to put them in their correct partitions:

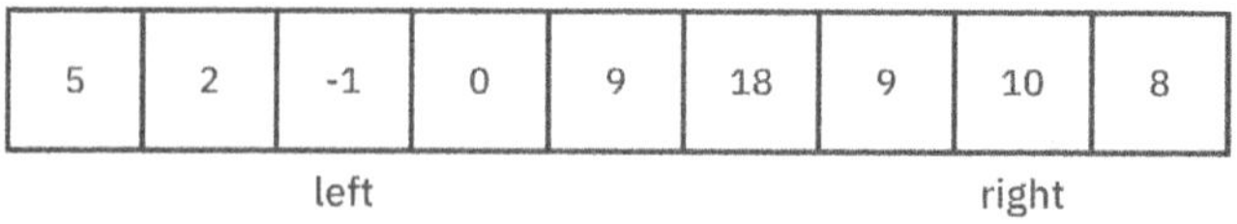

Keep moving the pointers inward. The left pointer will move until it hits **9**, and the right pointer will move until it hits **0**.

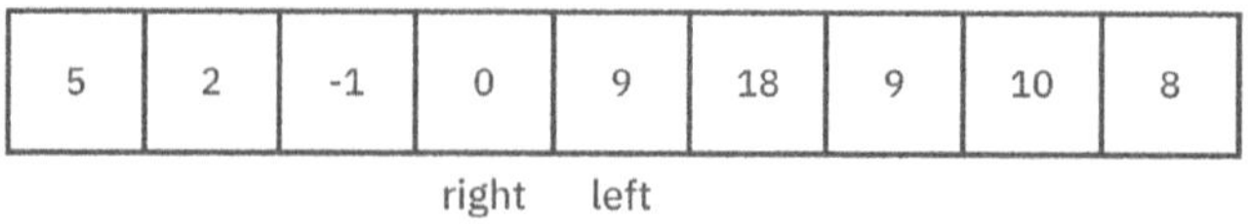

The pointers have crossed each other now, so the partitioning is finished. Note that the pivot value **8** isn't in the middle. That means Hoare partitioning really only creates two partitions rather than three.

There are far fewer swaps with Hoare's algorithm compared to Lomuto's algorithm. Isn't that nice?

Implementation

Add the Hoare partitioning function to **quicksort.dart**:

```
int _partitionHoare<E extends Comparable<E>>(
  List<E> list,
  int low,
  int high,
) {
  // 1
  final pivot = list[low];
  var left = low - 1;
  var right = high + 1;
  while (true) {
    // 2
    do {
      left += 1;
    } while (list[left].compareTo(pivot) < 0);
    // 3
    do {
      right -= 1;
    } while (list[right].compareTo(pivot) > 0);
    // 4
    if (left < right) {
      list.swap(left, right);
    } else {
      return right;
    }
  }
}
```

Here are the steps:

1. Select the first element as the pivot value.
2. Keep increasing the `left` index until it comes to a value greater than or equal to the pivot.
3. Keep decreasing the `right` index until it reaches a value less than or equal to the pivot.

4. Swap the values at `left` and `right` if they haven't crossed yet. Otherwise, return `right` as the new dividing index between the two partitions. It will be the high end of the left sublist on the next recursion.

You can now implement the `quicksortHoare` function. Add the following code to **quicksort.dart**:

```
void quicksortHoare<E extends Comparable<E>>(
  List<E> list,
  int low,
  int high,
) {
  if (low >= high) return;
  final leftHigh = _partitionHoare(list, low, high);
  quicksortHoare(list, low, leftHigh);
  quicksortHoare(list, leftHigh + 1, high);
}
```

The value passed back from `_partitionHoare` is the high value of the left partition. So to get the low value of the right partition just add one. You keep recursively passing these range indices back into `quicksortHoare` until the partitions all have a length of zero or one. At that point, the list is sorted.

Testing it Out

Try Hoare's quicksort out by running the following in `main`:

```
final list = <num>[8, 2, 10, 0, 9, 18, 9, -1, 5];
quicksortHoare(list, 0, list.length - 1);
print(list);
```

As before, you should see the sorted results:

```
[-1, 0, 2, 5, 8, 9, 9, 10, 18]
```

Effects of a Bad Pivot Choice

The most crucial part of implementing quicksort is choosing the right partitioning strategy.

You've looked at two different partitioning strategies so far:

1. Choosing the last element as a pivot.
2. Choosing the first element as a pivot.

What are the implications of choosing a bad pivot?

Take the following list as an example:

```
[8, 7, 6, 5, 4, 3, 2, 1]
```

If you use Lomuto's algorithm, the pivot will be the last element, **1**. This results in the following partitions:

- **less**: `[ ]`
- **equal**: `[1]`
- **greater**: `[8, 7, 6, 5, 4, 3, 2]`

An ideal pivot would split the elements evenly between the **less** and **greater** partitions. Choosing the first or last element of an already sorted list as a pivot makes quicksort perform much like **insertion sort**, which results in a worst-case performance of $O(n^2)$.

Median-of-Three Strategy

One way to address this problem is by using the **median-of-three** pivot selection strategy. Here, you find the median of the first, middle and last element in the list and use that as a pivot. This selection strategy prevents you from picking the highest or lowest element in the list.

Implementation

Add the following function to **quicksort.dart**:

```
int _medianOfThree<E extends Comparable<E>>(
  List<E> list,
  int low,
  int high,
) {
  final center = (low + high) ~/ 2;
  if (list[low].compareTo(list[center]) > 0) {
    list.swap(low, center);
  }
  if (list[low].compareTo(list[high]) > 0) {
    list.swap(low, high);
  }
  if (list[center].compareTo(list[high]) > 0) {
    list.swap(center, high);
  }
  return center;
}
```

Here, you find the median of `list[low]`, `list[center]` and `list[high]` by sorting them. The median will end up at index `center`, which is what the function returns.

Next, implement a variant of quicksort using this median of three:

```
void quicksortMedian<E extends Comparable<E>>(
  List<E> list,
  int low,
  int high,
) {
  if (low >= high) return;
  var pivotIndex = _medianOfThree(list, low, high);
  list.swap(pivotIndex, high);
  pivotIndex = _partitionLomuto(list, low, high);
  quicksortLomuto(list, low, pivotIndex - 1);
  quicksortLomuto(list, pivotIndex + 1, high);
}
```

This code is simply a variation on `quicksortLomuto` that chooses the median of the three elements as a first step.

Testing it Out

Try this out back in **bin/starter.dart** by replacing the contents of `main` with the following code:

```
final list = <num>[8, 7, 6, 5, 4, 3, 2, 1];
quicksortMedian(list, 0, list.length - 1);
print(list);
```

Run that, and you'll see the following sorted list:

```
[1, 2, 3, 4, 5, 6, 7, 8]
```

This strategy is an improvement, but there are still issues in some situations.

Dutch National Flag Partitioning

A problem with Lomuto's and Hoare's algorithms is that they don't handle duplicates well. With Lomuto's algorithm, duplicates end up in the **less** partition and aren't grouped together. With Hoare's algorithm, the situation is even worse as duplicates can be all over the place.

A solution to handle duplicate elements is **Dutch national flag partitioning**. This technique is named after the Dutch flag, which has three horizontal colored bands of red, white and blue. These three bands are analogous to the three partitions used in the sorting algorithm: values less than the pivot, equal to the pivot, and greater than the pivot. The key here is that when you have multiple values equal to the pivot, they all go in the middle partition. Dutch national flag partitioning is an excellent technique to use if you have a lot of duplicate elements.

Example

As before, walking through an example first will make this more clear. Start with the following unsorted list, noting all the duplicates:

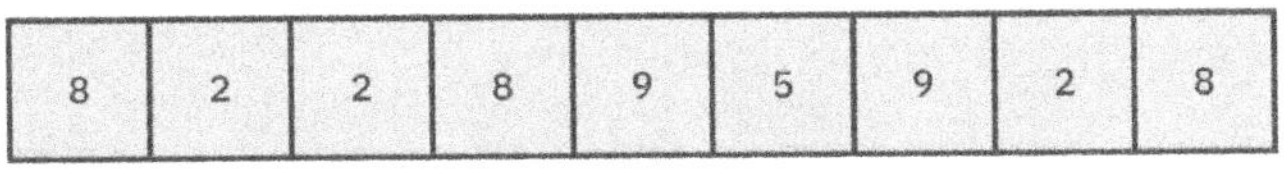

You'll use three pointers named `smaller`, `equal` and `larger`. The `smaller` and `equal` pointers start at the low end, and the `larger` pointer starts at the high end:

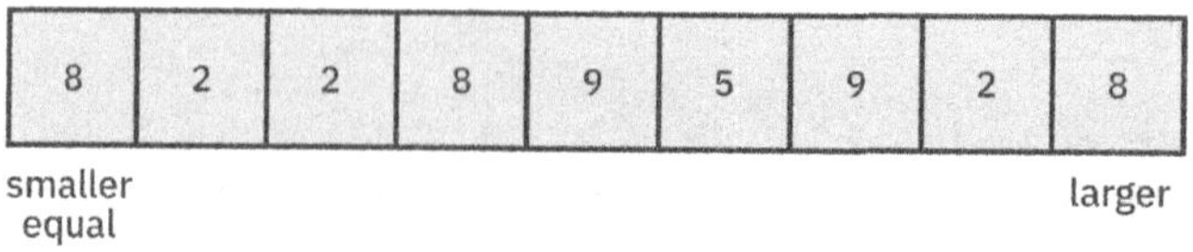

You could choose anything for the pivot, but for this example, choose the last value. That would be **8**. Then compare the value at `equal` to the pivot. They're the same, so move `equal` up. You now have one value in the "pivot" partition:

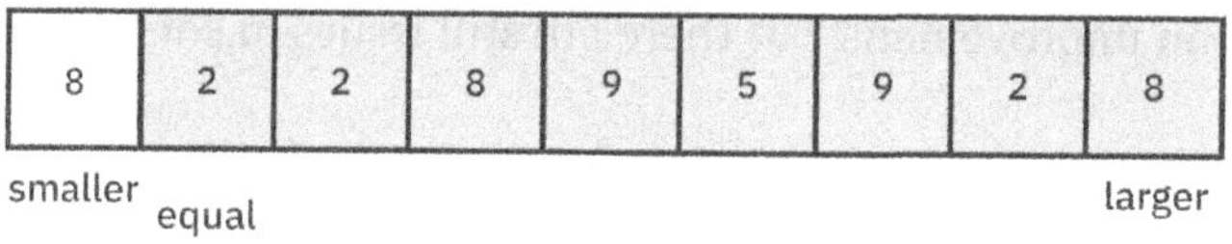

The value at `equal` is **2** now, which is smaller than the pivot **8**, so swap the values at `equal` and `smaller`. Then advance both pointers. You now have one value in the "smaller" partition as well:

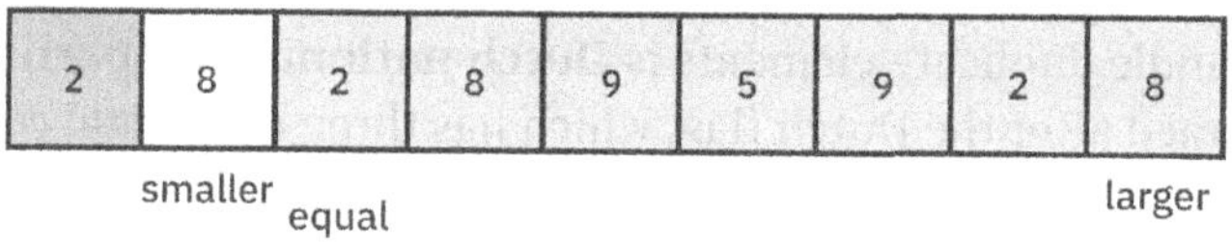

The value at `equal` is again **2**. Since this is smaller than **8**, swap `equal` and `smaller`. Then advance both pointers:

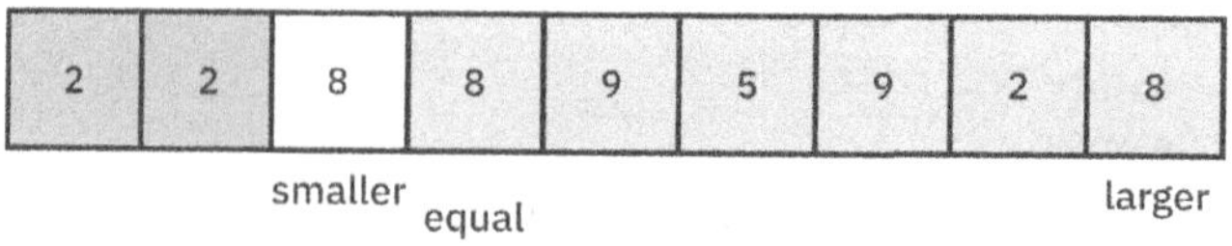

Now the value at `equal` is **8**. That's the same as the pivot, so advance the `equal` pointer:

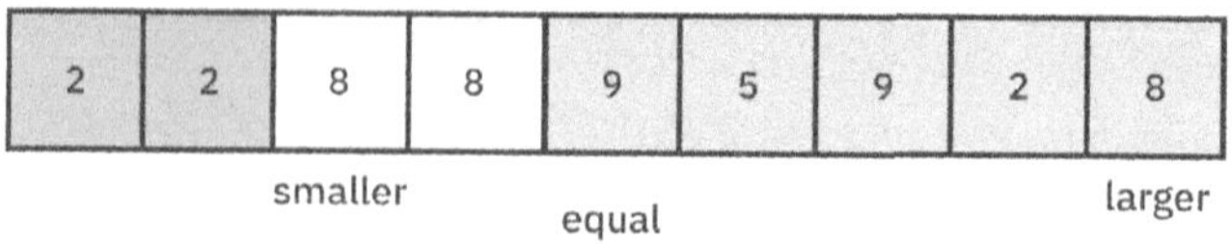

The value at `equal` is **9**, which is larger than **8**, so swap the values at `equal` and `larger`. Then move the `larger` pointer down. There's now a value in the "larger" partition:

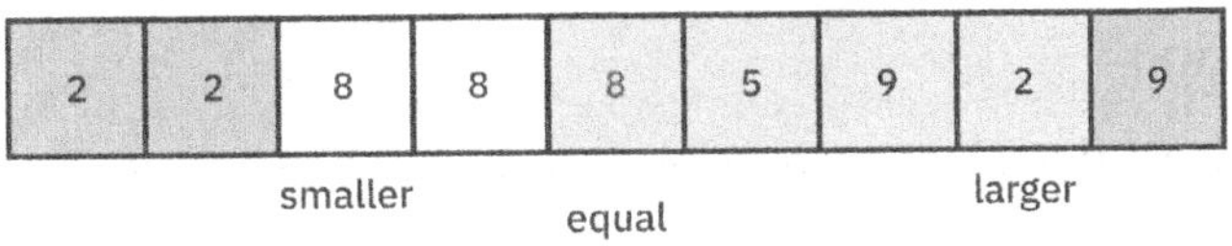

The `equal` pointer is pointing at another **8** so advance `equal`. There are three values in the middle partition now, that is, the pivot partition:

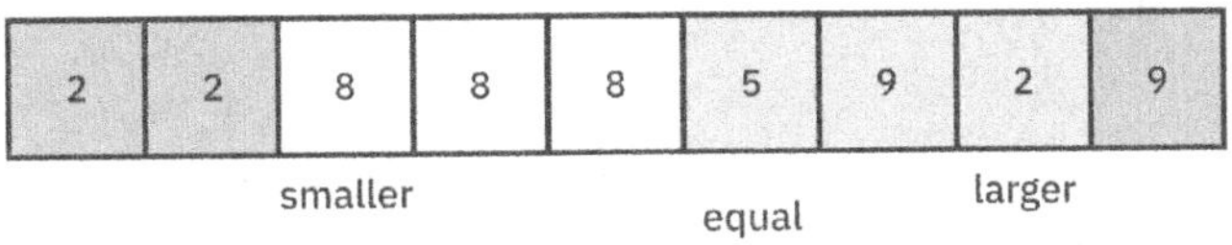

`equal` is pointing at **5**, which is smaller than **8**, so swap the values at `smaller` and `equal`. Then advance both of these pointers:

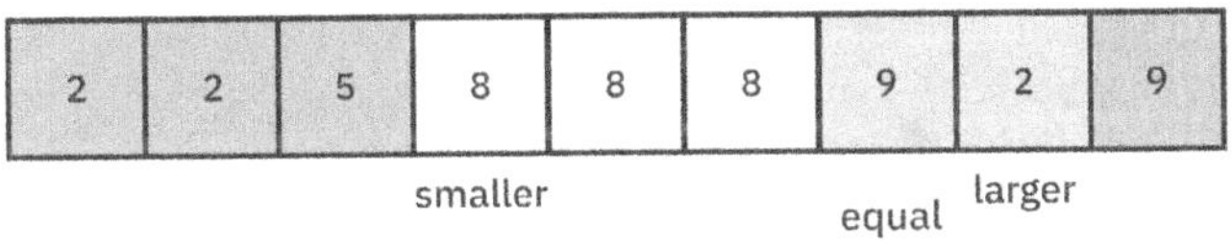

Now `equal` is pointing at **9**. This is larger than the pivot **8**, so swap the values at `equal` and `larger`. Then move `larger` down:

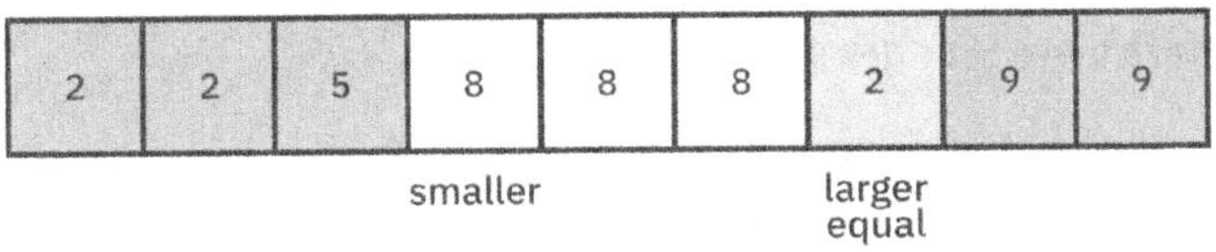

There's one more step. `equal` is pointing at **2**. Since this is smaller than **8**, swap the values at `smaller` and `equal`. Then advance both pointers:

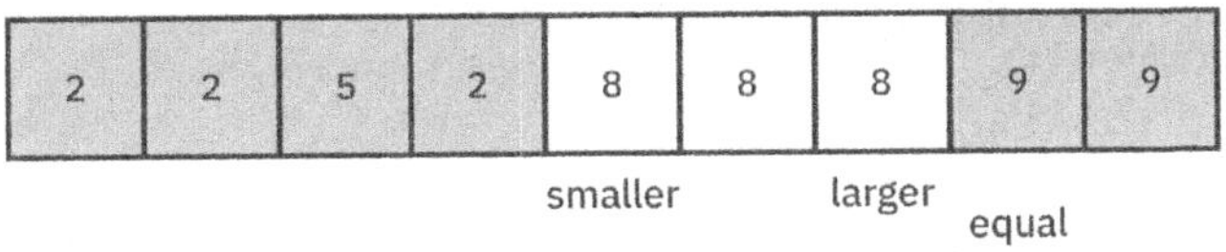

Now `equal` has passed `larger`. This means the partitioning is finished.

The ranges before `smaller` and after `larger` will be recursively partitioned using the same algorithm. However, the range from `smaller` to `larger` is the pivot partition and it's finished. It doesn't need to be further partitioned.

Implementation

Open **lib/quicksort.dart**. You need to keep track of the entire range of the pivot partition instead of just a single pivot index, so add a class for that:

```
class Range {
  const Range(this.low, this.high);
  final int low;
  final int high;
}
```

The parameters `low` and `high` are both inclusive. Range uses these names instead of `start` and end to avoid confusion since many APIs define end as an exclusive index.

Now add the partitioning function to **quicksort.dart** as well:

```
Range _partitionDutchFlag<E extends Comparable<E>>(
  List<E> list,
  int low,
  int high,
) {
  // 1
  final pivot = list[high];
  // 2
  var smaller = low;
  var equal = low;
  var larger = high;
  while (equal <= larger) {
    // 3
    if (list[equal].compareTo(pivot) < 0) {
      list.swap(smaller, equal);
      smaller += 1;
      equal += 1;
    } else if (list[equal] == pivot) {
      equal += 1;
    } else {
      list.swap(equal, larger);
      larger -= 1;
    }
  }
  // 4
  return Range(smaller, larger);
}
```

That code is a direct implementation of the algorithm you observed in the step-by-step description:

1. Choose the last value as the pivot. This choice is somewhat arbitrary. You could also use the median-of-three strategy.
2. Initialize `smaller` and `equal` at the beginning of the list and `larger` at the end of the list.
3. Compare the value at `equal` with the `pivot` value. Swap it into the correct partition if needed and advance the appropriate pointers.
4. The algorithm returns indices `smaller` and `larger`. These point to the first and last elements of the middle partition.

You're now ready to implement a new version of quicksort using Dutch national flag partitioning. Add the following method to **quicksort.dart**:

```
void quicksortDutchFlag<E extends Comparable<E>>(
  List<E> list,
  int low,
  int high,
) {
  if (low >= high) return;
  final middle = _partitionDutchFlag(list, low, high);
  quicksortDutchFlag(list, low, middle.low - 1);
  quicksortDutchFlag(list, middle.high + 1, high);
}
```

Notice how the function uses the `middle.low` and `middle.high` indices to determine the partitions that need to be sorted recursively. Because the elements equal to the pivot are grouped together, they can be excluded from the recursion.

Testing it Out

Try out your new quicksort by returning to **bin/starter.dart** and replacing the contents of `main` with the following:

```
final list = <num>[8, 2, 2, 8, 9, 5, 9, 2, 8];
quicksortDutchFlag(list, 0, list.length - 1);
print(list);
```

Run that, and you should see the sorted list below:

```
[2, 2, 2, 5, 8, 8, 8, 9, 9]
```

Nice, an efficient way to sort lists with lots of duplicates!

If any of the descriptions or code samples in this chapter were confusing, consider using the debugger in your IDE to step through each line one at a time. Explanations can be misleading, but code doesn't lie.

Challenges

Here are a couple of quicksort challenges to make sure you have the topic down. Try them out yourself before looking at the solutions, which you can find in the Challenge Solutions section at the end of the book.

Challenge 1: Iterative Quicksort

In this chapter, you learned how to implement quicksort recursively. Your challenge here is to implement it iteratively. Choose any partition strategy.

Challenge 2: Merge Sort or Quicksort

Explain when and why you would use merge sort over quicksort.

Key Points

- Lomuto's partitioning chooses the last element as the pivot.
- Hoare's partitioning chooses the first element as its pivot.
- An ideal pivot would split the elements evenly between partitions.
- Choosing a bad pivot can cause quicksort to perform in $O(n^2)$ time.
- Median of three finds the pivot by taking the median of the first, middle and last elements.
- Dutch national flag partitioning handles duplicate elements more efficiently.

Where to Go From Here?

The Dart `sort` method on `List` uses a quicksort when the list size is greater than 32. The quicksort implementations you made in this chapter used a single pivot value, but the Dart version uses a dual-pivot quicksort. To explore how it works, check out the source code:

- https://github.com/dart-lang/sdk/blob/3.0.0/sdk/lib/internal/sort.dart

Section V: Graphs

Graphs are an instrumental data structure that can model a wide range of things: webpages on the internet, the migration patterns of birds, and even protons in the nucleus of an atom. This section gets you thinking deeply (and broadly) about using graphs and graph algorithms to solve real-world problems.

Chapter 21: Graphs

What do social networks have in common with booking cheap flights around the world? You can represent both of these real-world models as graphs.

A **graph** is a data structure that captures relationships between objects. It's made up of **vertices** connected by **edges**.

Circles in the graph below represent the vertices, and the edges are the lines that connect them.

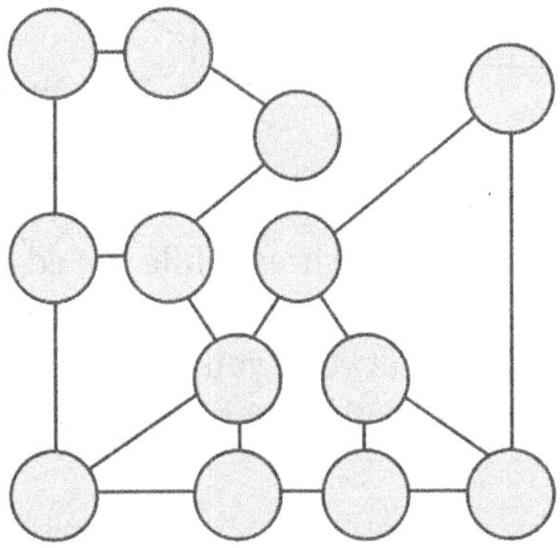

A graph

Types of Graphs

Graphs come in a few different flavors. The following sections will describe their characteristics.

Weighted Graphs

In a **weighted graph**, every edge has a weight associated with it that represents the cost of using this edge. These weights let you choose the cheapest or shortest path between two vertices.

Take the airline industry as an example. Here's a network with varying flight paths:

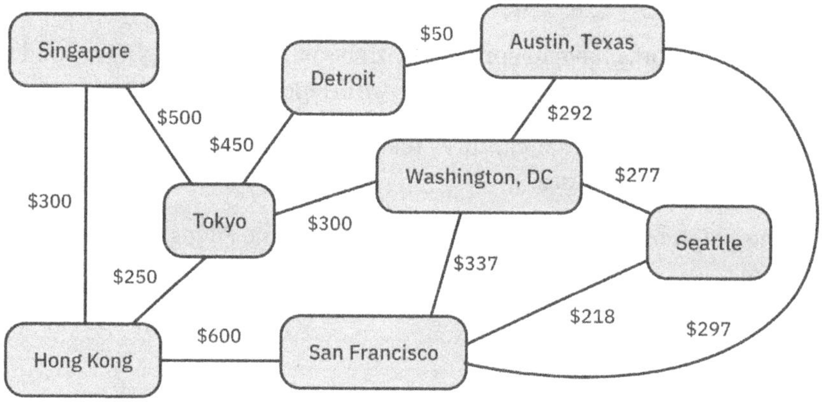

A weighted graph

In this example, the vertices represent cities, while the edges represent a route from one city to another. The weight associated with each edge represents the airfare between the two cities. Using this network, you can determine the cheapest flights from San Francisco to Singapore for all those budget-minded digital nomads out there!

Directed Graphs

As well as assigning a weight to an edge, your graphs can also have **direction**. Directed graphs are more restrictive to traverse because an edge may only permit traversal in one direction. The diagram below represents a directed graph.

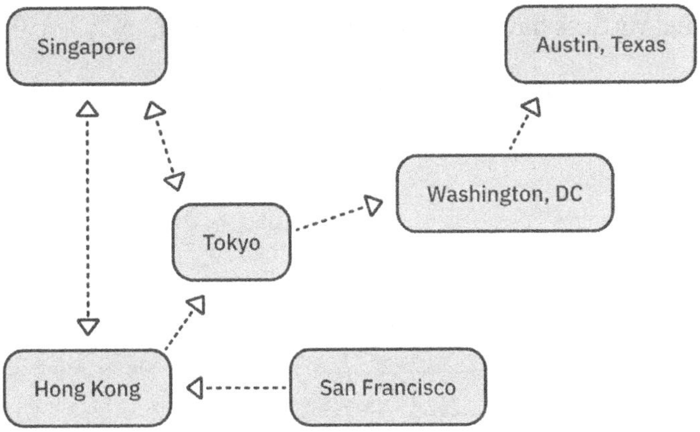

A directed graph

You can tell a lot from this diagram:

- There's a flight from Hong Kong to Tokyo.
- There's no direct flight from San Francisco to Tokyo.
- You can buy a roundtrip ticket between Singapore and Tokyo.
- There is no way to get from Tokyo to San Francisco.

Undirected Graphs

You can think of an undirected graph as a directed graph where all edges are bi-directional.

In an undirected graph:

- Two connected vertices have edges going back and forth.
- The weight of an edge applies to both directions.

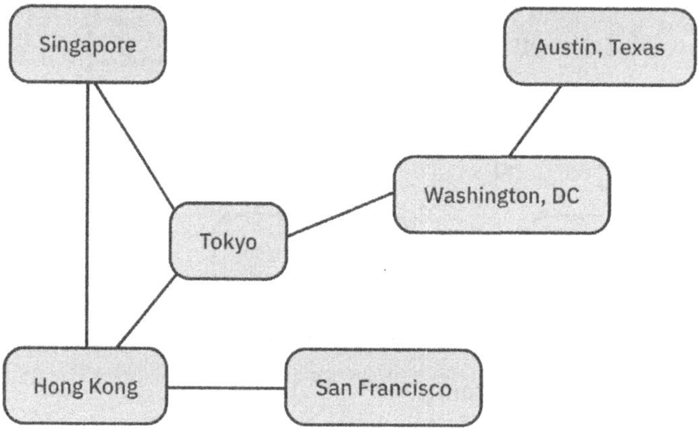

An undirected graph

Common Operations

There are a number of common operations that any graph needs to implement. Before you get to those, though, you need the basic building blocks, that is, the vertices and edges.

Open up the **starter** project for this chapter. Create a new **lib** folder in the root of the project, and create a file in there named **graph.dart**.

Defining a Vertex

The image below shows a collection of vertices. They're not yet a graph:

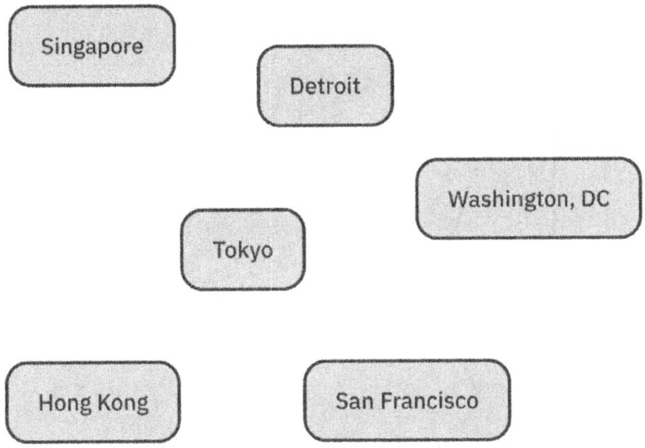

Unconnected vertices

To represent those vertices, add the following class inside **graph.dart**:

```
class Vertex<T> {
  const Vertex({
    required this.index,
    required this.data,
  });

  final int index;
  final T data;

  @override
  String toString() => data.toString();
}
```

Here, you've defined a generic `Vertex` class. A vertex has a unique index within its graph and holds a piece of data.

Defining an Edge

To connect two vertices, there must be an edge between them. These are the lines in the image below:

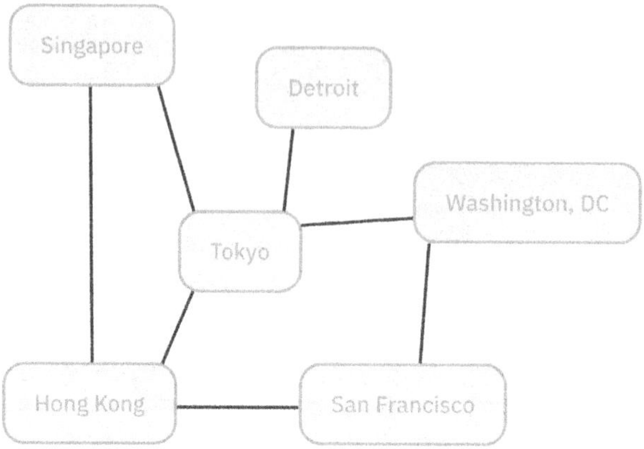

Edges added to the collection of vertices

Add an Edge class to **graph.dart**:

```
class Edge<T> {
  const Edge(
    this.source,
    this.destination, [
    this.weight,
  ]);

  final Vertex<T> source;
  final Vertex<T> destination;
  final double? weight;
}
```

Edge connects two vertices and has an optional weight. Not too complicated, is it?

Defining a Graph Interface

Now it's time to define the common operations that the various flavors of graphs all share.

Start by creating an EdgeType enum and adding it to **graph.dart**:

```
enum EdgeType { directed, undirected }
```

This will allow you to specify whether the particular graph you're constructing has directed or undirected edges.

Now add the following `Graph` interface below `EdgeType`:

```
abstract interface class Graph<E> {
  Iterable<Vertex<E>> get vertices;

  Vertex<E> createVertex(E data);

  void addEdge(
    Vertex<E> source,
    Vertex<E> destination, {
    EdgeType edgeType,
    double? weight,
  });

  List<Edge<E>> edges(Vertex<E> source);

  double? weight(
    Vertex<E> source,
    Vertex<E> destination,
  );
}
```

This interface describes the common operations for a graph:

- **vertices**: Returns all of the vertices in the graph.
- **createVertex**: Creates a vertex and adds it to the graph.
- **addEdge**: Connects two vertices in the graph with either a directed or undirected edge. The weight is optional.
- **edges**: Returns a list of outgoing edges from a specific vertex.
- **weight**: Returns the weight of the edge between two vertices.

In the following sections, you'll implement this interface in two ways, first using what's called an adjacency list, and second an adjacency matrix. Keep reading to find out what these terms mean.

Adjacency List

The first graph implementation you'll learn uses an **adjacency list**. For every vertex in the graph, the graph stores a list of outgoing edges.

Take the flight network you saw earlier as an example:

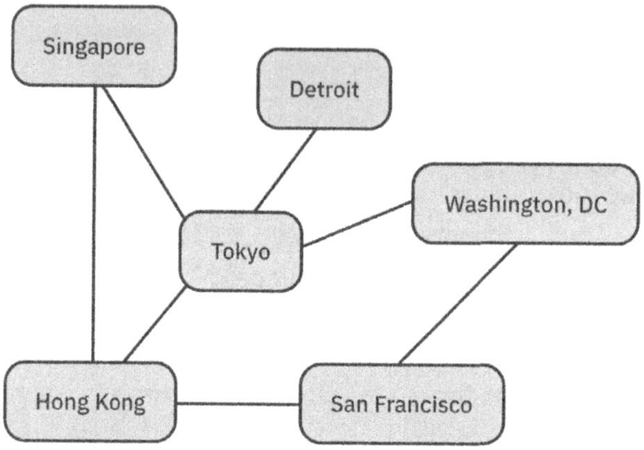

You can describe the relationship between the cities in this graph by listing out the adjacent cities for each location:

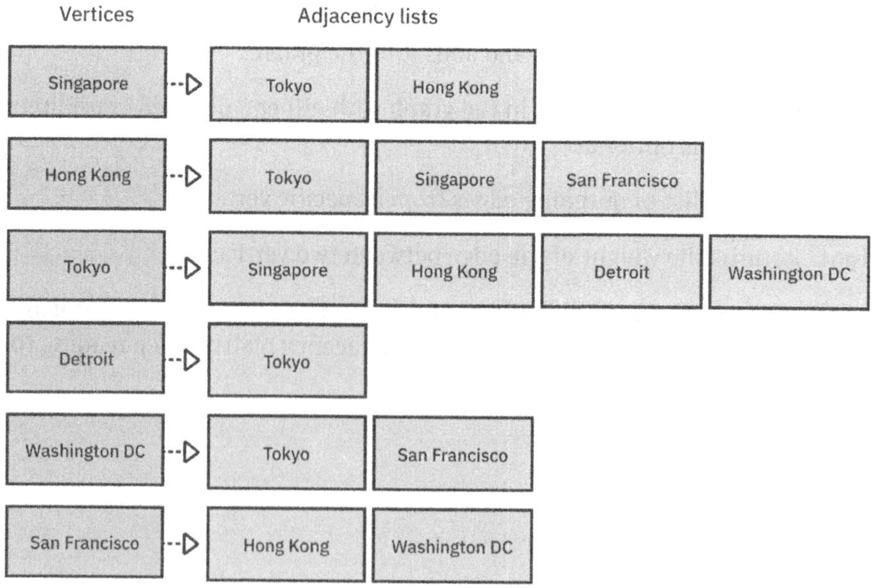

An adjacency list

There's a lot you can learn from this adjacency list:

1. Singapore's vertex has two outgoing edges, one to Tokyo and another to Hong Kong.
2. Detroit has the smallest number of outgoing flights.
3. Tokyo is the busiest airport, with the most outgoing flights.

In the next section, you'll create an adjacency list by storing a map of lists. Each key in the map is a vertex, and the value is the corresponding list of edges.

Implementation

An adjacency list is a graph, so you need to implement the `Graph` interface you created earlier. Add the following code to **graph.dart**:

```
class AdjacencyList<E> implements Graph<E> {

  final Map<Vertex<E>, List<Edge<E>>> _connections = {};
  var _nextIndex = 0;

  @override
  Iterable<Vertex<E>> get vertices => _connections.keys;

  // more to come ...
}
```

You've defined an `AdjacencyList` class that uses a map to store the outgoing edges for each vertex. You'll use `_nextIndex` to assign a unique index to each new vertex. If you need the vertices, you can obtain them from the `vertices` getter.

You still need to implement the various other methods of the `Graph` interface. You'll do that in the following sections.

Creating a Vertex

Add the missing `createVertex` method to `AdjacencyList`:

```
@override
Vertex<E> createVertex(E data) {
  // 1
  final vertex = Vertex(
    index: _nextIndex,
    data: data,
  );
  _nextIndex++;
  // 2
  _connections[vertex] = [];
  return vertex;
}
```

Here's what's happening:

1. You first create a new vertex with a unique index.
2. Then, add the vertex as a key in the `_connections` map. You haven't connected it to any other vertices in the graph yet, so the list of outgoing edges is empty.

Adding an Edge

To connect two vertices, you need to add an edge. Recall that there are directed and undirected edges:

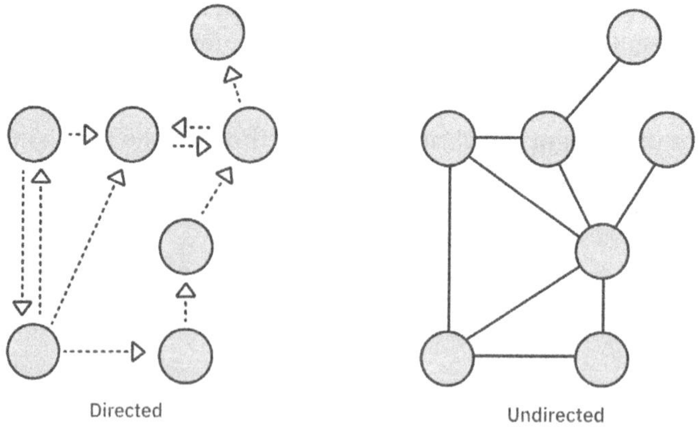

Every edge in an undirected graph can be traversed in both directions. So if it's an undirected graph, you need to add two edges, one from the source to the destination and another from the destination to the source.

Add the following method to AdjacencyList:

```
@override
void addEdge(
  Vertex<E> source,
  Vertex<E> destination, {
  EdgeType edgeType = EdgeType.undirected,
  double? weight,
}) {
  // 1
  _connections[source]?.add(
    Edge(source, destination, weight),
  );
  // 2
  if (edgeType == EdgeType.undirected) {
    _connections[destination]?.add(
      Edge(destination, source, weight),
    );
  }
}
```

Here's what's happening in the method body:

1. Since source is a vertex, check if it exists in the _connections map. If it does, create a new directed edge from the source to the destination. Then add it to the vertex's list of edges.
2. If this is an undirected graph, also add an edge going the other direction.

Retrieving the Outgoing Edges From a Vertex

Continue your work on implementing Graph by adding the edges method to AdjacencyList:

```
@override
List<Edge<E>> edges(Vertex<E> source) {
  return _connections[source] ?? [];
}
```

This gets the stored outgoing edges for the provided vertex. If source is unknown, the method returns an empty list.

Retrieving the Weight of an Edge

Recall that the weight is the cost of going from one vertex to another. For example, if the cost of a ticket between Singapore and Tokyo is $500, the weight of this bidirectional edge is 500:

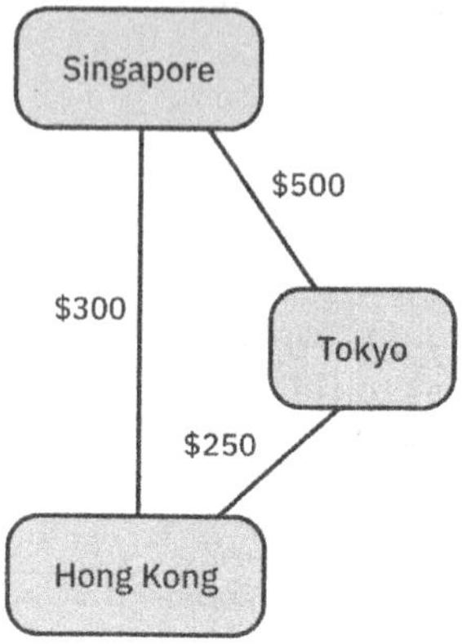

Implement the missing `weight` method in `AdjacencyList` by adding the following code to the class:

```
@override
double? weight(
  Vertex<E> source,
  Vertex<E> destination,
) {
  final match = edges(source).where((edge) {
    return edge.destination == destination;
  });
  if (match.isEmpty) return null;
  return match.first.weight;
}
```

Here, you search for an edge from `source` to `destination`. If it exists, you return its weight.

Making Adjacency List Printable

The required methods for `AdjacencyList` are complete now, but it would also be nice to be able to print a description of your graph. To do that, override `toString` like so:

```
@override
String toString() {
  final result = StringBuffer();
  // 1
  _connections.forEach((vertex, edges) {
    // 2
    final destinations = edges.map((edge) {
      return edge.destination;
    }).join(', ');
    // 3
    result.writeln('$vertex --> $destinations');
  });
  return result.toString();
}
```

Here's what's going on in the code above:

1. You loop through every key-value pair in `_connections`.
2. For every vertex, find all of the destinations and join them into a single, comma-separated string.
3. Put each vertex and its destinations on a new line.

This will produce output with lines in the following format:

```
Singapore --> Hong Kong, Tokyo
```

You've finally completed your first graph! Try it out by building a network in the next section.

Building a Network

For this example, you'll go back to the diagram you saw earlier and construct a network of flights with the prices as weights:

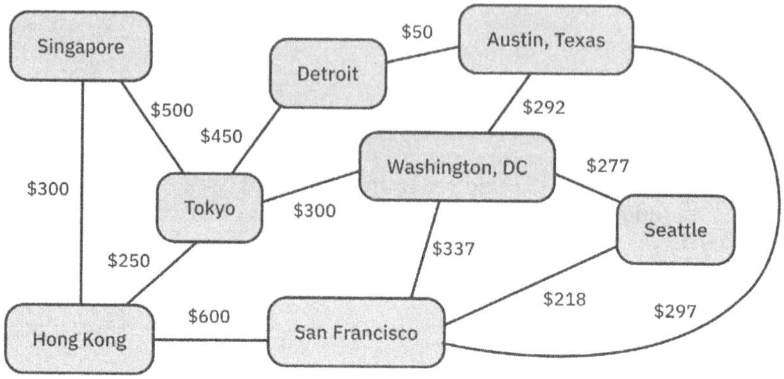

Open **bin/starter.dart** and replace the contents of the file with the following code:

```
import 'package:starter/graph.dart';

void main() {
  final graph = AdjacencyList<String>();

  final singapore = graph.createVertex('Singapore');
  final tokyo = graph.createVertex('Tokyo');
  final hongKong = graph.createVertex('Hong Kong');
  final detroit = graph.createVertex('Detroit');
  final sanFrancisco = graph.createVertex('San Francisco');
  final washingtonDC = graph.createVertex('Washington DC');
  final austinTexas = graph.createVertex('Austin Texas');
  final seattle = graph.createVertex('Seattle');

  graph.addEdge(singapore, hongKong, weight: 300);
  graph.addEdge(singapore, tokyo, weight: 500);
  graph.addEdge(hongKong, tokyo, weight: 250);
  graph.addEdge(tokyo, detroit, weight: 450);
  graph.addEdge(tokyo, washingtonDC, weight: 300);
  graph.addEdge(hongKong, sanFrancisco, weight: 600);
  graph.addEdge(detroit, austinTexas, weight: 50);
  graph.addEdge(austinTexas, washingtonDC, weight: 292);
  graph.addEdge(sanFrancisco, washingtonDC, weight: 337);
  graph.addEdge(washingtonDC, seattle, weight: 277);
  graph.addEdge(sanFrancisco, seattle, weight: 218);
  graph.addEdge(austinTexas, sanFrancisco, weight: 297);

  print(graph);
}
```

Run that, and you should get the following output:

```
Singapore --> Hong Kong, Tokyo
Tokyo --> Singapore, Hong Kong, Detroit, Washington DC
Hong Kong --> Singapore, Tokyo, San Francisco
Detroit --> Tokyo, Austin Texas
San Francisco --> Hong Kong, Washington DC, Seattle, Austin
Texas
Washington DC --> Tokyo, Austin Texas, San Francisco, Seattle
Austin Texas --> Detroit, Washington DC, San Francisco
Seattle --> Washington DC, San Francisco
```

This output shows a visual description of an adjacency list graph. You can see all the outbound flights from any city. Pretty nice, huh?

Finding the Weight

You can also obtain other helpful information, such as the cost of a flight from Singapore to Tokyo. This is the weight of the edge between those two vertices.

Add the following code at the bottom of the `main` function:

```
final cost = graph.weight(singapore, tokyo)?.toInt();
print('It costs \$$cost to fly from Singapore to Tokyo.');
// It costs $500 to fly from Singapore to Tokyo.
```

Getting the Edges

Do you need to know what all the outgoing flights from San Francisco are? For that, you just call `edges`.

Add the code below at the bottom of `main`:

```
print('San Francisco Outgoing Flights: ');
print('-------------------------------- ');
for (final edge in graph.edges(sanFrancisco)) {
  print('${edge.source} to ${edge.destination}');
}
```

Running that will display the flights:

```
San Francisco Outgoing Flights:
--------------------------------
San Francisco to Hong Kong
San Francisco to Washington DC
San Francisco to Seattle
San Francisco to Austin Texas
```

You've just created an adjacency list graph, which uses a map to store the outgoing edges for every vertex. In the next section, you'll learn a different approach to storing vertices and edges.

Adjacency Matrix

An **adjacency matrix** uses a two-dimensional grid or table to implement the graph data structure. Each vertex has its own row and column in the table. The cells where rows and columns intersect hold the edge weights. If any particular cell is empty, that is, if the weight is null, that means there is no edge between the row vertex and the column vertex.

Below is an example of a directed graph that depicts a flight network. As before, the weight represents the cost of the airfare:

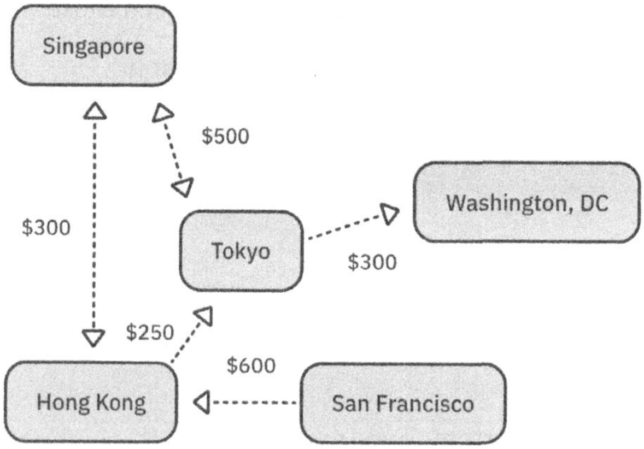

You can represent that network in matrix form by giving each of the five cities a row and a column in a table. Edges that don't exist between two cities are shown with a weight of **0** in the cells where the rows and columns intersect:

	Vertices
0	Singapore
1	Hong Kong
2	Tokyo
3	Washington DC
4	San Francisco

Source \ Destination	0	1	2	3	4
0	0	$300	$500	0	0
1	$300	0	$250	0	0
2	$500	0	0	$300	0
3	0	0	0	0	0
4	0	$600	0	0	0

Notes:

- As you recall, every vertex in a graph has its own index. These indices are used to label the rows and columns in the table.
- Read the row number as the source vertex and the column number as the destination vertex.
- There's a red line going down the middle of the matrix. When the row and column are equal, this represents an edge between a vertex and itself, which isn't allowed. You can't fly from Singapore to Singapore, right?

Here are a few examples of data points that you can read from the table above:

- `[0][1]` is **300**, so there is a flight from Singapore to Hong Kong for $300.
- `[2][1]` is **0**, so there's no flight from Tokyo to Hong Kong.
- `[1][2]` is **250**, so there *is* a flight from Hong Kong to Tokyo for $250.
- `[2][2]` is **0** because there's no flight from Tokyo to Tokyo!

You'll implement an adjacency matrix graph next.

Implementation

Add a new class to **graph.dart** called `AdjacencyMatrix`:

```
class AdjacencyMatrix<E> implements Graph<E> {

  final List<Vertex<E>> _vertices = [];
  final List<List<double?>?> _weights = [];
  var _nextIndex = 0;

  @override
  Iterable<Vertex<E>> get vertices => _vertices;

  // more to come ...
}
```

In `AdjacencyList` you used a map to store the vertices and edges. Here, though, you store the vertices in a list. You don't use `Edge` to store edges but rather a two-dimensional list of weights.

You've declared that you're implementing `Graph`, and so far you've only finished `vertices`. The following sections will help you add the other missing methods.

Creating a Vertex

For every new vertex that you create, you have to add an additional column and row to the matrix.

The first step is to create a new column by adding an additional empty destination at the end of every row. The destination is empty because no other vertices have created an edge to the new vertex yet. In the following diagram, you can see a new column 5 filled with empty weights:

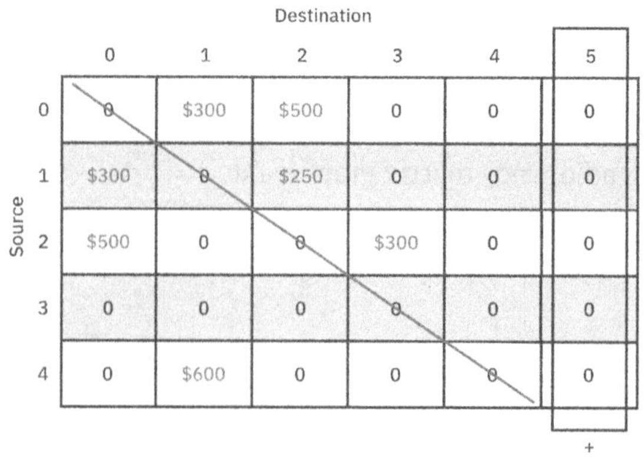

The next step is to add an additional row representing a new source vertex. The weights for this, too, are empty since you haven't yet added any edges. Row 5 in the image below shows the newly added source row:

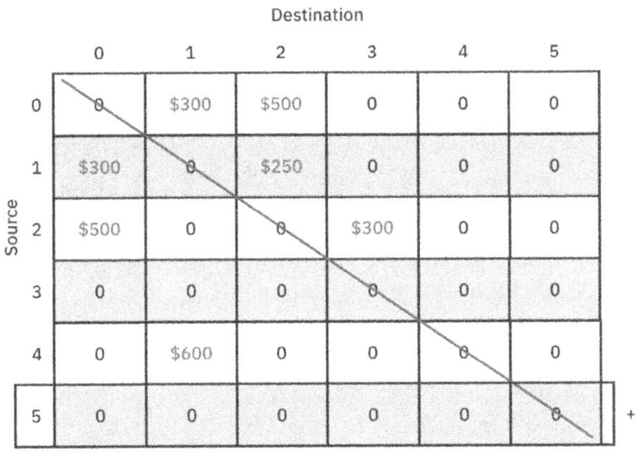

To implement the description above, add the `createVertex` method to `AdjacencyMatrix`:

```
@override
Vertex<E> createVertex(E data) {
  // 1
  final vertex = Vertex(
    index: _nextIndex,
    data: data,
  );
  _nextIndex++;
  _vertices.add(vertex);
  // 2
  for (var i = 0; i < _weights.length; i++) {
    _weights[i]?.add(null);
  }
  // 3
  final row = List<double?>.filled(
    _vertices.length,
    null,
    growable: true,
  );
  _weights.add(row);
  return vertex;
}
```

To create a vertex in an adjacency matrix, you perform the following tasks:

1. Add a new vertex to the list.
2. Append a `null` value at the end of every row. This, in effect, creates a new destination column in the matrix.
3. Add a new row to the matrix, again filled with `null` weight values.

Adding Edges

Creating edges is as simple as adding weights to the matrix. There's no `Edge` class to worry about.

Add the missing `addEdge` method to `AdjacencyMatrix`:

```
@override
void addEdge(
  Vertex<E> source,
  Vertex<E> destination, {
  EdgeType edgeType = EdgeType.undirected,
  double? weight,
}) {
  // 1
  _weights[source.index]?[destination.index] = weight;
  // 2
  if (edgeType == EdgeType.undirected) {
    _weights[destination.index]?[source.index] = weight;
  }
}
```

The logic here is similar to how you implemented `addEdge` in `AdjacencyList` previously:

1. Always add a directed edge.
2. If the edge type for the graph is undirected, also add another edge going from the destination to the source.

Retrieving the Outgoing Edges From a Vertex

Add the edges method to AdjacencyMatrix:

```
@override
List<Edge<E>> edges(Vertex<E> source) {
  List<Edge<E>> edges = [];
  // 1
  for (var column = 0; column < _weights.length; column++) {
    final weight = _weights[source.index]?[column];
    // 2
    if (weight == null) continue;
    // 3
    final destination = _vertices[column];
    edges.add(Edge(source, destination, weight));
  }
  return edges;
}
```

Remember that the columns represent destinations and that a source is a row:

1. To find all the edges for some source, you loop through all the values in a row.
2. Check for weights that aren't `null`. Every non-null weight implies an outgoing edge.
3. Use the column to look up the destination vertex.

Retrieving the Weight of an Edge

It's easy to get the weight of an edge. Simply look up the value in the adjacency matrix.

Implement `weight` like so:

```
@override
double? weight(Vertex<E> source, Vertex<E> destination) {
  return _weights[source.index]?[destination.index];
}
```

Making an Adjacency Matrix Printable

Finally, override `toString` so you can print out a readable description of your graph:

```
@override
String toString() {
  final output = StringBuffer();
  // 1
  for (final vertex in _vertices) {
    output.writeln('${vertex.index}: ${vertex.data}');
  }
  // 2
  for (int i = 0; i < _weights.length; i++) {
    for (int j = 0; j < _weights.length; j++) {
      final value = (_weights[i]?[j] ?? '.').toString();
      output.write(value.padRight(6));
    }
    output.writeln();
  }
  return output.toString();
}
```

Here are the steps:

1. You first create a list of the vertices.
2. Then, you build up a grid of weights, row by row.

Building a Network

You will reuse the same example from `AdjacencyList`:

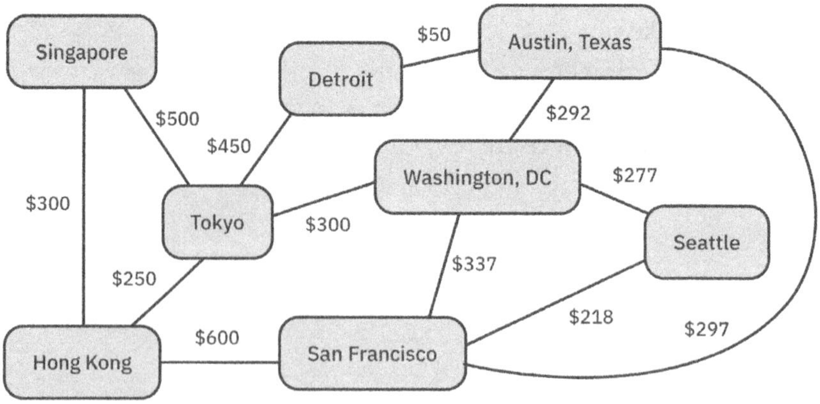

Go back to the `main` method in **bin/starter.dart** and replace this:

```
final graph = AdjacencyList<String>();
```

with the following:

```
final graph = AdjacencyMatrix<String>();
```

`AdjacencyMatrix` and `AdjacencyList` conform to the same `Graph` interface, so the rest of the code stays the same.

Run the code. The `print(graph)` portion of the code should give the following output:

```
0: Singapore
1: Tokyo
2: Hong Kong
3: Detroit
4: San Francisco
5: Washington DC
6: Austin Texas
7: Seattle
.     500.0 300.0 .     .     .     .     .
500.0 .     250.0 450.0 .     300.0 .     .
300.0 250.0 .     .     600.0 .     .     .
.     450.0 .     .     .     .     50.0  .
.     .     600.0 .     .     337.0 297.0 218.0
.     300.0 .     .     337.0 .     292.0 277.0
.     .     .     50.0  297.0 292.0 .     .
.     .     .     .     218.0 277.0 .     .
```

Graph Analysis

This chart compares the cost of different graph operations for adjacency lists and adjacency matrices. **V** represents the number of vertices, and **E** represents the number of edges.

Operations	Adjacency List	Adjacency Matrix
Storage Space	$O(V + E)$	$O(V^2)$
Add Vertex	$O(1)$	$O(V^2)$
Add Edge	$O(1)$	$O(1)$
Finding Edges and Weight	$O(V)$	$O(1)$

An adjacency list takes less storage space than an adjacency matrix. An adjacency list simply stores the number of vertices and edges needed. As for an adjacency matrix, recall that the number of rows and columns equals the number of vertices. This explains the quadratic space complexity of $O(V^2)$.

Adding a vertex is efficient in an adjacency list: Simply create a vertex and set its key-value pair in the map. It's amortized as $O(1)$. When adding a vertex to an adjacency matrix, you must add a column to every row and create a new row for the new vertex. This is at least $O(V)$, and if you choose to represent your matrix with a contiguous memory block, it can be $O(V^2)$.

Adding an edge is efficient in both data structures since they are both constant time. The adjacency list appends to the list of outgoing edges. The adjacency matrix simply sets a value in the two-dimensional list.

Adjacency list loses out when trying to find a particular edge or weight. To find an edge in an adjacency list, you have to obtain the list of outgoing edges and loop through every edge to find a matching destination. This happens in O(V) time. With an adjacency matrix, finding an edge or weight is a constant-time lookup in the two-dimensional list.

So which data structure should you choose to construct your graph?

If there are few edges in your graph, it's considered a **sparse graph**, and an adjacency list would be a good fit. An adjacency matrix would be a bad choice for a sparse graph because a lot of memory would be wasted since there aren't many edges.

If your graph has lots of edges, it's considered a **dense graph**, and an adjacency matrix would be a better fit since you'd be able to access your weights and edges far more quickly.

> **Note**: A dense graph in which every vertex has an edge to every other vertex is called a **complete graph**.

In the next few chapters, you'll learn different algorithms for visiting the nodes of a graph.

Challenges

Here's a challenge for you to apply your newfound knowledge of graphs. You can find the answer in the Challenge Solutions section as well as in the supplemental materials that accompany this book.

Challenge 1: Graph Your Friends

Megan has three friends: Sandra, Pablo and Edith. Pablo has friends as well: Ray, Luke, and a mutual friend of Megan's. Edith is friends with Manda and Vicki. Manda is friends with Pablo and Megan. Create an adjacency list that represents this friendship graph. Which mutual friend do Pablo and Megan share?

Key Points

- You can represent real-world relationships through vertices and edges.
- Think of vertices as objects and edges as the relationships between the objects.
- Weighted graphs associate a number with every edge.
- Directed graphs have edges that traverse in one direction.
- Undirected graphs have edges that point both ways.
- An adjacency list is a graph that stores a list of outgoing edges for every vertex.
- An adjacency matrix uses a two-dimensional list to represent a graph.
- An adjacency list is generally good for sparse graphs, which have a low number of edges.
- An adjacency matrix is generally suitable for dense graphs with many edges.

Chapter 22: Breadth-First Search

In the previous chapter, you explored using graphs to capture relationships between objects. Remember that objects are just vertices, and edges represent the relationships between them.

Several algorithms exist to traverse or search through a graph's vertices. One such algorithm is the **breadth-first search** (BFS) algorithm. The BFS algorithm visits the closest vertices from the starting vertex before moving on to further vertices.

BFS can be used to solve a wide variety of problems:

1. Generating a minimum-spanning tree.
2. Finding potential paths between vertices.
3. Finding the shortest path between two vertices.

How Breadth-First Search Works

A breadth-first search starts by selecting any vertex in a graph. The algorithm then explores all neighbors of this vertex before traversing the neighbors' neighbors and so forth.

You'll use the following undirected graph as an example to explore how BFS works:

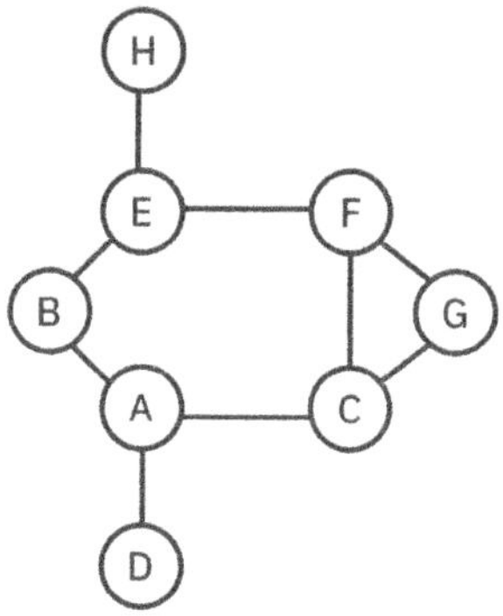

A **queue** will help you keep track of which vertices to visit next. The first-in-first-out approach of the queue guarantees that all of a vertex's neighbors are visited before you traverse one level deeper.

To begin, you pick a source vertex to start from, in this case, `A`. Then add it to the queue. Highlighted vertices will represent vertices that you've already visited:

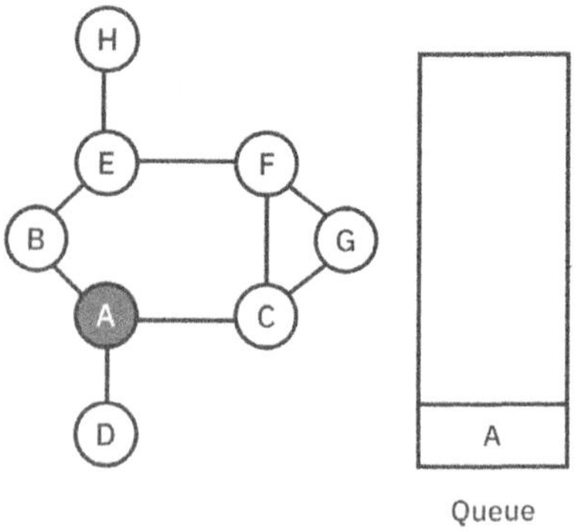

Next, you dequeue the `A` and add all of its neighboring vertices `[B, D, C]` to the queue:

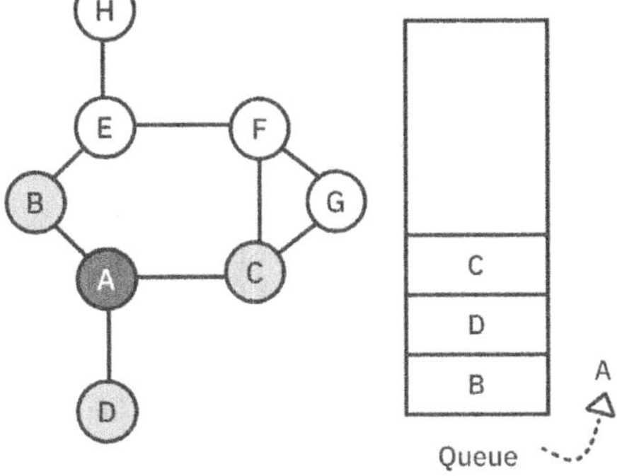

It's important to note that you only add a vertex to the queue when it has not yet been visited and is not already in the queue.

The queue isn't empty, so you dequeue and visit the next vertex, `B`. You then add `B`'s neighbor `E` to the queue. `A` has already been visited, so it isn't added. The queue now has `[D, C, E]`:

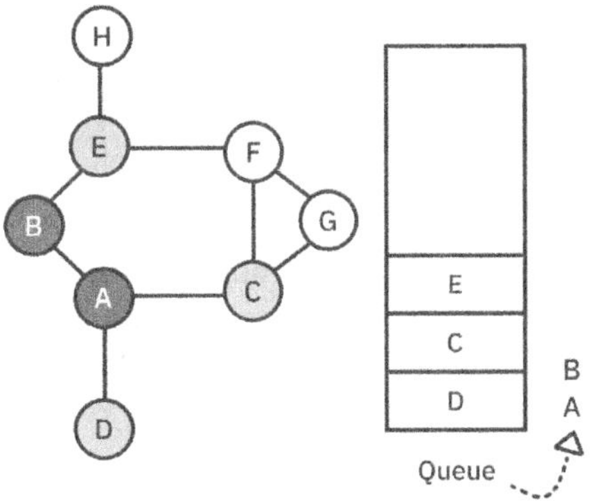

The next vertex to be dequeued is `D`. `D` doesn't have any neighbors that haven't been visited. The queue now has `[C, E]`:

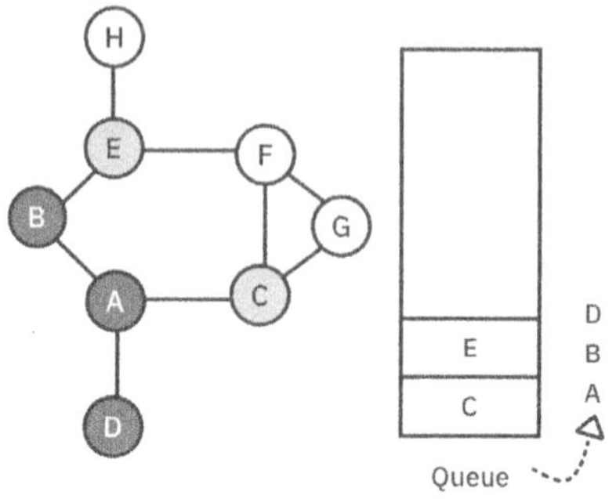

Next, you dequeue `C` and add its neighbors `[F, G]` to the queue. The queue now has `[E, F, G]`:

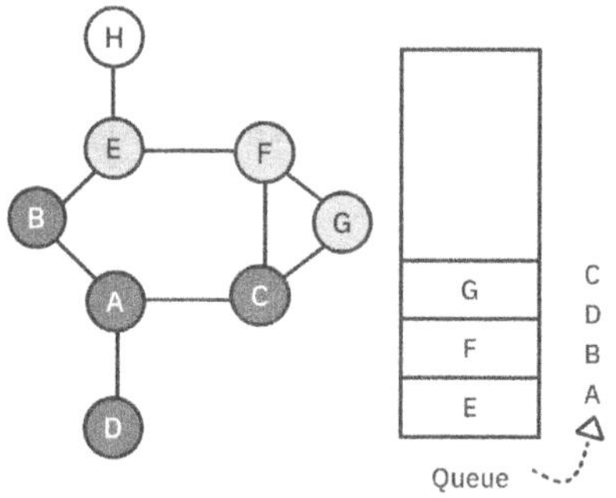

You've visited all of `A`'s neighbors! BFS now moves on to the second level of neighbors. You dequeue `E` and add `H` to the queue. The queue now has `[F, G, H]`. You don't add `B` or `F` to the queue because `B` has already been visited and `F` is already in the queue:

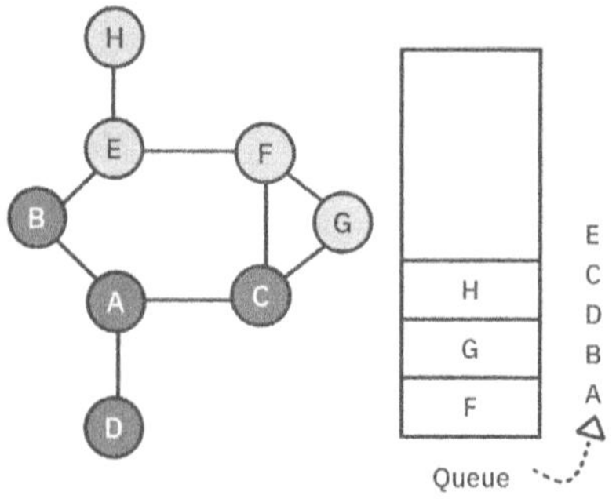

You dequeue `F`, and since all its neighbors are already in the queue or visited, you don't add anything to the queue:

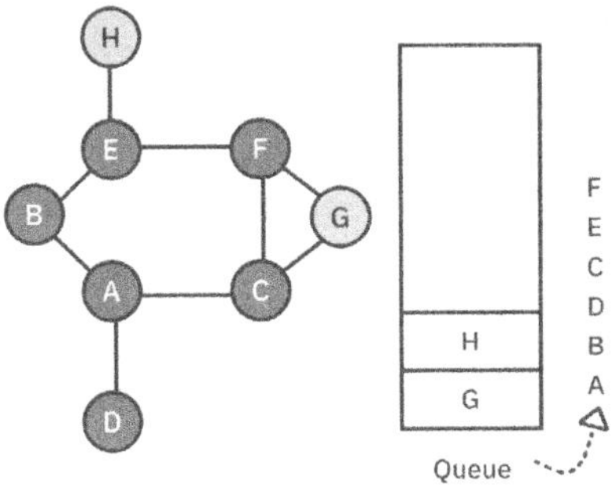

Like the previous step, you dequeue `G` and don't add anything to the queue:

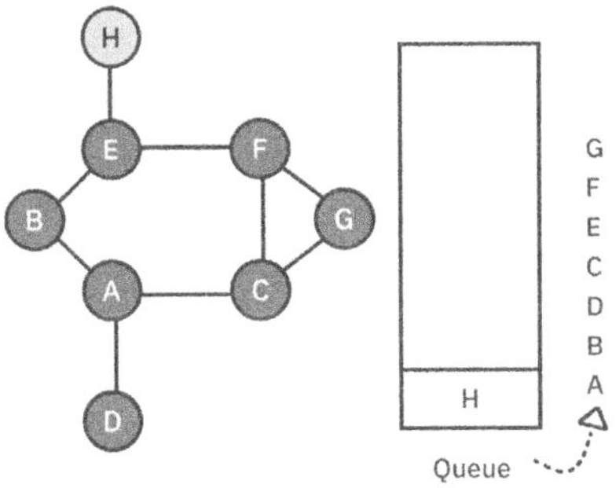

Finally, you dequeue `H`. The breadth-first search is complete since the queue is now empty!

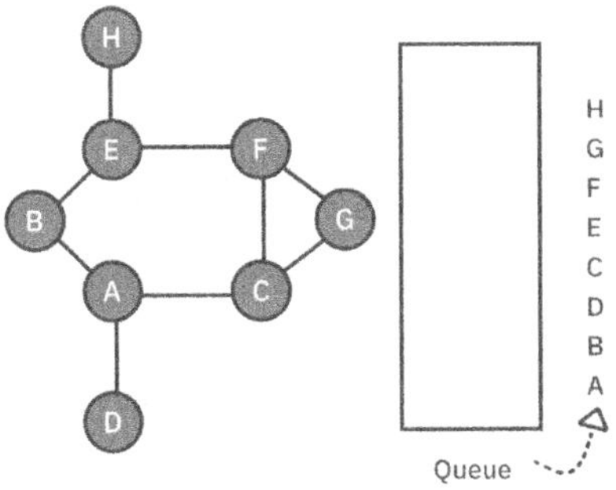

When exploring the vertices, you can construct a tree-like structure, showing the vertices at each level: first, the vertex you started from, then its neighbors, then its neighbors' neighbors and so on.

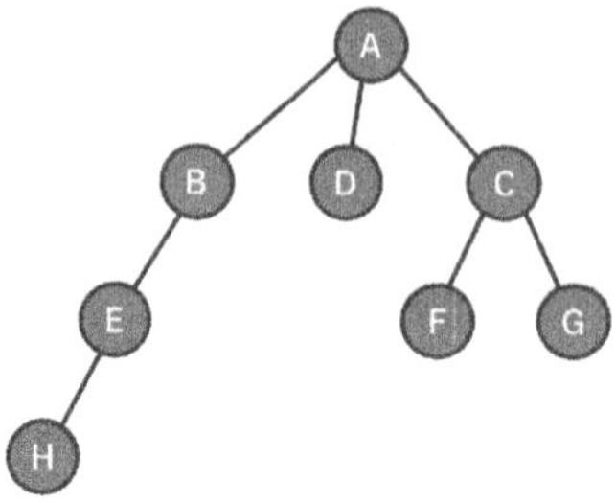

Implementation

Open up the **starter** project for this chapter. The **lib** folder contains the graph implementation you built in the previous chapter. It also includes the stack-based queue implementation that you made in Chapter 6, "Queues". You'll use both of these files to create your breadth-first search.

Extension on Graph

Rather than directly modifying `Graph`, you'll add an extension to it. Create a new file in **lib** named **breadth_first_search.dart**. Then add the following code to that file:

```
import 'queue.dart';
import 'graph.dart';

extension BreadthFirstSearch<E> on Graph<E> {
  List<Vertex<E>> breadthFirstSearch(Vertex<E> source) {
    final queue = QueueStack<Vertex<E>>();
    Set<Vertex<E>> enqueued = {};
    List<Vertex<E>> visited = [];

    // more to come

    return visited;
  }
}
```

You've defined an extension method on Graph called breadthFirstSearch, which takes in a starting vertex. The method uses three data structures:

1. queue keeps track of the neighboring vertices to visit next.
2. enqueued remembers which vertices have been enqueued before, so you don't enqueue the same vertex twice. You use Set so that lookup is cheap and only takes O(1) time. A list would require O(n) time.
3. visited is a list that stores the order in which the vertices were explored.

Next, complete the method by replacing the // more to come comment with the following:

```
// 1
queue.enqueue(source);
enqueued.add(source);

while (true) {
  // 2
  final vertex = queue.dequeue();
  if (vertex == null) break;
  // 3
  visited.add(vertex);
  // 4
  final neighborEdges = edges(vertex);
  for (final edge in neighborEdges) {
    // 5
    if (!enqueued.contains(edge.destination)) {
      queue.enqueue(edge.destination);
      enqueued.add(edge.destination);
    }
  }
}
```

Here's what's going on:

1. You initialize the BFS algorithm by first enqueuing the source vertex.
2. You continue to dequeue a vertex from the queue until the queue is empty.
3. Every time you dequeue a vertex from the queue, you add it to the list of visited vertices.
4. Then, you find all edges that start from the current vertex and iterate over them.
5. For each edge, you check to see if its destination vertex has been enqueued before, and, if not, you add it to the queue.

Testing it Out

That's all there is to implementing BFS! Give this algorithm a spin. Open **bin/starter.dart** and replace the contents of the file with the following code:

```
import 'package:starter/breadth_first_search.dart';
import 'package:starter/graph.dart';

void main() {
  final graph = AdjacencyList<String>();

  final a = graph.createVertex('A');
  final b = graph.createVertex('B');
  final c = graph.createVertex('C');
  final d = graph.createVertex('D');
  final e = graph.createVertex('E');
  final f = graph.createVertex('F');
  final g = graph.createVertex('G');
  final h = graph.createVertex('H');

  graph.addEdge(a, b, weight: 1);
  graph.addEdge(a, c, weight: 1);
  graph.addEdge(a, d, weight: 1);
  graph.addEdge(b, e, weight: 1);
  graph.addEdge(c, f, weight: 1);
  graph.addEdge(c, g, weight: 1);
  graph.addEdge(e, h, weight: 1);
  graph.addEdge(e, f, weight: 1);
  graph.addEdge(f, g, weight: 1);

  // more to come
}
```

This creates the same graph you saw earlier:

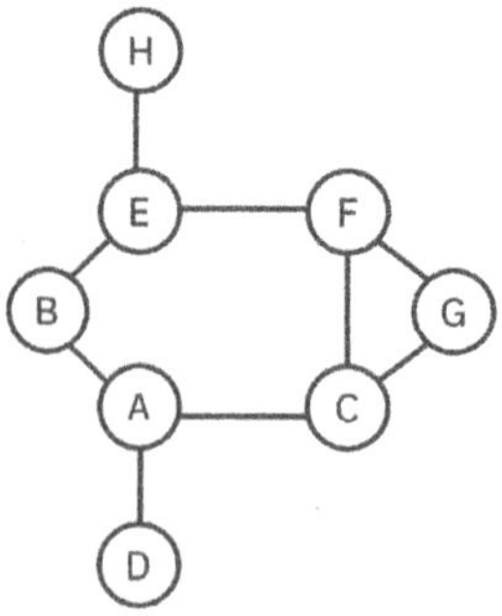

Now add the following code at the bottom of `main`:

```
final vertices = graph.breadthFirstSearch(a);
vertices.forEach(print);
```

Run that, and note the order that BFS explored the vertices in:

```
A
B
C
D
E
F
G
H
```

One thing to keep in mind with neighboring vertices is that the order in which you visit them is determined by how you construct your graph. You could have added an edge between `A` and `C` before adding one between `A` and `B`. In that case, the output would list `C` before `B`.

Performance

When traversing a graph using BFS, each vertex is enqueued once. This process has a time complexity of O(V). During this traversal, you also visit all the edges. The time it takes to visit all edges is O(E). Adding the two together means that the overall time complexity for breadth-first search is O(V + E).

The space complexity of BFS is O(V) since you have to store the vertices in three separate structures: `queue`, `enqueued` and `visited`.

Challenges

Ready to try a few challenges? If you get stuck, the answers are in the Challenge Solutions section and also in the supplemental materials accompanying this book.

Challenge 1: Maximum Queue Size

For the following undirected graph, list the **maximum** number of items ever in the queue. Assume that the starting vertex is **A**.

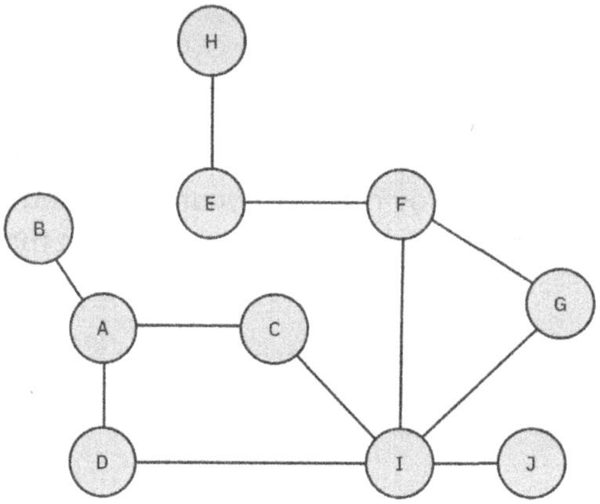

Challenge 2: Iterative BFS

In this chapter, you created an iterative implementation of breadth-first search. Now write a recursive solution.

Challenge 3: Disconnected Graph

Add a method to `Graph` to detect if a graph is disconnected. An example of a **disconnected graph** is shown below:

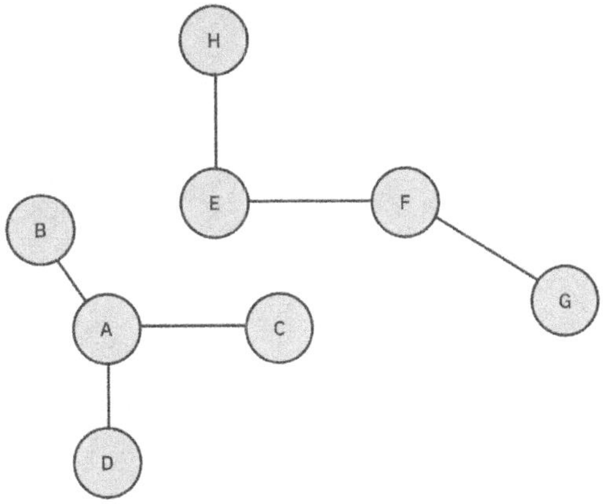

Key Points

- Breadth-first search (BFS) is an algorithm for traversing or searching a graph.
- BFS explores all the current vertex's neighbors before traversing the next level of vertices.
- It's generally good to use this algorithm when your graph structure has many neighboring vertices or when you need to find out every possible outcome.
- The queue data structure prioritises traversing a vertex's edges before diving down to a level deeper.

Chapter 23: Depth-First Search

In the previous chapter, you looked at breadth-first search (BFS), in which you had to explore every neighbor of a vertex before going to the next level. In this chapter, you'll look at **depth-first search** (DFS), another algorithm for traversing or searching a graph.

There are a lot of applications for DFS:

- Topological sorting.
- Detecting a cycle.
- Pathfinding, such as in maze puzzles.
- Finding connected components in a sparse graph.

To perform a DFS, you start with a given source vertex and attempt to explore a branch as far as possible until you reach the end. At this point, you backtrack and explore the next available branch until you find what you're looking for or until you've visited all the vertices.

How Depth-First Search Works

The following example will take you through a depth-first search. The graph below is the same as the one in the previous chapter so you can see the difference between BFS and DFS.

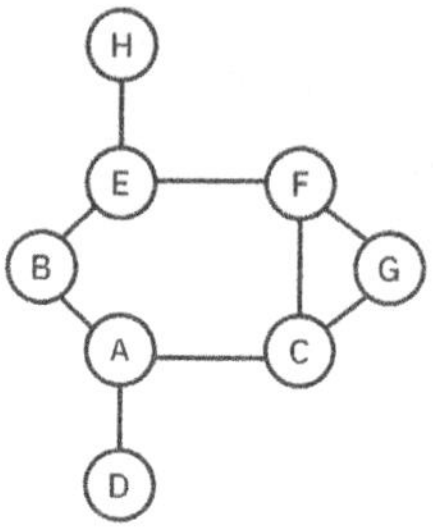

BFS used a queue to visit neighboring vertices first. However, DFS will use a stack to keep track of the levels you move through. The stack's last-in-first-out approach helps with backtracking. Every push on the stack means that you move one level deeper. You can pop to return to a previous level if you reach a dead end.

As in the previous chapter, you choose `A` as a starting vertex and add it to the stack:

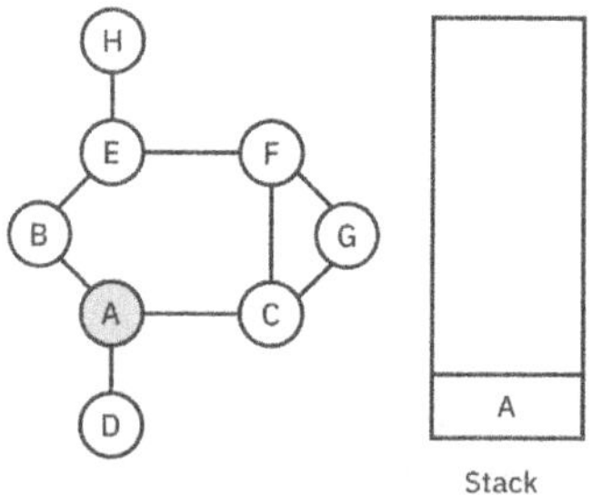

As long as the stack isn't empty, you visit the top vertex on the stack and push the first neighboring vertex that has yet to be visited. In this case, you visit `A` and push `B`:

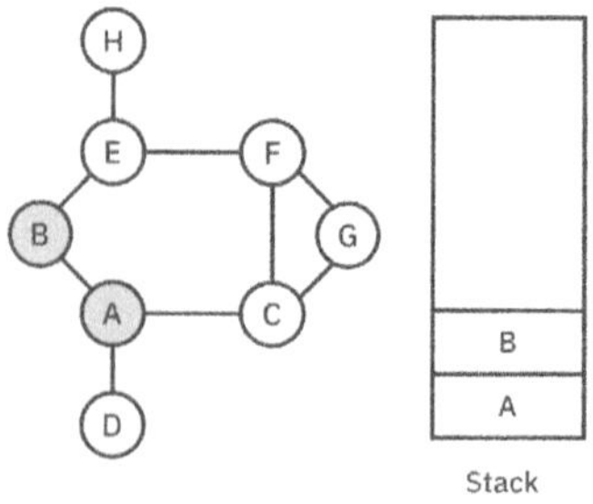

Remember that the order in which the edges were added influences the search result. In this case, the first edge added to A was to B, so B is pushed first.

You visit B and push E because A is already visited:

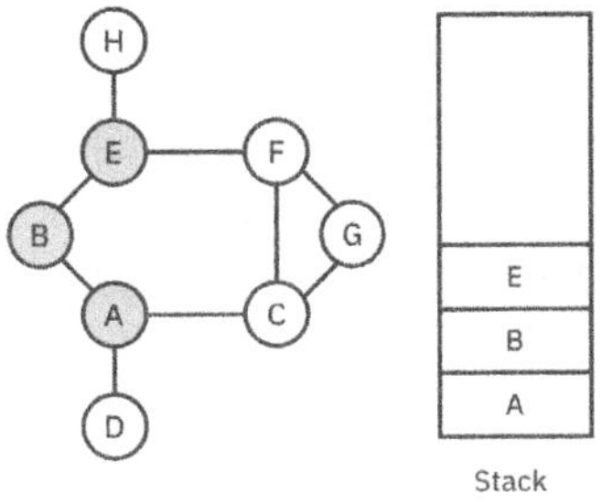

Every time you push onto the stack, you advance farther down a branch. Instead of visiting every adjacent vertex, you continue down a path until you reach the end. After that, you backtrack.

Next, visit E and push F.

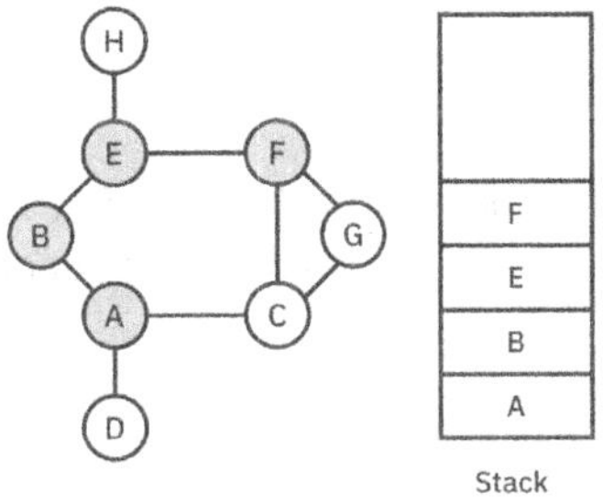

Again, the only reason you chose F instead of H is that F happened to be added first when the graph was created for this particular example. You can't see that from the diagram, but when you get to the code later on, you'll be able to observe the edge addition order.

Now visit `F` and push `G`:

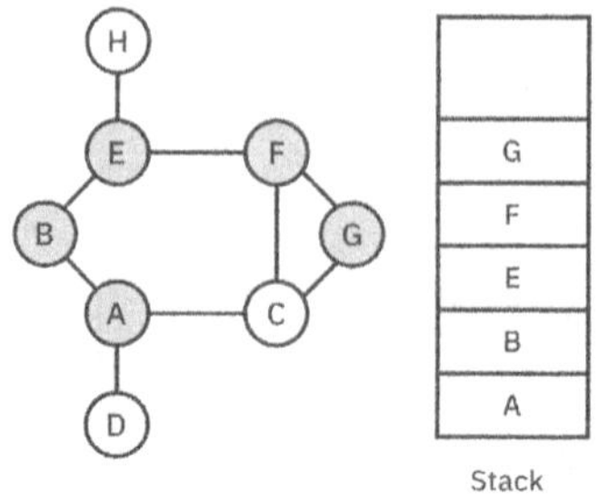

Then visit `G` and push `C`:

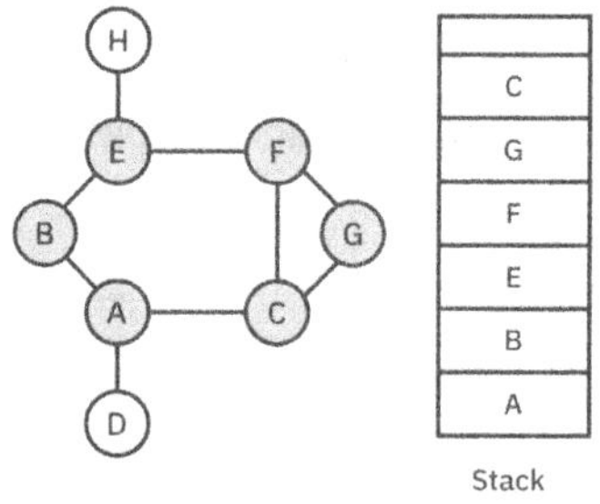

The next vertex to visit is `C`. It has neighbors `[A, F, G]`, but they all have already been visited. You've reached a dead end, so it's time to backtrack by popping `C` off the stack:

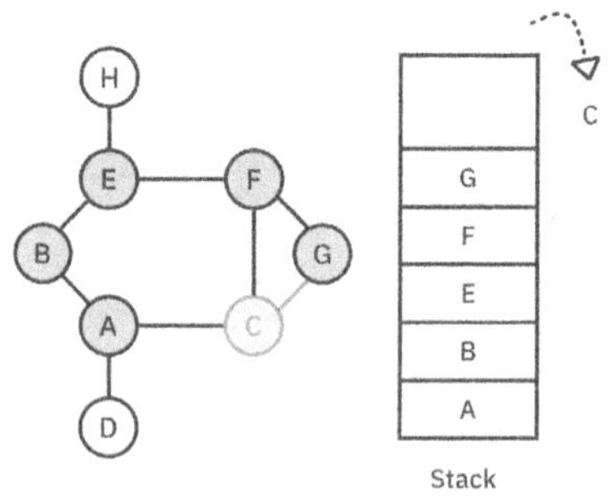

This brings you back to G. It has neighbors [F, C], but both of these have been visited. Another dead end, so pop G:

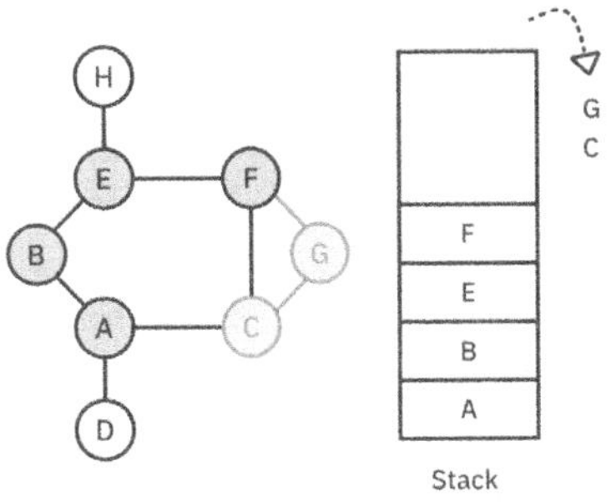

F also has no unvisited neighbors remaining, so pop F:

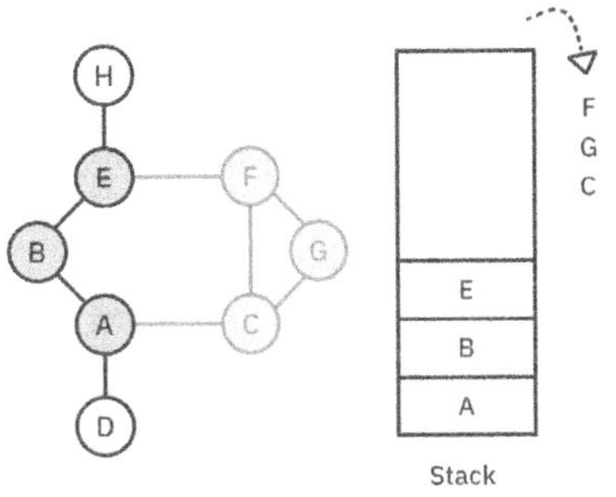

Now you're back at E. Its neighbor H is still unvisited, so you push H on the stack:

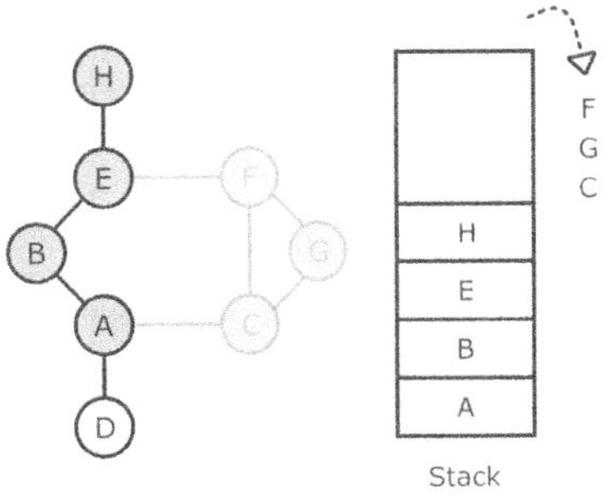

Visiting H results in another dead end, so pop H:

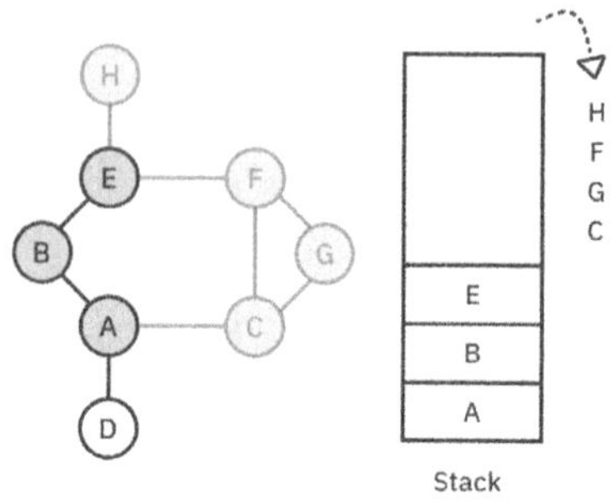

E doesn't have any available neighbors either, so pop it:

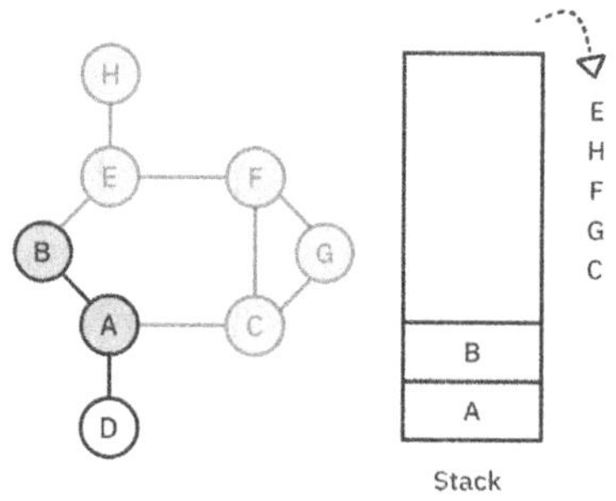

The same is true for B, so pop B:

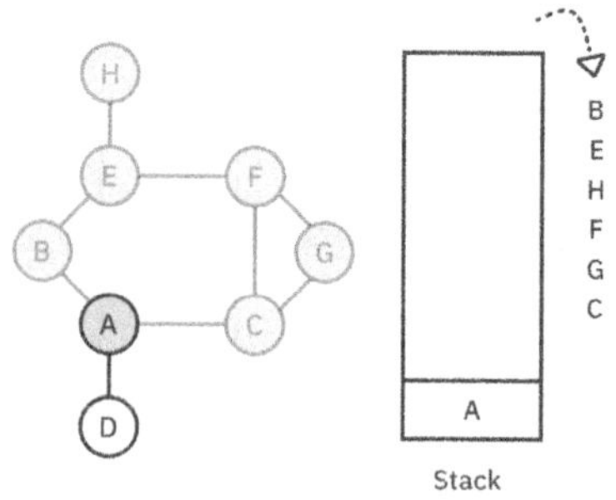

This brings you all the way back to A, whose neighbor D still needs to be visited, so you push D on the stack:

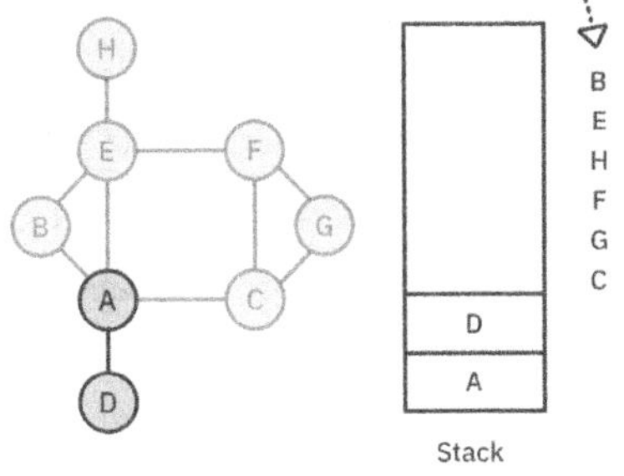

Visiting D results in another dead end, so pop D:

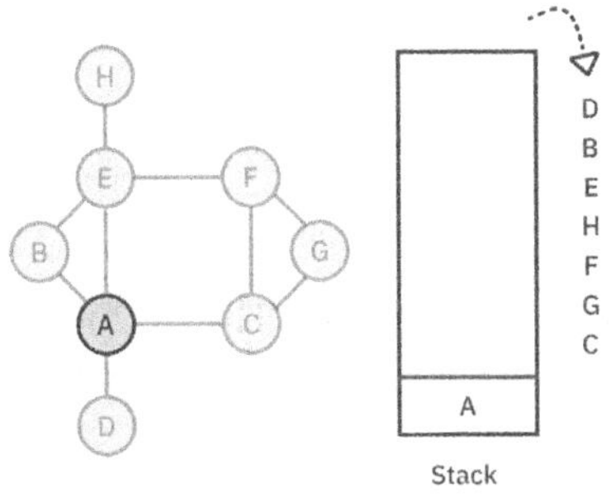

You're back at A, but this time, there are no available neighbors to push, so you pop A. The stack is now empty and DFS is complete!

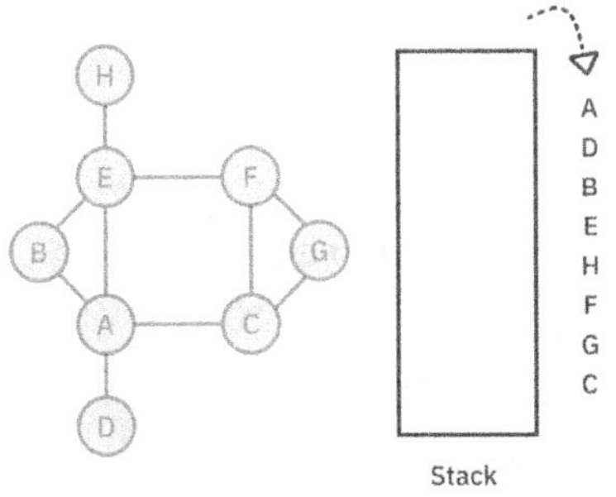

When exploring the vertices, you can construct a tree-like structure, showing the branches you've visited. You can see how deep DFS went compared to BFS:

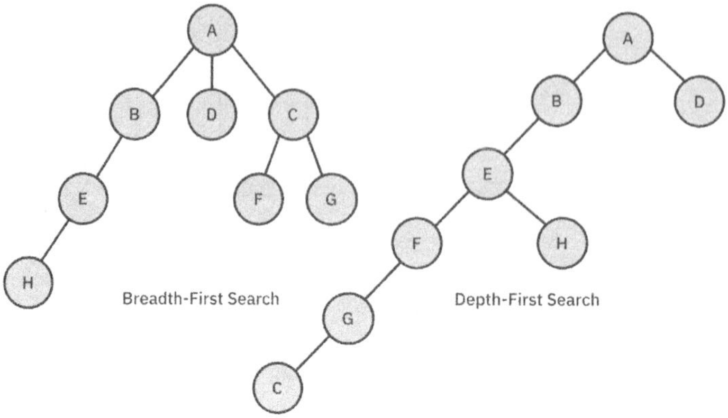

Implementation

Open up the **starter** project for this chapter. The **lib** folder contains an implementation of a graph as well as a stack, both of which you'll use to implement DFS.

Creating an Extension

Create a new file in **lib** called **depth_first_search.dart**. Add the following:

```
import 'stack.dart';
import 'graph.dart';

extension DepthFirstSearch<E> on Graph<E> {
  List<Vertex<E>> depthFirstSearch(Vertex<E> source) {
    final stack = Stack<Vertex<E>>();
    final pushed = <Vertex<E>>{};
    final visited = <Vertex<E>>[];

    stack.push(source);
    pushed.add(source);
    visited.add(source);

    // more to come

    return visited;
  }
}
```

Here, you've defined an extension method, `depthFirstSearch`, which takes in a starting vertex and returns a list of vertices in the order they were visited. It uses three data structures:

1. `stack` is used to store your path through the graph.
2. `pushed` is a set that remembers which vertices have been pushed before so that you don't visit the same vertex twice. Using `Set` ensures fast O(1) lookup.
3. `visited` is a list that stores the order in which the vertices were visited.

To initialize the algorithm, you add the `source` vertex to all three.

Traversing Vertices

Next, complete the method by replacing the `// more to come` comment with the following:

```
// 1
outerLoop:
while (stack.isNotEmpty) {
  final vertex = stack.peek;
  // 2
  final neighbors = edges(vertex);
  // 3
  for (final edge in neighbors) {
    if (!pushed.contains(edge.destination)) {
      stack.push(edge.destination);
      pushed.add(edge.destination);
      visited.add(edge.destination);
      // 4
      continue outerLoop;
    }
  }
  // 5
  stack.pop();
}
```

Here's what's going on:

1. You continue to check the top of the stack for a vertex until the stack is empty. You've labeled this loop `outerLoop` so that you have a way to continue to the next vertex, even from within a nested `for` loop.
2. You find all the neighboring edges for the current vertex.

3. Here, you loop through every edge connected to the current vertex and check if the neighboring vertex has been seen. If not, you push it onto the stack and add it to the `visited` list. It may seem a bit premature to mark this vertex as visited since you haven't peeked at it yet. However, vertices are visited in the order in which they're added to the stack, resulting in the correct order.

4. Now that you've found a neighbor to visit, you continue to `outerLoop` and peek at the newly pushed neighbor.

5. If the current vertex didn't have any unvisited neighbors, you know you've reached a dead end and can pop it off the stack.

Once the stack is empty, the DFS algorithm is complete! All you have to do is return the visited vertices in the order you visited them.

Testing it Out

To try out your code, open **bin/starter.dart** and replace the contents of the file with the following code:

```
import 'package:starter/graph.dart';
import 'package:starter/depth_first_search.dart';

void main() {
  final graph = AdjacencyList<String>();

  final a = graph.createVertex('A');
  final b = graph.createVertex('B');
  final c = graph.createVertex('C');
  final d = graph.createVertex('D');
  final e = graph.createVertex('E');
  final f = graph.createVertex('F');
  final g = graph.createVertex('G');
  final h = graph.createVertex('H');

  graph.addEdge(a, b, weight: 1);
  graph.addEdge(a, c, weight: 1);
  graph.addEdge(a, d, weight: 1);
  graph.addEdge(b, e, weight: 1);
  graph.addEdge(c, g, weight: 1);
  graph.addEdge(e, f, weight: 1);
  graph.addEdge(e, h, weight: 1);
  graph.addEdge(f, g, weight: 1);
  graph.addEdge(f, c, weight: 1);
}
```

This creates a graph with the edges added in an order that results in the DFS path you saw in the diagrams above.

Perform the depth-first search by adding the following two lines at the bottom of `main`:

```
final vertices = graph.depthFirstSearch(a);
vertices.forEach(print);
```

Run that, and observe the order in which DFS visited the indices:

```
A
B
E
F
G
C
H
D
```

Performance

DFS will visit every single vertex at least once. This process has a time complexity of O(V).

When traversing a graph in DFS, you have to check all neighboring vertices to find one available to visit. The time complexity of this is O(E) because you have to visit every edge in the graph in the worst case.

Overall, the time complexity for depth-first search is O(V + E).

The space complexity of depth-first search is O(V) since you have to store all the vertices in three separate data structures: `stack`, `pushed` and `visited`.

Cycles

A depth-first search is also useful for finding whether a graph contains cycles. A graph is said to have a **cycle** when a path of edges and vertices leads back to the same source.

For example, in the directed graph below, if you start at A, you can go to B, then to C, and then back to A again. Since it's possible to arrive back at the starting vertex, this is a **cyclic graph**:

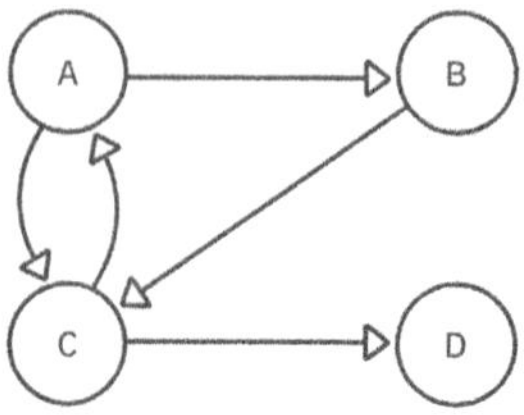

If you removed the C-to-A edge, this graph would become **acyclic**. That is, there would be no cycles. It would be impossible to start at any vertex and arrive back at the same vertex.

> **Note**: In this directed graph, there's also a cycle from A to C since the edges point in both directions. In an undirected graph, though, two vertices wouldn't count as a cycle. Undirected graphs need at least three vertices to make a cycle.

Checking for Cycles

Next, you'll write an algorithm to check whether a directed graph contains a cycle.

Return to **depth_first_search.dart** and create another extension on Graph:

```
extension CyclicGraph<E> on Graph<E> {
}
```

Add the following recursive helper method to `CyclicGraph`:

```
bool _hasCycle(Vertex<E> source, Set<Vertex<E>> pushed) {
  // 1
  pushed.add(source);
  // 2
  final neighbors = edges(source);
  for (final edge in neighbors) {
    // 3
    if (!pushed.contains(edge.destination)) {
      if (_hasCycle(edge.destination, pushed)) {
        return true;
      }
    // 4
    } else {
      return true;
    }
  }
  // 5
  pushed.remove(source);
  // 6
  return false;
}
```

Here's how it works:

1. Initialize the algorithm by adding the `source` vertex.
2. Visit every neighboring edge.
3. If the adjacent vertex has *not* been visited before, recursively dive deeper down a branch to check for a cycle.
4. If the adjacent vertex *has* been visited before, you've found a cycle.
5. Remove the `source` vertex so you can continue to find other paths with a potential cycle.
6. If you've reached this far, then no cycle was found.

To complete the code, add the public `hasCycle` method to `CyclicGraph`:

```
bool hasCycle(Vertex<E> source) {
  Set<Vertex<E>> pushed = {};
  return _hasCycle(source, pushed);
}
```

You're essentially performing a depth-first graph traversal by recursively diving down one path until you find a cycle and backtracking by popping off the stack to find another path. The time complexity is O(V + E).

Testing it Out

To create a graph that matches the image above, open **bin/starter.dart** and replace the content of `main` with the following:

```
final graph = AdjacencyList<String>();

final a = graph.createVertex('A');
final b = graph.createVertex('B');
final c = graph.createVertex('C');
final d = graph.createVertex('D');

graph.addEdge(a, b, edgeType: EdgeType.directed);
graph.addEdge(a, c, edgeType: EdgeType.directed);
graph.addEdge(c, a, edgeType: EdgeType.directed);
graph.addEdge(b, c, edgeType: EdgeType.directed);
graph.addEdge(c, d, edgeType: EdgeType.directed);

print(graph);
print(graph.hasCycle(a));
```

Run that, and you'll see the output below:

```
A --> B, C
B --> C
C --> A, D
D -->

true
```

If you comment out the `c`-to-`a` edge, the method will return `false`.

Challenges

Try out the following challenges to test your understanding of depth-first searches. You can find the answers in the back of the book or in the supplemental materials that accompany the book.

Challenge 1: BFS or DFS

For each of the following two examples, which traversal, depth-first or breadth-first, is better for discovering if a path exists between the two nodes? Explain why.

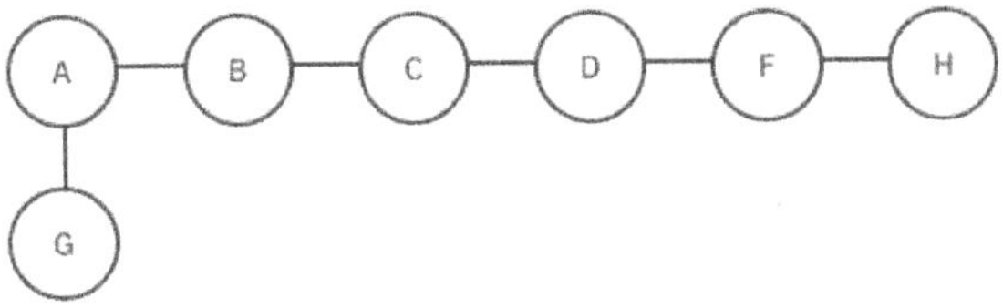

- Path from **A** to **F**.
- Path from **A** to **G**.

Challenge 2: Recursive DFS

In this chapter, you learned an iterative implementation of depth-first search. Now write a recursive implementation.

Key Points

- Depth-first search (DFS) is another algorithm to traverse or search a graph.
- DFS explores a branch as far as possible before backtracking to the next branch.
- The stack data structure allows you to backtrack.
- A graph is said to have a cycle when a path of edges and vertices leads back to the source vertex.

Chapter 24: Dijkstra's Algorithm

Have you ever used a map app to find the shortest distance or fastest time from one place to another? **Dijkstra's algorithm** is particularly useful in GPS networks to help find the shortest path between two locations. The algorithm works with weighted graphs, both directed and undirected, to calculate the optimal routes from one vertex to all others in the graph.

Dijkstra's algorithm is known as a **greedy** algorithm. That means it picks the most optimal path at every step along the way. It ignores solutions where some steps might have a higher intermediate cost but result in a lower overall cost for the entire path. Nevertheless, Dijkstra's algorithm usually arrives at a pretty good solution very quickly.

Some applications of Dijkstra's algorithm include:

1. Communicable disease transmission: Discovering where biological diseases are spreading the fastest.
2. Telephone networks: Routing calls to the highest-bandwidth paths available in the network.
3. Mapping: Finding the shortest and fastest paths for travelers.

> **Note**: On the off chance you've never seen the letters "jkstr" in combination and have no idea how you'd say that, "Dijkstra's" is pronounced ˈdaɪkstrəz. And if you aren't familiar with phonetic symbols, just combine the pronunciation of the words "dike" and "extras".

How Dijkstra's Algorithm Works

Imagine the directed graph below represents a road map. The vertices represent physical locations, and the edges represent one-way routes of a given cost between locations.

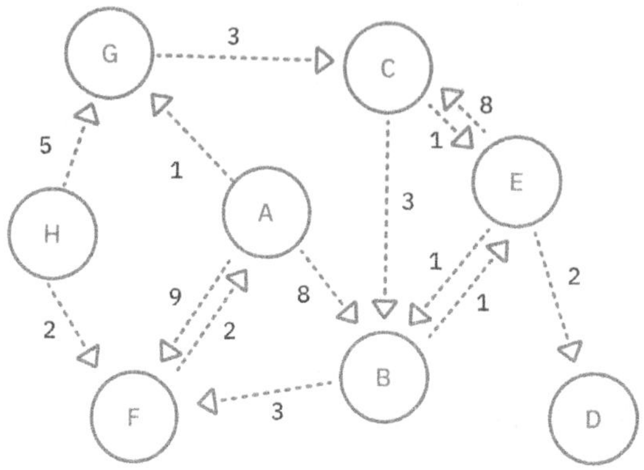

While edge weight can refer to the actual cost, it's also commonly referred to as **distance**, which fits the paradigm of finding the *shortest* route. However, if you like the word cost, you can think of route finding algorithms as looking for the *cheapest* route.

Initialization

In Dijkstra's algorithm, you first choose a **starting vertex** since the algorithm needs a starting point to find a path to the rest of the nodes in the graph. Assume the starting vertex you pick is vertex **A**.

You'll use a table to keep track of the shortest routes from **A** to the other vertices. In the beginning, you don't know anything, so fill in the table with `null` values:

	B	C	D	E	F	G	H
Start A	null	null	null	null	null	null	null

As you work through this example, you'll use each cell of the table to save two pieces of information:

1. The shortest known distance from **A** to this vertex.

2. The previous vertex in the path.

First Pass

From **vertex A**, look at all of the outgoing edges. In this case, there are three:

- **A** to **B** has a distance of **8**.
- **A** to **F** has a distance of **9**.
- **A** to **G** has a distance of **1**.

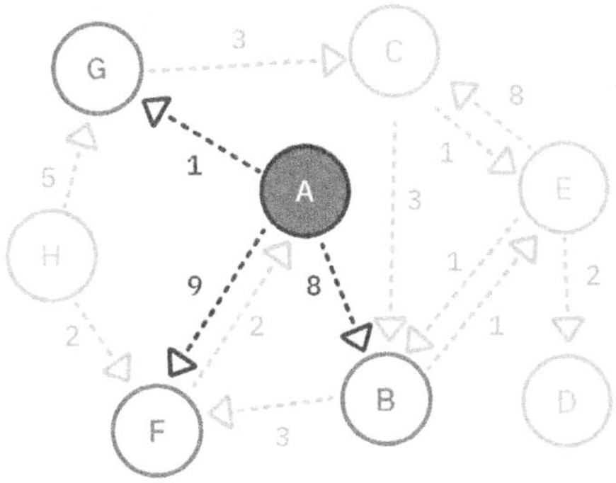

Since you know the distance of traveling from **A** to these three vertices, write the values in the table:

	B	C	D	E	F	G	H
Start A	8 A	null	null	null	9 A	1 A	null

You can see in the first cell that the distance from **A** to column **B** is **8**. Below the **8** you also write **A**. This means the previous vertex on the path to **B** is **A**. You'll update both the distance and the previous vertex if you find a better path to **B** in the future. Columns **F** and **G** follow the same pattern. The other vertices are still `null` since there's no known path to them from **A** yet.

Second Pass

In every round, Dijkstra's algorithm always takes the shortest path. Of the distances **8**, **9** and **1**, the shortest is **1**. That means column **G** with the **1** is the direction that Dijkstra will go:

	B	C	D	E	F	G	H
Start A	8 A	null	null	null	9 A	1 A	null

So the next step is to visit **G**:

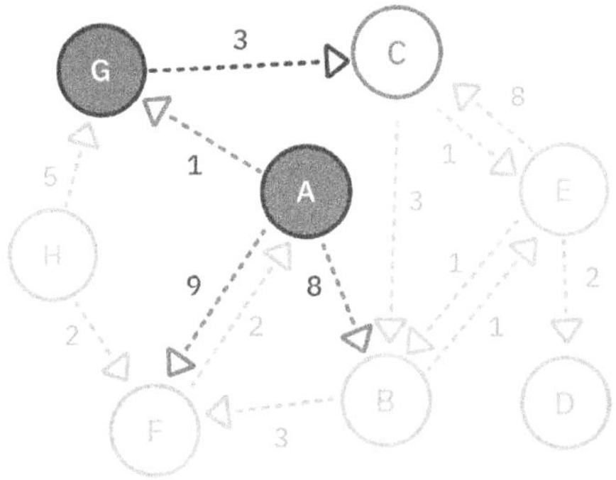

Now, look for **G**'s outgoing edges. It only has one, which goes to **C**, and the distance is **3**. That means the total distance of the **A** to **C** path is **1** + **3** = **4**. So write **4** and **G** in the **C** column. Again, the reason you write **G** is that **G** is the previous vertex on this path before reaching **C**:

	B	C	D	E	F	G	H
Start A	8 A	4 G	null	null	9 A	1 A	null

The filled-in vertices, both in the table and in the graph, are the ones you've visited. You already know the shortest routes to these vertices, so you don't need to check them anymore.

Third Pass

In the next pass, you look at the next-lowest distance. The distance to **B** is **8**, the distance to **C** is **4**, and the distance to **F** is **9**. That means **C** is the winner:

	B	C	D	E	F	G	H
Start A	8 A	(4) G	null	null	9 A	1 A	null

So now you visit **C**:

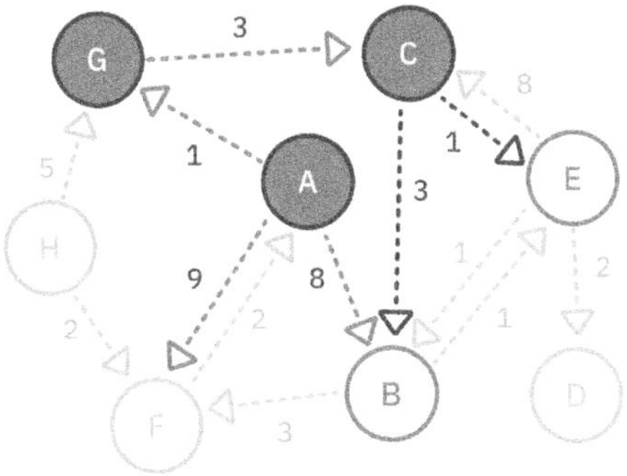

Look at all of **C**'s outgoing edges and add up the total cost it would take to get there from **A**:

- **C** to **E** has a total cost of **4** + **1** = **5**.
- **C** to **B** has a total cost of **4** + **3** = **7**.

It's actually cheaper to take this route to **B** than it was to go directly from **A** to **B**. Because of that, update the **B** column with a new value of **7** by way of vertex **C**. Also, fill in the **E** column since you know a route there now:

	B	C	D	E	F	G	H
Start A	(7) C	4 G	null	(5) C	9 A	1 A	null

Fourth Pass

Of the unvisited vertices, which path has the lowest distance now? According to the table, **E** does, with a total distance of **5**:

	B	C	D	E	F	G	H
Start A	7 C	4 G	null	5 C	9 A	1 A	null

Visit **E** and check its outgoing vertices. You've already visited **C**, so you can ignore that one. However, **B** and **D** are still unvisited:

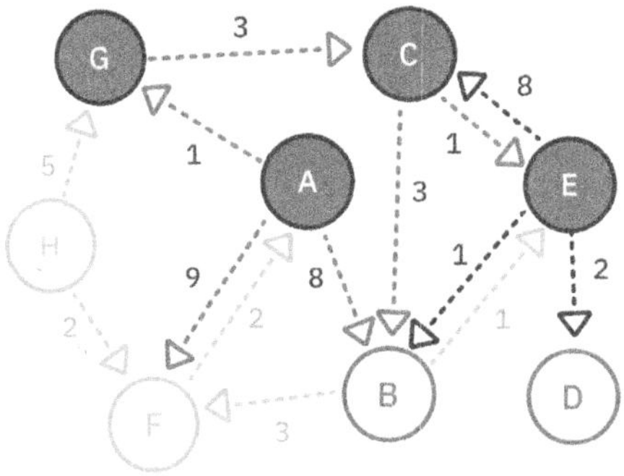

These are the distances from **A**:

- **E** to **D** has a total distance of **5 + 2 = 7**.
- **E** to **B** has a total distance of **5 + 1 = 6**.

You didn't know about **D** before, so you can fill in that column in the table. Also, when going to **B**, the path through **E** is even better than it was through **C**, so you can update the **B** column as well:

	B	C	D	E	F	G	H
Start A	6 E	4 G	7 E	5 C	9 A	1 A	null

Fifth Pass

Next, you continue the search from **B** since it has the next-lowest distance:

	B	C	D	E	F	G	H
Start A	6 E	4 G	7 E	5 C	9 A	1 A	null

Visit **B** and observe its edges:

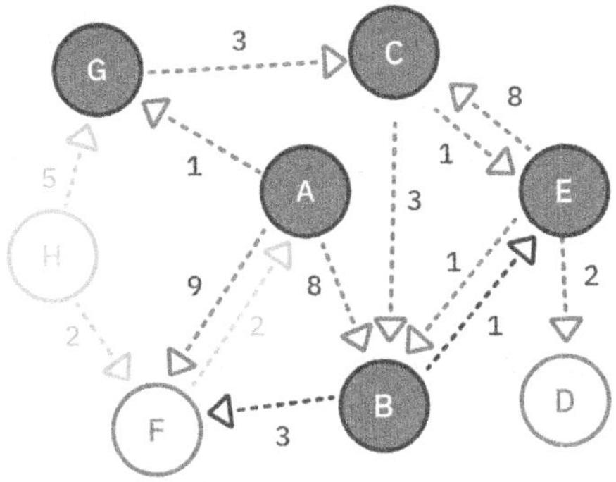

Of **B**'s neighbors, the only one you haven't visited yet is **F**. This has a total cost of **6 + 3 = 9**. From the table, you can tell that the current path to **F** from **A** also costs **9**. So, you can disregard this path since it isn't any shorter:

	B	C	D	E	F	G	H
Start A	6 E	4 G	7 E	5 C	9 A	1 A	null

Sixth Pass

Of the remaining unvisited vertices, **D** is closest to **A** with a distance of **7**:

	B	C	D	E	F	G	H
Start A	6 E	4 G	7 E	5 C	9 A	1 A	null

In this pass, continue the traversal from **D**:

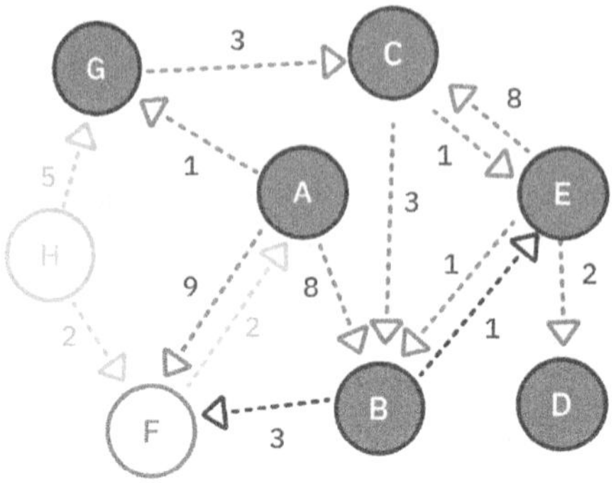

However, **D** has no outgoing edges, so it's a dead end. You can just move on.

Seventh Pass

F is up next. It's the only unvisited vertex that you have any information about:

	B	C	D	E	F	G	H
Start A	6 E	4 G	7 E	5 C	9 A	1 A	null

So visit **F** and observe its outgoing edges:

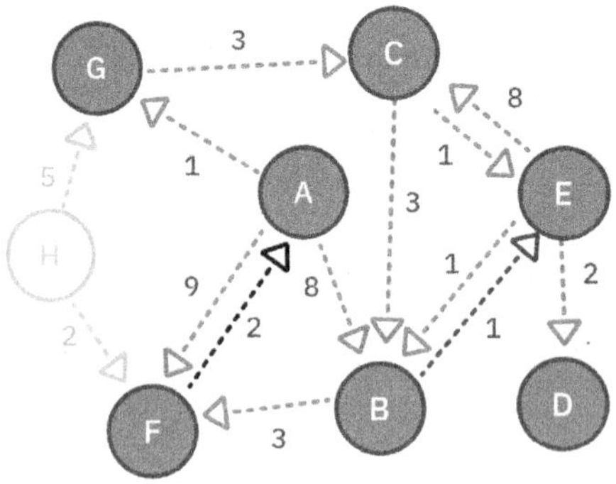

F has one outgoing edge to **A**, but you can disregard this edge since **A** is the starting vertex. You've already visited it.

Eighth Pass

You've covered every vertex except for **H**. **H** has one outgoing edge to **G** and one to **F**. However, there's no path from **A** to **H**:

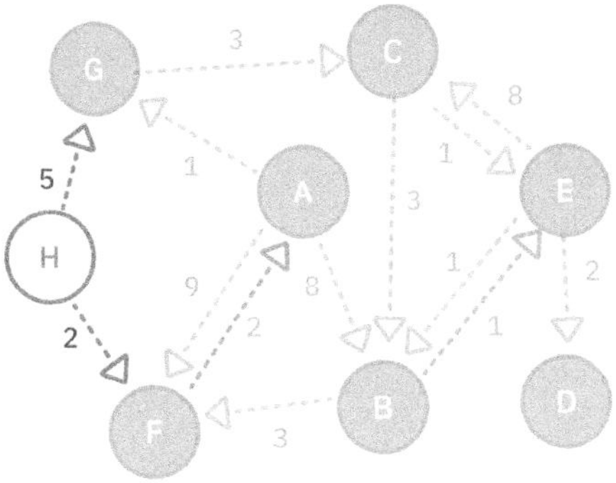

Because there's no path, the column for **H** is `null`:

	B	C	D	E	F	G	H
Start A	6 E	4 G	7 E	5 C	9 A	1 A	null

This step completes Dijkstra's algorithm since all the vertices that can be visited have been visited!

You can now check the table for the shortest paths and their distances. For example, the output tells you the distance you have to travel to get to **D** is **7**. To find the path, you backtrack. Each column in the table records the previous vertex that the current vertex is connected to. For example, to find the path to **D**, you start at **D** and backtrack. **D** points to **E**, which points to **C**, which points to **G**, which points to **A**, the starting vertex. So the path is **A-G-C-E-D**:

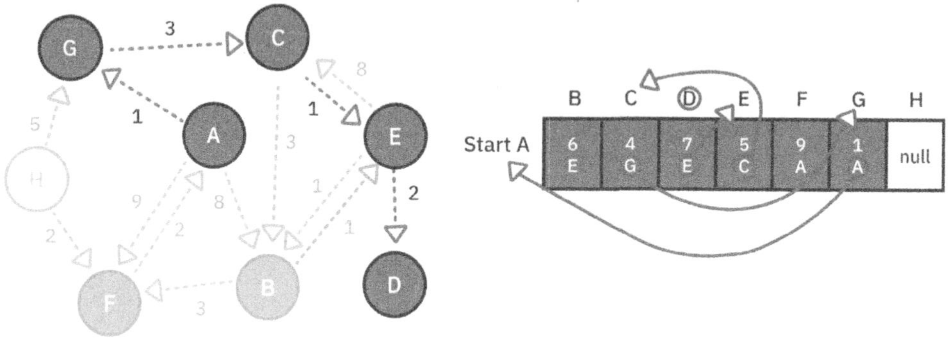

Backtrack from D to A

It's time to express these ideas in code now.

Implementation

Implementing Dijkstra's algorithm brings together a lot of the previous concepts that you've learned in this book. Besides the basic data structures of lists, maps and sets, you'll also use a priority queue, which itself is made from a min-heap, which is a partially sorted binary tree.

Open up the **starter** project for this chapter. The **lib** folder has an adjacency list graph and a priority queue.

You'll use the priority queue to store the vertices that haven't been visited. The queue uses a min-priority heap, which allows you to dequeue the shortest known path in every pass.

Creating Distance-Vertex Pairs

In the example diagrams above, you saw that the tables contained a distance-vertex pair for every destination vertex. You'll implement a class for this now to make it easier to pass these values around.

Create a new file in **lib** named **dijkstra.dart** and add the following code to it:

```
import 'graph.dart';

class Pair<T> implements Comparable<Pair<T>> {
  Pair(this.distance, [this.vertex]);

  double distance;
  Vertex<T>? vertex;

  @override
  int compareTo(Pair<T> other) {
    if (distance == other.distance) return 0;
    if (distance > other.distance) return 1;
    return -1;
  }

  @override
  String toString() => '($distance, $vertex)';
}
```

`Pair` extends `Comparable` because Dijkstra's algorithm hands the distance-vertex pairs to a priority queue. The internal heap requires comparable elements so that it can sort them. The comparison here is performed solely on the distance. Dijkstra will be on the lookout for the shortest distances.

Setting Up a Class for Dijkstra's Algorithm

Add the following class to **dijkstra.dart**:

```
class Dijkstra<E> {
  Dijkstra(this.graph);

  final Graph<E> graph;
}
```

`Dijkstra` allows you to pass in any graph that implements the `Graph` interface.

Generating the Shortest Paths

Now you're ready to start building the actual algorithm.

Initializing Dijkstra's Algorithm

First, import the file with your priority queue data structure at the top of **dijkstra.dart**:

```
import 'priority_queue.dart';
```

Then add the following method to `Dijkstra`:

```
Map<Vertex<E>, Pair<E>?> shortestPaths(Vertex<E> source) {
  // 1
  final queue = PriorityQueue<Pair<E>>(priority: Priority.min);
  final visited = <Vertex<E>>{};
  final paths = <Vertex<E>, Pair<E>?>{};
  // 2
  for (final vertex in graph.vertices) {
    paths[vertex] = null;
  }
  // 3
  queue.enqueue(Pair(0, source));
  paths[source] = Pair(0);
  visited.add(source);

  // more to come

  return paths;
}
```

This method takes in a `source` vertex and returns a map of all the paths. You begin the algorithm with the following content:

1. There are three data structures to help you out. The **priority queue** `queue` will allow you to visit the shortest route next in each pass. The **set** `visited` isn't strictly necessary, but using it will prevent you from unnecessarily checking vertices that you've already visited before. Finally, you'll use the **map** `paths` to store the distance and previous vertex information for every vertex in the graph. Building `paths` is what this method is all about.
2. Initialize every vertex in the graph with a `null` distance-vertex pair.

3. Initialize the algorithm with the source vertex. This is where the search will start from, so the distance to this vertex is zero. `queue` holds the *current* vertex, while `paths` stores a reference to the *previous* vertex. Since the source vertex doesn't have a previous vertex, using `Pair(0)` causes the previous vertex to default to `null`.

Visiting a New Vertex

Continue your implementation of `shortestPaths` by replacing the `// more to come` comment with the following `while` loop. Each loop handles visiting a new vertex:

```
// 1
while (!queue.isEmpty) {
  final current = queue.dequeue()!;
  // 2
  final savedDistance = paths[current.vertex]!.distance;
  if (current.distance > savedDistance) continue;
  // 3
  visited.add(current.vertex!);

  // more to come
}
```

This is how Dijkstra's algorithm works here:

1. The queue holds the vertices that are known but haven't been visited yet. As long as the queue isn't empty, you're not done exploring!
2. Later on, you'll decrease the distances of certain paths as you find shorter routes. However, if you update the distance in `paths`, you should really update the same distance in `queue`. The problem is, your priority queue doesn't have a way to do that. Don't forget that the internal heap needs to maintain its min-heap property. Instead of implementing any new features in the priority queue, though, you'll just add the same vertex again with a new distance. When the old, obsolete distance-vertex pair comes through, the code at `// 2` will ignore it.
3. Add the current vertex to the `visited` set so you can skip over it later. You already know the shortest route to this vertex.

Looping Over Outgoing Edges

You're almost done. Now replace the `// more to come` comment inside the `while` loop with the following code. This `for` loop iterates over the outgoing edges of the current vertex:

```
for (final edge in graph.edges(current.vertex!)) {
  final neighbor = edge.destination;
  // 1
  if (visited.contains(neighbor)) continue;
  // 2
  final weight = edge.weight ?? double.infinity;
  final totalDistance = current.distance + weight;
  // 3
  final knownDistance = paths[neighbor]?.distance
    ?? double.infinity;
  // 4
  if (totalDistance < knownDistance) {
    paths[neighbor] = Pair(totalDistance, current.vertex);
    queue.enqueue(Pair(totalDistance, neighbor));
  }
}
```

Here's what's happening:

1. If you've previously visited the destination vertex, then ignore it and go on.
2. Find the total distance from the source to the neighboring vertex.
3. Compare the known distance to that vertex with the new total you just calculated. Newly discovered vertices will get a default distance of infinity.
4. If you've found a shorter route this time around, then update `paths` and enqueue this vertex for visiting later. No worries if the same vertex is already enqueued. You'll discard the obsolete one when it shows up.

Once all the discoverable vertices have been visited and the priority queue is empty, you return the map of the shortest paths. Dijkstra's algorithm is complete.

Trying it Out

Navigate to **bin/starter.dart** and replace the contents of the file with the following code:

```
import 'package:starter/dijkstra.dart';
import 'package:starter/graph.dart';

void main() {
  final graph = AdjacencyList<String>();

  final a = graph.createVertex('A');
  final b = graph.createVertex('B');
  final c = graph.createVertex('C');
  final d = graph.createVertex('D');
  final e = graph.createVertex('E');
  final f = graph.createVertex('F');
  final g = graph.createVertex('G');
  final h = graph.createVertex('H');

  graph.addEdge(a, b, weight: 8, edgeType: EdgeType.directed);
  graph.addEdge(a, f, weight: 9, edgeType: EdgeType.directed);
  graph.addEdge(a, g, weight: 1, edgeType: EdgeType.directed);
  graph.addEdge(g, c, weight: 3, edgeType: EdgeType.directed);
  graph.addEdge(c, b, weight: 3, edgeType: EdgeType.directed);
  graph.addEdge(c, e, weight: 1, edgeType: EdgeType.directed);
  graph.addEdge(e, b, weight: 1, edgeType: EdgeType.directed);
  graph.addEdge(e, d, weight: 2, edgeType: EdgeType.directed);
  graph.addEdge(b, e, weight: 1, edgeType: EdgeType.directed);
  graph.addEdge(b, f, weight: 3, edgeType: EdgeType.directed);
  graph.addEdge(f, a, weight: 2, edgeType: EdgeType.directed);
  graph.addEdge(h, g, weight: 5, edgeType: EdgeType.directed);
  graph.addEdge(h, f, weight: 2, edgeType: EdgeType.directed);
}
```

This recreates the graph that you saw in the example at the beginning of the chapter:

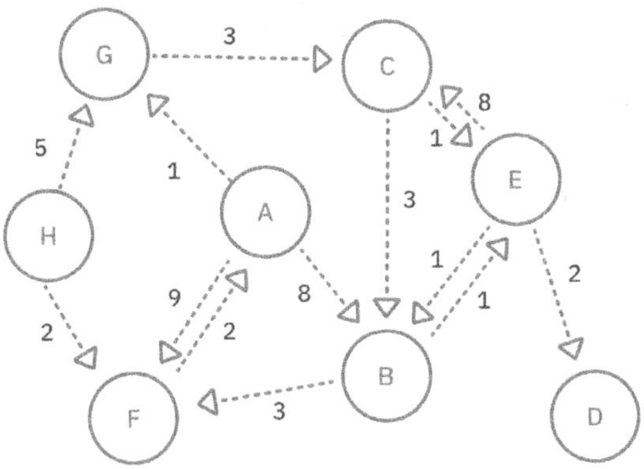

Now add the following code at the end of `main`:

```
final dijkstra = Dijkstra(graph);
final allPaths = dijkstra.shortestPaths(a);
print(allPaths);
```

Run that, and you should see the following output:

```
{A: (0.0, null), B: (6.0, E), C: (4.0, G), D: (7.0, E), E: (5.0,
C), F: (9.0, A), G: (1.0, A), H: null}
```

This matches the results that the example described earlier.

Finding a Specific Path

The `shortestPaths` method found the shortest route to *all* of the other reachable vertices. Often you just want the shortest path to a *single* destination, though. You'll add one more method to accomplish that.

Return to **lib/dijkstra.dart** and add the following method to `Dijkstra`:

```
List<Vertex<E>> shortestPath(
  Vertex<E> source,
  Vertex<E> destination, {
  Map<Vertex<E>, Pair<E>?>? paths,
}) {
  // 1
  final allPaths = paths ?? shortestPaths(source);
  // 2
  if (!allPaths.containsKey(destination)) return [];
  var current = destination;
  final path = <Vertex<E>>[current];
  // 3
  while (current != source) {
    final previous = allPaths[current]?.vertex;
    if (previous == null) return [];
    path.add(previous);
    current = previous;
  }
  // 4
  return path.reversed.toList();
}
```

After providing the source and destinations vertices to this method, here's what happens:

1. You find all of the paths. Providing `paths` as an argument is an optimization if you need to call `shortestPath` multiple times on the same graph. No need to recalculate Dijkstra's algorithm over and over.
2. Ensure that a path actually exists.
3. Build the path by working backwards from the destination.
4. Since you built the list by starting from the back, you need to reverse the list before returning it.

Trying it Out

Open **bin/starter.dart** and add the following two lines at the end of `main`:

```
final path = dijkstra.shortestPath(a, d);
print(path);
```

Run your code again and you should see the ordered list of vertices showing the shortest path from **A** to **D**:

```
[A, G, C, E, D]
```

Just like in the example!

Performance

When performing Dijkstra's algorithm, you need to visit every edge. That means the time complexity is at least O(E). After visiting an edge, you add the destination vertex to a priority queue if the distance for this edge is shorter. However, in a worst-case scenario where every edge is shorter that the previous ones, you'd still have to enqueue a vertex for every edge. Since enqueuing and dequeuing with your heap-based priority queue has a logarithmic time complexity, this operation would be O(log E). Repeating that for every edge would thus be O(E log E).

What about when you visited all of the vertices at the beginning of the algorithm to set the paths to `null`? That operation was O(V), so you could say the overall time complexity is O(V + E log E). However, you can assume that for a connected graph, V will be less than or approximately equal to E. That means you can replace O(V + E log E) with O(E + E log E). You can rearrange that as O(E × (1 + log E)). Then drop the 1 to again leave you with O(E log E). Remember that Big O notation is just a generalized way to talk about the complexity of an algorithm as the number of components increases. Constant values can be ignored.

> **Note**: Special thanks to bradfieldcs.com for inspiration on the algorithm used in this chapter and to Google Engineer David Eisenstat on Stack Overflow for help analyzing the complexity. See the following links for details:
>
> https://bradfieldcs.com/algos/graphs/dijkstras-algorithm
>
> https://stackoverflow.com/a/70436868

Challenges

Here are a few challenges to help you practice your new knowledge about Dijkstra's algorithm. As always, you can find the answers in the Challenge Solutions section at the back of the book as well as in the downloadable supplemental materials.

Challenge 1: Dijkstra Step-by-Step

Given the following graph, step through Dijkstra's algorithm yourself to produce the shortest path to every other vertex starting from vertex **A**.

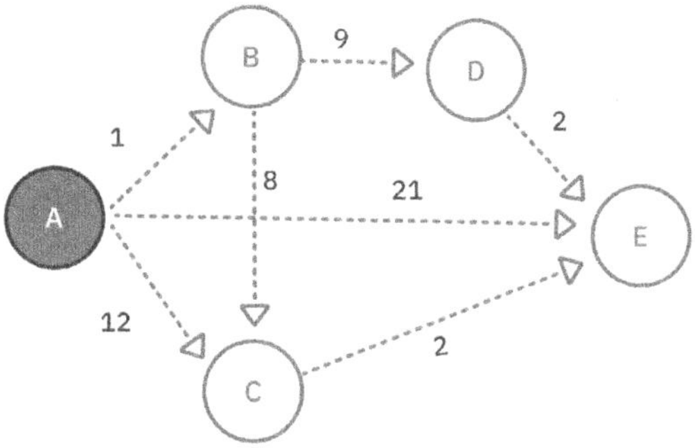

Challenge 2: Find All the Shortest Paths

Add an extension on `Dijkstra` that returns all the shortest paths in list form from a given starting vertex. Here's the method signature to get you started:

```
Map<Vertex<E>, List<Vertex<E>>> shortestPathsLists(
  Vertex<E> source,
)
```

Key Points

- Dijkstra's algorithm finds the shortest path from a starting vertex to the rest of the vertices in a graph.
- The algorithm is greedy, meaning it chooses the shortest path at each step.
- The priority queue data structure helps to efficiently return the vertex with the shortest path.

25 Conclusion

Congratulations! You've made it to the end of the book. You have a solid foundation now in data structures and algorithms. Even so, there's still a lot more to learn. Don't let that scare you, though. Each new data structure and algorithm will be its own adventure.

Approaching a Difficult Problem

At times, you may not even know what data structure or algorithm you should use to solve a particular problem. Here are a few ideas to help with that:

- Draw a diagram to model the issue.
- Talk through the problem with another developer.
- Just get started by writing some code that "works", even if it's horribly slow and inefficient.
- Analyze what the time and space complexity are of your current implementation. How could they be improved?
- Step through your current implementation line by line in a debugger. This often shows you useless tasks that your algorithm is performing.
- Keep reading and watching videos about data structures and algorithms that you're unfamiliar with. The more you know, the more naturally a solution will pop into your head when you come up against a hard problem.

Learning Tips

Whenever you hear about a new data structure or algorithm that you'd like to learn, here are some steps you can take to maximize your learning experience:

1. Try to get an intuitive grasp of how the data is structured or how the algorithm works. Find illustrations or videos that describe it well. Draw yourself pictures or manipulate objects such as playing cards.
2. After you understand the data structure or algorithm on a conceptual level, try to implement it in code by yourself. Don't look at other people's implementations just yet. Imagine that you're a computer scientist in the 1950s!
3. Finally, check out the implementations in other languages like C or Java or Python. Then convert them to Dart.

Where to Go From Here?

Don't know what to study next? Here are some suggestions:

- Try out the **A* pathfinding algorithm**. Dijkstra's algorithm is good for finding *all* the shortest paths in a graph, but it does a lot of unnecessary work if you only need the single shortest path between two vertices.
- Many online sites provide provide coding challenges to improve your algorithmic thinking. One such example is codeforces.com. Start with the easier problems and work up to the more challenging ones.

If you have any questions or comments as you work through this book, please stop by our forums at https://forums.kodeco.com and look for the particular forum category for this book.

Thank you again for purchasing this book. Your continued support is what makes the books, tutorials, videos and other things we do at Kodeco possible. We truly appreciate it!

– The *Data Structures & Algorithms in Dart* team

Section VI: Challenge Solutions

This section contains all of the solutions to the challenges throughout the book. They're printed here for your convenience and to aid your understanding, but you'll receive the most benefit if you attempt to solve the challenges yourself before looking at the answers.

The code for all of the solutions is also available for download in the supplemental materials that accompany this book.

Chapter 4 Solutions

Solution to Challenge 1

One of the prime use cases for stacks is to facilitate backtracking. If you push a sequence of values into the stack, sequentially popping the stack will give you the values in reverse order.

```
void printInReverse<E>(List<E> list) {
  var stack = Stack<E>();

  for (E value in list) {
    stack.push(value);
  }

  while (stack.isNotEmpty) {
    print(stack.pop());
  }
}
```

If you try it with `['d', 'r', 'a', 'w', 'e', 'r']` you'll get a reward. :]

The time complexity of pushing all list elements into the stack is O(n). The time complexity of popping the stack to print the values is also O(n). Overall, the time complexity of this algorithm is O(n).

Since you're allocating a container (the stack) inside the function, you also incur an O(n) space complexity cost.

> **Note**: The way you should reverse a list in production code is to call the `reversed` method that `List` provides. This method is O(1) in time and space. This is because, as an iterable, it's **lazy** and only creates a reversed view into the original collection. If you traverse the items and print out all of the elements, it predictably makes the operation O(n) in time while remaining O(1) in space.

Solution to Challenge 2

To check if there are balanced parentheses in the string, you need to go through each string character. When you encounter an opening parenthesis, you'll push that onto a stack. Conversely, if you encounter a closing parenthesis, you should pop the stack.

Here's what the code looks like:

```
bool areParenthesesBalanced(String text) {
  var stack = Stack<String>();
  for (int i = 0; i < text.length; i++) {
    final character = text[i];
    if (character == '(') {
      stack.push(character);
    } else if (character == ')') {
      if (stack.isEmpty) {
        return false;
      } else {
        stack.pop();
      }
    }
  }
  return stack.isEmpty;
}
```

The time complexity of this algorithm is O(n), where *n* is the number of code units in the string. This algorithm also incurs an O(n) space complexity cost due to using the `Stack` data structure.

Chapter 5 Solutions

Solution to Challenge 1

One solution is to have two references traverse down the list nodes, where one is twice as fast as the other. Once the faster reference reaches the end, the slower reference will be in the middle. Update the function to the following:

```
Node<E>? getMiddle<E>(LinkedList<E> list) {
  var slow = list.head;
  var fast = list.head;

  while (fast?.next != null) {
    fast = fast?.next?.next;
    slow = slow?.next;
  }

  return slow;
}
```

In the `while` loop, `fast` checks the next two nodes, while `slow` only gets one. This is known as the **runner's technique**.

Write the following in your `main` function:

```
var list = LinkedList<int>();
list.push(3);
list.push(2);
list.push(1);
print(list);

final middleNode = getMiddle(list);
print('Middle: ${middleNode?.value}');
```

You should see the following output:

```
1 -> 2 -> 3
Middle: 2
```

The time complexity of this algorithm is O(n) since you traversed the list in a single pass. The runner's technique helps solve a variety of problems associated with a linked list.

Solution to Challenge 2

To reverse a linked list, you must visit each node and update the `next` reference to point in the other direction. This can be a tricky task since you'll need to manage multiple references to multiple nodes.

The Easy Way

You can trivially reverse a list by using the `push` method along with a new temporary list. Either add a `reverse` method to `LinkedList` or create an extension like so:

```
extension ReversibleLinkedList<E> on LinkedList<E> {
  void reverse() {
    final tempList = LinkedList<E>();
    for (final value in this) {
      tempList.push(value);
    }
    head = tempList.head;
  }
}
```

You first start by pushing the current values in your list to a new temporary list. This will create a list in reverse order. After that, point the `head` of the list to the reversed nodes.

O(n) time complexity, short and sweet!

But Wait...

Although O(n) is the optimal time complexity for reversing a list, there's a significant resource cost in the previous solution. As it is now, `reverse` will have to allocate new nodes for each `push` method on the temporary list. You can avoid using the temporary list entirely and reverse the list by manipulating the `next` pointers of each node. The code ends up being more complicated, but you reap considerable benefits in terms of performance.

Replace the reverse method with the following:

```
void reverse() {
  tail = head;
  var previous = head;
  var current = head?.next;
  previous?.next = null;

  // more to come...
}
```

You begin by assigning `head` to `tail`. Next, you create two references — `previous` and `current` — to keep track of traversal. The strategy is fairly straightforward: each node points to the next node down the list. You'll traverse the list and make each node point to the previous node instead:

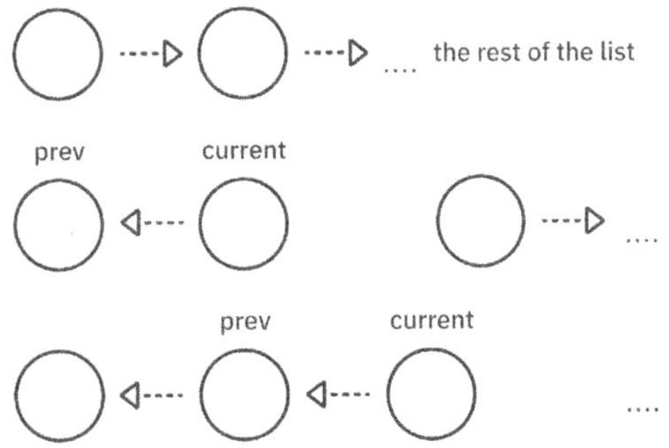

As you can see from the diagram, it gets a little tricky. By pointing `current` to `previous`, you've lost the link to the rest of the list. Therefore, you'll need to manage a third pointer. Add the following at the bottom of the `reverse` method:

```
while (current != null) {
  final next = current.next;
  current.next = previous;
  previous = current;
  current = next;
}
```

Each time you perform the reversal, you create a new reference to the next node. After every reversal procedure, you move the two pointers to the next two nodes.

Once you've finished reversing all the pointers, you'll set the `head` to the last node of this list. Add the following at the end of the `reverse` method:

```
head = previous;
```

Try it Out!

Test the `reverse` method by writing the following in `main`:

```
var list = LinkedList<int>();
list.push(3);
list.push(2);
list.push(1);

print('Original list: $list');
list.reverse();
print('Reversed list: $list');
```

You should see the following output:

```
Original list: 1 -> 2 -> 3
Reversed list: 3 -> 2 -> 1
```

The time complexity of your new `reverse` method is still O(n), the same as the trivial implementation discussed earlier. However, you didn't need to use a temporary list or allocate any new `Node` objects, which significantly improves the performance of this algorithm.

Solution to Challenge 3

This solution traverses down the list, removing all nodes that match the element you want to remove. Each time you perform a removal, you need to reconnect the predecessor node with the successor node. While this can get complicated, it's well worth it to practice this technique. Many data structures and algorithms will rely on clever uses of pointer arithmetic.

There are a few cases you need to consider. The first case to consider is when the head of the list contains the value that you want to remove.

Trimming the Head

Suppose you want to remove **1** from the following list:

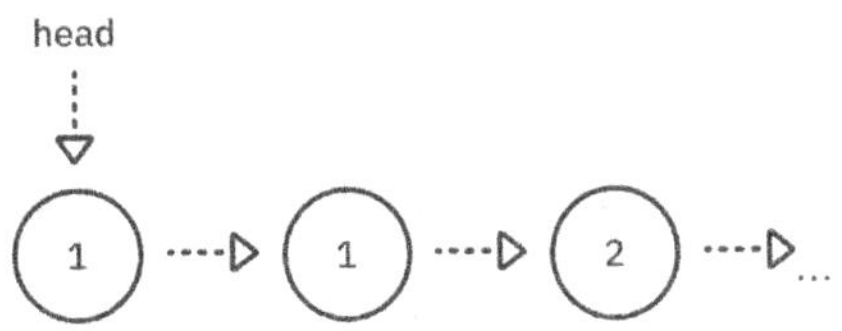

You'd want your new head to point to **2**.

Create an extension on `LinkedList` and add a `removeAll` method to it:

```
extension RemovableLinkedList<E> on LinkedList<E> {
  void removeAll(E value) {

  }
}
```

Then add the following `while` loop to `removeAll`:

```
while (head != null && head!.value == value) {
  head = head!.next;
}
```

Since it's possible to have a sequence of nodes with the same value, the `while` loop ensures that you remove them all. The loop will finish if you get to the end of the list or when the value is different.

Unlinking the Nodes

Like many of the algorithms associated with linked lists, you'll leverage your pointer arithmetic skills to unlink the nodes. Write the following at the bottom of `removeAll`:

```
var previous = head;
var current = head?.next;
while (current != null) {
  if (current.value == value) {
    previous?.next = current.next;
    current = previous?.next;
    continue;
  }
  // more to come
}
```

You need to traverse the list using two pointers: `previous` and `next`. The `if` block will trigger if it's necessary to remove a node.

You modify the list so that you bypass the node you don't want:

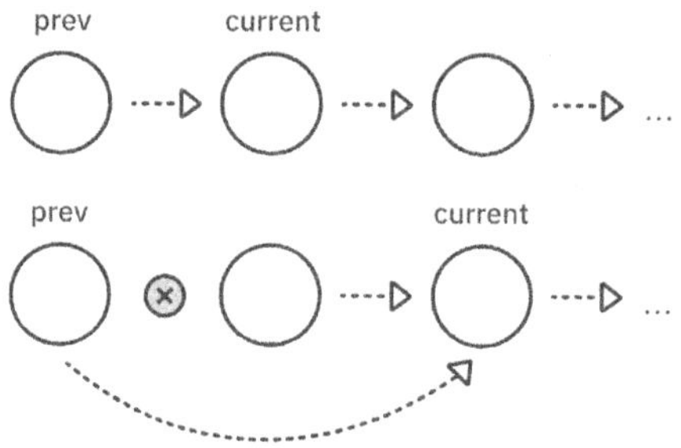

Keep Traveling...

Can you tell what's missing? As it is right now, the `while` loop may never terminate. You need to move the `previous` and `current` pointers along. Write the following at the bottom of the `while` loop, replacing the `// more to come` comment:

```
previous = current;
current = current.next;
```

Finally, you'll update the `tail` of the linked list. This is necessary when the original tail is a node containing the value you wanted to remove. Add the following to the end of `removeAll`:

```
tail = previous;
```

And that's it for the implementation!

Try it Out!

Write the following in `main`:

```
final list = LinkedList<int>();
list.push(3);
list.push(2);
list.push(2);
list.push(1);
list.push(1);

list.removeAll(3);
print(list);
```

You should see the following output:

```
1 -> 1 -> 2 -> 2
```

This algorithm has a time complexity of O(n) since you need to go through all the elements.

Chapter 6 Solutions

Solution to Challenge 1

Queues have a behavior of first-in-first-out. What comes in first must come out first. Items in the queue are inserted from the rear and removed from the front.

Queue Examples:

1. **Line in a movie theatre**: You would hate for people to cut the line at the movie theatre when buying tickets!
2. **Printer**: Multiple people could print documents from a printer in a similar first-come-first-serve manner.

Stacks have a behavior of last-in-first-out. Items on the stack are inserted at the top and removed from the top.

Stack Examples:

1. **Stack of plates**: You stack plates on top of each other and remove the top plate every time you use one. Isn't this easier than grabbing the one at the bottom?
2. **Undo functionality**: Imagine typing words on a keyboard. Clicking Ctrl-Z will undo the most recent text you typed.

Solution to Challenge 2

List

Keep in mind that whenever the list is full, and you try to add a new element, a new list will be created with twice the capacity and existing elements will be copied over.

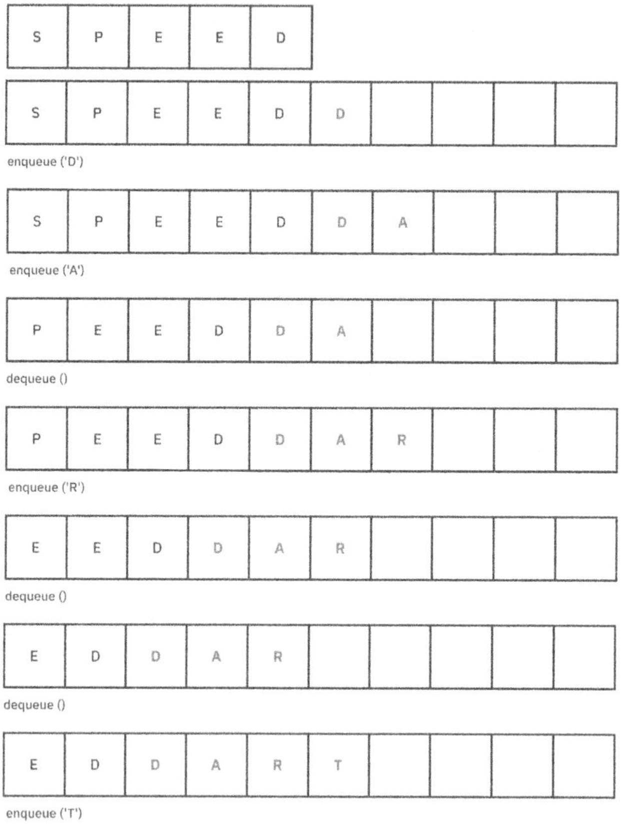

Linked List

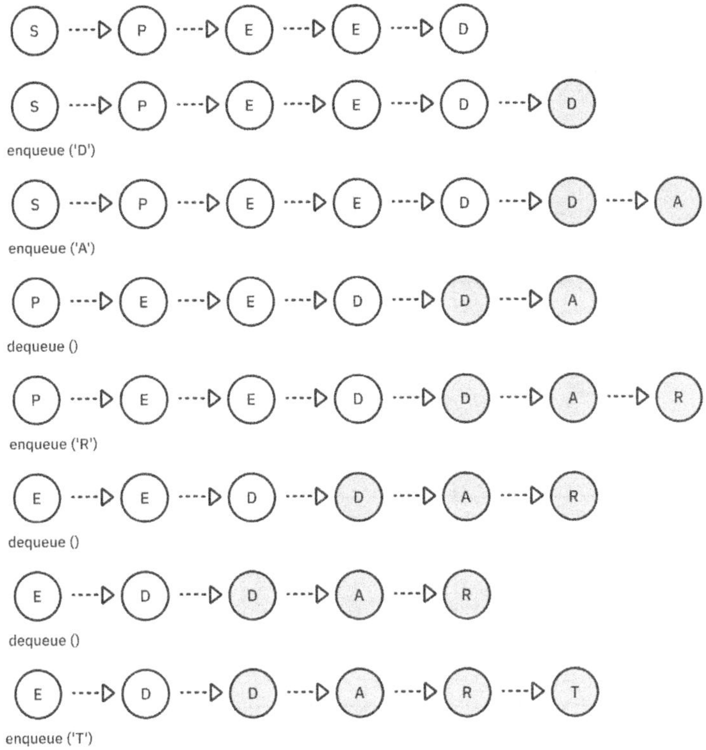
S P E E D
S P E E D D
enqueue ('D')
S P E E D D A
enqueue ('A')
P E E D D A
dequeue ()
P E E D D A R
enqueue ('R')
E E D D A R
dequeue ()
E D D A R
dequeue ()
E D D A R T
enqueue ('T')

Ring Buffer

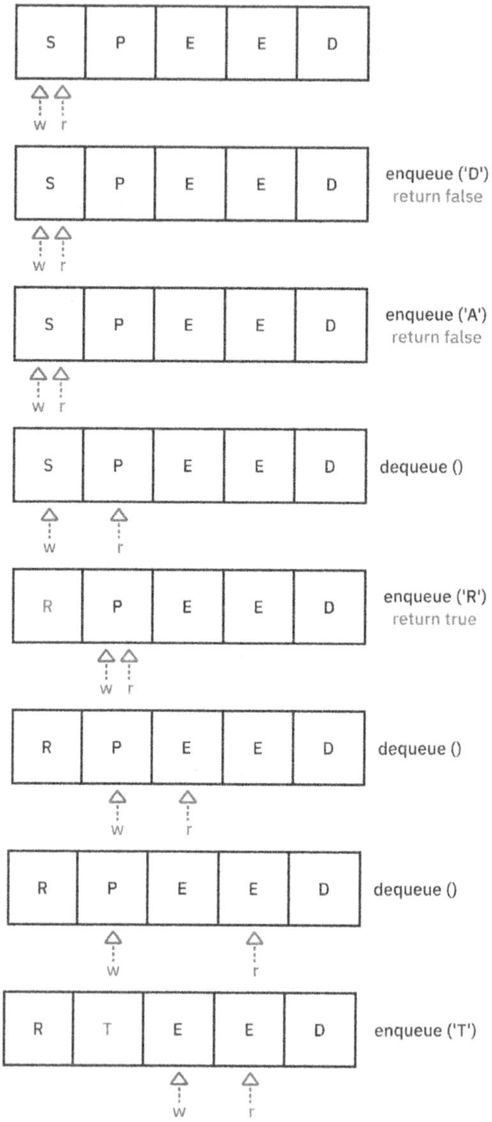
S
P
E
E
D
w
r
enqueue ('D')
return false
enqueue ('A')
return false
dequeue ()
R
enqueue ('R')
return true
dequeue ()
dequeue ()
T
enqueue ('T')

Double Stack

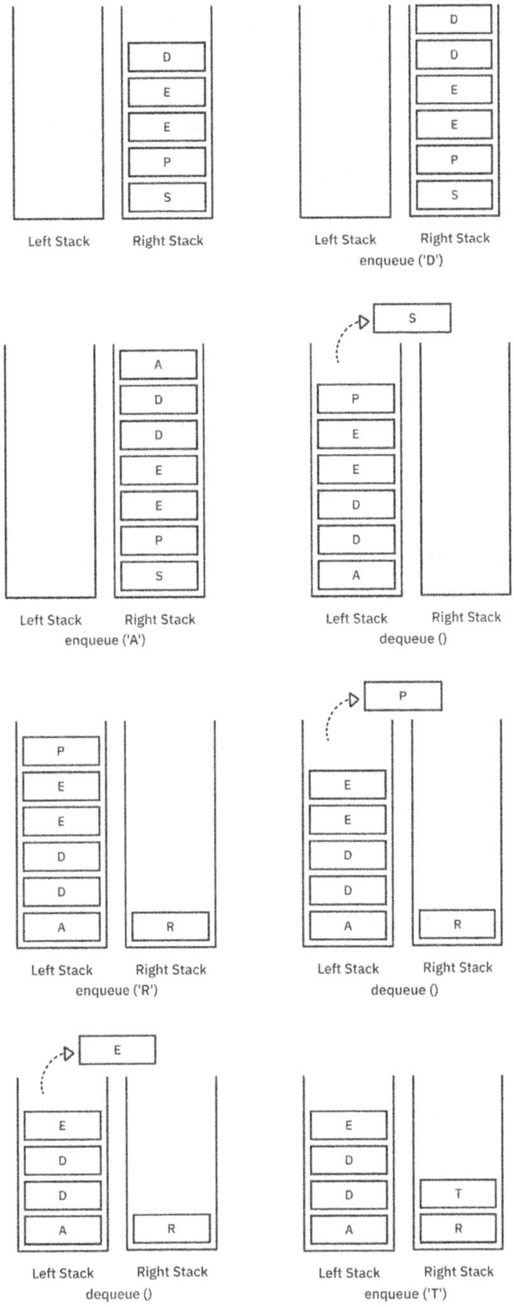

Solution to Challenge 3

Creating a board game manager is straightforward. All you care about is whose turn it is. A queue data structure is the perfect choice for that!

```
extension BoardGameManager<E> on QueueRingBuffer<E> {
  E? nextPlayer() {
    final person = dequeue();
    if (person != null) {
      enqueue(person);
    }
    return person;
  }
}
```

Dequeuing a player tells you who is next. Enqueuing them again puts them at the back of the queue.

For the small number of players you're dealing with in a Monopoly game, you aren't going to have any noticeable performance difference no matter what queue type you choose. However, a ring-buffer-based queue is great for Monopoly since there are a set number of players and you don't need to worry about overfilling the buffer.

Test it out:

```
final monopolyTurn = QueueRingBuffer<String>(4);
monopolyTurn.enqueue('Ray');
monopolyTurn.enqueue('Vicki');
monopolyTurn.enqueue('Luke');
monopolyTurn.enqueue('Pablo');

String? player;
for (var i = 1; i <= 20; i++) {
  player = monopolyTurn.nextPlayer();
  print(player);
}
print('$player wins!');
```

Solution to Challenge 4

Deque is made up of common operations from the Queue and Stack data structures. There are many ways to implement a Deque. The solution below makes use of a linked list to construct a Deque.

First setup the linked list deque as shown below:

```
class DequeLinkedList<E> implements Deque<E> {
  final _list = LinkedList<E>();

}
```

Now you have to conform to the Deque interface. First, implement isEmpty by checking if the linked list is empty. This is an O(1) operation.

```
@override
bool get isEmpty => _list.isEmpty;
```

Next, you need a way to look at the value from the front or back of the Deque.

```
@override
E? peek(Direction from) {
  switch (from) {
    case Direction.front:
      return _list.head?.value;
    case Direction.back:
      return _list.tail?.value;
  }
}
```

To peek at the element from the front or back, check the list's head and tail values. This is an O(1) operation.

Now you need a way to add elements to the front or back of `Deque`.

```
@override
bool enqueue(E value, Direction to) {
  switch (to) {
    case Direction.front:
      _list.push(value);
      break;
    case Direction.back:
      _list.append(value);
      break;
  }
  return true;
}
```

Adding an element to the front or back of `Deque`:

1. **Front**: push an element to the front of the list. Internally the linked list will update the new node as the head of the linked list.
2. **Back**: append an element to the back of the list. Similarly, the linked list will update the new node as the tail of the linked list.

These are both O(1) operations since all you have to do is update the internal pointers.

Now that you have a way to add elements, how about a way to remove elements?

```
@override
E? dequeue(Direction from) {
  switch (from) {
    case Direction.front:
      return _list.pop();
    case Direction.back:
      return _list.removeLast();
  }
}
```

Removing an element from the front or back of a `Deque` is simple:

1. **Front**: Call `pop` to remove the `head` node in the list.
2. **Back**: Similarly, call `removeLast` to remove the `tail`.

Note: If you recall from Chapter 5, "Linked Lists", `pop` is an O(1) operation, but `removeLast` is an O(n) operation. That's unfortunate because users of your `Deque` are probably expecting dequeue to be O(1) no matter which direction they choose. One solution would be to replace `LinkedList` with `DoublyLinkedList`, which you can find in the Chapter 5 challenge folder in the supplemental materials. A doubly linked list has O(1) performance for `removeLast`. Another solution would be to use a double stack. If you chose one of those already, good for you!

Lastly, override `toString` so you can test your `Deque`.

```
@override
String toString() => _list.toString();
```

Add the following code to `main` to test your implementation:

```
final deque = DequeDoublyLinkedList<int>();
deque.enqueue(1, Direction.back);
deque.enqueue(2, Direction.back);
deque.enqueue(3, Direction.back);
deque.enqueue(4, Direction.back);

print(deque);

deque.enqueue(5, Direction.front);

print(deque);

deque.dequeue(Direction.back);
deque.dequeue(Direction.back);
deque.dequeue(Direction.back);
deque.dequeue(Direction.front);
deque.dequeue(Direction.front);
deque.dequeue(Direction.front);

print(deque);
```

Run that, and you'll see the following in the console:

```
1 -> 2 -> 3 -> 4
5 -> 1 -> 2 -> 3 -> 4
Empty list
```

Chapter 7 Solutions

Solution to Exercise 1

One way to count by fives to 100 iteratively is like so:

```
for (int i = 5; i <= 100; i += 5) {
  print(i);
}
```

You can accomplish the same task recursively like this:

```
void countByFivesRecursively([int i = 5]) {
  if (i > 100) return;
  print(i);
  countByFivesRecursively(i + 5);
}
```

Solution to Exercise 2

You can print the square integers up to 100 iteratively using a while loop:

```
int i = 1;
int square = 1;
while (square <= 100) {
  print(square);
  i++;
  square = i * i;
}
```

Here is how you would accomplish the same task recursively:

```
void printSquaresRecursively([int i = 1]) {
  final square = i * i;
  if (square > 100) return;
  print(square);
  printSquaresRecursively(i + 1);
}
```

Solution to Challenge 1

1. A computer's file system uses a tree-like structure of folders and files. To print every file name, you would need to backtrack after completing the files in any particular folder. So **recursion** would be an appropriate solution.
2. There is nothing especially tree-like about calculating a factorial, so using **iteration** would be just fine.
3. While a family tree is indeed tree-like, no backtracking is needed to follow the matrilineal line, so **iteration** would be sufficient.
4. JSON uses a tree-like structure with nested objects and arrays. To navigate in and out of them, backtracking would be required. So **recursion** would be an appropriate solution here.

Solution to Challenge 2

First, you count the current rabbit, and then you recursively add any babies it has. The base case is when a rabbit has no babies, or you've finished iterating through them.

```
int countSize(Rabbit family) {
  int count = 1;
  final babies = family.babies;
  if (babies != null) {
    for (final baby in babies) {
      count += countSize(baby);
    }
  }
  return count;
}
```

Solution to Challenge 3

Although you could use a map, an efficient solution would be to use a list to cache the numbers of the Fibonacci sequence that you've already calculated. The index is *n*, and the value is the number in the sequence.

```
// 1
final List<int> _memo = [0, 1, 1];

int fibonacci(int n) {
  // 2
  if (n < _memo.length) {
    return _memo[n];
  }
  // 3
  for (int i = _memo.length; i <= n; i++) {
    int temp = _memo[i - 1] + _memo[i - 2];
    _memo.add(temp);
  }

  return _memo[n];
}
```

Here are a few notes:

1. Initialize the list with the first three Fibonacci values.
2. If your cached value is already in the list, you can return it immediately with an O(1) time complexity.
3. For new Fibonacci numbers that are not yet in the list, you must calculate the values. This has an O(n) time complexity, but since you cache every value leading up to it, you'll only need to do this once.

If you only ever call `fibonacci` once, it'll still have a linear time complexity, but since future calls for values of *n* less than or equal to previous ones have a constant time, the overall efficiency will average out to constant time. This is also known as **amortized** constant time.

One more thing to be aware of is that for any value of *n* higher than 92, a signed 64-bit integer will overflow.

Chapter 8 Solutions

Solution to Challenge 1

A straightforward way to print the nodes in level-order is to leverage the level-order traversal using a `Queue` data structure. The tricky bit is determining when a newline should occur. For that, it would be useful to know the number of elements in the queue. The queues you made in the last chapter don't have a `length` property, but you can add one now.

Open your `QueueStack` implementation and add the following line:

```
int get length => _leftStack.length + _rightStack.length;
```

You implemented the double-stack queue using two lists, so finding the length is still an O(1) operation. This would not be true if you used the linked-list implementation.

Now you're ready to deal with the challenge:

```
void printEachLevel<T>(TreeNode<T> tree) {
  final result = StringBuffer();
  // 1
  var queue = QueueStack<TreeNode<T>>();
  var nodesLeftInCurrentLevel = 0;
  queue.enqueue(tree);
  // 2
  while (!queue.isEmpty) {
    // 3
    nodesLeftInCurrentLevel = queue.length;
    // 4
    while (nodesLeftInCurrentLevel > 0) {
      final node = queue.dequeue();
      if (node == null) break;
      result.write('${node.value} ');
      for (var element in node.children) {
        queue.enqueue(element);
      }
      nodesLeftInCurrentLevel -= 1;
    }
    // 5
    result.write('\n');
  }
  print(result);
}
```

1. You begin by initializing a `Queue` data structure to facilitate the level-order traversal. You also create `nodesLeftInCurrentLevel` to keep track of the number of nodes you'll need to work on before you print a new line.

2. Your level-order traversal continues until your queue is empty.

3. Inside the first `while` loop, you begin by setting `nodesLeftInCurrentLevel` to the number of current elements in the queue.

4. Using another `while` loop, you dequeue the first `nodesLeftInCurrentLevel` number of elements from the queue. Every element you dequeue is added to `result` *without* establishing a new line. You also enqueue all the children of the node.

5. At this point, you append a new line to `result`. In the next iteration, `nodesLeftInCurrentLevel` will be updated with the count of the queue, representing the number of children from the previous iteration.

This algorithm has a time complexity of O(n). Since you initialize the `Queue` data structure as an intermediary container, this algorithm also uses O(n) space.

Solution to Challenge 2

When building a UI widget tree it's easier if you can pass the children in as parameters in the constructor. Here is one version of what the nodes could look like:

```
class Widget {}

class Column extends Widget {
  Column({this.children});
  List<Widget>? children;
}

class Padding extends Widget {
  Padding({this.value = 0.0, this.child});
  double value;
  Widget? child;
}

class Text extends Widget {
  Text([this.value = '']);
  String value;
}
```

Now you can easily build a Flutter-like widget tree:

```
final tree = Column(
  children: [
    Padding(
      value: 8.0,
      child: Text('This'),
    ),
    Padding(
      value: 8.0,
      child: Text('is'),
    ),
    Column(
      children: [
        Text('my'),
        Text('widget'),
        Text('tree!'),
      ],
    ),
  ],
);
```

Chapter 9 Solutions

You can use the following code to create a demo tree for both challenges:

```
//    ┌──25
//    │  └──17
// 15
//    │  ┌──12
//    └──10
//       └──5
BinaryNode<int> createBinaryTree() {
  final n15 = BinaryNode(15);
  final n10 = BinaryNode(10);
  final n5 = BinaryNode(5);
  final n12 = BinaryNode(12);
  final n25 = BinaryNode(25);
  final n17 = BinaryNode(17);

  n15.leftChild = n10;
  n10.leftChild = n5;
  n10.rightChild = n12;
  n15.rightChild = n25;
  n25.leftChild = n17;

  return n15;
}
```

Solution to Challenge 1

A recursive approach for finding the height of a binary tree doesn't take much code:

```
import 'dart:math';

int height(BinaryNode<int>? node) {
  // 1
  if (node == null) return -1;

  // 2
  return 1 +
      max(
        height(node.leftChild),
        height(node.rightChild),
      );
}
```

1. This is the base case for the recursive solution. If the node is `null`, you'll return -1.
2. Here, you recursively call the `height` function. For every node you visit, you add one to the height of the highest child.

This algorithm has a time complexity of O(n) since you need to traverse through all the nodes. This algorithm incurs a space cost of O(n) since you need to make the same *n* recursive calls to the call stack.

Solution to Challenge 2

There are many ways to serialize and deserialize a binary tree. Your first task when encountering this question is to decide on the traversal strategy.

This solution will use the **pre-order** traversal strategy.

Traversal

Define the following extension in your project:

```
extension Serializable<T> on BinaryNode<T> {
  void traversePreOrderWithNull(void Function(T? value) action)
{
    action(value);
    if (leftChild == null) {
      action(null);
```

```
      } else {
        leftChild!.traversePreOrderWithNull(action);
      }
      if (rightChild == null) {
        action(null);
      } else {
        rightChild!.traversePreOrderWithNull(action);
      }
    }
  }
```

This function implements pre-order traversal. However, it differs from the `traversePreOrder` function you wrote when going through the chapter because this one performs `action` even when the children are `null`. It's essential to record those for serialization and deserialization.

As with all traversal functions, this algorithm goes through every node in the tree once, so it has a time complexity of O(n).

Serialization

For serialization, you simply traverse the tree and store the values into a list. The list elements have type `T?` since you need to keep track of the `null` nodes. Write the following function to perform the serialization:

```
List<T?> serialize<T>(BinaryNode<T> node) {
  final list = <T?>[];
  node.traversePreOrderWithNull((value) => list.add(value));
  return list;
}
```

`serialize` will return a new list containing the values of the tree in pre-order.

The time complexity of the serialization step is O(n). Since you're creating a new list, this also incurs an O(n) space cost.

Deserialization

In the serialization process, you performed a pre-order traversal and assembled the values into a list. The deserialization process is to take each value of the list and reassemble it back into a tree.

Your goal is to iterate through the list and reassemble the tree in pre-order format. Add the following function to your project:

```
// 1
BinaryNode<T>? deserialize<T>(List<T?> list) {
  // 2
  if (list.isEmpty) return null;
  final value = list.removeAt(0);
  if (value == null) return null;
  // 3
  final node = BinaryNode<T>(value);
  node.leftChild = deserialize(list);
  node.rightChild = deserialize(list);
  return node;
}
```

Here's how the code works:

1. `deserialize` takes a mutable list of values. This is important because you'll be able to make mutations to the list in each recursive step and allow future recursive calls to see the changes.
2. This is the base case. If the list is empty, you'll end recursion here. You also won't bother making any nodes for `null` values in the list.
3. You reassemble the tree by creating a node from the current value and recursively calling `deserialize` to assign nodes to the left and right children. Notice this is very similar to the pre-order traversal, except you build nodes rather than extract their values.

Your algorithm is now ready for testing! Write the following in `main`:

```
final tree = createBinaryTree();
final list = serialize(tree);
final newTree = deserialize(list);
print(newTree);
```

You should see the result below in your console:

```
  ┌── null
 ┌──25
 │ └── 17
15
 │ ┌── 12
 └──10
  └── 5
```

Your deserialized tree mirrors the original one. This is the behavior you want.

However, the time complexity of this function isn't desirable. Since you're calling `removeAt(0)` as many times as elements in the list, this algorithm has an $O(n^2)$ time complexity. Fortunately, there's an easy way to remedy that.

Write the following function just after `deserialize`:

```
BinaryNode<T>? deserializeHelper<T>(List<T?> list) {
  return deserialize(list.reversed.toList());
}
```

This is a helper function that first reverses the list before calling the main `deserialize` function. In `deserialize`, find the `removeAt(0)` function call and change it to the following:

```
final value = list.removeLast();
```

This tiny change has a big effect on performance. `removeAt(0)` is an $O(n)$ operation because, after every removal, every element after the removed element must shift left to take up the missing space. In contrast, `removeLast` is an $O(1)$ operation.

Finally, find and update the call site of `deserialize` to use the new helper function that reverses the list:

```
final tree = createBinaryTree();
final list = serialize(tree);
final newTree = deserializeHelper(list);
```

You should see the same tree before and after the deserialization process. The time complexity, though, for this solution has now improved to $O(n)$. Because you've created a new reversed list and chosen a recursive solution, this algorithm has a space complexity of $O(n)$.

Chapter 10 Solutions

Solution to Challenge 1

A binary search tree is a tree where every left child is less than its parent, and every right child is greater than or equal to its parent.

An algorithm that verifies whether a tree is a binary search tree involves going through all the nodes and checking for this property.

Write the following in your project. You'll need access to the `BinaryNode` class you created in Chapter 9.

```
import 'binary_node.dart';

extension Checker<E extends Comparable<E>> on BinaryNode<E> {
  bool isBinarySearchTree() {
    return _isBST(this, min: null, max: null);
  }

  bool _isBST(BinaryNode<E>? tree, {E? min, E? max}) {
    // 1
    if (tree == null) return true;

    // 2
    if (min != null && tree.value.compareTo(min) < 0) {
      return false;
    } else if (max != null && tree.value.compareTo(max) >= 0) {
      return false;
    }

    // 3
    return _isBST(tree.leftChild, min: min, max: tree.value) &&
        _isBST(tree.rightChild, min: tree.value, max: max);
  }
}
```

`isBinarySearchTree` is the method that you'll expose for external use. Meanwhile, the magic happens in `_isBST`, which is responsible for recursively traversing through the tree and checking that the BST rules are followed. It needs to keep track of progress via a reference to a `BinaryNode`, and also keep track of the `min` and `max` values to verify the BST rules. Here are the details:

1. This is the base case. If `tree` is `null`, there are no nodes to inspect. A `null` node is a binary search tree, so you'll return `true` in that case.

2. This is essentially a bounds check. If the current value exceeds the bounds of `min` and `max`, the current node violates binary search tree rules.

3. This statement contains the recursive calls. When traversing through the left children, the current value is passed in as the `max` value. This is because any nodes on the left side cannot be greater than the parent. Conversely, when traversing to the right, the `min` value is updated to the current value. Any nodes on the right side must be greater than or equal to the parent. If any recursive calls evaluate `false`, the `false` value will propagate back to the top.

The time complexity of this solution is O(n) since you need to traverse through the entire tree once. There is also an O(n) space cost since you're making *n* recursive calls.

Solution to Challenge 2

Testing equality is relatively straightforward. For two binary trees to be equal, both trees must have the same elements in the same order. Here's what the solution looks like:

```
bool treesEqual(BinarySearchTree first, BinarySearchTree second)
{
  return _isEqual(first.root, second.root);
}

// 1
bool _isEqual<T>(
  BinaryNode<Comparable<T>>? first,
  BinaryNode<Comparable<T>>? second,
) {
  // 2
  if (first == null || second == null) {
    return first == null && second == null;
  }
  // 3
  return first.value == second.value &&
      _isEqual(first.leftChild, second.leftChild) &&
      _isEqual(first.rightChild, second.rightChild);
}
```

The commented numbers refer to the following notes:

1. `_isEqual` will recursively check two nodes and their descendants for equality.

2. This is the base case. If one or more of the nodes are `null`, then there's no need to continue checking. If both nodes are `null`, they're equal. Otherwise, one is `null` and one isn't `null`, so they must not be equal.

3. Here, you check the value of the first and second nodes for equality. You also recursively check the left children and right children for equality.

The time complexity of this function is O(n). The space complexity of this function is also O(n).

> **Note**: Trees are mutable, and testing for equality on mutably data structures is an inherently tricky business. That's why this solution didn't have you override the == operator and `hashCode` method on `BinarySearchTree`.

Solution to Challenge 3

Your goal is to create a method that checks if the current tree contains all the elements of another tree. In other words, the values in the current tree must be a superset of the values of the other tree. Here's what the solution looks like:

```
extension Subtree<E extends Comparable<E>> on
BinarySearchTree<E> {
  bool containsSubtree(BinarySearchTree subtree) {
    // 1
    final set = <E>{};
    root?.traverseInOrder((value) {
      set.add(value);
    });

    // 2
    var isEqual = true;

    // 3
    subtree.root?.traverseInOrder((value) {
      isEqual = isEqual && set.contains(value);
    });
    return isEqual;
  }
}
```

1. You begin by inserting all the elements of the current tree into a set.
2. `isEqual` is there to store the end result. You need this because `traverseInOrder` takes a closure, and you can't directly return from inside the closure.
3. For every element in the subtree, you check if the set contains the value. If at any point `set.contains(value)` evaluates as `false`, you'll make sure `isEqual` stays `false` even if subsequent elements evaluate as `true`.

The time and space complexity for this algorithm is O(n).

Chapter 11 Solutions

Solution to Challenge 1

A perfectly balanced tree is a tree where all the leaves are in the same level, and that level is completely filled:

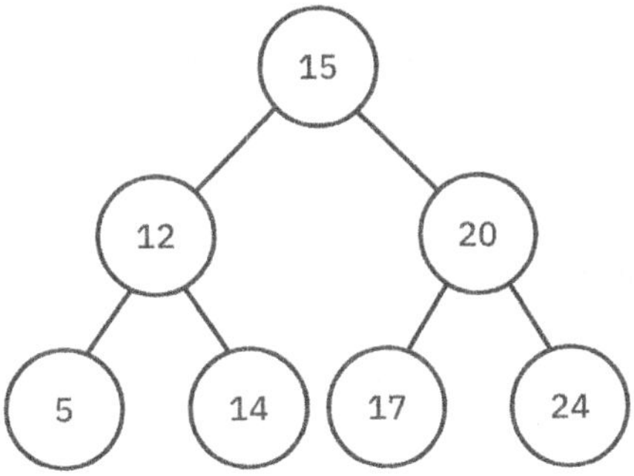

Recall that a tree with just a root node has a height of zero. Thus, the tree in the example above has a height of two. You can extrapolate that a tree with a height of three would have **eight** leaf nodes.

Since each node has two children, the number of leaf nodes doubles as the height increases. You can calculate the number of leaf nodes with a simple equation:

```
int leafNodes(int height) {
  return math.pow(2, height).toInt();
}
```

Solution to Challenge 2

Since the tree is perfectly balanced, the number of nodes in a perfectly balanced tree of height 3 can be expressed by the following:

```
int nodes(int height) {
  int nodes = 0;
  for (int h = 0; h <= height; h++) {
    nodes += math.pow(2, h).toInt();
  }
  return nodes;
}
```

Although this certainly gives you the correct answer of **15**, there's a faster way. If you examine the results of a sequence of height inputs, you'll realize that the total number of nodes is one less than the number of leaf nodes of the next level.

Thus, a faster version of this is the following:

```
int nodes(int height) {
  return math.pow(2, height + 1).toInt() - 1;
}
```

Solution to Challenge 3

First, open **avl_node.dart** and add the following interface to the top of the file:

```
abstract class TraversableBinaryNode<T> {
  T get value;
  TraversableBinaryNode<T>? get leftChild;
  TraversableBinaryNode<T>? get rightChild;

  void traverseInOrder(void Function(T value) action) {
    leftChild?.traverseInOrder(action);
    action(value);
    rightChild?.traverseInOrder(action);
  }

  void traversePreOrder(void Function(T value) action) {
    action(value);
    leftChild?.traversePreOrder(action);
    rightChild?.traversePreOrder(action);
  }

  void traversePostOrder(void Function(T value) action) {
    leftChild?.traversePostOrder(action);
    rightChild?.traversePostOrder(action);
    action(value);
  }
}
```

Next, replace the first few lines of `AvlNode` to include `TraversableBinaryNode` and the `@override` annotations:

```
class AvlNode<T> extends TraversableBinaryNode<T> {
  AvlNode(this.value);

  @override
  T value;

  @override
  AvlNode<T>? leftChild;

  @override
  AvlNode<T>? rightChild;

  // ...
```

You can also delete the traversal methods in `AvlNode` since they are already included in `TraversableBinaryNode`.

Finally, run the following to test it out:

```
import 'avl_tree.dart';

void main() {
  final tree = AvlTree<num>();
  for (var i = 0; i < 15; i++) {
    tree.insert(i);
  }
  tree.root?.traverseInOrder(print);
}
```

Verify that you're getting the following results in the console:

```
0
1
2
3
4
5
6
7
8
9
10
11
12
13
14
```

Chapter 12 Solutions

Solution to Challenge 1

You'll implement `allStrings` as a stored property. Inside `StringTrie`, add the following new property:

```
final Set<String> _allStrings = {};
Set<String> get allStrings => _allStrings;
```

This property is a `Set` that will separately store all the strings represented by the code unit collections in the trie. Making `allStrings` a getter prevents the property from being tampered with from the outside.

Next, in the `insert` method, find the line `current.isTerminating = true` and add the following below it:

```
_allStrings.add(text);
```

In the remove function, find the line `current.isTerminating = false` and add the following just below that line:

```
_allStrings.remove(text);
```

This ensures that your string set will stay in sync with the trie.

Adding the `count` and `isEmpty` properties is straightforward now that you're keeping track of all the strings:

```
int get length => _allStrings.length;

bool get isEmpty => _allStrings.isEmpty;
```

That's it!

> **Note**: Just because you can do something doesn't mean you should. Now that you're storing all of the strings in your trie separately as a set, you've lost the space complexity benefits that trie gave you.

Solution to Challenge 2

In `StringTrie`, you only dealt with code unit collections. Now you have to generalize the task to handle any collection. Since you need to be able to loop through the elements of whatever collection you're inserting, searching for, or removing, a generic trie should require any input to be iterable.

Create a new file called **trie.dart** and add the following class to it:

```
import 'trie_node.dart';

class Trie<E, T extends Iterable<E>> {
  TrieNode<E> root = TrieNode(key: null, parent: null);
}
```

`T` represents the iterable collections that you'll add to the trie while `E` represents the type for the `TrieNode` key. For example, given a list of code units, `E` is `int` for the code unit while `T` is `List<int>` for the collection.

Now that you have the generic types set up, you can implement the `insert` method like so:

```
void insert(T collection) {
  var current = root;
  for (E element in collection) {
    current.children[element] ??= TrieNode(
      key: element,
      parent: current,
    );
    current = current.children[element]!;
  }
  current.isTerminating = true;
}
```

This is almost identical to your `StringTrie` implementation except that now you iterate through the more generic elements of type `E` in a collection of type `T`.

The process to update `contains` and `remove` are similar:

- Parameter inputs are `T collection`.
- Use `for (E element in collection)` to loop through the elements.

Try out your generic `Trie` by running the following in `main`:

```
import 'trie.dart';

void main() {
  final trie = Trie<int, List<int>>();
  trie.insert('cut'.codeUnits);
  trie.insert('cute'.codeUnits);
  if (trie.contains('cute'.codeUnits)) {
    print('cute is in the trie');
  }
  trie.remove('cut'.codeUnits);
  assert(!trie.contains('cut'.codeUnits));
}
```

Run that, and you'll see the following results:

```
cute is in the trie
cut has been removed
```

From the user's perspective, the code above isn't quite as concise as your `StringTrie` was. However, the advantage is that your new `Trie` can handle any iterable collection, not just the code units of strings.

Chapter 13 Solutions

Solution to Challenge 1

In this challenge, you implement binary search as a free function. Here's what it looks like:

```
int? binarySearch<E extends Comparable<E>>(List<E> list, E
value) {
  var start = 0;
  var end = list.length;
  while (start < end) {
    final size = end - start;
    final middle = start + size ~/ 2;
    if (list[middle] == value) {
      return middle;
    } else if (list[middle].compareTo(value) < 0) {
      start = middle + 1;
    } else {
      end = middle;
    }
  }
  return null;
}
```

The only major difference from the extension that you made earlier is that now you also need to pass the list in as a parameter.

Don't forget that you need to specify the function's generic type as num:

```
final list = [1, 5, 15, 17, 19, 22, 24, 31, 105, 150];
final index = binarySearch<num>(list, 31);
print('Found at index $index'); // 7
```

Solution to Challenge 2

Here's how you would implement `binarySearch` as a recursive function:

```
int? binarySearch<E extends Comparable<E>>(
  List<E> list,
  E value, [
  int? startIndex,
  int? endIndex,
]) {
  final start = startIndex ?? 0;
  final end = endIndex ?? list.length;

  if (start >= end) {
    return null;
  }

  final size = end - start;
  final middle = start + size ~/ 2;

  if (list[middle] == value) {
    return middle;
  } else if (list[middle].compareTo(value) < 0) {
    return binarySearch(list, value, middle + 1, end);
  } else {
    return binarySearch(list, value, start, middle);
  }
}
```

On each recursion, you move `start` and end closer and closer to each other until you finally get the value...or find nothing. The base case is when `start` meets end.

Solution to Challenge 3

First, create a class to hold the start and end indices:

```
class Range {
  const Range(this.start, this.end);
  final int start;
  final int end;

  @override
  String toString() => 'Range($start, $end)';
}
```

`start` is inclusive and `end` is exclusive.

An unoptimized but elegant solution to find a range of indices that match a value is quite simple:

```
Range? findRange(List<int> list, int value) {
  final start = list.indexOf(value);
  if (start == -1) return null;
  final end = list.lastIndexOf(value) + 1;
  return Range(start, end);
}
```

The time complexity of this solution is O(n), which isn't terrible. However, the solution can be optimized to O(log n).

Whenever you hear that a collection is *sorted*, your mind should jump to binary search. The binary search you implemented in this chapter, though, isn't powerful enough to tell you whether the index is a start or end index. You'll modify the binary search to accommodate for this new rule.

First, write a helper method to find the start index:

```
int? _startIndex(List<int> list, int value) {
  if (list[0] == value) return 0;
  var start = 1;
  var end = list.length;
  while (start < end) {
    final size = end - start;
    final middle = start + size ~/ 2;
    if (list[middle] == value && list[middle - 1] != value) {
      return middle;
    } else if (list[middle] < value) {
      start = middle + 1;
    } else {
      end = middle;
    }
  }
  return null;
}
```

This method not only checks that the value is correct but also that it's the first one if there are multiple elements of the same value.

Add another method to find the end index:

```
int? _endIndex(List<int> list, int value) {
  if (list[list.length - 1] == value) return list.length;
  var start = 0;
  var end = list.length - 1;
  while (start < end) {
    final size = end - start;
    final middle = start + size ~/ 2;
    if (list[middle] == value && list[middle + 1] != value) {
      return middle + 1;
    } else if (list[middle] > value) {
      end = middle;
    } else {
      start = middle + 1;
    }
  }
  return null;
}
```

The logic is the same except for new adjustments to make sure you've found the very *last* element of a series.

Once you can find the start and end indices, obtaining the range is straightforward:

```
Range? findRange(List<int> list, int value) {
  if (list.isEmpty) return null;
  final start = _startIndex(list, value);
  final end = _endIndex(list, value);
  if (start == null || end == null) return null;
  return Range(start, end);
}
```

Test out your solution by running the following in `main`:

```
final list = [1, 2, 3, 3, 3, 4, 5, 5];
final range = findRange(list, 3);
print(range);
```

You should see the output below in the console:

```
Range(2, 5)
```

This function improves the time complexity from O(n) to O(log n).

Chapter 14 Solutions

Solution to Challenge 1

There are many ways to solve for the *n*th smallest number in an unsorted list. This chapter is about heaps, so the solution here will use a min-heap.

```
num? getNthSmallestElement(int n, List<num> elements) {
  var heap = Heap<num>(
    elements: elements,
    priority: Priority.min,
  );
  num? value;
  for (int i = 0; i < n; i++) {
    value = heap.remove();
  }
  return value;
}
```

Since `heap.remove` always returns the smallest element, you just loop through *n* times to get the *n*th smallest number.

Solution to Challenge 2

Given the following unsorted list:

```
[21, 10, 18, 5, 3, 100, 1]
```

The diagrams below show the steps it would take to convert that list into a min-heap. First sift the **18**, then the **10**, and finally the **21**:

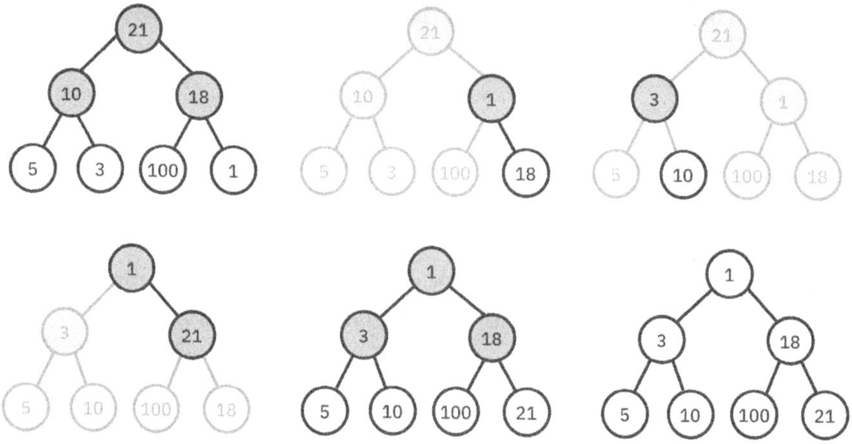

Solution to Challenge 3

To combine two heaps, add the following method to Heap:

```
void merge(List<E> list) {
  elements.addAll(list);
  _buildHeap();
}
```

You first combine both lists, which is O(m), where *m* is the size of the heap you're merging. Building the heap takes O(n), where *n* is the new total number of elements. Overall the algorithm runs in O(n) time.

Solution to Challenge 4

To satisfy the min-heap requirement, every parent node must be less than or equal to its left and right child nodes.

Here's how you can determine if a list is a min-heap:

```
bool isMinHeap<E extends Comparable<E>>(List<E> elements) {
  // 1
  if (elements.isEmpty) return true;
  // 2
  final start = elements.length ~/ 2 - 1;
  for (var i = start; i >= 0; i--) {
    // 3
    final left = 2 * i + 1;
    final right = 2 * i + 2;
    // 4
    if (elements[left].compareTo(elements[i]) < 0) {
      return false;
    }
    // 5
    if (right < elements.length &&
        elements[right].compareTo(elements[i]) < 0) {
      return false;
    }
  }
  // 6
  return true;
}
```

1. If the list is empty, it's a min-heap!
2. Loop through all parent nodes in the list in reverse order.
3. Get the left and right child index.
4. Check if the left element is less than the parent.
5. Check if the right index is within the list's bounds. Then check if the right element is less than the parent.
6. If every parent-child relationship satisfies the min-heap property, return true.

The time complexity of this solution is O(n). This is because you still have to check the value of every element in the list.

Chapter 15 Solutions

Solution to Challenge 1

Start with the following `Person` type:

```
class Person implements Comparable<Person> {
  Person({
    required this.name,
    required this.age,
    required this.isMilitary,
  });

  final String name;
  final int age;
  final bool isMilitary;

  @override
  int compareTo(other) => throw UnimplementedError();
}
```

Since a priority queue needs to compare elements, `Person` also needs to be `Comparable`.

Given a list of people on the waitlist, you would like to prioritize the people in the following order:

1. Military background.
2. Seniority, by age.

The key to solving this problem is to finish implementing the `compareTo` method in `Person` so that you can use a priority queue to tell you the order of people on the waitlist. Replace `compareTo` with the following code:

```
@override
int compareTo(other) {
  if (isMilitary == other.isMilitary) {
    return age.compareTo(other.age);
  }
  return isMilitary ? 1 : -1;
}
```

If two people have the same military background, then age is used to see who has the highest priority. But if the military background is different, then the one having a military background is prioritized.

Before you test your implementation out, override `toString` so that `Person` is printable:

```
@override
String toString() {
  final military = (isMilitary) ? ', (military)' : '';
  return '$name, age $age$military';
}
```

Import the `PriorityQueue` that you made earlier in the chapter if you haven't already. Then run the following example in `main`:

```
final p1 = Person(name: 'Josh', age: 21, isMilitary: true);
final p2 = Person(name: 'Jake', age: 22, isMilitary: true);
final p3 = Person(name: 'Clay', age: 28, isMilitary: false);
final p4 = Person(name: 'Cindy', age: 28, isMilitary: false);
final p5 = Person(name: 'Sabrina', age: 30, isMilitary: false);

final waitlist = [p1, p2, p3, p4, p5];

var priorityQueue = PriorityQueue(elements: waitlist);
while (!priorityQueue.isEmpty) {
  print(priorityQueue.dequeue());
}
```

You should see the output below:

```
Jake, age 22, (military)
Josh, age 21, (military)
Sabrina, age 30
Clay, age 28
Cindy, age 28
```

Solution to Challenge 2

To make a list-based priority queue, all you have to do is implement the Queue interface. Instead of a heap, you use a list data structure.

Here's the Queue interface that you've used previously:

```
abstract interface class Queue<E> {
  bool enqueue(E element);
  E? dequeue();
  bool get isEmpty;
  E? get peek;
}
```

Getting Started

First, add the following code to a project that contains the Queue interface:

```
enum Priority { max, min }

class PriorityQueueList<E extends Comparable<E>> implements
Queue<E> {
  PriorityQueueList({List<E>? elements, Priority priority =
Priority.max}) {
    _priority = priority;
    _elements = elements ?? [];
  }

  late List<E> _elements;
  late Priority _priority;

  // more to come
}
```

So far, this is nearly the same as your heap implementation. This time, though, you have a list.

Which Is the High Priority End?

At this point, you need to make a decision. You can either put the high priority elements at the start of the list or at the end of the list. It might seem logical to put the high priority elements at the start of the list since that's how you implemented heap. However, think about the properties of a list and what you need to accomplish in a queue. Inserting and removing from the beginning of a list is slow. If you make the start of the list the high priority end, then every single dequeue will be slow.

On the other hand, if you put the high priority elements at the end of the list, then dequeuing will be a lightning-fast `removeLast` operation. Enqueuing will be slow no matter what you choose, but you might as well make dequeuing fast!

The code in the rest of this answer will assume that the end of the list is the high priority side.

Sorting an Initial List

Replace the `PriorityQueueList` constructor with the following code:

```
PriorityQueueList({List<E>? elements, Priority priority =
Priority.max}) {
  _priority = priority;
  _elements = elements ?? [];
  _elements.sort((a, b) => _compareByPriority(a, b));
}

int _compareByPriority(E a, E b) {
  if (_priority == Priority.max) {
    return a.compareTo(b);
  }
  return b.compareTo(a);
}
```

`_compareByPriority` returns an `int` following the requirements of the list's `sort` function. Like you've seen before with `Comparable` values, a comparison result of `1` means the first value is larger, `-1` means the second is larger, and `0` means they're equal. The `sort` algorithm in Dart has a time complexity of O(n log n) for large lists.

Implementing isEmpty and peek

Add the following methods to begin implementing the `Queue` interface:

```
@override
bool get isEmpty => _elements.isEmpty;

@override
E? get peek => (isEmpty) ? null : _elements.last;
```

Since the high priority side is the end of the list, peeking returns the *last* element.

Implementing enqueue

Next, add the enqueue method:

```
@override
bool enqueue(E element) {
  // 1
  for (int i = 0; i < _elements.length; i++) {
    // 2
    if (_compareByPriority(element, _elements[i]) < 0) {
      // 3
      _elements.insert(i, element);
      return true;
    }
  }
  // 4
  _elements.add(element);
  return true;
}
```

To enqueue an element in a list-based priority queue, perform the following tasks:

1. Start at the low priority end of the list and loop through every element.
2. Check if the element you're adding has an even lower priority than the current element.
3. If it does, insert the new element at the current `index`.
4. If you get to the end of the list, that means every other element was lower priority. Add the new element to the end of the list as the new highest priority element.

This method has an overall time complexity of O(n) since you have to go through every element to check the priority against the new element you're adding. Also, if you're inserting in between elements in the list, you have to shift all of the remaining elements to the right by one.

> **Note**: Since you're working with a *sorted* list, you could improve the efficiency of this algorithm by using the binary search you learned about in Chapter 13. Insertion would still be O(n) in the worst case, but at least the search part would be O(log n).

Implementing dequeue

Next, add the dequeue method:

```
@override
E? dequeue() => isEmpty ? null : _elements.removeLast();
```

Here is where the benefit of putting the high priority elements at the end of the list comes in. removeLast is O(1) since you don't have to shift anything, so that makes dequeue also O(1). That's even better than the heap implementation!

Making the Queue Printable

Finally, override toString so that you can print your priority queue in a friendly format:

```
@override
String toString() => _elements.toString();
```

Alternatively, if you wanted to hide the fact that the high-priority items are at the end, then you could reverse the list with _elements.reversed.

There you have it! A list-based priority queue.

Testing it Out

To test out the priority queue, run the following in main:

```
final priorityQueue = PriorityQueueList<num>(
  elements: [1, 12, 3, 4, 1, 6, 8, 7],
);
print(priorityQueue);
priorityQueue.enqueue(5);
priorityQueue.enqueue(0);
priorityQueue.enqueue(10);
print(priorityQueue);
while (!priorityQueue.isEmpty) {
  print(priorityQueue.dequeue());
}
```

You should see the output below:

```
[1, 1, 3, 4, 6, 7, 8, 12]
[0, 1, 1, 3, 4, 5, 6, 7, 8, 10, 12]
12
10
8
7
6
5
4
3
1
1
0
```

This challenge was an exercise in implementing an interface from scratch. However, because of the slowness of enqueuing elements, you probably wouldn't want to use your `PriorityQueueList` in a real project. The heap implementation performs better overall. On the other hand, if you have an application where you need dequeuing to be O(1) and you don't care about enqueuing time, the list-based implementation might be the better choice.

Chapter 16 Solutions

Solution to Challenge 1

If you start with the following list:

```
[4, 2, 5, 1, 3]
```

Here are the steps a **bubble sort** would take:

```
[2, 4, 5, 1, 3] // 4-2 swapped
[2, 4, 5, 1, 3] // 4-5 not swapped
[2, 4, 1, 5, 3] // 5-1 swapped
[2, 4, 1, 3, 5] // 5-3 swapped

[2, 4, 1, 3, 5] // 2-4 not swapped
[2, 1, 4, 3, 5] // 4-1 swapped
[2, 1, 3, 4, 5] // 4-3 swapped

[1, 2, 3, 4, 5] // 2-1 swapped
[1, 2, 3, 4, 5] // 2-3 not swapped

[1, 2, 3, 4, 5] // 1-2 not swapped
```

Bubble sort needed the full $O(n^2)$ traversal to finish the sort. It made ten comparisons and six swaps.

Solution to Challenge 2

Given the following list:

```
[4, 2, 5, 1, 3]
```

These are the steps a **selection sort** would take:

```
[4, 2, 5, 1, 3] // start, lowest: 4

[4, 2, 5, 1, 3] // compare 2-4, lowest: 2
[4, 2, 5, 1, 3] // compare 5-2, lowest: 2
[4, 2, 5, 1, 3] // compare 1-2, lowest: 1
[4, 2, 5, 1, 3] // compare 3-1, lowest: 1

// swap 4-1, reset lowest: 2

[1, 2, 5, 4, 3] // compare 5-2, lowest: 2
[1, 2, 5, 4, 3] // compare 4-2, lowest: 2
[1, 2, 5, 4, 3] // compare 3-2, lowest: 2

// no swap needed, reset lowest: 5

[1, 2, 5, 4, 3] // compare 4-5, lowest: 4
[1, 2, 5, 4, 3] // compare 3-4, lowest: 3

// swap 5-3, reset lowest: 4

[1, 2, 3, 4, 5] // compare 5-4, lowest: 4

// no swap needed
```

This solution also needed the full $O(n^2)$ traversal with its ten comparisons. However, selection sort completed the task with only two swaps.

Solution to Challenge 3

Using the following list:

```
[4, 2, 5, 1, 3]
```

An **insertion sort** would perform the steps below:

```
[2, 4, 5, 1, 3] // 4-2 swapped

[2, 4, 5, 1, 3] // 4-5 not swapped

[2, 4, 1, 5, 3] // 5-1 swapped
[2, 1, 4, 5, 3] // 4-1 swapped
[1, 2, 4, 5, 3] // 2-1 swapped

[1, 2, 4, 3, 5] // 5-3 swapped
[1, 2, 3, 4, 5] // 4-3 swapped
[1, 2, 3, 4, 5] // 2-3 not swapped
```

Insertion sort was able to do a little better than $O(n^2)$ since on the second and fourth passes it found some presorted elements. Those steps are marked with "not swapped" in the comments above. Overall this solution required eight comparisons and six swaps.

Solution to Challenge 4

Each of the sort algorithms below is working on the following sorted collection:

```
[1, 2, 3, 4, 5]
```

Bubble Sort

Here are the steps bubble sort would take:

```
[1, 2, 3, 4, 5] // 1-2 not swapped
[1, 2, 3, 4, 5] // 2-3 not swapped
[1, 2, 3, 4, 5] // 3-4 not swapped
[1, 2, 3, 4, 5] // 4-5 not swapped
```

Since bubble sort completed an entire pass without needing to swap any elements, it could exit early after only one pass. This is O(n) time complexity. However, if you simply moved the **1** to the end of the list, bubble sort would suddenly become $O(n^2)$ again.

Selection Sort

These are the steps selection sort would take:

```
[1, 2, 3, 4, 5] // compare 2-1, lowest: 1
[1, 2, 3, 4, 5] // compare 3-1, lowest: 1
[1, 2, 3, 4, 5] // compare 4-1, lowest: 1
[1, 2, 3, 4, 5] // compare 5-1, lowest: 1

// no swap needed, reset lowest: 2

[1, 2, 3, 4, 5] // compare 3-2, lowest: 2
[1, 2, 3, 4, 5] // compare 4-2, lowest: 2
[1, 2, 3, 4, 5] // compare 5-2, lowest: 2

// no swap needed, reset lowest: 3

[1, 2, 3, 4, 5] // compare 4-3, lowest: 3
[1, 2, 3, 4, 5] // compare 5-3, lowest: 3

// no swap needed, reset lowest: 4

[1, 2, 3, 4, 5] // compare 5-4, lowest: 4

// no swap needed
```

Even with a fully sorted list, selection sort is still $O(n^2)$.

Insertion Sort

And these are the steps insertion sort would take:

```
[1, 2, 3, 4, 5] // 1-2 not swapped
[1, 2, 3, 4, 5] // 2-3 not swapped
[1, 2, 3, 4, 5] // 3-4 not swapped
[1, 2, 3, 4, 5] // 4-5 not swapped
```

Like bubble sort, insertion sort is able to determine that the list is sorted with a single pass, giving it a time complexity of O(n). However, unlike bubble sort, moving **1** to the end of the list wouldn't cause insertion sort to jump all the way back up to $O(n^2)$.

Chapter 17 Solutions

Solution to Challenge 1

Stepping through the code of `mergeSort` one line at a time is probably the easiest way to understand what's happening.

A few strategically placed print statements can also help:

```
List<E> mergeSort<E extends Comparable<E>>(List<E> list) {
  if (list.length < 2) {
    print('recursion ending:  $list');
    return list;
  } else {
    print('recursion list in: $list');
  }

  final middle = list.length ~/ 2;
  final left = mergeSort(list.sublist(0, middle));
  final right = mergeSort(list.sublist(middle));

  final merged = _merge(left, right);
  print('recursion ending:  merging $left and $right ->
$merged');
  return merged;
}
```

Here's the output for sorting the list `[[4, 2, 5, 1, 3]`:

```
recursion list in: [4, 2, 5, 1, 3]
recursion list in: [4, 2]
recursion ending:  [4]
recursion ending:  [2]
recursion ending:  merging [4] and [2] -> [2, 4]
recursion list in: [5, 1, 3]
recursion ending:  [5]
recursion list in: [1, 3]
recursion ending:  [1]
recursion ending:  [3]
recursion ending:  merging [1] and [3] -> [1, 3]
recursion ending:  merging [5] and [1, 3] -> [1, 3, 5]
recursion ending:  merging [2, 4] and [1, 3, 5] -> [1, 2, 3, 4,
5]

[1, 2, 3, 4, 5]
```

Solution to Challenge 2

The tricky part of this challenge is the limited capabilities of `Iterable`. Traditional implementations of merge sort rely on using the indices of a list. Since `Iterable` types have no notion of indices, though, you'll make use of their iterator.

Recreate `_merge` in this way:

```
List<E> _merge<E extends Comparable<E>>(
  Iterable<E> first,
  Iterable<E> second,
) {
  // 1
  var result = <E>[];
  // 2
  var firstIterator = first.iterator;
  var secondIterator = second.iterator;
  // 3
  var firstHasValue = firstIterator.moveNext();
  var secondHasValue = secondIterator.moveNext();

  // more to come
}
```

Setting up the algorithm involves the following steps:

1. Create a new list to store the merged iterables.

2. Grab the iterators. Iterators are objects that know how to get the next value in the iterable.

3. Create two variables to track when the iterators have reached the end of their content. `moveNext` returns `true` if the iterator found a next element, or `false` if the end of the collection was reached.

Using the iterators, you'll decide which element should be appended into the `result` list by comparing the values. Write the following at the end of the `_merge` function:

```
while (firstHasValue && secondHasValue) {
  // 1
  final firstValue = firstIterator.current;
  final secondValue = secondIterator.current;
  // 2
  if (firstValue.compareTo(secondValue) < 0) {
    result.add(firstValue);
    firstHasValue = firstIterator.moveNext();
  // 3
  } else if (firstValue.compareTo(secondValue) > 0) {
    result.add(secondValue);
    secondHasValue = secondIterator.moveNext();
  // 4
  } else {
    result.add(firstValue);
    result.add(secondValue);
    firstHasValue = firstIterator.moveNext();
    secondHasValue = secondIterator.moveNext();
  }
}

// more to come
```

Here are some notes on the numbered comments above:

1. Grab the values using your iterators' `current` property.
2. If the first value is less than the second one, you'll add the first value to `result`, and then move the iterator to the next value.
3. If the first value is greater than the second, you'll do the opposite.
4. If both values are equal, you'll add them both and move the iterators on.

This process will continue until one of the iterators runs out of values to dispense. In that scenario, if the other iterator still has any values left, they'll be equal to or greater than the ones in `result`.

To add the rest of those values, write the following at the end of the `_merge` function:

```
if (firstHasValue) {
  do {
    result.add(firstIterator.current);
  } while (firstIterator.moveNext());
}

if (secondHasValue) {
  do {
    result.add(secondIterator.current);
  } while (secondIterator.moveNext());
}

return result;
```

That completes your new implementation of `_merge`.

Confirm that `mergeSort` still works by running the following in `main`:

```
final list = <num>[7, 2, 6, 3, 9];
final sorted = mergeSort(list);
print(sorted);
```

You should see the console output below:

```
[2, 3, 6, 7, 9]
```

Chapter 18 Solutions

Solution to Challenge 1

You're starting with the following list:

```
var list = [46, 500, 459, 1345, 13, 999];
```

LSD-Radix Sort

Modify your `radixSort` extension by adding the following `print` statement at the bottom of the `while` loop:

```
print(buckets);
```

Then when you call `list.radixSort()`, you'll see the following output:

```
[[500], [], [], [13], [], [1345], [46], [], [], [459, 999]]
[[500], [13], [], [], [1345, 46], [459], [], [], [], [999]]
[[13, 46], [], [], [1345], [459], [500], [], [], [], [999]]
[[13, 46, 459, 500, 999], [1345], [], [], [], [], [], [], [],
[]]
```

This shows the values in the buckets at the end of all four rounds.

MSD-Radix Sort

To see the items in your buckets on each recursion, add the following line to `_msdRadixSorted` right above where you set `bucketOrder`:

```
print(buckets);
// final bucketOrder = ...
```

Now when you call `list.lexicographicalSort()`, you should see the following output:

```
[[], [1345, 13], [], [], [46, 459], [500], [], [], [], [999]]
[[], [], [], [1345, 13], [], [], [], [], [], []]
[[], [], [], [], [1345], [], [], [], [], []]
[[], [], [], [], [], [459], [46], [], [], []]
```

The **13** is missing from the third set of buckets since it's in the priority bucket.

Solution to Challenge 2

You can find the number of unique UTF-16 code units in a list of words by adding each code unit to a set:

```
int uniqueCharacters(List<String> words) {
  final uniqueChars = <int>{};
  for (final word in words) {
    for (final codeUnit in word.codeUnits) {
      uniqueChars.add(codeUnit);
    }
  }
  return uniqueChars.length;
}
```

Here's the example list:

```
final words = ['done', 'ad', 'eel', 'zoo', 'adept', 'do'];
print(uniqueCharacters(words)); // 9
```

In this case, there are nine different letters used to write the words in the list. If you were implementing a bucket sort, you would need nine buckets.

Solution to Challenge 3

Rather than just checking if you've reached the most significant digit of the largest number, you can count how many numbers are left to sort. If there's only one, then you're finished.

```
extension RadixSort on List<int> {
  void radixSort() {
    const base = 10;
    var place = 1;
    // 1
    var unsorted = length;
    // 2
    while (unsorted > 1) {
      // 3
      unsorted = 0;
      final buckets = List.generate(base, (_) => <int>[]);
      forEach((number) {
        final remainingPart = number ~/ place;
        final digit = remainingPart % base;
        buckets[digit].add(number);
        // 4
        if (remainingPart ~/ base > 0) {
          unsorted++;
        }
      });
      place *= base;
      clear();
      addAll(buckets.expand((element) => element));
    }
  }
}
```

The numbered comments show the parts that have changed:

1. Initialize the `unsorted` count with however many numbers are in the list.
2. Proceed with another round of sorting as long as there is more than one number left to sort.
3. Start counting over at the beginning of each round.
4. If the current number has more significant digits left, increment the `unsorted` count.

In this way, the algorithm will stop as soon as it's sorted all of the digits in all of the numbers except the remaining ones of the last big number. They don't need to be sorted since this number will always be last.

Chapter 19 Solutions

Solution to Challenge 1

Heapsort requires two steps:

1. Converting a list to a heap.
2. Repeatedly moving the root of the heap to an ordered list.

Step one is where you'll find the difference in the number of comparisons needed.

5, 4, 3, 2, 1

`[5, 4, 3, 2, 1]` will yield the fewest number of comparisons since it's already a max-heap and no swaps take place.

When building a max-heap, you only look at the parent nodes because these are the nodes that might need to sift down. In this case, there are two parent nodes, each with two comparisons. You compare **4** with **2** and **1**. Then you compare **5** with **4** and **3**. Since none of these comparisons requires a swap, no further comparisons are necessary.

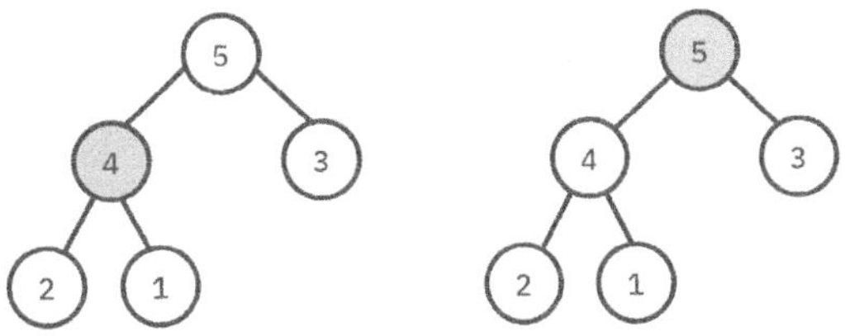

1, 2, 3, 4, 5

`[1, 2, 3, 4, 5]` will yield the most number of comparisons. You first compare **2** with **4** and **4** with **5**. Since **2** is smaller, you swap it with **5**. Then you compare **1** with **5** and **5** with **3**. Since **1** is smaller, you sift it down, swapping it with the **5**. The down-sift now requires comparing **1** with **4** and **4** with **2**, which will lead to swapping **1** with **4**.

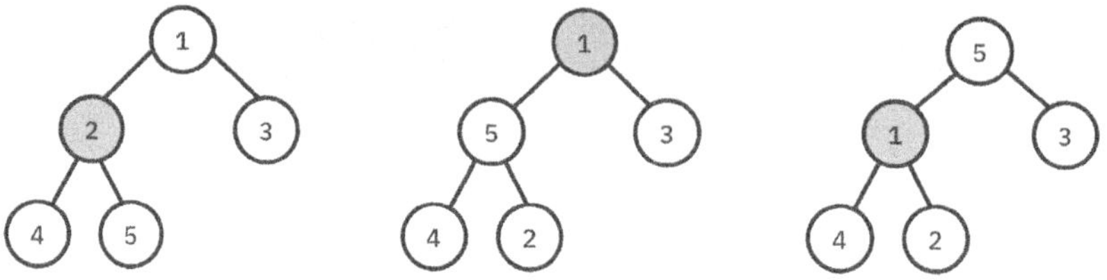

The sorting itself will take additional comparisons, but these are equivalent since both lists have already been converted to heaps.

Solution to Challenge 2

There are multiple ways to sort in descending order.

Using reversed

The easiest solution is to simply use the `reversed` method on `List`:

```
final list = <num>[6, 12, 2, 26, 8, 18, 21, 9, 5];
final ascending = heapsort(list);
final descending = ascending.reversed;
```

This gives you an iterable, but you can convert it to a list with `toList` if needed.

Reimplementing Heapsort

If you're using the `heapsort` function that you implemented earlier in the chapter, then replace `Priority.min` with `Priority.max`.

```
List<E> descendingHeapsort<E extends Comparable<E>>(List<E>
list) {
  final heap = Heap<E>(
    elements: list.toList(),
    priority: Priority.max, // changed
  );
  final sorted = <E>[];
  while (!heap.isEmpty) {
    final value = heap.remove();
    sorted.add(value!);
  }
  return sorted;
}
```

This will fill the list by pulling the max values off of the heap, resulting in a list of descending values.

Reimplementing heapsortInPlace

It's also easy to reimplement your `heapsortInPlace` extension to sort in ascending order. Again, all you have to do is change the heap priority.

Go to `_siftDown` and look for the two comparisons:

```
this[left].compareTo(this[chosen]) > 0
// and
this[right].compareTo(this[chosen]) > 0
```

Then switch `> 0` to `< 0`:

```
this[left].compareTo(this[chosen]) < 0
// and
this[right].compareTo(this[chosen]) < 0
```

This will create an internal min-heap so that during the sorting step, the *lowest* values will be pulled off the heap and placed at the *end* of the list.

Chapter 20 Solutions

Solution to Challenge 1

In this chapter, you implemented quicksort recursively. Here's how you might do it iteratively.

This solution uses Lomuto's partitioning strategy. You'll leverage a stack to store pairs of `high` and `low` indices for sublist partitions.

```
void quicksortIterativeLomuto<E extends Comparable<E>>(
  List<E> list,
) {
  // 1
  var stack = Stack<int>();
  // 2
  stack.push(0);
  stack.push(list.length - 1);
  // 3
  while (stack.isNotEmpty) {
    // 4
    final high = stack.pop();
    final low = stack.pop();
    // 5
    final pivot = _partitionLomuto(list, low, high);
    // 6
    if (pivot - 1 > low) {
      stack.push(low);
      stack.push(pivot - 1);
    }
    // 7
    if (pivot + 1 < high) {
      stack.push(pivot + 1);
      stack.push(high);
```

```
      }
    }
  }
```

Here's how the solution works:

1. Create a stack that stores indices.
2. Push the starting low and high boundaries on the stack as initial values.
3. When the stack is empty, quicksort is complete.
4. Get the pair of `high` and `low` indices from the stack.
5. Perform Lomuto's partitioning with the current indices. Recall that Lomuto picks the last element as the pivot and splits the partitions into three parts: elements that are less than the pivot, the pivot, and finally, elements that are greater than the pivot.
6. Once the partitioning is complete, add the lower bound's `low` and `high` indices to partition the lower half later.
7. Similarly, add the upper bound's `low` and `high` indices to partition the upper half later.

The results are the same as with the recursive version:

```
final list = <num>[8, 2, 10, 0, 9, 18, 9, -1, 5];
quicksortIterativeLomuto(list);
print(list);
// [-1, 0, 2, 5, 8, 9, 9, 10, 18]
```

Solution to Challenge 2

Merge sort is preferable over quicksort when you need stability. Merge sort is stable and guarantees O(n log n). These characteristics are not the case with quicksort, which isn't stable and can perform as badly as $O(n^2)$.

Merge sort works better for larger data structures or data structures where elements are scattered throughout memory. Quicksort works best when elements are stored in a contiguous block.

Chapter 21 Solutions

Solution to Challenge 1

This solution uses the `AdjacencyList` API you built in this chapter. You can use any non-null weight, but a good default is 1.

```
final graph = AdjacencyList<String>();

final megan = graph.createVertex('Megan');
final sandra = graph.createVertex('Sandra');
final pablo = graph.createVertex('Pablo');
final edith = graph.createVertex('Edith');
final ray = graph.createVertex('Ray');
final luke = graph.createVertex('Luke');
final manda = graph.createVertex('Manda');
final vicki = graph.createVertex('Vicki');

graph.addEdge(megan, sandra, weight: 1);
graph.addEdge(megan, pablo, weight: 1);
graph.addEdge(megan, edith, weight: 1);
graph.addEdge(pablo, ray, weight: 1);
graph.addEdge(pablo, luke, weight: 1);
graph.addEdge(edith, manda, weight: 1);
graph.addEdge(edith, vicki, weight: 1);
graph.addEdge(manda, pablo, weight: 1);
graph.addEdge(manda, megan, weight: 1);

print(graph);
```

You can simply look at the graph to find the common friend:

```
Megan --> Sandra, Pablo, Edith, Manda
Sandra --> Megan
Pablo --> Megan, Ray, Luke, Manda
Edith --> Megan, Manda, Vicki
Ray --> Pablo
Luke --> Pablo
Manda --> Edith, Pablo, Megan
Vicki --> Edith
```

Turns out to be Manda, which was stated pretty directly in the question. :]

If you want to solve it programmatically, you can find the intersection of the set of Megan's friends with the set of Pablo's friends.

```
final megansFriends = Set.of(
  graph.edges(megan).map((edge) {
    return edge.destination.data;
  }),
);

final pablosFriends = Set.of(
  graph.edges(pablo).map((edge) {
    return edge.destination.data;
  }),
);

final mutualFriends = megansFriends.intersection(pablosFriends);
```

Chapter 22 Solutions

Solution to Challenge 1

The maximum number of items ever in the queue is 3. You can observe this by adding `print` statements after every enqueue and dequeue in `breadthFirstSearch`.

Solution to Challenge 2

You already know how to implement the breadth-first search algorithm iteratively. Here's how you would implement it recursively.

Create an extension on `Graph`:

```
extension RecursiveBfs<E> on Graph<E> {

}
```

Then add a recursive helper method to it:

```
void _bfs(
  QueueStack<Vertex<E>> queue,
  Set<Vertex<E>> enqueued,
  List<Vertex<E>> visited,
) {
  final vertex = queue.dequeue();
  // 1
  if (vertex == null) return;
  // 2
  visited.add(vertex);
  final neighborEdges = edges(vertex);
  // 3
  for (final edge in neighborEdges) {
    if (!enqueued.contains(edge.destination)) {
      queue.enqueue(edge.destination);
      enqueued.add(edge.destination);
    }
  }
  // 4
  _bfs(queue, enqueued, visited);
}
```

You'll use this method soon. Here's what it does:

1. This is the base case. The recursion stops when the queue is empty.
2. Mark the vertex as visited.
3. For every edge of the current `vertex`, check if the adjacent vertices have been visited before inserting them into the queue.
4. Recursively call this function until the queue is empty.

Now add the public `bfs` method above `_bfs`:

```
List<Vertex<E>> bfs(Vertex<E> source) {
  final queue = QueueStack<Vertex<E>>();
  final Set<Vertex<E>> enqueued = {};
  List<Vertex<E>> visited = [];

  queue.enqueue(source);
  enqueued.add(source);

  _bfs(queue, enqueued, visited);
  return visited;
}
```

This method is much the same as the implementation you wrote earlier in the chapter. The difference now is that you call the recursive helper function rather than using a `while` loop.

Test it out using the same graph as the one in the chapter text:

```
final vertices = graph.bfs(a);
vertices.forEach(print);
```

Run that, and you should again see `A` to `H` printed line by line.

The overall time complexity for this breadth-first search implementation is also O(V + E).

Solution to Challenge 3

A graph is said to be **disconnected** if no path exists between two nodes.

Create an extension on `Graph` like so:

```
extension Connected<E> on Graph<E> {
  bool isConnected() {
    // 1
    if (vertices.isEmpty) return true;
    // 2
    final visited = breadthFirstSearch(vertices.first);
    // 3
    for (final vertex in vertices) {
      if (!visited.contains(vertex)) {
        return false;
      }
    }
    return true;
  }
}
```

The commented numbers refer to the following points:

1. If there are no vertices, treat the graph as connected.
2. Perform a breadth-first search starting from the first vertex. This process will return all the visited nodes.
3. Go through every vertex in the graph and check if it has been visited before.

The graph is disconnected if a vertex is missing in the `visited` set.

Chapter 23 Solutions

Solution to Challenge 1

- Path from **A** to **F**: Use depth-first because the path you're looking for is deeper in the graph.
- Path from **A** to **G**: Use breadth-first because the path you're looking for is near the root.

Solution to Challenge 2

In this chapter, you learned how to implement a depth-first search iteratively. Here's how you would implement it recursively.

Create an extension on `Graph`:

```
extension RecursiveDfs<E> on Graph<E> {

}
```

Then add a recursive helper method to it:

```
void _dfs(
  Vertex<E> source,
  List<Vertex<E>> visited,
  Set<Vertex<E>> pushed,
) {
  // 1
  pushed.add(source);
  visited.add(source);
  // 2
  final neighbors = edges(source);
  for (final edge in neighbors) {
    // 3
    if (!pushed.contains(edge.destination)) {
      _dfs(edge.destination, visited, pushed);
    }
  }
}
```

You'll use this method soon. Here's what it does:

1. Mark the source vertex as visited.
2. Visit every neighboring edge.
3. As long as the adjacent vertex has not been visited yet, continue to dive deeper down the branch recursively.

Now add the public `dfs` method above `_dfs`:

```
List<Vertex<E>> dfs(Vertex<E> start) {
  List<Vertex<E>> visited = [];
  Set<Vertex<E>> pushed = {};
  _dfs(start, visited, pushed);
  return visited;
}
```

This method initializes `visited` and `pushed` and then starts the recursion process. Unlike the iterative solution you wrote earlier, there's no `stack` here. That's because recursion itself implicitly uses a stack.

Grab the same graph as the one you used in the chapter text. Then add the following:

```
final vertices = graph.dfs(a);
vertices.forEach(print);
```

Run that, and you should see the same result as the iterative solution:

```
A
B
E
F
G
C
H
D
```

Chapter 24 Solutions

Solution to Challenge 1

These are the shortest paths from **A** to the following vertices:

- Path to B: **A** - (1) - **B**
- Path to C: **A** - (1) - **B** - (8) - **C**
- Path to D: **A** - (1) - **B** - (9) - **D**
- Path to E: **A** - (1) - **B** - (8) - **C** - (2) - **E**

Solution to Challenge 2

To get the shortest paths from the `source` vertex to every other vertex in the graph, use the following extension on `Dijkstra`:

```
extension ShortestPaths<E> on Dijkstra<E> {
  Map<Vertex<E>, List<Vertex<E>>> shortestPathsLists(
    Vertex<E> source,
  ) {
    // 1
    final allPathsLists = <Vertex<E>, List<Vertex<E>>>{};
    // 2
    final allPaths = shortestPaths(source);
    // 3
    for (final vertex in graph.vertices) {
      final path = shortestPath(
        source,
        vertex,
        paths: allPaths,
      );
      allPathsLists[vertex] = path;
    }
    return allPathsLists;
  }
}
```

This is how it works:

1. The map stores the path to every vertex from the `source` vertex.
2. Perform Dijkstra's algorithm to find all the paths from the `source` vertex.
3. For every vertex in the graph, generate the list of vertices that makes up the path.

Made in the USA
Monee, IL
08 November 2026

67811053R20273